DESIGN-BASED RESEARCH IN EDUCATION

Also Available

*Developing Strategic Young Writers through Genre Instruction:
Resources for Grades K–2*
Zoi A. Philippakos and Charles A. MacArthur

*Developing Strategic Writers through Genre Instruction:
Resources for Grades 3–5*
Zoi A. Philippakos, Charles A. MacArthur,
and David L. Coker Jr.

*Differentiated Literacy Instruction in Grades 4 and 5:
Strategies and Resources, Second Edition*
Sharon Walpole, Michael C. McKenna,
Zoi A. Philippakos, and John Z. Strong

*Effective Read-Alouds for Early Literacy:
A Teacher's Guide for PreK–1*
Katherine A. Beauchat, Katrin L. Blamey,
and Zoi A. Philippakos

DESIGN-BASED RESEARCH IN EDUCATION

Theory and Applications

edited by

Zoi A. Philippakos
Emily Howell
Anthony Pellegrino

Foreword by David Reinking

THE GUILFORD PRESS
New York   London

Copyright © 2021 The Guilford Press
A Division of Guilford Publications, Inc.
370 Seventh Avenue, Suite 1200, New York, NY 10001
www.guilford.com

All rights reserved

No part of this book may be reproduced, translated, stored in a retrieval system, or transmitted, in any form or by any means, electronic, mechanical, photocopying, microfilming, recording, or otherwise, without written permission from the publisher.

Printed in the United States of America

This book is printed on acid-free paper.

Last digit is print number: 9 8 7 6 5 4 3 2 1

Library of Congress Cataloging-in-Publication Data

Names: Philippakos, Zoi A., editor.
Title: Design-based research in education : theory and applications / edited by Zoi A. Philippakos, Emily Howell, Anthony Pellegrino ; foreword by David Reinking.
Other titles: Design-based research in education
Description: New York : The Guilford Press, [2021] | Includes bibliographical references and index.
Identifiers: LCCN 2021025278 | ISBN 9781462547371 (Paperback : acid-free paper) | ISBN 9781462547388 (Hardcover : acid-free paper)
Subjects: LCSH: Education—Research—Methodology. | Curriculum planning. | Teachers—In-service training. | BISAC: EDUCATION / Research | SOCIAL SCIENCE / Methodology
Classification: LCC LB1028 .D4427 2021 | DDC 370.72—dc23
LC record available at *https://lccn.loc.gov/2021025278*

About the Editors

Zoi A. Philippakos, PhD, is Associate Professor in the Department of Theory and Practice in Teacher Education at The University of Tennessee, Knoxville. Her research interests include reading and writing instruction in K–12 and postsecondary classrooms, strategy instruction with self-regulation, and teacher professional development. She collaborates with teachers to design and evaluate instructional approaches through design-based research methodologies and engages in experimental studies. Dr. Philippakos has published her research in leading journals and presents her work at national and international conferences.

Emily Howell, PhD, is a faculty member in literacy in the Department of Education and Human Development at Clemson University. She has taught English and writing at the secondary and collegiate levels and currently teaches preservice teachers and graduate students in education. Her research interests include multiliteracies, adolescent literacy, writing instruction, and digital tools. Dr. Howell approaches research through partnerships with teachers using methodologies such as design-based research. Her research has been published in leading journals of education.

Anthony Pellegrino, PhD, is Associate Professor in the Department of Theory and Practice in Teacher Education at The University of Tennessee, Knoxville. Prior to his work in higher education, he worked in K–12 classrooms and in public school administration for a decade. Dr. Pellegrino's research interests include student learning of difficult history and counternarratives in history/social studies education, as well as the experiences of preservice educators in clinical practice.

Contributors

Arthur Bakker, PhD, Freudenthal Institute, University of Utrecht, Utrecht, Netherlands

Kristi Tamte Bergeson, PhD, Department of Teacher Development, St. Cloud State University, St. Cloud, Minnesota

Melissa Campanella, doctoral candidate, Department of Learning Sciences and Human Development, University of Colorado Boulder, Boulder, Colorado

Kelly Chandler-Olcott, EdD, Department of Reading and Language Arts, Syracuse University, Syracuse, New York

Susan Cridland-Hughes, PhD, Department of Teaching and Learning, Clemson University, Clemson, South Carolina

Sharon Dotger, PhD, Department of Science Teaching, Syracuse University, Syracuse, New York

Paul Drijvers, PhD, Freudenthal Institute, University of Utrecht, Utrecht, Netherlands

Douglas Fisher, PhD, Department of Educational Leadership, San Diego State University, San Diego, California

Nancy Frey, PhD, Department of Educational Leadership, San Diego State University, San Diego, California

Alejandro Gonzalez Ojeda, EdD, Department of Educational Leadership, San Diego State University, San Diego, California

Kathleen A. Hinchman PhD, Department of Reading and Language Arts, Syracuse University, Syracuse, New York

Contributors

Margret A. Hjalmarson, PhD, College of Education and Human Development, George Mason University, Fairfax, Virginia

Emily Howell, PhD, Department of Education and Human Development, Clemson University, Clemson, South Carolina

Amy C. Hutchison, PhD, Division of Elementary, Literacy, and Secondary Education, George Mason University, Fairfax, Virginia

Lorraine Jacques, PhD, Department of Curriculum Instruction and Leadership, Louisiana Tech University, Ruston, Louisiana

Kalle Juuti, PhD, Department of Education, University of Helsinki, Helsinki, Finland

Diane Lapp, EdD, Department of Teacher Education, San Diego State University, San Diego, California

Jari Lavonen, PhD, Department of Education, University of Helsinki, Helsinki, Finland

Charles A. MacArthur, PhD, School of Education, University of Delaware, Newark, Delaware

Ryan McCarty PhD, Reading and Language Department, National Louis University, Chicago, Illinois

Susan McKenney, PhD, Department of Teacher Professional Development, University of Twente, Enschede, Netherlands

Albert Moes, MSc, HU University of Applied Sciences Utrecht, Utrecht, Netherlands

Keith O. Newvine, MS, doctoral candidate, Department of Reading and Language Arts, Syracuse University, Syracuse, New York

Nienke Nieveen, PhD, Department of Teacher Professional Development, University of Twente, Enschede, Netherlands

Tim Pappageorge, PhD, Maine West High School, Des Plaines, Illinois

Allison Ward Parsons, PhD, Division of Elementary, Literacy, and Secondary Education, George Mason University, Fairfax, Virginia

Seth A. Parsons, PhD, Division of Elementary, Literacy, and Secondary Education, George Mason University, Fairfax, Virginia

Anthony Pellegrino, PhD, Department of Theory and Research, The University of Tennessee, Knoxville, Knoxville, Tennessee

William Penuel, PhD, School of Education, University of Colorado Boulder, Boulder, Colorado

Zoi A. Philippakos, PhD, Department of Theory and Research, The University of Tennessee, Knoxville, Knoxville, Tennessee

Thomas Reeves, PhD, Department of Career and Information Studies, University of Georgia, Athens, Georgia

Claudia Rueda-Alvarez, PhD, Maine West High School, Des Plaines, Illinois

Mary-Celeste Schreuder, PhD, Clemson University, Clemson, South Carolina

Michelle Stephan, EdD, Department of Middle/Secondary Mathematics, University of North Carolina at Charlotte, Charlotte, North Carolina

Jan van den Akker, PhD, Department of Curriculum, University of Twente, Enschede, Netherlands

Nathalie J. van der Wal, PhD, Freudenthal Institute, University of Utrecht, Utrecht, Netherlands

Heather Waymouth, PhD, Literacy Department, West Chester University, West Chester, Pennsylvania

Phillip Wilder, PhD, Department of Teacher Education, Clemson University, Clemson, South Carolina

Foreword

A casual stroll through the history of education research may be an informative backdrop for this welcome book and for contextualizing its contribution to design-based research (DBR). Entwined with that history, and I hope also enlightening to readers, is my personal journey as an education researcher interested in literacy who was attracted to DBR shortly after its origins among education researchers in the early 1990s. These histories, the field's and mine, reveal a rationale and justification for DBR and its place within the current landscape of education research. They also illustrate why DBR continues to attract more researchers, to expand the range of its application, and to continue its steady move into the mainstream of education research.

Historically, the major players and relevant developments of what is now the field of education research emerged at the turn of the 19th and 20th centuries.[1] A young John Dewey was already a central figure. His was the iconic voice of progressive education and American pragmatism, and he wrote prolifically, and with deft clarity, about educational practice and research. To Dewey, there was no separation between practice and research. Knowledge isolated from educational practice was inert. To be useful, he argued, knowledge fluidly evolves from and is absorbed into practice.[2]

---

[1] For a more detailed account of the much condensed and simplified historical account here, see Lagemann (2000).

[2] For a detailed explication of Dewey's views of research and practice, see Biesta and Burbules (2003).

In his early years at the University of Chicago, Dewey was given the reins of the University's laboratory school along with his wife, Alice, who served as a teacher and principal. The school became a testing ground for their progressive vision of child-centered instruction and their commitment to instilling democratic ideals. Historical accounts suggest that these lofty ideals met the hard realities of day-to-day instruction, and the school was not an unmitigated success. Yet, confronting the inevitable challenges of implementing their vision no doubt honed Dewey's thinking and understanding, as did his close professional relationships with the laboratory school's teachers. Throughout his career, for Dewey, practice was research, and research was practice.

Moving to Teachers College, Columbia University in 1904, where he would remain a professor of philosophy until his retirement almost three decades later, Dewey walked the same hallways with another iconic figure in education research: Edward L. Thorndike. Thorndike, though younger, was already an accomplished scholar when Dewey arrived. He was well on his way to making a name for himself as a psychologist interested in education, and his accomplishments during a long career have led many to identify him as the founder of educational psychology.

But his views about research's role in education and its practice couldn't have been more different from Dewey's. Research in education, Thorndike argued, should be scientific and modeled after the experimental research and statistical analyses in the physical sciences and in basic psychological research. Scientific studies, conducted in a laboratory under carefully controlled conditions gathering quantitative data analyzed statistically, would, he believed, provide scientific guidance for educational practice. Furthermore, he argued, education research and scholarship would not be taken seriously until it adopted a scientific approach—a point of view that some contemporary critics have characterized pejoratively as "physics envy." Regrettably, Thorndike was also an elitist who saw researchers (then, invariably white men) as intellectually superior, and teachers of children (then, invariably women) as lower-level technicians who should follow the dictates of psychological research.[3] He is also reported to have advised his doctoral students that they should not waste their time in schools. A laboratory was their professional home.

As any education researcher of my generation knows, Thorndike's views triumphed over Dewey's for decades,[4] although not entirely intact. Like others pursuing a PhD in education during the early 1980s, my doctoral program was designed to prepare (one might even say indoctrinate) me to become a researcher in the

---

[3] In July 2020, Thorndike Hall at Columbia University, named 50 years ago to commemorate his accomplishments, was renamed because of his support of eugenics and his racist, sexist, and anti-Semitic views (see *www.tc.columbia.edu/articles/2020/july/important-announcement-from-the-president—chair-of-the-board-of-trustees*).

[4] Due in some measure to the fact that his son (Robert L.) and grandson (Robert M.) followed in his footsteps, keeping his legacy alive.

scientific mold Thorndike envisioned, but with some key differences. There was an increasing number of women professors and doctoral students, most of us had been classroom teachers, and we at least occasionally did research in schools. Consequently, like my fellow doctoral students, I enrolled in a bevy of courses on statistics, experimental design, and assessment. We didn't always work literally in laboratories (although, as a research assistant, one of my responsibilities was to use sophisticated equipment that collected eye-movement data while "subjects" read texts), but the laboratory was metaphorically how my professors and fellow students approached education research, even in schools. And, I must confess that I was developing a professional aloofness that made me even more an interloper in the classrooms that I *used* for my research. For the first 10 years or so of my career as a university professor and researcher, I dutifully embraced that paradigm with enough success to receive tenure and eventually promotion to the rank of professor.

Then, as occasionally happens when one obtains that level of professional security, and presumably maturity, I began to reflect more deeply on the research methods I had been taught and had used. One event, in particular, was akin to a conversion experience. A conventional experiment I was conducting in a middle school with several doctoral students went disappointingly awry. For example, just before we were to initiate the intervention into a treatment classroom, the school principal decided to move a cohort of academically challenged students into the class. That decision made perfect sense because the teacher was one of the most experienced and successful teachers in the school. But it was disturbingly problematic for our experimental design and statistical analysis. Then, during the intervention, when teachers in the control classrooms decided that the treatment intervention was too appealing to resist, they decided to do it as well, which also undermined the scientific integrity of our experiment.

But, the moment of conversion came during a debriefing with the doctoral students, essentially a "wake" for our failed experiment. During the discussion, we discovered that we had learned much about our intervention, just not in quantifiable terms that could fit reliably into our statistical analysis. For example, it seemed significant that the teachers in the control condition couldn't wait to use it. Then, one of the doctoral students said something I'll never forget. Offered in a spirit of consolation, the student said, "The problem is that the teacher is a nuisance variable." We all paused and looked at each other. That was true in an experimental, statistical sense, but it seemed irreverent. We had all been teachers. Did we conceptualize our former classroom teaching lives that way? What did it say about our research if a teacher was in any sense a nuisance? Shortly thereafter, I read an article in *Educational Researcher* (Newman, 1990) that resonated perfectly with the intellectual and emotional turmoil I was starting to feel. It was my introduction to DBR. But, more history is needed to fully grasp DBR's unique niche in the landscape of education research and why I was attracted to it.

The conceptual appearance of DBR in the early 1990s was preceded by a higher-profile challenge to the use of quantitative experimental methods in education research.[5] In the 1980s, the education research community ruptured into factions leading to the so-called paradigm wars. Many education researchers found that raw empiricism, coldly formulated in statistical analyses, was at odds with the complex, often subjectively human and sociocultural factors in, with, and around instruction. They gravitated toward naturalistic methods and qualitative analyses using methods imported from the social sciences, often driven by critical theory that focused on issues of morality and power. Much of that research included becoming observers, not laboratory experimenters, in schools and classrooms. If the scientific quantitative experimental approach was guided by a laboratory metaphor, the metaphor for qualitative researchers was a lens through which subjective observations were made. But, like different individuals looking with different lenses at the same object under a microscope, qualitative research was mostly descriptive observation accommodating diverse, and often abstract, theoretical interpretations. But it, too, paved a way for the evolution of DBR, which relies heavily on close observation, but in a much different frame that goes beyond observing and describing.

Heated debates about the legitimacy of these two different worldviews and approaches to research continued into the 1990s. However, as blood pressures lowered and the debates cooled, a rapprochement of sorts took hold, opening the way for some researchers to promote the use of mixed methods.[6] Mixed methods created a middle plank of educational research suggesting that it could take the best of both worlds, quantitative and qualitative, and generate research findings that were richer than the sum of its two parts. It also conveniently side-stepped the epistemological arguments offered to defend either quantitative or qualitative approaches. Instead, it claimed pragmatism as its epistemological foundation[7]—a small, but notable, step toward a return to Deweyan views.

Yet, since Dewey, none of these three approaches and their variations have dealt satisfactorily with the most enduring and central failure of education research. Since Dewey, the education research literature has had a distinctly unimpressive record of positively affecting, or effecting, practice, especially when weighed against mountains of published education research. In every decade during the previous century, it is easy to find laments about this longstanding gap between research and practice. The more disingenuous of these chide practitioners for not paying attention to research, more or less absolving researchers of any complicity.

For the most part, those who identify as quantitative, qualitative, or mixed-methods researchers have conducted and reported research that is about, and

---

[5] For a detailed account and analysis of the 1980 paradigm wars at the end of the decade and three scenarios of where it might lead, including one prediction that suggests an approach similar to DBR, see Gage (1989). Interestingly, all of Gage's scenarios occurred to some extent, but failed to become productively integrated, as he had hoped.

[6] For a detailed history of mixed-methods research, see Maxwell (2016).

[7] For an explication of mixed methods and an epistemological justification for them, see Tashakkori and Teddlie (1998).

maybe in, but not directly for, practice. The boundary between research and practice is more permeable today than the wall that Thorndike advocated, but for conventional quantitative and qualitative approaches, it is nothing like the oneness Dewey saw. For too many researchers, the link between their research and practice remains superficial, at best. For example, it might be limited to a section entitled "Implications for Instruction" tacked on to the end of a research report, or heeding the advice of a mentor to consider how a doctoral dissertation might be published in a researcher journal but then spun into an article for a practitioner journal, or an occasional inservice session after the school day for teachers.

For me, closing this long-lamented gap between research and practice figured prominently in my decision to become a DBR researcher. In that sense, it continues to remind me that it is the most logical and appropriate way to conduct research that meets my, and I think the field's, presumed professional commitment to inform practice. Originally, it responded to my sense of frustration as I came to realize that the methods I had been trained to use cut across the grain of real classrooms and reinforced my aloofness as an education researcher, while suppressing my instincts as a former classroom teacher.[8] It gave me a sense of purpose in my research that was notably lacking earlier in my career.

Admittedly, it also makes me less patient with my colleagues who use other approaches and who sometimes show relatively little interest in how their research informs practice. If professors in schools and colleges of education are not fully engaged in research that directly informs practice, who, we might ask, will do that research? In that regard, a colleague and I (Reinking & Yaden, 2021) have proposed a dynamic continuum along which theory (and research) can be placed to characterize productivity in relation to informing practice. On one end is theory/research that is *scholarship about education.* Those who do scholarship about education focus more abstractly on education as a societal institution, view its practitioners as a group to be studied, and may aspire, but not feel necessarily obligated, to inform educational practice. Such theories, and the research they inspire, often address laudable goals, but they provide little concrete guidance about how to achieve them. For researchers in this realm, education is often positioned as if it were a subtopic of other disciplines (e.g., history, sociology, economics, philosophy, public policy, critical studies). At the other end of the continuum is theory/research for education aimed at determining how those goals can be achieved. Those who theorize and do research in this realm view practitioners as an audience to inform, and they accept a fundamental responsibility to do so. It is at this end of the continuum that DBR exists.

That DBR reunites education research with practice was evident from its conceptual origins, which can be traced most directly to two publications, one by Alan Collins (1992) and another by Ann Brown (1992). Both of these researchers had

---

[8] For an argument suggesting that former teachers who wish to become education researchers must exchange their instincts from practical experience for a theoretical orientation, see Labaree (2003).

roots in cognitive psychology and were associated with an eclectic group of noted scholars who represented expertise in diverse fields including cognition, artificial intelligence, textual meaning, computer programming, instructional design, and social anthropology. The thread unifying this group, which founded what is now called the *learning sciences*,[9] was an interest in developing instructional interventions, often with new digital technologies, that could be used effectively in real classrooms. It was out of this amalgam, thanks mainly to Collins and Brown, that DBR was birthed.

Their articles, both published in 1992, were coincidentally complementary. Collins, in a book chapter entitled "Toward a Design Science in Education," outlined the broad parameters of a new methodological approach. Brown's article, published in the then fledgling *Journal of Learning Sciences*, described a more detailed personal journey toward what both she and Collins called *design experiments*. She referred to herself as a "design scientist" who came to realize that the laboratory methods she had used to research and develop a theory of metacognition while reading texts was of little use in studying how that understanding could be translated into instruction integrated successfully into the complexities of classroom instruction.

To illustrate her design work, she used an intervention she called reciprocal teaching, a technique to enhance the metacognitive aspects of reading comprehension that arose out of her previous laboratory work. Subsequently, that approach became not only one of the most well-researched interventions in literacy instruction (using conventional experiments and DBR), it also became widely used and laid the foundation for strategy instruction as a domain of teaching reading comprehension. Clearly, from its earliest days, DBR directly informed and influenced instructional practice in a way that other mainstream approaches did not. I believe that it is also noteworthy that DBR is the only methodological frame endogenous to education, not being imported from the physical or other social sciences.[10]

Brown's article is also where this brief history of education research comes full circle. She wrote discursively in her article about the compatibility of design experiments with Dewey's views about education, educational practice, and knowledge. In addition, she addressed how research that involved introducing innovative practices often necessitated addressing the challenge of teachers' natural inclination to resist moving away from established practices, which can be a pervasive issue for DBR researchers. She also made it clear that her work as a design scientist was methodologically neutral in terms of data collection and analysis. Although DBR employs analytical tools familiar to quantitative and qualitative researchers, it repositions those tools within a different epistemology and paradigmatic frame well suited, if not essential, to education. Within the philosophy of science, that frame is an expression of instrumentalism (about which Dewey also wrote), and

---

[9] For a history of the learning sciences, see Lee (2018).

[10] DBR has actually been imported from education into other fields of study such as public health political science.

thus methodologically related to mixed methods, although Brown noted that qualitative observations and analyses were necessary.

DBR is not just another approach to collecting and analyzing data. Instead, it offers a different ethos that foregrounds an entirely different domain of research questions. Quantitative experimental methods, guided by a laboratory metaphor applied to instructional options, ask, "How can we identify the best instructional practice?" Qualitative naturalistic methods, guided by a lens metaphor, ask, "How can we deeply understand instructional environments and interventions through systematic observation?" DBR, on the other hand, guided by an engineering metaphor, asks, "How can we gain deep understanding of pedagogy by designing interventions that accomplish valued goals?" DBR embraces any form of data collection and analysis that serves that purpose, typically undergirded by a strong base of experience in classrooms. Consistent with Dewey, DBR blurs the distinction between research and practice, treating practitioners as collegial partners, and sometimes as fellow researchers. It also views classrooms as complex ecologies in which one, sometimes seemingly small adaptation or change can have cascading effects, positively or negatively. This is a dynamic that anyone who has been a classroom teacher clearly knows and understands. Any researcher who does not acknowledge and accept that complexity is either delusional or dishonest, and failing to address that complexity abdicates researchers' responsibility to help practitioners deal with it.

Since its inception and continuing to the present, the community of DBR researchers has grown in number and diversity. Although its core ethos has remained solid, methodologically it has morphed into a diverse array of frames and approaches. For better or worse, they are described with a panoply of terms, several of which are on display in this volume's chapters. Some of these conceptualizations and approaches include Collins's and Brown's original term, design experiment, but now include others as well, such as development research, formative experiment, design-based implementation research, and participatory design research, and may include links to action research and improvement science (McKenney & Reeves, 2020). Arguably, all fit reasonably well under the umbrella of the DBR ethos. Also arguable is that various approaches to DBR are better suited to particular contexts and purposes, which is amply illustrated in the remainder of this book. For example, the chapters that follow illustrate how DBR can be applied somewhat differently to designing curriculum, creating classroom interventions aimed at accomplishing specific goals in different subject areas, initiating large-scale reforms within school districts, conducting effective professional development, and implementing interventions aimed at increasing social diversity. In my view, there is no one correct way to do design experiments, beyond engaging systematically in goal-oriented design that is formative and practically informative, and that generates theories of pedagogy embedded in practice.

This diversity might also be comparable to diverse approaches available within quantitative and qualitative research methods (e.g., qualitative methods include ethnographies, case studies, interviews, and phenomenological approaches). Yet, the DBR community has not clearly come to terms with firm categories or boundaries that separate them—and perhaps it shouldn't. In fact, in one sense this diversity and continuous evolution are consistent with DBR's ethos. That is, DBR itself might be expected to be designed and redesigned as needed in local circumstances, or as it is applied to new contexts and particular goals. Put another way, we may need to guard against the excesses of what has been called "hardening of the categories."

Returning to my personal history, I remain engaged in an ongoing journey in contemplating the totality of DBR—one now approaching three decades. Semi-retirement provides even more time for reflection. It has been a rewarding journey that has included conducting and publishing DBR studies, serving as an editor and reviewer of DBR manuscripts, coauthoring a book about DBR, and the gracious invitation to write this foreword. It also includes reading journal articles and books, such as this one, where I learn how others have interpreted DBR and applied it in different ways and in diverse contexts. Invariably, I have learned, and continue to learn, something new from each experience in my own research and writing, from serving on many doctoral dissertation committees guiding a DBR project, and from engaging vicariously with the work and thinking of DBR colleagues such as the editors of and contributors to this volume. I am continuously learning its subtleties and refining my own understandings.

In that vein, occasionally I list 10 personal things I think I know or value about DBR. Each list is never quite the same or in the same order. I have found this exercise also useful in teaching graduate courses on DBR. During a semester, I ask students to develop and update a list of 10 things they think are particularly unique, valuable, and personally attractive about DBR. Here is my personal list on this occasion, no doubt influenced by having read this book:

1. *DBR is guided by an explicit goal.* A goal not only gives concrete purpose to a research project, it anchors coherence (but see also item 2). Interestingly, when I require my students to develop a one-sentence goal, they find it quite challenging. It can take me hours to satisfactorily hone the wording of an overarching goal for a study. But, the process of doing so is an important and insightful step. I also insist, for them and for myself, that a goal be justified in the literature and often in the realm of democratic values à la Dewey.

2. *DBR makes space for the unexpected.* All instructional moves, from the mundane (e.g., changing a seating arrangement) to the more profound (e.g., engaging in less teacher talk), have unintended as well as intended consequences. My data collection and analysis always include a category for unintended consequences, so I attend to that reality. It can inform a current study and may lead to further research. It also makes me wonder, especially with regard to those who use medical research as a model for education research, why education researchers don't specify the possible side effects of our "treatments."

3. *DBR foregrounds consequential validity and case-to-case generalization.* These could be separate items, but they are related. Experimental studies seek to balance internal validity (setting up an experiment to make valid causal connections) and external validity (experimental tasks like those occurring naturally). But, increasing one often decreases the other—a catch-22. External validity isn't an issue for DBR. It is always conducted in naturally occurring complex learning environments. Neither is internal validity, because it is nigh impossible to identify precise causal chains among the many interacting variables in classrooms. Instead, DBR seeks consequential validity (Messick, 1992), achieving valued goals more or less reliably and in the process identifying consequential (i.e., influential), not unequivocal causal variables. Likewise, experimental studies seek generalization from a sample (a few representative cases) to a population (everyone who might use a particular intervention). DBR seeks case-to-case generalization (Firestone, 1993), which essentially means that the more a teacher's situation (i.e., case) is like the one in a particular DBR study, the more likely findings will hold (again, like a medical doctor diagnosing a case). That means replication is particularly useful and important in DBR, which is another idea that could be a separate item in this list.

4. *DBR offers recommendations, not prescriptions, for practice.* This aspect counters the conceit, most evident among quantitative researchers, and policymakers looking for final answers, that the object of education research is to identify best practice for every teacher anywhere (Thorndike's legacy lives on). Most prominent is the U.S. Department of Education's What Works Clearinghouse, which, from a DBR perspective, might be recast as "What It *Takes* to Work Clearinghouse." Using research findings as dictates removes all of teachers' professional judgment from the equation (see item 10). I have written elsewhere (Reinking, 2007) that the concept of best, or so-called evidence-based, practice is unreasonable and should instead be a quest to determine good and better practice.

5. *DBR reveals and naturally attends to failure, treating it as data that open up possibilities for deep understanding.* Engineers, as designers, systematically investigate failure (e.g., wind tunnels that determine conditions that will lead an airplane's wing to fail). Failure does not have to be manufactured in DBR research. It happens naturally. As Decker Walker (2006) has argued poetically, our goal as design-based researchers is not to create an intervention that is immune to failure, but one that might fail more gracefully. A major historical limitation of education research is that there is virtually no systematic analysis of failure, which, since failure is routine in the physical sciences, calls into question whether education research is truly scientific.

6. *DBR is intellectually stimulating, because it requires creative, diagnostic problem solving.* DBR researchers are inevitably problem solvers. They must continuously be attuned to the question "What is really happening here?" because making reliable, stable predictions associated with teaching is incredibly difficult, if not impossible.

Instructional environments are unbounded spaces that entail radical uncertainty in the domain of "wicked problems" (Kay & King, 2020). They entail diagnosis and creative thinking about solutions, and diagnostic thinking has been argued to be more generative, divergent, and creative than causal thinking (Sloman & Fernbach, 2017). In DBR, there are invariably multiple challenging obstacles to achieving success, and thus is fertile ground to learn something that no one has seen clearly or thought about before. I think of the scene from the movie *Apollo 13* with the three astronauts trying to make it back to Earth in their damaged spacecraft and running out of oxygen. The chief engineer on the ground gathers his team, saying we must figure out how to make this fit into that using only this, while throwing a box of miscellaneous items found on the spacecraft onto a table. It is a great analogy for DBR. Designing instruction is engaging because it is difficult, but potentially deeply revealing.

7. *DBR looks beyond effectiveness to aspects such as appeal and efficiency—and importance* (Reigeluth & Frick, 1999). Put simply, what good is an intervention that results in measurable gains in learning or competence in a skill that is unnecessary, that is implemented in a way that practitioners and students/users dislike, or that requires so much time and resources that it is completely unfeasible? What can work (under controlled conditions) isn't always important, and doesn't always work under less than ideal conditions in a way that is completely satisfying to those who must implement it.

8. *DBR is productively theoretical.* Some critics have unfairly criticized DBR for being atheoretical, that is, only aimed at designing something that works. That criticism is no more valid than saying that the Wright brothers' efforts to design an airplane were atheoretical (Stokes, 1997). They knew well and used Bernoulli's theory of lift in their design, but their genius was to build a machine that would enable controlled flight, consequently founding the field of aerodynamics. Similarly, and just as important, DBR produces theories that are more productive. They inherently test existing theory in practice and generate new pedagogical theories that are more immediately applicable to practice. These new theories have been called "local" or "humble" or even more modestly labeled not as theories but as "assertions" or "conjectures" (Bell, 2004; Cobb, Confrey, diSessa, Lehrer, & Schauble, 2003). They must necessarily be so because they are contextually contingent, which makes them productively useful to practice in the spirit of instrumentalism.

9. *DBR is about infidelity, not fidelity.* No, not that kind. Fidelity means prescriptively (see item 4) following an instructional protocol precisely without variation (think recipes). It is promoted as a necessary and desirable aspect of experimental studies. It is also one of two convenient "excuses" offered when a so-called evidence-based intervention doesn't work: (1) lack of fidelity, or (2) not enough time applying fidelity for the expected effects to appear. Any teacher knows that good instruction needs to be adapted to particular students, the instructional context, available resources, and so forth. So do DBR researchers. That reality means

infidelity is necessary and useful, and, more importantly, informative. Fidelity is a fantasy and a product of conceptualizing classrooms as laboratories (Thorndike's legacy).

10. *DBR respects and values the professional judgment of practitioners.* A common narrative trope is a supervisor, senior military officer, and so forth, who has little experience but who thinks they know more than the longtime repairman or noncommissioned officer engaged in day-to-day practice (Thorndike, again). One of my greatest assets as a DBR researcher has been having the good fortune to be married for 45 years to a highly successful, and well-loved, elementary schoolteacher. She has been a sounding board and reality check for my theoretical musings and interpretations of research.

Readers of this book will get glimpses of these personally attractive and useful aspects of DBR and many others that might be listed. The editors have assembled a group of contributors who are well positioned to share their ongoing work using DBR and the insights they have gained along the way. The contributors include seasoned researchers who, like me, came to know, understand, and use DBR after many years of conducting and publishing research within more established paradigms of education research. Others are mid-career, and a few are newer scholars who have used DBR in their dissertation studies and who are now building their careers around DBR research. Collectively, they and their respective chapters testify to the attraction of DBR and to how it has slowly, but steadily, moved into the mainstream of education research. This book is an important milestone in that historical progress.

DAVID REINKING, PhD
University of Georgia

REFERENCES

Bell, P. (2004). On the theoretical breadth of design-based research in education. *Educational Psychologist, 39,* 243–253.

Biesta, J. J., & Burbules, N. C. (2003). *Pragmatism and educational research.* Lanham, MD: Rowman & Littlefield.

Brown, A. L. (1992). Design experiments: Theoretical and methodological challenges in creating complex interventions in classroom settings. *Journal of Learning Sciences, 2*(2), 141–178.

Cobb, P., Confrey, J., diSessa, A., Lehrer, R., & Schauble, L. (2003). Design experiments in educational research. *Educational Researcher, 32*(1), 9–13.

Collins, A. (1992). Toward a design science of education. In E. Scanlon & T. O'Shea (Eds.), *New directions in educational technology* (pp. 15–22). Berlin: Springer-Verlag.

Firestone, W. A. (1993). Alternative arguments for generalizing from data as applied to qualitative research. *Educational Researcher, 22*(4), 16–23.

Gage, N. L. (1989). The paradigm wars and their aftermath: A "historical" sketch of research on teaching since 1989. *Educational Researcher, 18*(7), 4–10.

Kay, J. A., & King, M. A. (2020). *Radical uncertainty*. London: Bridge Street Press.

Labaree, D. F. (2003). The peculiar problems of preparing educational researchers. *Educational Researcher, 32*(4), 13–22.

Lagemann, E. C. (2000). *An elusive science: The troubling history of education research*. Chicago: University of Chicago Press.

Lee, V. (2018). A short history of the learning sciences. In R. E. West (Ed.), *Foundations of learning and instructional design technology*. EdTech Books. Retrieved from *https://edtechbooks.org/lidtfoundations/history_of_learning_sciences*

Maxwell, J. A. (2016). Expanding the history and range of mixed methods research. *Journal of Mixed Methods Research, 10*(1), 12–27.

McKenney, S., & Reeves, T. C. (2020). Educational design research: Portraying, conducting, and enhancing productive scholarship. *Medical Education.*

Messick, S. (1992). The interplay of evidence and consequences in the validation of performance assessments. *Educational Researcher, 23*(2), 13–23.

Newman, D. (1990). Opportunities for research on the organizational impact of school computers. *Educational Researcher, 19*, 8–13.

Reigeluth, C. M., & Frick, T. W. (1999). Formative research: A methodology for creating and improving design theories. In C. M. Reigeluth (Ed.), *Instructional-design theories and models: Vol. II. A new paradigm of instructional theory* (pp. 633–651). Mahwah, NJ: Erlbaum.

Reinking, D. (2007). Toward a good or better understanding of best practice. *Journal of Curriculum and Instruction*. Retrieved December 15, 2007, from *www.joci.ecu.edu/index.php/JoCI*

Reinking, D., & Yaden Jr., D. B. (2021). Do we need more productive theorizing? A commentary. *Reading Research Quarterly, 56*(3), 383–399.

Sloman, S., & Fernbach, F. (2017). *The knowledge illusion: Why we never think alone*. New York: Riverhead.

Stokes, D. E. (1997). *Pasteur's quadrant*. Washington, DC: Brookings Institution Press.

Tashakkori, A., & Teddlie, C. (1998). *Mixed methodology: Combining qualitative and quantitative approaches*. Thousand Oaks, CA: SAGE.

Walker, D. (2006). Toward productive design studies. In J. van den akker, K. Gravemeijer, S. Mckenney, & N. Nieveen (Eds.), *Educational design research* (pp. 8–13). New York: Routledge.

Preface

In 2015, Catherine Snow argued that education is in need of research that values partnerships between research and practice. Although this was not a new assertion, it did reflect a growing sense that more must be done to ensure connections between research and practice that were robust and elemental to better understand teaching and learning. Snow also responded to those who may see this perspective as incongruent with sound research practices, by asserting that such partnerships and associated research methods are "not an alternative to rigor, though it may impose an altered definition of rigor" (p. 465). In some fields, such as literacy, research has methodologically extended the repertoire of approaches used for design and analysis of findings to address questions involving individuals, groups, and larger populations. Establishing collaborative partnerships between researchers and practitioners has led to a fertile orientation in which the purpose of research is driven by the classroom (e.g., Howell, Perez, & Abraham, 2021; Traga Philippakos, MacArthur, & Munsell, 2018). As acceptance of research methodologies has expanded in these ways, it is important to deeply understand them, so they become an avenue for exploration and further learning rather than a source of tension leading to fragmentation of research. In this process, it becomes of paramount importance to leverage the efforts to accurately portray the realities of classroom learning and recognize the ways research shapes classroom environments, while also being shaped by them.

One approach that gives attention to both the outcome and the process of learning is design-based research (DBR). DBR focuses on understanding the environment, the transformation of tasks and individuals, and modifications needed in a complex classroom ecology. At its core, DBR is a researcher–practitioner collaborative effort based on a specific theory and on the design and testing of approaches within an authentic instructional context through iterative cycles. The specificity in design and execution of DBR works in concert with its responsiveness to the dynamic needs associated with working in classrooms. As such, DBR responds to classroom needs and is shaped by the reality of classrooms. Contrary to traditional experimental methodologies that are interested in answering what works and generalize findings, DBR is interested in addressing how an intervention works and how it can best work within the context of a real classroom and school. Notably, DBR does not exclude follow-up with experimental methodologies; thus, it can enrich the narrative of *what works* with *how, for whom,* and *when*.

While DBR is increasingly common across education research, it remains more accepted in the learning sciences than in other fields within educational research (such as literacy; see Parsons, Gallagher, & the George Mason University Content Analysis Team, 2016). And while an increasing number note DBR as a methodological approach, the development and refinement of the principles of DBR continue and warrant continued examination (Sandoval, 2014). The lack of a deep publication record on DBR coupled with challenges associated with engaging in such research does not seem due to an unwillingness of journal editors to broaden perspectives of the research they publish, but is possibly due to needed understanding of the purpose, principles, and practices that make DBR a vital approach to education research.

Goals of This Book

As the editors of this book, we have set as a goal to showcase the relevancy of DBR to education and provide specific examples of its application across educational contexts and subjects. We hope that this work will encourage current and future researchers to utilize DBR in their educational research settings.

We hope that this book and the content of this work will allow DBR to become more fully known and possibly available to researchers and graduate students. DBR is more than the implementation and observation of concrete control and treatment variables. It is messy, with continual negotiations between the research team and co-constructing solutions to a continual flux of factors. Large amounts of data are often collected that inform both anticipated and unexpected factors that influence the goal of research. With this in mind, DBR is not just one approach, but a combination of approaches that can lead to refinement of instruction, theories, or resources to an applied educational context (Barab & Squire, 2004). The ambiguity in this combination at times leads to challenges on well-designed DBR receiving research merit and becoming part of a published corpus. Thus, we anticipate that the provided chapters, with a close examination and identification of DBR principles across contexts of educational learning, can provide continual development and clarity of DBR in practice to better differentiate between DBR studies and other designs, and to demonstrate the value of DBR to education research.

We are thankful for our contributing authors and are hopeful for future DBR studies that may emerge from this work. The field of education is a complex construct; answers to questions on "what works" should be more inclusive and contextual. Research and researchers have a lot to learn from teachers in this reciprocal learning process.

Organization of the Book

The authors of chapters in this book explain the rigor, procedures, and benefits of implementing DBR at an international level, across educational contexts (e.g., science, literacy), grade levels (e.g., elementary, secondary), foci (e.g., intervention design, professional development, assessment, technical education), and populations (e.g., graduate students, researchers, preservice learners), while also presenting a thorough view of the history and components of high-quality DBR.

Part I provides a comprehensive explanation of DBR as a research methodology, with Chapter 1 commenting on its principles of design and Chapter 2 explaining its function in research.

Part II addresses curriculum development across a range of subjects and grades. Chapter 3 examines the process of curriculum development and the role of teachers as partners within a DBR methodological setting. Chapter 4 offers an example of the use of DBR in science, and Chapter 5 addresses the use of DBR in mathematics with explicit explanations of a design and application with young learners. Chapter 6 comments on the use of DBR to develop a middle school curriculum in reading and writing.

Part III includes specific applications of DBR in educational settings. Chapter 7 explains how DBR is applied in reading intervention; Chapter 8 addresses the application of digital literacies in secondary settings; Chapter 9 comments on the application of DBR methodologies to best support multilingual learners; and Chapter 10 describes the use of DBR in assessment and specifically in the development of think-aloud measures.

Part IV addresses the relationship of teachers and researchers within DBR methodologies. Chapter 11 examines the design and application of a professional development model on genre-based strategy instruction; Chapter 12 addresses the design and application of professional development in disciplinary literacy; Chapter 13 explains how DBR can be used in teacher preparation and its affordances with preservice teachers; Chapter 14 explores DBR as a means for dissertation research and its utilization by graduate students; and, finally, Chapter 15 applies DBR in higher technical education.

Acknowledgments

We would like to acknowledge that this work was developed during a pandemic that greatly affected the lives of citizens of our world, including the authors of these chapters. We would like to thank our contributing authors for diligently working to complete this work even though life as we all knew it was not the same. Furthermore, we would like to thank Professor David Reinking, who has been a leader in the field of DBR in literacy, for writing the foreword for this book. In addition, we would like to thank our editor at The Guilford Press, Craig Thomas, for supporting a book on DBR methodologies and for offering advice and guidance throughout the process. Finally, we would like to thank all our graduate students, teachers, and collaborators across educational settings and strata for working with us while we applied DBR in our own research and allowed us to learn from them and with them in a true partnership that is a hallmark of DBR.

REFERENCES

Barab, S., & Squire, K. (2004). Design-based research: Putting a stake in the ground. *Journal of the Learning Sciences, 13*(1), 1–14.

Howell, E., Perez, S., & Abraham, W. T. (2021). Toward a professional development model for writing as a digital, participatory process. *Reading Research Quarterly, 56*(1), 95–117.

Parsons, S. A., Gallagher, M. A., & the George Mason University Content Analysis Team. (2016). A content analysis of nine literacy journals, 2009–2014. *Journal of Literacy Research, 48*(4), 476–502.

Sandoval, W. (2014). Conjecture mapping: An approach to systematic educational design research. *Journal of the Learning Sciences, 23*(1), 18–36.

Snow, C. E. (2015). 2014 Wallace Foundation Distinguished Lecture: Rigor and realism: Doing educational science in the real world. *Educational Researcher, 44*(9), 460–466.

Traga Philippakos, Z., MacArthur, C., & Munsell, S. (2018). Collaborative reasoning with strategy instruction for opinion writing in primary grades: Two cycles of design research. *Reading and Writing Quarterly, 34*(6), 485–504.

Contents

PART I. UNDERSTANDING DESIGN-BASED RESEARCH

1. Design-Based Research in Educational Settings: 3
Motivations, Crosscutting Features, and Considerations
for Design
Melissa Campanella and William R. Penuel

2. Addressing Publication Challenges in Design-Based Research 23
**Margret A. Hjalmarson, Allison Ward Parsons, Seth A. Parsons,
and Amy C. Hutchison**

PART II. DESIGN-BASED RESEARCH AND CURRICULUM DEVELOPMENT

3. Combining Curriculum and Teacher Development 45
through Design Research
Jan van den Akker and Nienke Nieveen

4. Curriculum Development in Science 64
Kalle Juuti and Jari Lavonen

5. Classroom Design-Based Research: Designing for Proportional Reasoning in Mathematics Education ... 83
Michelle Stephan

6. Curriculum Development of Reading and Writing in the Middle Grades ... 103
Zoi A. Philippakos and Charles A. MacArthur

PART III. DESIGN-BASED RESEARCH AND SPECIFIC APPLICATIONS

7. Literacy Is Transformative: Secondary Reading Interventions Using Design-Based Research ... 127
Alejandro Gonzalez Ojeda, Nancy Frey, Douglas Fisher, and Diane Lapp

8. Collaborative Design to Support Digital Literacies across the Curriculum ... 147
Kelly Chandler-Olcott, Sharon Dotger, Kathleen A. Hinchman, Heather Waymouth, and Keith O. Newvine

9. Multilingual Students and Design-Based Research: Developing Opportunities in Partnerships ... 167
Ryan McCarty, Tim Pappageorge, and Claudia Rueda-Alvarez

10. Using Design-Based Research to Develop a Formative Assessment Tool ... 187
Kristi Tamte Bergeson

PART IV. DESIGN-BASED RESEARCH AND TEACHER-RESEARCHERS

11. Professional Development on Genre-Based Strategy Instruction on Writing ... 209
Zoi A. Philippakos

12. Improving Disciplinary Literacy Teaching: A Formative Experiment Exploring Professional Development in Disciplinary Settings ... 231
Phillip Wilder, Emily Howell, Lorraine Jacques, Susan Cridland-Hughes, and Mary-Celeste Schreuder

13. Purposeful Clinical Practices in Teacher Preparation through Design-Based Research 253
Anthony Pellegrino

14. Graduate Students Writing Design-Based Research Dissertations 272
Susan McKenney and Thomas Reeves

15. Fostering Techno-Mathematical Literacies in Higher Technical Education: Reflections on Challenges and Successes of Design-Based Implementation Research 296
Nathalie J. van der Wal, Arthur Bakker, Albert Moes, and Paul Drijvers

Index 317

PART I
UNDERSTANDING DESIGN-BASED RESEARCH

CHAPTER 1

Design-Based Research in Educational Settings
Motivations, Crosscutting Features, and Considerations for Design

Melissa Campanella and William R. Penuel

> Most educational research describes or evaluates education as it currently is. Some educational research analyzes education as it was. Design research, however, is about education as it could be or even as it should be.
> —BAKKER (2018, p. 3)

Design-based research (DBR) as it is practiced today can trace its origins to Vygotsky and his followers, as well as a number of other influences. One of those followers, Davydov (1988), coined the term *teaching experiment* to refer to a method he used: testing out approaches to supporting students' mathematical concept development, observing how students responded, and articulating potential trajectories of learning at the conclusions of his investigations. In the learning sciences, where DBR might be called a *signature methodology*, Davydov's approach inspired multiple lines of research in Holland and the United States in mathematics education (e.g., Cobb, McClain, & Gravemeijer, 2003). These researchers adapted the idea of a "teaching experiment" to the design and testing of conjectures about how to support mathematics learning. DBR within the learning sciences has also been inspired by participatory design traditions of Scandinavia (Ehn, 1992) and workplace ethnography (e.g., Orr & Crowfoot, 1992), and by psychologists and cognitive scientists seeking to create practical applications of theories and knowledge for education (e.g., Brown, 1992; Collins, 1992).

DBR is neither a single methodology nor a static one. It can be challenging to conceptualize, in part because it draws on methods from multiple traditions, from ethnography to human–computer interaction, and also because the purposes for DBR are so varied and continually evolving. For example, while DBR focused on supporting subject matter learning during much of the decade of the 1990s, and typically involved close collaborations between researchers and one or more classroom teachers, today, DBR encompasses research on outcomes such as civic participation (Kirshner & Polman, 2013; York & Kirshner, 2015; York, 2015) and can involve multileveled partnerships between researchers and practitioners (Severance, Leary, & Johnson, 2014). Furthermore, whereas DBR has focused primarily in the past on generating powerful concepts about learning like Vygotsky's zone of proximal development (ZPD) that help us to *see* learning in new ways (diSessa & Cobb, 2004), today's DBR also aims to help us generate new forms of relationships—not only among researchers, practitioners, and community members, but also within larger ecosystems (Bang, Faber, Gurneau, Marin, & Soto, 2016).

When Is DBR a Good Choice as an Approach?

Before addressing what DBR *is*, it is useful to consider *when* DBR might be a good approach for a given problem, phenomenon, or goal. DBR, like all approaches to inquiry, can address some research questions more suitably than others (Bakker, 2018; Penuel & Frank, 2016). Furthermore, its pragmatic commitments to changing educational practice make it different from research that is primarily descriptive or critical in nature. DBR, however, can and does take critical perspectives (e.g., Khalil & Kier, 2017), and descriptive analyses are common in reports of design studies.

In this connection, one situation where DBR is a good choice is when the design team hopes to *intervene* in the situation. The purpose of intervention may be to improve an outcome that is already a goal within a school or community organization, but DBR is especially well suited to intervention where new goals are being identified and pursued that may not be reflected in current standards or practice (Cobb, Confrey, diSessa, Lehrer, & Schauble, 2003; Shaffer & Squire, 2006). The goals of intervention may also include transformation of systems (e.g., Wingert, Riedy, Campanella, & Penuel, 2020) and of relationships between institutions in a community (e.g., families and schools; Ishimaru & Takahashi, 2017).

Not all intervention research questions, however, can be addressed in DBR. When the question of whether something works or not is central, experimental research—in which participants or groups are randomly assigned to treatment or control conditions—is more appropriate to use than DBR. Experimental research answers the question of what would have happened if the participants did not participate in the intervention (cf. Rubin, 1974). By contrast, DBR answers questions of a "How can . . . ?" variety, such as *How can tools for assessment design help teachers develop more equitable assessments for students?* Causal questions can be answered, but they answer questions about the roles of designed tools and practices in supporting specific learning processes (Sandoval, 2014).

Another situation where DBR is a suitable approach is when the purpose is to develop theory and knowledge related to some aspect of learning and development.

Edelson (2002) wrote that DBR is a good approach for developing theory and knowledge related to particular outcomes of learning and routes or means to supporting learning. He also argued that DBR could help develop theory and knowledge related to how to go about designing a particular class of innovations. An example of this type of DBR comes from the inquiryHub partnership, which has iterated over many years on a process of collaborative design of science curriculum materials, with the purpose of refining an approach to balance a focus on standards with student interest (Penuel et al., 2018).

A review of the past two decades of DBR in education might lead one to conclude that DBR focuses exclusively on subject matter learning, particularly in science, technology, engineering, and mathematics (STEM). But DBR can be fitting for intervention research focused on any domain of learning and development at any age and in any context, from socioemotional learning of young children in preschools to the sociopolitical development of adolescents in community-based organizations to the civic learning of adults in a community science project in a museum. It can also be used to generate knowledge related to differences in values in a community of practitioners (Kaplan, Riedy, Van Horne, & Penuel, 2019).

Another occasion when DBR is appropriate is when researchers aim to directly affect practice through their research. At its core, DBR is pragmatic in aspiration (Brown, 1992), seeking to bring about changes in the world. Practical tools such as professional development (PD) designs and curriculum materials may result from DBR studies, even though those designs and materials are only sometimes shared widely. For some learning scientists, the pragmatic approach embedded in DBR means that designs should aspire to be usable within current contexts of learning (e.g., Blumenfeld, Fishman, Krajcik, Marx, & Soloway, 2000). But for others, the goal of influencing practice is interpreted more in line with a Marxist or post-Marxist notion of *praxis* (e.g., Gutiérrez & Vossoughi, 2010). For these design researchers, it is not enough to support existing goals of institutions or even of researcher-developed learning goals; rather, DBR is oriented to support a kind of "social dreaming" (McLaren, 1991) of new possibilities not only for learning but also of a just society.

What Makes Something a Design Study?

In this section, we describe some crosscutting features of DBR. Our description differs from previous efforts to characterize what makes something a design study (e.g., Cobb et al., 2003; Design-Based Research [DBR] Collective, 2003; Reimann, 2011; Anderson & Shattuck, 2012), in that it both builds from those and derives from the collective effort of a group of graduate students to make sense of this broad, and continuing changing approach to research. The students read both earlier descriptions of DBR as an approach, as well as examples of DBR studies that have been widely cited in the field for decades and studies that have been published over the last few years. The crosscutting features we describe below reflect their synthesis of key features, which extend earlier efforts at synthesis to encompass where DBR is headed as an approach in the learning sciences today.

DBR Is Future Oriented

DBR asks questions about what could be learned about the world by changing it. It asks what *could* or *should* be, and how can we get there? It seeks to imagine new possible social futures (New London Group, 1996) via the design or organization of learning environments. What could be goes beyond just the design of a particular program or curriculum: behind any DBR effort is a *design politic* (Tzou et al., 2019b), that is, an image of the social world as it could be and how to bring it about.

The particular imagined social futures and design politics of design researchers vary widely. Whereas some research posits subject-matter mastery as the desired end of learning and imagines that mastery at each grade level prepares students to develop successively more sophisticated understandings of subject matter (e.g., Wiser, Smith, & Doubler, 2012), other DBR raises significant questions about whether subject-matter learning as traditionally conceived can truly benefit people and communities in ways imagined (e.g., Bang, Warren, Rosebery, & Medin, 2012). Explicit commitments to equity and justice, to remediating and repairing relationships in human communities and with the Earth, as well as to cultural sustainability and resurgence, are increasingly goals of DBR (e.g., Bang et al., 2016; Bang & Vossoughi, 2016; Teeters & Jurow, 2018). Thus, the *design politic* of DBR can involve a critique of existing social and educational inequities, and it can also begin with an envisioning of radical new possibilities for learning.

Being future oriented also means that design researchers often invent methods for doing what has not yet been done in classrooms. For example, in the 1970s, mathematics teacher-researchers at the University of Utrecht in the Netherlands wanted students to have more control over their learning after years of top-down, direct instruction methods. They rejected existing educational research methods that began in controlled laboratory settings, which produced findings on a timeline that was too slow to be of practical use. They decided to set up shop in classrooms, testing their design ideas in real time and making immediate refinements. Over time, they developed a domain-specific theory, Realistic Mathematics Education (RME), which included both principles for math learning and for the design of math learning environments. This approach emphasized that the "development of learning environments and the development of theory were intertwined" (Bakker, 2018, p. 30). These mathematics education researchers imagined a possible future where students learned in ways that were more authentic to real-life experiences, and they envisioned—and brought about—new methods for studying teaching that supported this way of learning. In sum, DBR is future oriented with respect to both the ends of learning and means of supporting it.

DBR Builds Theory and Knowledge about Learning *and* Design

A design study is always engaged in building knowledge and theory about both learning and design. That is to say, the products of design are not the only thing that matters in DBR. The interventions are intended to embody theory and help understand the relations among theory, designs, and practice (DBR Collective, 2003; Sandoval, 2014).

Pinkard, Erete, Martin, and McKinney de Royston's (2017) study of narrative-driven curriculum in the Digital Youth Divas (DYD) project illustrates these intertwined priorities. Drawing on Nasir and Cooks's (2009) notion of identity resources, they sought to create a program that could support Black and Brown middle school girls' STEM interests and identities by developing new ideas about valued learning goals (ideational resources), new connections with peers and mentors (relational resources), and curriculum (material resources). The team designed a project-based curriculum anchored to an interactive virtual program whose narrative mirrored real life in middle school and integrated authentic STEM tasks into the episodes of the story line. Featuring virtual mentors with realistic intersectional identities, the curriculum allowed girls to immerse in the story virtually and then contribute in concrete ways to solving problems in the real world, with their real-life mentors (for instance, building a circuit board like the one that would be needed to light a LED bouquet of flowers in the episode).

Testing this conjecture allowed the team to continue to refine ideas about how different identity resources could support learning. They found that authentic, interactive narratives were motivating to girls, and that the curriculum offered material, relational, and ideational resources that supported the girls' identity development in STEM and computer science; the study also helped team members learn how to improve their design. For example, co-design of the narrative became an important part of the design. Team members believed that, to be relevant, the story needed to include input from the girls they hoped would benefit from it. After co-designing narratives with the girls, they found that this turned out to be the case, with the girls giving invaluable feedback about how to refine situations and characters to make them more relatable.

DBR Is Intended to Be Useful

Usability is both a motivation for and a crosscutting feature of DBR. In DBR, both the theories that guide design and the products need to be practical. To be of use in DBR, theories must do real "design work in generating, selecting and validating design alternatives at the level at which they are consequential" (diSessa & Cobb, 2004, p. 77). In this connection, the kind of theories that are useful tend to be *small* or *humble* (Cobb et al., 2003) in nature, focused on a specific domain of learning and development (e.g., how to support elementary-aged students' statistical reasoning; Cobb, McClain, & Gravemeijer, 2003), rather than *grand* theories that provide mainly general frameworks or guidance for design (e.g., the idea of *scaffolding* to support learning in the ZPD).

Theory can inform efforts to create designs that are usable in a wide range of contexts as well. For example, Ahn and colleagues (Ahn, Campos, Hays, & DiGiacomo, 2019) used ideas from human–computer interaction research to inform their efforts to design and test a learning analytics dashboard that instructional coaches could use to support the improvement of mathematics teaching. The theories they drew on helped them make explicit to their partners design rationales for work, but also supported productive adaptations and uses of the dashboard for a variety of users.

Ahn and colleagues' (2019) approach of involving end users or implementers in design is becoming more common, as more design researchers embrace the idea that participation is key to creating usable designs. Though participation in co-design is not always a part of DBR in education (e.g., Alvarez, 2012), design researchers often view at least some participation as essential to design itself. We return to this conversation during our discussion of considerations for design.

DBR Is Iterative

Iteration, that is, revising a design based on a study of its enactment, is essential to DBR (Anderson & Shattuck, 2012). It is through iteration and careful documentation of the iterative process that designs are improved, and knowledge and theory are refined. Design researchers use a variety of strategies for documenting and interpreting the process of iteration, from developing design narratives (e.g., Ahn et al., 2019) to analyzing design tensions (e.g., Tatar, 2007), to tracing shifts in conjectured relations between design features and learning interactions (e.g., Wilkerson, 2017). Each of these methods helps design researchers coordinate changes in designs with evidence gathered about how designs are taken up in practice. Iteration also provides a means to help test theories that emerge from testing designs in practice (Gravemeijer & Cobb, 2013).

Design researchers do not always write about their iterations, or sometimes write only about one phase of iteration in their published studies; still other design researchers trace the evolution of the intervention over multiple iterations. Iteration does not always serve the same purpose, or provide the same benefit, but it is an essential part of design. For example, for Gutiérrez and Jurow (2016), iteration centered on attending to emerging issues of equity, and partners and communities were meaningfully involved in the process of iteration, with researchers holding themselves accountable for the ways that they promoted more equitable relationships in the community (e.g., Gutiérrez & Jurow, 2016). For Tzou and colleagues (2019a), iteration focused on the participatory design process, and the relational components that helped transform traditional power dynamics and roles taken up in DBR partnerships.

Bang and colleagues (2016) described yet another form of iteration that can take place in DBR in the context of a search for axiological innovations in learning, that is, innovations in the ways people relate to one another and to other living beings in their environment. Initial efforts in this project on Indigenous science learning focused on crafting formal processes and agreements among researchers, community-based educators, and community members, as well as consultations with elders about the project (Bang, Medin, Washinawatok, & Chapman, 2010). Over time, to help support more transformative relations among those involved in the effort, the team developed activities to help facilitate relationship building:

> Increasingly we worked to develop design practices to surface and acknowledge our collective experiences and help us to work toward imagining new possible futures. For example we often engaged in "river of life" activities, which is a visual narrative method that supports collaborators in telling their stories, perspectives, and diverse expertises about the past, present, and future by creating a collective visual artifact, working toward unpacking the trajectories that made the present moment possible and helped to imagine future trajectories. (p. 35)

In addition to illustrating how the focus of iteration can center on relationships, this project highlights ways that iteration can take place within participatory or co-design processes.

Examples of DBR That Illustrate Its Crosscutting Features

In this section, we present two different examples of DBR that illustrate each of the crosscutting features named above. The examples were chosen to reflect two common contexts of DBR, schools and communities. The first is a line of DBR that we have conducted in the context of a long-term research practice partnership (Farrell, Penuel, Daniel, Steup, & Coburn, 2020). The second is an example of community-based DBR conducted in partnership with parents in schools.

Case 1: Preparing Teachers to Develop Five-Dimensional Science Assessments

The inquiryHub research–practice partnership, which began in 2007, is a collaboration between the Denver Public Schools and the University of Colorado Boulder, and includes a number of other partners that support its work. The primary work of the partnership is in STEM education. Since the partnership's inception, it has (1) created a technology platform for supporting science teachers to customize their instruction that has been in continuous use within the district since 2009 (Sumner & the Curriculum Customization Service Team, 2010); (2) developed routines and formative assessments supporting middle school science teachers to use responsive pedagogies (Penuel et al., 2017); (3) developed software tools and processes supporting algebra teachers to identify and select high-quality mathematical tasks (Johnson, Severance, Penuel, & Leary, 2016); (4) developed a yearlong, project-based biology curriculum (Affolter et al., 2018) aligned with the Next Generation Science Standards (NGSS Lead States, 2013). The line of research described below focuses on supporting teachers in learning to design new science assessments that embody the vision for teaching and learning proposed in A Framework for K–12 Science Education (National Research Council [NRC], 2012).

Future-Oriented

The vision of the NRC framework calls for new forms of assessment that are uncommon in today's schools, that is, assessments that require students to apply knowledge of science and use science and engineering practices to solve problems and explain phenomena in the world (NRC, 2014). The vision is oriented toward an imagined future in which science and engineering can be resources or tools in service of community priorities and civic engagement (Penuel, 2016). Moreover, the call of assessments to connect to students' interests and identities in meaningful ways to promote equity invites teachers to consider how their classrooms are promoting agency and epistemic justice in classrooms that address ways in which students of color, girls and gender nonconforming students, emerging multilinguals, and students with disabilities historically have not been seen as *knowers* capable of doing science (Penuel & Watkins, 2019). The focus of this line of DBR—to prepare teachers to develop and use assessments that address all *five dimensions* (5D) of the NRC framework (core ideas, practices, crosscutting concept, interest, and identity)—is a means to bringing about a future with different kinds of assessments and relationships among students and between students and teachers in science classrooms.

Developing Theory and Knowledge

The high-level conjecture of this current iteration of the project posits that supporting teachers to design these 5D tasks using tools and feedback can shift teachers' visions for science teaching and improve the quality of tasks they develop. Supporting this conjecture is the theory and practice of evidence-centered design (Mislevy & Haertel, 2006), which proposes that a careful analysis of the domain of learning to be assessed, coupled with the use of specialized templates called *design patterns*, can support developers to create valid assessments. Evidence-centered design is typically an expert-driven process (i.e., by professional assessment developers); the research sought to investigate whether templates could support teachers with limited experience in designing assessments to create 5D tasks. A design study was undertaken in which a small sample of teachers received these templates with instructions on how to use them independently, while another sample took part in a 2-day workshop where they created assessments under the guidance of researchers, using the same templates. The study showed that both groups could, in fact, use the templates, and the use of those templates supported higher-quality assessments aligned with the vision of the framework (Penuel et al., 2019). Thus, the findings helped extend the range of applicability of evidence-based design to teachers and built knowledge of the ways tools could support design.

Supports for Usability

So that it would usable by teachers, the design team made significant modifications to the standard, evidence-centered design process. The team created a nine-step protocol for 5D task design, as well as a range of smaller, lightweight tools to support each step in the design. These tools included simplified templates that scaffold how to build science and engineering practices into tasks, question frames to support the incorporation of crosscutting concepts into prompts, sample exit tickets, a task screener that includes a rubric with checklist items, and reflective questions designed to help evaluate the "5D-ness" of existing tasks.

Iteration within the Project

One finding that emerged from the first iteration of the PD workshops was that in addition to templates, teachers found the feedback researchers gave on their assessments to be particularly useful. The design team had intended the feedback to be primarily a vehicle to share key findings with teachers as to how their tasks were being evaluated for research purposes. But, teachers found the feedback to be constructive and useful in helping them better understand 5D science assessment design. Therefore, the team incorporated feedback as a formal aspect of the learning design into a subsequent iteration, attending more to the structure of the feedback.

Case 2: PRIMES Project

Our second example concerns a line of DBR focused on supporting parent engagement in mathematics. The PRIMES project, which stands for Parents Rediscovering and Interacting with Math and Engaging Schools, was funded by the National Science Foundation. The goal of the project, led by Stanford researchers Angela Booker and Shelley Goldman, was to increase parents' confidence with reform-based mathematics teaching and with engaging with their child's school. The PRIMES project resulted in a small number of research publications, as well as a number of parent resources, including parent workshops, a television special called *The Family Angle* that aired on a digital public television channel, and a parent guide.

Future-Oriented

In contrast to projects that seek to engage parents on the typical terms that schools impose (Jay, Rose, & Simmons, 2017), the design team in PRIMES began with the premise that parents themselves bring important resources to accomplish this task. The researchers assumed that parents already engaged in some forms of mathematics in their household, some with their children, and that these could form the basis for supporting their children in school-based mathematics (Goldman & Booker, 2009). Therefore, as part of the research, they set out to take note of these resources and practices using ethnographic methods and a participatory design process to develop additional tools and resources for parents to support their engagement.

A key aspect of their vision for the future was one in which parents' relationship to mathematics—including school mathematics—was *repaired*. Math shame and fear were common among the parents in their study and hindered advocating for their children's learning. If parents could begin to feel like they were *math people*, they would be able to better advocate for their children and would themselves feel more comfortable in math learning spaces. The focus on repair, moreover, illustrates how one of the key goals of DBR can be centered on changing relationships among and between people and disciplinary practices.

Developing Theory and Knowledge

There were two key aims of the project, one related to developing knowledge of conditions under which repair of parents' relationship to mathematics might be facilitated, and one on how to support parents' participation in design.

A key concept guiding the researchers' efforts to promote repair was the sense of *epistemic authority* in mathematics (Booker & Goldman, 2016, p. 231), which forms a basis for supporting parents' agency and advocacy for their children's learning. Epistemic authority here refers to a confidence in speaking up about what parents know from using mathematics in their everyday lives and claiming its relevance to school mathematics that their children will encounter. The researchers also sought to cultivate among parents "the understanding that school math success is dependent on many factors that involve parents, ones that are quite independent of their understanding of classroom math" (Goldman, 2006, p. 58). The team's work started with the initial premise that "we could displace parents' fears of math by naming our everyday math practices and letting them start building new confidences" (Booker & Goldman, 2016, p. 224). This also depended on changing conditions in schools where other adults (e.g., teachers, administrators) positioned parents as not having competence in mathematics and were therefore treated as less than expert in their children's learning. The DBR tested this premise through developing and iterating in a series of workshops (described below) and documenting in a selected case study parents' changing sense of epistemic authority and agency over successive iterations of the workshops.

Rather than seeking to make a product that could *scale*, the design team sought to engage parents as co-designers and to develop knowledge of potentially replicable processes for co-design. The assumption that parents could be equal partners in design came from the researchers' commitment to a *competence-based* view of parents (Goldman, 2006). With that, PRIMES included four teams in a design consortium coordinated by researchers from Stanford University, each composed of parents, educators, and researchers. Two teams were based in school districts, and two were based in community organizations. Based on their experience of participatory design with parents, the researchers concluded that " 'open-ended social innovations' are crucial to systemic repair and that scaling method rather than product is a challenge for which PDR is well matched" (Booker & Goldman, 2016, p. 233).

Supports for Usability

Over the course of the partnership, the PRIMES project produced a number of resources that parents helped design and that were offered to parents outside the project sphere. A total of nine different workshops were created and delivered to multiple groups not only in the San Francisco Bay Area, but also across the country. The workshops were made available to others, too, to guide them independently of the research group. The team produced a television program for a digital channel of the Public Broadcasting Service (PBS). And, the design team produced a booklet detailing strategies parents could use to approach the school around aspects of school math during the middle school years. This booklet included topics from expectations around homework, to decisions about when to take algebra, to how to approach teacher conferences, and how to turn everyday math problem-solving opportunities into family math engagements.

According to the project's final report to the National Science Foundation, the workshops reached a total of 168 parents in three different locations: the San Francisco Bay Area, New York City, and rural Michigan. The San Francisco Unified School District shared the parent resource with every one of its parent liaisons to schools. The report also indicated that the television special aired in 2002 to more than 60,000 people. A total of 14 PBS and other educational stations additionally aired the feed.

Iteration within the Project

In the initial workshops with parents, researchers retained their position as experts—inadvertently supported by parents themselves—resulting in a significant early failure. According to Booker and Goldman (2016), the initial "workshop, and the kind of math problem solving accomplished, felt a lot like school, and as such, it reproduced the systemic rift we were seeking to repair" (p. 227). To address this issue, the team decided it would be more effective to reposition the teacher as a learner, and to build the next workshop around an open-ended planter box building project. This iteration proved more effective in some ways—the debrief conversation engaged parents more. But, the teacher still functioned as the owner of knowledge, and teachers struggled to position families' cultures and personal experiences as valuable. It was not until a parent, who was active as a partner in co-design, became a facilitator that the dynamic shifted, with the parent proposing different kinds of activities that involved a design activity where doing mathematics was required but was also in the background to a greater degree. Importantly, the failures from each of these workshop iterations supported the team so they could better understand the nature of the math rift. Ultimately, the team synthesized their learning into four design principles: sustained open dialogue, learner authority/positioning, collaborative data analysis, muting individual and cultural deficit.

What Should Design Researchers Consider When Planning and Carrying Out Studies?

While working through the sorts of difficulties and failures described in the examples above is a feature of DBR, some more serious critiques of DBR have emerged over the years (e.g., Shavelson et al., 2003), each of which has resulted in clarification of the underlying principles of the approach as well as advances within it. The different types of critiques could also be used as considerations for design researchers when planning and carrying out DBR.

Attending to Methodological Rigor

DBR has been subject to various methodological critiques, and design researchers should care about the methodological rigor of their studies. For us, two criticisms rise to the top. First, since design researchers conduct their *experiments* in complex settings with a multitude of uncontrolled variables, some have argued that it is difficult for design researchers to meet scientifically rigorous standards for making reliable and valid claims (Kelly, 2004; Shavelson et al., 2003). Second, since design studies can produce huge amounts of data, some have pointed out that design researchers can easily *cherry-pick* results (Brown, 1992; Derry et al., 2010).

Making scientifically rigorous claims in DBR is different from doing so in other interventionist or descriptive approaches to research, but it is not impossible. First, it is important to understand how DBR arguments differ from these other approaches. At the root of these differences is the fact that DBR is not a single or static methodology. Some approaches have what can be distinguished as a shared *argumentative grammar* (Kelly, 2004), such as experiments, where there are common understandings (a grammar) for evaluating studies based on whether threats to validity have been addressed adequately through random assignment. But, design researchers follow different argumentative grammars (Bell, 2004). They draw on a variety of both experimental and observational methods. Rather than beginning with a shared argumentative grammar then, DBR arguments lead with substantive theoretical conjectures about how best to organize for different forms of learning (Sandoval, 2014). Underlying each of these conjectures is a set of values about what is most worth learning, which themselves may become objects of critique and argument (Penuel & Shepard, 2016).

Conjecture maps are tools for figuring out if the things we believe promote the forms of learning we are trying to support are actually doing so. In a conjecture map, design researchers articulate their ideas about how particular designs will support particular kinds of learning by starting with a high-level conjecture. Design researchers then think through what it would look like if learners were to take up designs as intended by considering how learners embody designs via their tools and materials, prescribed roles for teachers and learners in the setting, and discursive practices (Sandoval, 2014). How learners interact with designs mediates their learning processes. Considering what we might see in these observable interactions between learners and designs, as well as in the artifacts learners produce through these processes, helps us begin to imagine what might actually happen as they take up designs (and thus articulate evidence for design successes and failures). Finally, design researchers consider how these mediating processes are intended to produce desired learning outcomes. Using a tool like a conjecture map, or some other means for keeping track of our ideas and how we are testing them, to explain our ideas about how both mediating processes of learning and embodiment of designs contribute to the kinds of change we are trying to make through our interventions helps us do a better job of evaluating how our designs function, and how those functions support particular kinds of learning (Sandoval, 2014, p. 25).

Supporting the Agency of Participants in Research

As we've emphasized, one of the crosscutting features of DBR is an attention to usability. Many design researchers believe that to create useful designs, their methods must be at least in some way participatory or collaborative (e.g., Couso, 2016). Design researchers differ in the level of agency they support for participants in design, as well as in the form agency takes in the process (Ormel, Roblin, McKenney, Voogt, & Pieters, 2012). In some instances, the agency of participants can extend to the DBR process itself (Severance, Penuel, Sumner, & Leary, 2016). Factors such as time, interest, and what is at stake all shape what level of agency participants have in design; determining roles and agency in design is often an ongoing (re)negotiation within teams (Penuel, Coburn, & Gallagher, 2013).

A number of scholars have pointed specifically to the question of *Who designs?* (Booker & Goldman, 2016; Engeström, 2011; Philip, Bang, & Jackson, 2018). Raising this question challenges design teams to consider what stakeholder groups are at the table in DBR, from teachers to parents to students. It demands that teams raise questions about the racial composition of their teams, and their preparedness to design both for and with particular groups. And, when particular groups cannot be at the table during the design process, how their input might be solicited is an important consideration, as is the creation of structures for *answerability* (Patel, 2015) to those groups.

When different groups are at the table in co-design, inevitably questions arise as to *participation for what?* (Ormel et al., 2012). There are multiple motivations for engaging in design, as reviewed above, and these can sometimes come into conflict. Leal (2007) highlights how the co-optation of participation by institutions like the World Bank have made *participation* a buzzword. Participation must be structured in such a way that attends to power differences involved in participation in design (O'Connor, Hanny, & Lewis, 2011), and to the ways that participation can simultaneously enable some forms of action (and actors' agency) while inhibiting other forms of action (and actors' agency) (Golob & Giles, 2013).

Promoting Socioecological and Racial Justice

Many design researchers have not and do not always do a good job of mapping positionality, race, and power, and how these factors impact design. Vakil, McKinney de Royston, Nasir, and Kirshner (2016) write that DBR, with its future orientation and concern with usable theory, "marks an important departure in the educational sciences toward investigations of cognition and learning that recognize the centrality of context" (p. 3), but that explicitly treating race and power in designs is currently lacking and is "critical for DBR to fulfill its potential to contribute towards equity and realize its potential as a democratizing methodology that can intervene in educational practice" (p. 4). Missing particularly are treatments of how "race and power mediate researcher-researched relationships within DBR projects" (p. 4). Khalil and Kier (2017) offer an emerging antiracist methodological approach for integrating critical race theory into DBR in education that presents one approach for better theorizing race and power in design. They propose three principles or pillars: attending to interest convergence, critiquing liberalism, and privileging counternarratives in DBR.

There is more than a single justice project, or even a single notion of justice. For example, Indigenous scholars remind us that repairing relations with living beings beyond the human is an important justice project (Bang et al., 2016; Tuck & Yang, 2018). Important justice projects being pursued by design researchers include decolonization (e.g., Tzou et al., 2019a), as well as abolition, that is, the effort to eliminate *carceral thinking*, which emphasizes policing and control over thriving and liberation, from our social institutions (Agid, 2018). As an aid to these projects, a lens of *critical historicity*, that is, attention to the history of relations among institutions, communities, and with the land, can be beneficial (Bang et al., 2016).

Toward a Critical Pragmatism in DBR

In this chapter, we have sought to represent DBR as an evolving, heterogeneous family of approaches with common features. At its root, all forms of DBR are deeply pragmatic in their approaches to developing and testing interventions with the potential to promote more equitable outcomes for students. DBR teams seek to change or transform practice through organizing and supporting new forms of learning. Whether cast as a form of *use-inspired research* (Stokes, 1997) or as a means of supporting "expansive notions of learning and mediated praxis fundamental to a transformative education for students from nondominant communities" (Gutiérrez & Vossoughi, 2010, p. 101), pragmatism suffuses DBR.

As DBR turns increasingly to tackle questions of race, power, and politics (Esmonde & Booker, 2016), it is important to bring one aspect of Dewey's pragmatism to the fore: the idea that education should prepare young people for participation in a democratic society. What kind of democracy, though, should DBR help prepare young people to join? DBR always makes bets on claims that a certain form of learning will bring young people into a particular future (Penuel & O'Connor, 2010); we would be wise to remain conscious of what those futures should be.

Emerging developments within the field point to the need for a more *critical pragmatist* (Feinberg, 2015) stance, that is, one that attends to both history and power. A critical pragmatism is a pragmatism "with teeth" that engages with conflict and pluralism (Hildreth, 2009, p. 798) and with questions of race (Eldridge, 2004). In this connection, new developments toward social design experiments as a form of DBR that engages systems of power directly, and that embraces a critical-historical perspective on systems, strike us as a promising direction (Gutiérrez & Jurow, 2016).

Emerging developments also point toward the need to develop new strategies for structuring co-participation in the context of a profoundly inequitable society, to promote ideals of engagement within a multiracial democracy. Here, promising developments include those being explored within the Family Leadership Design Collaborative (2017), where teams of researchers, families, and communities have been exploring ways to structure participation to amplify the voices of those who rarely have decision-making power in conversations about how to improve education. Similarly, emerging models for community-based partnerships show promise for multidirectional mentoring models, where senior researchers, junior scholars, and community members can learn together in the context of change efforts (Ghiso, Campano, Scheab, Asaah, & Rusoja, 2019).

One of the strengths of DBR has been its power to evolve in response to critiques. The current directions of DBR suggest that its evolution continues in this way. For this reason, we are hopeful that DBR is here to stay and continues to develop as a promising approach for promoting equitable change and justice in schools and communities.

ACKNOWLEDGMENTS

We express sincere appreciation to Danielle Shaw Attaway, Srinjita Bhaduri, Alexandra Chakarov, Laura Hamman, William Lindsay, Ali Raza, Kristina

Stamatis, Rachel von Holst, and Sari Widman, whose insights and reflections were instrumental to our thinking in this chapter.

REFERENCES

Affolter, R., Brown, V., Carter, J. F., Whitt, K. C., Devaul, H., Edwards, K., . . . Watkins, D. (2018). *Why don't antibiotics work like they used to?* Boulder, CO, and Evanston, IL: University of Colorado and Northwestern University.

Agid, S. (2018). "Dismantle, change, build": Designing abolition at the intersections of local, large-scale, and imagined infrastructures. *Design Studies, 59,* 95–116.

Ahn, J., Campos, F., Hays, M., & DiGiacomo, D. (2019). Designing in context: Reaching beyond usability in learning analytics dashboard design. *Journal of Learning Analytics, 1*(1), 1–10.

Alvarez, L. (2012). Reconsidering academic language in practice: The demands of Spanish expository reading and students' bilingual resources. *Bilingual Research Journal, 35*(1), 32–52.

Anderson, T., & Shattuck, J. (2012). Design-based research: A decade of progress in education research? *Educational Researcher, 41*(1), 16–25.

Bakker, A. (2018). *Design research in education: A practical guide for early career researchers.* New York: Routledge.

Bang, M., Faber, L., Gurneau, J., Marin, A., & Soto, C. (2016). Community-based design research: Learning across generations and strategic transformations of institutional relations toward axiological innovations. *Mind, Culture, and Activity, 23*(6), 28–41.

Bang, M., Medin, D., Washinawatok, K., & Chapman, S. (2010). Innovations in culturally based science education through partnerships and community. In M. S. Khine & M. I. Saleh (Eds.), *New science of learning: Cognition, computers, and collaboration in education* (pp. 569–592). New York: Springer.

Bang, M., & Vossoughi, S. (2016). Participatory design research and educational justice: Studying learning and relations within social change making. *Cognition and Instruction, 34*(3), 173–193.

Bang, M., Warren, B., Rosebery, A., & Medin, D. (2012). Desettling expectations in science education. *Human Development, 55,* 302–318.

Bell, P. (2004). On the theoretical breadth of design-based research in education. *Educational Psychologist, 39*(4), 243–253.

Blumenfeld, P., Fishman, B. J., Krajcik, J., Marx, R. W., & Soloway, E. (2000). Creating usable innovations in systemic reform: Scaling up technology-embedded project-based science in urban schools. *Educational Psychologist, 35*(3), 149–164.

Booker, A., & Goldman, S. V. (2016). Participatory design research as a practice for systemic repair: Doing hand-in-hand math research with families. *Cognition and Instruction, 34*(3), 223–235.

Brown, A. L. (1992). Design experiments: Theoretical and methodological challenges in creating complex interventions in classroom settings. *Journal of the Learning Sciences, 2*(2), 141–178.

Cobb, P. A., Confrey, J., diSessa, A. A., Lehrer, R., & Schauble, L. (2003). Design experiments in educational research. *Educational Researcher, 32*(1), 9–13.

Cobb, P. A., McClain, K., & Gravemeijer, K. (2003). Learning about statistical covariation. *Cognition and Instruction, 21*(1), 1–78.

Collins, A. (1992). Toward a design science of education. In E. Scanlon & T. O'Shea (Eds.), *New directions in educational technology* (pp. 15–22). Berlin: Springer-Verlag.

Couso, D. (2016). Participatory approaches to curriculum design from a design research perspective. In D. Psillos & P. Kariotoglou (Eds.), *Iterative design of teaching-learning sequences* (pp. 47–71). Dordrecht, the Netherlands: Springer.

Davydov, V. V. (1988). Problems of developmental teaching: The experience of theoretical and experimental research. *Soviet Education, 30*, 8–10.

Derry, S. J., Pea, R. D., Barron, B., Engle, R. A., Erickson, F., Goldman, R., . . . Sherin, B. L. (2010). Conducting video research in the learning sciences: Guidance on selection, analysis, technology, and ethics. *Journal of the Learning Sciences, 19*(1), 3–53.

Design-Based Research Collective. (2003). Design-based research: An emerging paradigm for educational inquiry. *Educational Researcher, 32*(1), 5–8.

diSessa, A. A., & Cobb, P. A. (2004). Ontological innovation and the role of theory in design experiments. *Journal of the Learning Sciences, 13*(1), 77–103.

Edelson, D. C. (2002). Design research: What we learn when we engage in design. *Journal of the Learning Sciences, 11*(1), 105–121.

Ehn, P. (1992). Scandinavian design: On participation and skill. In P. S. Adler & T. A. Winograd (Eds.), *Usability: Turning technologies into tools* (pp. 96–132). New York: Oxford University Press.

Eldridge, M. (2004). Dewey on race and social change. In D. F. Koch & B. E. Lawson (Eds.), *Pragmatism and the problem of race* (pp. 11–21). Bloomington: Indiana University Press.

Engeström, Y. (2011). From design experiments to formative interventions. *Theory & Psychology, 21*(5), 598–628.

Esmonde, I., & Booker, A. N. (2016). *Power and privilege in the learning sciences: Critical and sociocultural theories of learning.* New York: Routledge.

Family Leadership Design Collaborative. (2017). *Solidarity-driven decision making: Enacting equity in partnering and decision making.* Phase 2 Process Brief. Seattle, WA: Author.

Farrell, C. C., Penuel, W. R., Daniel, J., Steup, L., & Coburn, C. E. (2020). *Research–practice partnerships: The state of the field.* Boulder: National Center for Research in Policy and Practice, University of Colorado Boulder.

Feinberg, W. (2015). Critical pragmatism and the appropriation of ethnography by philosophy of education. *Studies in Philosophy and Education, 34*, 149–157.

Ghiso, M. P., Campano, G., Scheab, E. R., Asaah, D., & Rusoja, A. (2019). Mentoring in research–practice partnerships: Toward democratizing expertise. *AERA Open, 5*(4), 1–12.

Goldman, S. V. (2006). A new angle on families: Connecting the mathematics of life with school mathematics. In Z. Bekerman, N. C. Burbules, & D. Silberman-Keller (Eds.), *Learning in places: The informal education reader* (pp. 55–76). New York: Peter Lang.

Goldman, S. V., & Booker, A. (2009). Making math a definition of the situation: Families as sites for mathematical practices. *Anthropology and Education Quarterly, 40*, 369–387.

Golob, M. I., & Giles, A. R. (2013). Challenging and transforming power relations within community-based participatory research: The promise of a Foucauldian analysis. *Qualitative Research in Sport, Exercise and Health, 5*, 356–372.

Gravemeijer, K., & Cobb, P. (2013). Design research from a learning design perspective. In J. van den Akker, K. Gravemeijer, S. E. McKenney, & N. Nieveen (Eds.), *Educational design research* (pp. 73–112). New York: Routledge.

Gutiérrez, K. D., & Jurow, A. S. (2016). Social design experiments: Toward equity by design. *Journal of the Learning Sciences, 25*, 565–598.

Gutiérrez, K. D., & Vossoughi, S. (2010). Lifting off the ground to return anew: Mediated praxis, transformative learning, and social design experiments. *Journal of Teacher Education, 61*(1–2), 100–117.

Hildreth, R. W. (2009). Reconstructing Dewey on power. *Political Theory, 37*(6), 780–807.

Ishimaru, A. M., & Takahashi, S. (2017). Disrupting racialized institutional scripts: Toward parent–teacher transformative agency for educational justice. *Peabody Journal of Education, 92,* 343–362.

Jay, T., Rose, J., & Simmons, B. (2017). Finding "mathematics": Parents questioning school-centered approaches to involvement in children's mathematics learning. *School Community Journal, 27*(1), 201–230.

Johnson, R., Severance, S., Penuel, W. R., & Leary, H. A. (2016). Teachers, tasks, and tensions: Lessons from a research–practice partnership. *Journal of Mathematics Teacher Education, 19*(2), 169–185.

Kaplan, R. G., Riedy, R., Van Horne, K., & Penuel, W. R. (2019). Going on a statewide listening tour: Involving education leaders in the process of research to enhance the practical value of qualitative research. *Evidence & Policy: A Journal of Research, Debate and Practice, 15*(2), 179–196.

Kelly, A. E. (2004). Design research in education: Yes, but is it methodological? *Journal of the Learning Sciences, 13*(1), 113–128.

Khalil, D., & Kier, M. (2017). Critical race design: An emerging methodological approach to anti-racist design and implementation research. *International Journal of Adult Vocational Education, 8*(2), 54–71.

Kirshner, B., & Polman, J. L. (2013). Adaptation by design: A context-sensitive, dialogic approach to design. In B. J. Fishman, W. R. Penuel, A.-R. Allen, & B. H. Cheng (Eds.), *Design-based implementation research: Theories, methods, and exemplars* (pp. 215–236). New York: Teachers College Record.

Leal, P. A. (2007). Participation: The ascendancy of a buzzword in the neo-liberal era. *Development in Practice, 17,* 539–548.

McLaren, P. (1991). Critical pedagogy: Constructing an arch of social dreaming and a doorway to hope. *Journal of Education, 173*(1), 9–34.

Mislevy, R. J., & Haertel, G. D. (2006). Implications of evidence-centered design for educational testing. *Educational Measurement: Issues and Practice, 25*(4), 6–20.

Nasir, N. S., & Cooks, J. (2009). Becoming a hurdler: How learning settings afford identities. *Anthropology and Education Quarterly, 40*(1), 41–61.

National Research Council. (2012). *A framework for K–12 science education: Practices, crosscutting concepts, and core ideas.* Washington, DC: National Academies Press.

National Research Council. (2014). *Developing assessments for the Next Generation Science Standards.* Washington, DC: The National Academies Press.

New London Group. (1996). A pedagogy of multiliteracies: Designing social futures. *Harvard Educational Review, 66,* 60–92.

NGSS Lead States. (2013). *Next Generation Science Standards: For states, by states.* Washington, DC: National Academies Press.

O'Connor, K., Hanny, C., & Lewis, C. (2011). Doing "business as usual": Dynamics of voice in community organizing talk. *Anthropology and Education Quarterly, 42*(2), 154–171.

Ormel, B. J. B., Roblin, N. N. P., McKenney, S. E., Voogt, J. M., & Pieters, J. M. (2012). Research–practice interactions as reported in recent design studies: Still promising, still hazy. *Educational Technology Research and Development, 60*(6), 967–986.

Orr, J. E., & Crowfoot, N. C. (1992). Design by anecdote: The use of ethnography to guide the application of technology to practice. In M. J. Muller, S. Kuhn, & J. A. Meskill (Eds.), *PDC '92: Proceedings of the Participatory Design Conference* (pp. 31–37). Palo Alto, CA: Computer Professionals for Social Responsibility.

Patel, L. (2015). *Decolonizing educational research: From ownership to answerability*. New York: Routledge.

Penuel, W. R. (2016). Studying science and engineering learning in practice. *Cultural Studies of Science Education, 11*(1), 89–104.

Penuel, W. R., Coburn, C. E., & Gallagher, D. (2013). Negotiating problems of practice in research–practice partnerships focused on design. In B. J. Fishman, W. R. Penuel, A.-R. Allen, & B. H. Cheng (Eds.), *Design-based implementation research: Theories, methods, and exemplars* (pp. 237–255). New York: Teachers College Record.

Penuel, W. R., DeBarger, A. H., Boscardin, C. K., Moorthy, S., Beauvineau, Y., Kennedy, C., & Allison, K. (2017). Investigating science curriculum adaptation as a strategy to improve teaching and learning. *Science Education, 101*(1), 66–98.

Penuel, W. R., & Frank, K. A. (2016). Modes of inquiry in educational psychology and learning sciences. In L. Corno & E. M. Anderman (Eds.), *Handbook of educational psychology* (pp. 16–28). New York: Routledge.

Penuel, W. R., Lo, A. S., Jacobs, J. K., Gardner, A., Stuhlsatz, M. A. M., & Wilson, C. (2019). *Tools for supporting teachers to build quality 3D assessment tasks*. Paper presented at the NARST Annual Meeting, Baltimore.

Penuel, W. R., & O'Connor, K. (2010). Learning research as a human science: Old wine in new bottles? *National Society for the Study of Education Yearbook, 109*(1), 268–283.

Penuel, W. R., Reiser, B. J., Novak, M., McGill, T., Frumin, K., Van Horne, K., Sumner, T., & Watkins, D. A. (2018). *Using co-design to test and refine a model for three-dimensional science curriculum that connects to students' interests and experiences*. Paper presented at the Annual Meeting of the American Educational Research Association, New York.

Penuel, W. R., & Shepard, L. A. (2016). Assessment and teaching. In D. H. Gitomer & C. A. Bell (Eds.), *Handbook of research on teaching* (pp. 787–851). Washington, DC: American Educational Research Association.

Penuel, W. R., & Watkins, D. A. (2019). Assessment to promote equity and epistemic justice: A use-case of a research–practice partnership in science education. *Annals of the American Academy of Political and Social Science, 683*, 201–216.

Philip, T. M., Bang, M., & Jackson, K. (2018). Articulating the "how," the "for what," the "for whom," and the "with whom" in concert: A call to broaden the benchmarks of our scholarship. *Cognition and Instruction, 36*(2), 83–88.

Pinkard, N., Erete, S., Martin, C. K., & McKinney de Royston, M. (2017). Digital Youth Divas: Exploring narrative-driven curriculum to spark middle school girls' interest in computational activities. *Journal of the Learning Sciences, 26*, 477–516.

Reimann, P. (2011). Design-based research. *Methodological Choice and Design, 9*(2), 37–50.

Rubin, D. B. (1974). Estimating causal effects of treatments in randomized and nonrandomized studies. *Journal of Educational Psychology, 66*, 688–701.

Sandoval, W. A. (2014). Conjecture mapping: An approach to systematic educational design research. *Journal of the Learning Sciences, 23*(1), 18–36.

Severance, S., Leary, H., & Johnson, R. (2014). Tensions in a multi-tiered research partnership. In J. L. Polman, E. Kyza, D. K. O'Neill, I. Tabak, A. S. Jurow, K. O'Connor, & W. R. Penuel (Eds.), *Proceedings of the 11th International Conference of the Learning Sciences* (Vol. 2, pp. 1171–1175). Boulder, CO: ISLS.

Severance, S., Penuel, W. R., Sumner, T., & Leary, H. (2016). Organizing for teacher agency in curriculum design. *Journal of the Learning Sciences, 25*, 531–564.

Shaffer, D. W., & Squire, K. (2006). The Pasteurization of education. *Advances in Education and Administration, 8*, 43–55.

Shavelson, R. J., Phillips, D. C., Towne, L., & Feuer, M. J. (2003). On the science of education design studies. *Educational Researcher, 32*(1), 25–28.

Stokes, D. E. (1997). *Pasteur's quadrant: Basic science and technological innovation.* Washington, DC: Brookings Institution.

Sumner, T., & the Curriculum Customization Service Team. (2010). Customizing instruction with educational digital libraries. In J. Hunter, C. Lagoze, L. Giles, & Y.-F. Li (Eds.), *Proceedings of the 10th Annual Joint Conference on Digital Libraries* (pp. 353–356). New York: Association for Computing Machinery.

Tatar, D. (2007). The design tensions framework. *Human–Computer Interaction, 22*(4), 413–451.

Teeters, L. A., & Jurow, A. S. (2018). Relationships *de Confianza* and the organisation of collective social action. *Ethnography and Education, 13*(1), 84–99.

Tuck, E., & Yang, K. W. (Eds.). (2018). *Toward what justice: Describing diverse dreams of justice in education.* New York: Routledge.

Tzou, C. T., Bell, P., Bang, M., Kuver, R., Twito, A., & Braun, A. (2019a). Building expansive family STEAM programming through participatory design research. In V. R. Lee & A. L. Phillips (Eds.), *Reconceptualizing libraries: Perspectives from the information and learning sciences* (pp. 72–93). New York: Routledge.

Tzou, C., Meixi, Suárez, E., Bell, P., LaBonte, D., Starks, E., & Bang, M. (2019b). Storywork in STEM-Art: Making, materiality and robotics within everyday acts of Indigenous presence and resurgence. *Cognition and Instruction, 37*, 306–326.

Vakil, S., de Royston, M. M., Nasir, N. S., & Kirshner, B. (2016). Rethinking race and power in design-based research: Reflections from the field. *Cognition and Instruction, 34*(3), 194–209.

Wilkerson, M. H. (2017). Teachers, students, and after-school professionals as designers of digital tools for learning. In B. DiSalvo, J. Yip, E. Bonsignore, & C. DiSalvo (Eds.), *Participatory design for learning: Perspectives from practice and research* (pp. 125–138). New York: Routledge.

Wingert, K., Riedy, R., Campanella, M., & Penuel, W. R. (2020). Equity across state systems: Possibilities and tensions in understanding scale. In M. S. Gresalfi, I. S. Horn, N. Enyedy, H.-J. So, V. Hand, K. Jackson, . . . T. M. Philip (Eds.), *Proceedings of the International Conference of the Learning Sciences* (pp. 2453–2560). Nashville, TN: International Conference of the Learning Sciences.

Wiser, M., Smith, C. L., & Doubler, S. (2012). Learning progressions as tools for curriculum development: Lessons from the Inquiry Project. In A. C. Alonzo & A. W. Gotwals (Eds.), *Learning progressions in science: Current challenges and future directions* (pp. 359–404). Rotterdam, the Netherlands: Sense.

York, A. (2015). *The social organization of learning opportunities in creative civic practices.* Unpublished diss., University of Colorado Boulder.

York, A., & Kirshner, B. (2015). How positioning shapes student engagement in action civics. *Teachers College Record, 117*(13), 103–118.

CHAPTER 2

Addressing Publication Challenges in Design-Based Research

Margret A. Hjalmarson, Allison Ward Parsons,
Seth A. Parsons, and Amy C. Hutchison

The beginning of design-based research (DBR) is often credited to Ann Brown's 1992 paper about design experiments. Brown suggested a movement to classroom-based research in order to understand how designs for teaching and learning work in practice within the context. Other authors continued the discussion of DBR for studying learning interventions and developing theory in context (Collins, 1992; Collins, Joseph, & Bielaczyc, 2004; Gravemeijer, 1994). However, a special issue of *Educational Researcher* in 2003 and a special issue of *The Journal of the Learning Sciences* in 2004 marked increased visibility of DBR in education and researchers in multiple disciplines. A challenge at that time introduced by Kelly's (2004) paper captures the central question in the title: *But is it methodological?* Early papers on the topic explored the argumentative grammar (Kelly, 2004, 2006) and underlying epistemological perspective about DBR (Collins, 1992; Collins et al., 2004; Gravemeijer, 1994). A reframing of the research enterprise from a design-based (or design-focused, perhaps) perspective leads to reframing sources of evidence and the nature of the claims that might be made in DBR projects.

As design-based methods expanded, there was also an emergence of descriptors of this methodology (e.g., design experiments, DBR, design-based implementation research, formative experiment). Central to all of the methodological descriptors was the notion of design as a process and the source of evidence for the researcher. While design experiments originated in classrooms, DBR has since expanded to contexts including school districts (e.g., Cobb & Jackson, 2011, 2012; Penuel & Fishman, 2012), communities (Hermes, Bang, & Marin, 2012; Santo, Ching, Peppler, & Hoadley, 2018), and informal learning settings (e.g., Land & Zimmerman, 2015). Participatory design research was the focus of a special issue of *Cognition &*

Instruction (Bang & Vossoughi, 2016). This expansion of terminology and framing is not unusual for a new approach to research; however, it can impede comprehensive understanding in the field, thereby slowing advancement. This expansion of use from classrooms to school systems and beyond demonstrates the power and applicability of this approach to study enhancement in understanding and outcomes.

In this chapter, we explore how the epistemological framing of research from a design-based perspective shapes publication and distribution of findings, outcomes, and results. The framing shapes how DBR is reviewed and published. We also explore the state of DBR in terms of publication rates in leading journals. Finally, we present possible implications and suggestions for publishing, promotion guidelines, and overall research practice that would support DBR in the field. Another chapter in this volume will speak about the application of DBR in graduate studies and dissertations (see Chapter 14).

What Are the Methodological Affordances of DBR?

In this section, we will not provide an extensive review of DBR, its principles, and educational implications. Chapter 1 effectively addresses the theory and genesis of DBR. We will briefly situate the methodological affordances of DBR and their benefits for educational settings. There are many reasons that researchers choose DBR methods to investigate educational problems and innovations. DBR methods afford researchers unique opportunities to understand how, when, and why educational innovations work in practice (Penuel, Fishman, Cheng, & Sabelli, 2011). For researchers interested in understanding *if* and *how* innovations may work beyond a single context, DBR is a beneficial approach. Some of the key benefits of DBR are outlined in this section.

A fundamental affordance of DBR is that it enables researchers to iteratively and flexibly refine an educational intervention to meet a contextually sensitive goal. Although DBR is flexible, it is also highly systematic. Researchers using this approach typically first identify a problem to be solved (Edelson, 2002). Identifying a problem leads researchers to generate a possible solution(s) or goal for their educational intervention. Researchers then use that goal as a continual reference point for collecting and analyzing data and determining the need for refinements to the intervention (Reinking & Bradley, 2008). This flexibility differs from other methodologies that require strict adherence to an intervention, regardless of whether it is working in a way that aligns with a desired outcome. Rather, with DBR research, researchers iteratively analyze data, often in cycles or predetermined periods of time, and make refinements to the intervention until the desired goal is met. The combination of being both systematic and flexible not only leads to an intervention that works, but also ensures that researchers understand how and why it works (Cobb, Confrey, diSessa, Lehrer, & Schauble, 2003).

A second affordance of DBR is that the research is situated and carried out in the real-world setting for which the intervention is intended (Kelly, 2006). This situated approach differs from other forms of research in which interventions are studied in clinical or lab settings, or in small subgroups or samples of the intended recipients. By situating the research in real-world settings and applying quantitative and/or qualitative methods, researchers can better understand how the intervention works in classroom settings and can iteratively modify it within that setting until the predetermined intervention goal is met. Ecological validity—the degree to which outcomes of a study are predictive of outcomes in real-world settings (Schmuckler, 2001)—has long been an important concern among the research community (e.g., Orne & Holland, 1968), particularly because ecological validity decreases as the controlled conditions of a research setting increase. Design research accounts for the importance of ecological validity by enabling researchers to ensure that the intervention can be effectively applied in real-world contexts.

A third affordance of DBR is that it enables researchers to work collaboratively with teachers (and other stakeholders) to develop and test specific pedagogical theories based on instructional practice, rather than only overarching theories of teaching and learning (Reinking & Bradley, 2008; e.g., see Chapters 3, 4, 5, 6, 11, and 12, this volume). On a larger scale, *design-based implementation research* might include district or school-based leaders as part of the research team to test models for change (e.g., Cobb & Jackson, 2011; Penuel & Fishman, 2012). Variations such as *participatory design research* engage community members throughout the entire endeavor (Bang & Vossoughi, 2016). This approach often enables researchers to produce findings that are more useful to teachers or practitioners to whom the findings would be most applicable.

One tactic used in DBR is to determine the factors that both enhance and inhibit progress toward the desired outcomes of an intervention. By systematically and continuously examining these factors to make refinements to an intervention, researchers are better able to construct theories and findings that are of benefit to practitioners. Instead of being "locked in" to an intervention to fidelity, as is required by an experimental design, DBR allows researchers and practitioners to adjust implementation to magnify the enhancing features of an intervention while reducing or eliminating the features that inhibit progress toward the desired outcomes. Gravemeijer and Cobb (2006) recommend planning the DBR intervention in a series of interconnected data collection and analysis cycles in order to ensure that factors that impact the intervention are noted, analyzed, and adapted if needed to improve the design or working theory supporting the design conjectures. Cycles of data collection and analysis may be considered micro, meaning that they repeat over a brief time frame, such as a daily microcycle or lesson microcycle, and in turn a series of microcycles may be further examined in a macrocycle to gain overall perspective of a complete DBR experiment (Gravemeijer & Cobb, 2006). Reinking and Bradley (2008) suggest that larger DBR studies may need additional cycle designations, noting that a single classroom may create a microcycle for data collection and analysis, followed by macrocycles looking across classrooms within a study. By establishing a clear framework of data collection and analysis cycles, DBR researchers can nimbly adjust a design that is not working as planned, noting the contextual or design factors that inhibited progress. In other cases, researchers may notice an unintended enhancing factor that they want to keep close tabs on in order to understand how it is positively influencing the outcome. The cyclical framework should be included in the intervention description of the method section.

Current State of Publications of DBR

The central goal of this chapter is to understand how DBR should and could be viewed by the research community, by editors, and by publishers. We recognize that peer review is an invaluable part of vetting research contributions to the field, and the role is to read and interrogate each manuscript, weighing details and ensuring that the journal or conference audience will clearly understand the final piece. We use the term *reader* to describe the reviewers, editors, publishers, and ultimately, the intended audience. Salient features of DBR should be included in publications in order to distinguish a DBR project from other types of research (see Chapter 1 for an explanation). In the following section, this explanation is provided not from the perspective of the researcher and writer but from the perspective of the reader.

Publication Rate of DBR and Presence in High-Tier Journals

Because DBR is a relatively new methodology (Easterday, Rees Lewis, & Gerber, 2014) and it has been variably applied in different fields of educational research (e.g., see Chapters 3, 4, 8, and 15, this volume), there is diverse understanding about the methodology used. This diverse understanding influences how reviewers and editors respond to and evaluate DBR studies. Nevertheless, DBR studies are published in different journals at varying rates. Therefore, researchers using DBR need to be intentional and strategic in selecting an outlet for their work—more so than they have traditionally been because unlike researchers using quantitative and qualitative methods, DBR researchers face a real chance that journal editorial review boards may not have a DBR methodological expert to review the study. As a result, the work of DBR researchers is often evaluated by reviewers who do not fully understand the methodology.

In order to explore the publication rate of DBR, we used two strategies. First, we used an existing dataset (Parsons, Gallagher, & the George Mason University Content Analysis Team, 2016; Parsons, Gallagher, Leggett, Ives, & Lague, 2020) to explore the frequency of DBR in 15 literacy journals from 2007 to 2016. We chose to examine data from this project because it included articles across a 10-year time period; because it is a large dataset (4,305 articles); and because it *pulls* publications from a wide range of literacy journals, many that would be identified as *top-tier* journals in education research broadly, such as *Reading Research Quarterly, Scientific Studies of Reading, Elementary School Journal,* and *Journal of Literacy Research.*

Second, we explored the methodologies used in current volumes (i.e., 2019 and 2020) of journals publishing empirical research that we identified as those with the highest impact factors. This analysis provides readers with an idea of how DBR is currently received and represented in the educational journals that are most "prestigious" in our field. Such information provides a touchpoint for future understanding of the development and use of DBR in the field. To identify the 10 journals with the highest impact factors, we consulted two journal-ranking databases: Journal Citations Reports (2018) and SCImago (2018). In the Educational Research categories, we listed the 30 journals with the highest impact factors from each database. Next, we removed journals focused on reviews of research. Then, we cross-checked the lists to identify journals appearing on each list, resulting in 13 journals. We added the rank of each journal from each list, and ordered them from the lowest (i.e., the highest impact factor would be ranked number 1). We examined the methods of each article published in each publication to see how many studies used DBR as the methodology.

The previous analysis of journals that publish literacy research included the journals presented in Table 2.1. In the 4,305 articles analyzed in this study, 21 used DBR. Researchers adhered to the following rules for coding research designs in this dataset: the research design needed to be explicitly stated in the article. "Where a research design was not explicitly stated, coders classified the study as general qualitative (referred to as qualitative throughout), general quantitative (referred to as quantitative), mixed methods, or nonempirical" (Parsons et al., 2020, p. 349). We recognize that this coding rule is restrictive, but it ensured accuracy in coding. Nevertheless, it is clear that DBR was not a common research design in the 4,305 articles coded in this research.

The journals that emerged through our process of identifying the educational research journals with the highest impact factors resulted in the analysis of the journals presented in Table 2.2. In the 149 articles reviewed in the two most recent issues of the high-impact-factor journals, seven used DBR.

There are a few possible reasons for low publication rates in the high-impact-factor journals. It may be the situated, context-based nature of DBR such that the work is often grounded in a specific content area (e.g., literacy, mathematics, engineering) and thus less likely to address topics of general interest for some journals, or authors may seek out discipline-based journals for publishing DBR findings. Some journals may publish more about the theoretical perspective (e.g., *Educational Researcher*) than studies themselves as guidance to the field. As we argue in the next section, it may be that some editors or reviewers are unfamiliar with DBR and, therefore, are more likely to offer unfavorable ratings and recommendations.

TABLE 2.1. Journals in the Analysis of Literacy Publications

Journal	Journal Citation Reports	SCImago
Elementary School Journal	1.140	1.269
English Journal	N/A	N/A
Language Arts	N/A	N/A
Literacy Research and Instruction	N/A	0.800
Journal of Adolescent and Adult Literacy	1.250	0.737
Journal of Educational Psychology	5.178	3.459
Journal of Literacy Research	1.886	1.385
Journal of Research in Reading	1.323	0.894
Reading Psychology	N/A	0.530
Reading Research Quarterly	2.696	2.064
The Reading Teacher	1.168	0.609
Reading and Writing Quarterly	0.934	0.530
Research in the Teaching of English	1.675	1.621
Reading and Writing	1.942	1.462
Scientific Studies of Reading	2.470	2.101

TABLE 2.2. Journals with High Impact Factors

Journal	Journal Citation Reports	SCImago
Internet and Higher Education	5.284	3.307
Educational Researcher	3.386	3.621
Sociology of Education	3.146	4.334
Educational Evaluation and Policy Analysis	3.127	5.021
American Educational Research Journal	3.170	3.176
Journal of Teacher Education	3.263	3.009
Journal of Engineering Education	3.244	3.032
Journal of the Learning Sciences	3.545	2.752
Computers and Education	5.627	2.323
Learning and Instruction	3.917	2.494

Reviewing DBR and DBR under Review

Reviewing DBR research requires an understanding of the components and principles of this type of research. Readers will ask as they process a manuscript and study on DBR, *What distinguishes a DBR project from other types of research?* First and foremost, there should be a description of what is being designed. For example, is there a new curriculum? A model for professional development (PD)? The design of a learning environment in a science museum? What is being designed, why, and for what purpose? Using the term *design* as a noun to describe the study-created product or tool that will effectively address the goal of the research is a shift for many readers, who are accustomed to viewing *design* as a verb that describes the research technique. It is incumbent on the researcher to clearly describe what is being designed, and why it is needed to achieve the particular study goal. For example, if the study goal is to better teach vocabulary to students, the design is the multimodal instructional approach that was created, tested, and refined during the intervention (see Parsons & Bryant, 2016).

The second element of DBR is its focus on the design principles or conjectures. Sandoval (2004, 2014) characterizes this as starting with a set of conjectures about the design that both support iterations and revisions but are also questioned throughout the project. The researchers must collect and analyze data to determine if the initial conjectures about the design continue to hold throughout, or if (and how) they need to be revised. Guiding principles are a commonly used element of design research projects (Anderson & Shattuck, 2012; Gravemeijer & Cobb, 2006; Sandoval, 2004). Guiding principles should inform the design but also need to be interrogated themselves since a product of the research endeavor can be the design principles themselves. Testing, investigating, and documenting how the conjectures or principles play out in practice through the design and implementation process are the focus of gathering evidence.

A third feature of DBR is the iterative nature of the process and the focus on the process itself as well as products. Therefore, DBR should document the decision making on the part of the research team that supported design, implementation, and revision of what was being designed. This documentation of process (and related design decisions) should include how evidence was used to make decisions about revisions to what was being designed. So, if research teams are anticipating revisions to a product, what data are they gathering to support that decision making? For example, in developing curriculum, are the researchers gathering artifacts of student work to support revision? Authors should distinguish between micro and macro levels of iteration and modifications (e.g., Reinking & Bradley, 2008).

The focus on design process is a key distinction between DBR and other types of education research. An overarching goal of DBR is to share the inner workings of the research project, thereby making the implicit elements visible or explicit to the reader. The researcher must describe the underlying work within an intervention in order to explain how and why the design product iteratively evolved to address the research goal. To use learning environments as an example of a product, DBR documents not only what happened in the implementation but also the underpinnings of the design of the learning environment (e.g., Gravemeijer & van Eerde, 2009). This supports the understanding of specific curriculum materials and additionally how those materials were developed to inform future design. Tasks for students and teachers should be culturally relevant and meaningful. Therefore, tasks do not exist in a vacuum, but rather are likely to be revised or adjusted over time. DBR provides principles that undergird the curriculum design such as *culturally relevant contexts* to support the curriculum, which allow tasks to shift in context but still be assessed. Since the conjectures or principles are tested and revised over time, the project can create sharable resources and tools as well as guidelines to support the development and adaptation of resources.

Critiques of DBR and Recommendations for Publications

> This journal doesn't publish action research.
>
> More clarity in the methodology is needed.
>
> Your organization of the design-based research work into the phases identified by Gravemeijer and Cobb is useful; however, I'm not sure how these sections fit into the methods section.
>
> You have a section on inhibiting factors, but that doesn't match a research question.

While more researchers are using DBR, it remains misunderstood in educational research settings. The comments above are representative of those received by us in the process of pursuing publication of various DBR studies. Given that the method is somewhat novel, we are placed in the position of explaining our choices more explicitly than researchers using, for example, experimental design or case study. Simply stated, the onus remains on researchers using DBR to explain not only why the methodology works for their study but also how the methodology works. This explication is particularly relevant if the target journal has not published DBR previously. Researchers seeking publication are regularly advised to review recent issues of their target journal in order to match writing style and format; we suggest that reviewing for methodology is of equal importance, as discussed in the above section. In this manner, researchers can explore which methods are more frequently published in the target journal, as well as how other authors have described their methodological choices. In this section, we explore a few of the common critiques of DBR and present corresponding recommendations to resolve the issues, thereby enhancing publication chances. In publishing, as in sports, often the best defense is a good offense!

Critique: DBR Isn't Methodological

In the early days of DBR, the question of whether it was methodological was raised. Kelly (2004) published a paper titled "Yes, But Is It Methodological?" More recently, Bakker (2018) questioned whether DBR is a method or methodology. Sandoval (2014) explains that DBR may not be a methodology as Kelly (2004) notes, because there's no identifiable set of clear-cut methods for DBR, but design researchers have demonstrated that they can use many methods to effectively enact designs in specific learning environments in order to pair outcomes with intervention (p. 20). Anderson and Shattuck (2012) explain that DBR "is largely agnostic when it comes to epistemological challenges to the choice of methodologies used" (p. 17) and is pragmatically oriented, meaning that researchers often employ mixed methods in DBR studies. Many researchers emphasize the idea that DBR frames research not in terms of qualitative, quantitative, or mixed methods, but rather is a framing of the endeavor of research itself. Components of a DBR project may use varied methodological approaches depending on the goals and objectives of the research. In this sense, it is not only about a choice of methodological tools and resources. It is also about how we frame the purpose and goals of research itself.

Bakker (2018) discusses a related critique that design-based researchers may "cherry-pick" findings and conclusions that suit their predetermined goals. In a similar vein, there are questions about local theory development grounded in context: Are DBR findings and conclusions unique to the specific study context? Or, what is learned in the local context that can inform work in other contexts? To address these concerns, design-based researchers need to examine and carefully explain how they have warranted their conclusions and findings. In addition, DBR also typically yields findings as well as other "products" of research that are useful in other settings, such as principles to guide decision making or to design learning experiences that can be situated elsewhere (e.g., Hira & Hynes, 2019).

Recommendation: Explain Methods—But Methods Section Is Long

DBR has hopefully moved beyond earlier questions about whether it was methodological or empirical. Significant studies exist in both larger-scale (e.g., Cobb & Jackson, 2012; Ketelhut, Nelson, Clarke, & Dede, 2010; Penuel & Fishman, 2012) and smaller-scale work (e.g., Newstetter, 2005; Strobel, Jonassen, & Jonas, 2008) that contribute to the development of educational theory and findings for educational questions. However, even small-scale design studies are complex, and it can be challenging to describe a study within the confines of a 30- to 40-page journal article format.

Methodology sections for a DBR project are complex and therefore lengthy because DBR is by nature interventionist while also studying intervention. This means that DBR researchers must explain the intervention itself and how the accompanying investigation unfolded. In this manner, DBR researchers address not only "if" something worked, as in an experimental design, but "how" it worked in the research context. Cherry-picking claims (see Bakker, 2018) may be warded off by details that describe when and where the design elicits learning, and the nature of that learning.

Reinking and Bradley (2008) describe the importance of a clear intervention framework on which to base the study. We suggest that the intervention framework be depicted in a figure to illustrate which elements are stable, when and how data are collected, and when cycles of iterative analysis occurred to determine how well the design met the study's pedagogical goal, informing the need (or not) for design modifications. Most DBR interventions are set within complex contexts and researchers must document the nature of the context, the nature of the intervention, and the cycles of data collection and revision. Appendices that show key design products or study-developed data collection tools such as questionnaires or response prompts also add important detail in a reader-friendly format. By using figures and other graphics to show their thinking to reviewers, authors can maximize manuscript space for a detailed description of design revisions and outcomes. Furthermore, researchers can look for journals that offer online space, such as repositories for supplemental materials. Many DBR projects boast a wealth of collected data, and online supplements that connect design process and product can provide readers and reviewers with important details to deeply understand the study.

We have found it useful to carefully describe the methodology with relevant citations to support the DBR framework and cyclical data collection and analysis. Offering a clear description of the study design, along with explicit treatment of design choices, iterative data collection and analysis, plus enhancing and inhibiting factors that informed design adaptations is critical. Without a clear description of those elements that are unique to DBR, it is impossible for reviewers and editors to truly understand the research presented in the manuscript. And, a confusing methodology often leads to a rejected submission.

Critique: Everything Is Local, So What Generalizes to Other Research?

A defining feature of DBR is that it is deeply embedded in the study context. However, that embeddedness also raises questions about what aspects of the DBR study can be generalized and what theory is being built. Anderson and Shattuck (2012, p. 22) note that DBR produces rich contextual description, implementation detail, development and design processes, and design principles that emerged as the project evolved, which should result in clear pictures of specific local intervention that researchers can then adapt in their own settings.

In a related vein, the researchers' role in the project may be as members of a partnership, and they are likely the designers of the learning environment, which raises further questions of generalizability (e.g., Barab & Squire, 2004). Other researchers acknowledge this critique and note that qualitative researchers are long accustomed to it, and in fact, the depth of a researcher's involvement makes

DBR more successful than other situated approaches (Anderson & Shattuck, 2012; Onwuegbuzie & Leech, 2007). Anderson and Shattuck go on to explain that the "insider knowledge" of the DBR researcher engaged in a project can simultaneously add to and detract from study validity, declaring that a solid understanding of the difference between objectivity and bias, and the willingness to carefully tread that line define quality DBR (p. 18). Connected to validity, arguments can be made that because the findings, principles, and products are grounded in and guided by the local setting, they have greater validity. As with methodology, the DBR products should be described clearly to ensure broad understanding of what kinds of claims are being made and what outcomes may be generalizable to other settings.

Recommendation: Explain Theory Used and Theory Developed

While all methods should be consistently examined and interrogated for rigor and quality assurance, many of the earlier critiques of DBR appear to be somewhat ameliorated by later design research from the same authors. For example, compare Dede's (2004) early stance that DBR lacks methodological rigor with his later participation in the highly successful, multiyear, grant-funded River City project (see Ketelhut et al., 2010). It is possible that earlier reviewers and publishers of DBR studies were less focused on describing theory and conjectures that grounded and evolved during their study process, and were more focused on describing "what works" as a result of an intervention since the experimental/postpositivist lens was highly valued in the 2000s as randomized controlled trials (RCTs) were considered the gold standard for educational research. In the current climate, with the focus of DBR on both intervention and design in context, it follows that shifting to more explanatory detail, particularly in the rationale and intervention description, especially conjectures and working theories to inform design choices, would help address much of this. Sandoval (2014) called out previous researchers for not explaining enough of their approach or design components, decisions, and working theory for design choices, noting that conjecture mapping may make design relationships concrete. Since conjecture mapping is gaining visibility, we note that older DBR publications are unlikely to include such elements. As such, authors may increase their chances of achieving publication by finding recent published work on which to model their own manuscripts, clearly noting the connections between their working theories, or conjectures, and connected design decisions.

Theoretical and conceptual frameworks play a dual role in DBR. A paradox of DBR is that it is simultaneously driven by local context (e.g., including stakeholders, situated in the setting) and driven to produce and respond to theory that transcends the local context. Design conjectures and principles should be grounded in theory, and the results of the study should contribute to theory. However, the use of theory and the meaning of theory are far from uniform in DBR (Svihla & Reeves, 2016). Some researchers also describe local theory (e.g., Gravemeijer & Cobb, 2006) that both situates the design and the process, but also points to theory development that may go beyond the local setting and is transportable to other settings, thereby developing grounded theory (e.g., Glaser & Strauss, 1965). So, a design-based researcher needs to explain how theory was used throughout the study, how decisions were made carefully, and how data were analyzed critically to avoid claims of "what you see is what you get." Providing theoretical details aids reader understanding and further reveals the implicit decisions and elements within the study.

For publishing, then, it makes sense that authors should include explicit details to support initial design decisions for the intervention. To illustrate their thinking while saving text space, authors may consider including figures that depict their conjecture mapping. They should then explain how designs are embodied throughout the intervention. In that way, readers can better visualize the research and connect the data-supported outcomes to iterative design evolution, finishing with a well-justified working theory that can then be considered in other contexts.

Critique: Everything Is Changing and Nothing Seems Fixed

As discussed previously, a feature of DBR is implementing cycles of data collection, analysis, and revisions in order to analyze changes to the design as resources and tools might be operationalized in different settings. Readers accustomed to an experimental or post-positivist lens may wonder what elements are fixed in the setting, and what is being tested or examined. Or, if everything is open to revision, then what is known at the end of the study? Furthermore, reviewers might question the interventionist role of the researcher/designer in the context and wonder about influence on the results and conclusions. When the researcher is both changing the system and studying the system, it raises a conundrum identified by Phillips and Dolle (2006) about Hawthorne effects. Reviewers may ask, "Is the researcher reporting only what he or she wants to see? What is the person's role in the study, and does it become predictive given that he or she is also the designer?"

Recommendation: Explain Cycles, Phases, or Strands Clearly

A second challenge for publication is that a paper may be focused on one phase of the study, but researchers may need to describe other phases to explain their design decisions for the current phase. When this occurs, researchers must describe the underlying or implicit work within an intervention, making their design processes visible to the reader to explain how and why the design product iteratively evolved to address the research goal. The phases or strands of the study may interact in complex ways (e.g., teacher PD interacts with student-level data that interact with school-level interventions). These interactions and overlaps add length along with crucial detail. It also becomes challenging to determine the appropriate level of context to include for a particular paper. Separation of intervention and design framework from the discussion of individual cycles and resulting revisions can also help ensure clarity for readers. We suggest noting early what the scope of the study described within the paper is so that reviewers know what to read for and how to consider the overall implications. Reviewers accustomed to experimental research reports may expect a direct, linear description of variable manipulation leading to an outcome, but DBR requires more nuanced discussion of how the study unfolded as a result of the design testing and revision process.

Since a characteristic of DBR is iteration and cyclic development of resources, authors must clearly explain design decisions from cycle to cycle. Authors also need to justify changes that are likely to occur from cycle to cycle with evidence from the data. The changes may also be grounded in the local context but must be explained and justified in order to have a coherent analysis. The variation in the implementation cycles may also be a source of learning and implications as the design improves over time and leads to greater understanding. This is a challenge for reviewers who want to understand what remains fixed and "testable" in the study or the balance between description and intervention on the part of the researcher (Bakker, 2018).

In our experience, there is an ongoing challenge between including too much or too little detail in any one phase of the study; we thus strive to include just the right amount to not be overwhelming, but to clearly explain the phase being explored. Similarly, researchers might opt to focus on one aspect of the study in a given manuscript. For example, a large design-based study exploring teacher PD through a dual approach of classroom interventions with students and district-level work may be best separated into more than one paper. The focus of one paper might be the teachers' learning and development even though the larger project included school-based leaders, students, and district leadership. Other papers may focus on the design process itself (e.g., Svihla & Reeves, 2016). To support the description of the phases and strands of the study, researchers may include figures or tables that explain the design process, phases of the study, or guiding framework. A sample DBR framework from a yet-unpublished, yearlong literacy professional learning project is shown in Figure 2.1.

Advice to Authors Writing about DBR

Design-based researchers should consider that while the use of DBR is increasing, they may encounter reviewers who are not familiar with or have misconceptions about its premises. In this section, we offer some tips for authors to help facilitate the review process. First, suggest reviewers when submitting a paper. Some journals have a specific section for suggesting reviewers when submitting. Another place to make suggestions is within the reference list. Including a robust list of references corresponding to both the methodology and related DBR studies provides journal editors with another source to seek reviewers.

As a publishing strategy, design-based researchers may need to think about dividing a large project into multiple, related papers for different outlets that may provide additional information too extensive for one paper (e.g., the MIST Project, *https://peabody.vanderbilt.edu/departments/tl/teaching_and_learning_research/mist*). The creation of online resources and tools can also expand the space available for reporting on a DBR study. Similarly, creating a repository for all of the resources developed in a project, including items for practitioners, research tools, and reporting papers as a collection, can help other researchers identify the impact of the project and find resources for different aspects of the work.

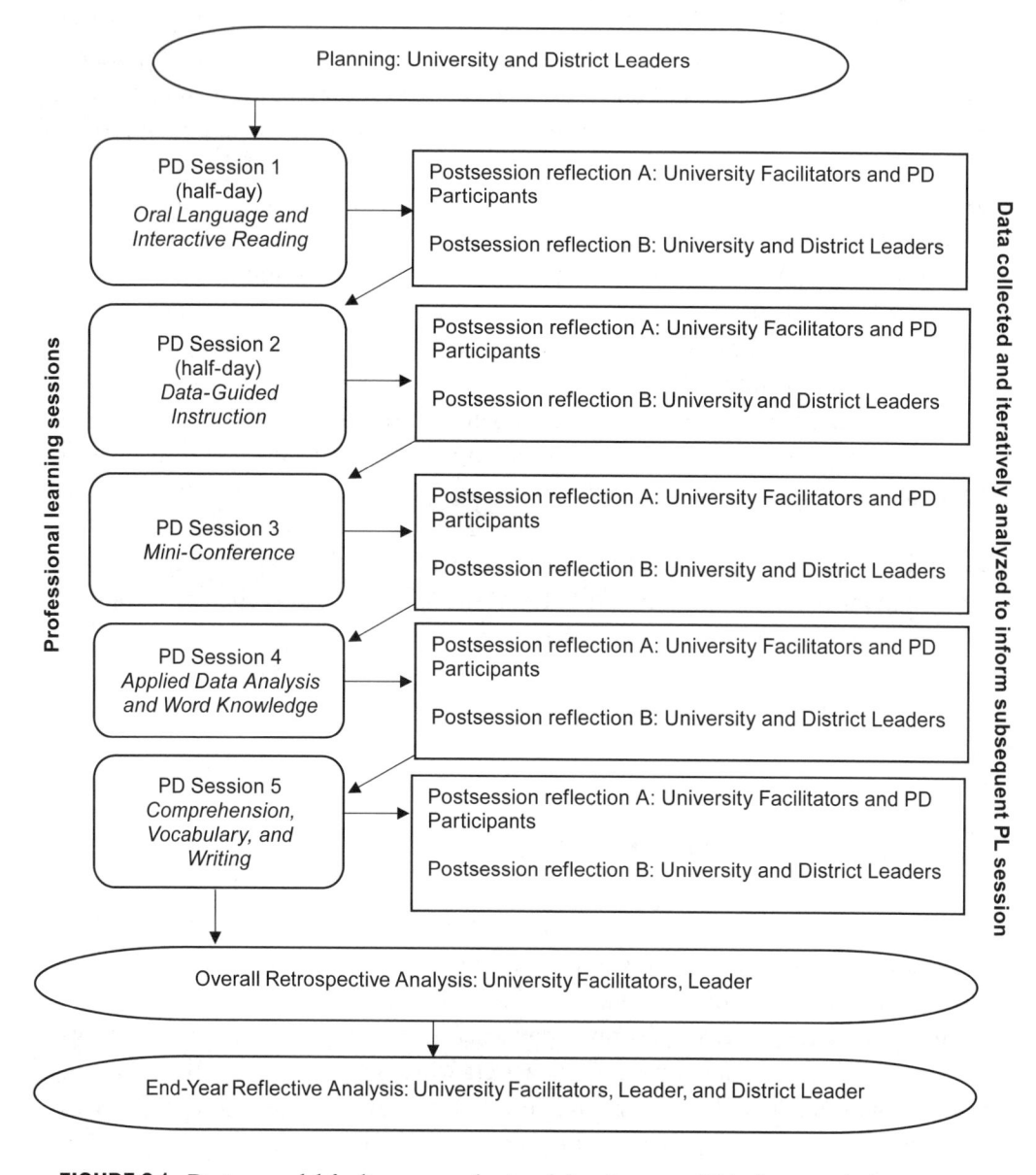

FIGURE 2.1. Design model for literacy professional development. This framework depicts iterative data collection and analysis cycles to guide the research.

As a research methodology that is grounded on research collaborations with practitioners, research teams should consider greater inclusion of practitioners in publications and presentations as writing collaborators. In addition, DBR teams should also consider outlets beyond the research community for publications that appeal to teachers, district leaders, community leaders, and other stakeholders in search of findings or sharable resources that can support learning needs within their communities. As practitioners should be closely involved in the project, resources developed by the project should be useful beyond the research community of traditional journal articles and presentations for researchers.

Returning to the above recommendation of thoroughly understanding the journal to which you are submitting, it is wise to cite other DBR studies recently published that align with your methods. This approach does two things: First, it reminds editors that DBR has successfully appeared in the journal or related journals. Second, it offers editors a connection for peer reviewers who reviewed the articles cited and the option of inviting authors of the cited research to review your manuscript. A reviewer with greater experience with DBR offers the work a more robust and sound review. Matching reviewers with manuscripts can be challenging, and a key element for a thoughtful review is to pair reviewers with methodologies and methods that they understand and (hopefully) use in their own work.

Visions for Publishing, Promotion, and Tenure

In this section, we offer recommendations for the field of education research to help promote the affordances of DBR.

Promotion and Tenure

Promotion and tenure guidelines in colleges of education may privilege publications such as peer-reviewed journal articles that may not be the best outlet for reporting on DBR studies. We have suggested other formats (e.g., online resources, books) that are also high-quality, impactful products that should be counted as scholarly contributions toward tenure and promotion. DBR may also result in the creation of curriculum, assessments, technology, or other resources that could be included as scholarly products. Early career design-based researchers should not be hampered by narrow tenure guidelines in determining appropriate methodologies and approaches for their work. Education research has long suffered from a disconnect between research and practice. DBR is an approach to filling that gap and mediating the disconnect with work that engages stakeholders, the community, and schools in the research. The intent of DBR is that findings and products should be relevant to the communities where they are created. This impact should, in turn, be supported by the community of education research scholars.

In addition to broadening the types of outlets, tenure and promotion guidelines (and the perceptions of education researchers, even if not explicitly stated) may privilege solo-authored works or first-author works in tenure cases. While we recognize that scholars should identify a clear trajectory in their work, we also challenge the field to consider team-based work and jointly authored publications as essential to creating impact on the field and findings that are relevant to the groups we intend to impact as a field. This includes involving research stakeholders such as participants and practitioners (e.g., teachers, school leaders) as coauthors. This kind of team-based work can be time-consuming and challenging, and the contributions of the team should be honored through shared publications and the recognition that impactful work takes a team. Given the collective value our field places on collaborative learning, we should also value collaborative scholarship.

Promotion guidelines will also sometimes reward impact and influence within a field of education. Evaluators will look for leading publications within the field. As a naturally interdisciplinary endeavor, DBR projects could result in publications across multiple fields within education. Researchers should be rewarded for this kind of cross-disciplinary work that has implications for different aspects of education. Early career researchers should be supported for work not only in their own disciplines but also across disciplines. We recommend that early career researchers who have the opportunity to suggest external reviewers for tenure and promotion dossiers take the time to explore the various methodologies of experts in their chosen research area, much as we suggested above that authors analyze journals for previously published DBR studies. If a well-regarded peer also publishes DBR, it may be a wise choice to add that peer to a list of potential external reviewers.

Journals and Conference Proceedings

Given the challenges in describing DBR in sufficient detail in journal publications and conference proceedings, we challenge journal editors, authors, and publishers to consider how supplementary material might be used to provide more information for readers. Publishing tools and resources for data gathering as online supplementary materials would support the community and be another type of product generated from DBR. However, current publishing formats do not regularly support their inclusion. Authors could also consider Web-based formats for providing collections of resources from their DBR studies. These can include tools and resources (e.g., interview protocols, observation instruments) and collections of publications.

A second challenge for design-based researchers can be the content boundaries of some journals and conferences either by discipline or by audience (e.g., focus on teachers or principals, but not both). Properly aligning a manuscript or proposal with a venue can be challenging for DBR that may focus simultaneously on teaching and learning, curriculum and professional development, literacy and computational thinking. So, are there articles that design-based researchers would like to publish that do not fit within current journal boundaries? For example, there are a large number of journals focused on mathematics or science education, but a smaller number that focus on both disciplines.

Book Publishing

We also suggest that book publishing may be another format for creating collections of articles about a DBR project. DBR projects also often have teams of investigators, teachers, school leaders, and other players. A book or monograph can provide opportunities for inclusion of multiple different perspectives on the project. Furthermore, a book can fully depict the design details and sample artifacts, offering insights that can inform adaptability to other contexts and thereby lending elements of generalizability and accessibility to DBR. The book can then serve as a reference for authors to point to when writing journal articles for information about the design-based study in its entirety, such as the MIST Project (Cobb, Jackson, Henrick, & Smith, 2018).

Conclusion and Discussion

Although DBR may have transcended the initial challenges it faced regarding quality and methodological acceptance, there are still a limited number of publications about DBR projects. The analysis of the existing articles we present shows that DBR is beginning to take hold; it is not being outright rejected by leading journals. However, room for improvement exists. A further analysis that explores variation among disciplines in education would also likely reveal different patterns of adoption of DBR methodologies over time.

As a field that should be concerned with the connected implications, influence, and impact of research on practice as well as the implications, influence, and impact of practice on research, we see DBR as an exciting avenue for the distribution of information and publication opportunities that can reach multiple audiences who may be influenced by our work. DBR offers unique insight into the implicit elements of research that often are left unspoken, and therefore invites readers and researchers alike to know why and how a project evolved and what design products can be applied or adapted for use in other contexts. The underlying issue that each research team (and editorial review team) must address is which design phases and details to include to provide adequate detail without overwhelming the reader. It is very easy to include too much detail in a given publication, since details influence design decisions.

As a field, we need to continue to explore different mechanisms for sharing the design outcomes and resources produced by this type of work. Book-length reports that include the multiple voices and perspectives of the stakeholders involved in a project, and online repositories that researchers can reference when sharing their work in peer-reviewed, but page-limited journals, are two viable options. Both options offer a deeper exploration of project nuance and further invite explicit understanding of the various design decisions made throughout the project.

Finally, we also need to continue to advocate for how DBR is valued by our field's guidelines for professional advancement and tenure. In our minds, research that is grounded in problems of practice, context-driven, and collaborative has great potential to effectively and positively impact education. DBR paradigms were founded on those very tenets. We stress that early-career researchers who are drawn to problems of practice and research questions that can be addressed effectively by DBR paradigms should have the support of the field to pursue their research while also achieving their professional goals.[1]

REFERENCES

Anderson, T., & Shattuck, J. (2012). Design-based research: A decade of progress in education research? *Educational Researcher, 41*(1), 16–25.

Bakker, A. (2018). *Design research in education: A practical guide for early career researchers.* New York: Routledge.

Bang, M., & Vossoughi, S. (2016). Participatory design research and educational justice: Studying learning and relations within social change making. *Cognition and Instruction, 34*(3), 173–193.

Barab, S., & Squire, B. (2004). Design-based research: Putting a stake in the ground. *Journal of the Learning Sciences, 13*, 1–14.

Brown, A. (1992). Design experiments: Theoretical and methodological challenges in creating complex interventions in classroom settings. *Journal of the Learning Sciences, 2*(2), 141–178.

Cobb, P., Confrey, J., diSessa, A., Lehrer, R., & Schauble, L. (2003). Design experiments in educational research. *Educational Researcher, 32*(1), 9–13.

Cobb, P., & Jackson, K. (2011). Towards an empirically grounded theory of action for improving the quality of mathematics teaching at scale. *Mathematics Teacher Education & Development, 13*(1), 6–33.

Cobb, P., & Jackson, K. (2012). Analyzing educational policies: A learning design perspective. *Journal of the Learning Sciences, 21*(4), 487–521.

Cobb, P., Jackson, K., Henrick, E., & Smith, T. M. (2018). *Systems for instructional improvement: Creating coherence from the classroom to the district office.* Cambridge, MA: Harvard Education Press.

Collins, A. (1992). Toward a design science of education. In E. Scanlon & T. O'Shea (Eds.), *New directions in educational technology* (pp. 15–22). Berlin: Springer-Verlag.

Collins, A., Joseph, D., & Bielaczyc, K. (2004). Design research: Theoretical and methodological issues. *The Journal of the Learning Sciences, 13*(1), 15–42.

Dede, C. (2004). If design-based research is the answer, what is the question? *Journal of the Learning Sciences, 13*, 105–114.

---

[1] This material is based upon work completed while Margret Hjalmarson served as a program officer at the National Science Foundation. Any opinions, findings, and conclusions or recommendations expressed in this material are those of the authors and do not necessarily reflect the views of the National Science Foundation.

Easterday, M., Rees Lewis, D., & Gerber, E. (2014). Design-based research process: Problems, phases, and applications. In J. L. Polman, E. A. Kyza, D. K. O'Neill, I. Tabak, W. R. Penuel, A. S. Jurow, . . . L. D. Amico (Eds.), *Learning and becoming in practice: The International Conference of the Learning Sciences 2014* (Vol. 1, pp. 317–324). Boulder, CO: International Society of the Learning Sciences.

Edelson, D. (2002). Design research: What we learn when we engage in design. *Journal of the Learning Sciences, 11*(1), 105–121.

Glaser, B. G., & Strauss, A. L. (1965). Discovery of substantive theory: A basic strategy underlying qualitative research. *American Behavioral Scientist, 8*, 5–12.

Gravemeijer, K. (1994). Educational development and developmental research in mathematics education. *Journal for Research in Mathematics Education, 25*(5), 443–471.

Gravemeijer, K., & Cobb, P. (2006). Design research from a learning design perspective. In J. van den Akker, K. Gravemeijer, S. McKenney, & N. Nieveen (Eds.), *Educational research design* (pp. 17–51). New York: Routledge.

Gravemeijer, K., & van Eerde, D. (2009). Design research as a means for building a knowledge base for teachers and teaching in mathematics education. *Elementary School Journal, 109*(5), 510–524.

Hermes, M., Bang, M., & Marin, A. (2012). Designing indigenous language revitalization. *Harvard Educational Review, 82*(3), 381–402.

Hira, A., & Hynes, M. M. (2019). Design-based research to broaden participation in pre-college engineering: Research and practice of an interest-based engineering challenges framework. *European Journal of Engineering Education, 44*(1–2), 103–122.

Kelly, A. E. (2004). Design research in education: Yes, but is it methodological? *The Journal of the Learning Sciences, 13*(1), 115–128.

Kelly, A. E. (2006). Quality criteria for design research: Evidence and commitments. In J. van den Akker, K. Gravemeijer, S. McKenney, & N. Nieveen (Eds.), *Educational design research* (pp. 107–118). New York: Routledge.

Ketelhut, D. J., Nelson, B. C., Clarke, J., & Dede, C. (2010). A multiuser virtual environment for building higher order inquiry skills in science: An exploratory investigation in River City, a multi-user virtual environment. *British Journal of Educational Technology, 41*, 56–68.

Land, S., & Zimmerman, H. (2015). Socio-technical dimensions of an outdoor mobile learning environment: A three-phase design-based research investigation. *Educational Technology Research & Development, 63*(2), 229–255.

Newstetter, W. C. (2005). Designing cognitive apprenticeships for biomedical engineering. *Journal of Engineering Education, 94*(2), 207–213.

Onwuegbuzie, A., & Leech, N. (2007). Validity and qualitative research: An oxymoron? *Quality and Quantity, 41*, 233–249.

Orne, M. T., & Holland, C. H. (1968). On the ecological validity of laboratory deceptions. *International Journal of Psychiatry, 6*, 282–293.

Parsons, A. W., & Bryant, C. L. (2016). Deepening kindergarteners' science vocabulary: A design study. *Journal of Educational Research, 109*, 375–390

Parsons, S. A., Gallagher, M. A., & the George Mason University Content Analysis Team. (2016). A content analysis of nine literacy journals, 2009–2014. *Journal of Literacy Research, 48*, 476–502.

Parsons, S. A., Gallagher, M. A., Leggett, A. B., Ives, S. T., & Lague, M. (2020). An analysis of 15 journals' literacy content, 2007–2016. *Journal of Literacy Research, 52*(3), 341–367.

Penuel, W. R., & Fishman, B. J. (2012). Large-scale science education intervention research we can use. *Journal of Research in Science Teaching, 49*(3), 281–304.

Penuel, W. R., Fishman, B. J., Cheng, B. H., & Sabelli, N. (2011). Organizing research and development at the intersection of learning, implementation, and design. *Educational Researcher, 40*(7), 331–337.

Phillips, D. C., & Dolle, J. R. (2006). From Plato to Brown and beyond: Theory, practice, and the promise of design experiments. In L. Verschaffel, F. Dochy, M. Boekaerts, & S. Vosniadou (Eds.), *Instructional psychology: Past, present, and future trends: Sixteen essays in honor of Erik DeCorte* (pp. 277–293). Amsterdam, The Netherlands: Elsevier.

Reinking, D., & Bradley, B. A. (2008). *Formative and design experiments: Approaches to language and literacy research*. New York: Teachers College Press.

Sandoval, W. (2004). Developing learning theory by refining conjectures embodied in educational designs. *Educational Psychologist, 39*, 213–223.

Sandoval, W. (2014). Conjecture mapping: An approach to systematic educational design research. *Journal of the Learning Sciences, 23*, 18–36.

Santo, R., Ching, D., Peppler, K., & Hoadley, C. M. (2018). Messy, sprawling and open: Research-practice partnership methodologies for working in distributed interorganizational networks. In B. Bevan & W. R. Penuel (Eds.), *Connecting research and practice for educational improvement: Ethical and equitable approaches* (pp. 100–118). New York: Routledge.

Schmuckler, M. (2001). What is ecological validity? A dimensional analysis. *Infancy, 2*, 419–436

Strobel, J., Jonassen, D. H., & Ionas, I. G. (2008). The evolution of a collaborative authoring system for non-linear hypertext: A design-based research study. *Computers & Education, 51*(1), 67–85.

Svihla, V., & Reeve, R. (2016). *Design as scholarship: Case studies from the learning sciences*. New York: Routledge.

PART II
DESIGN-BASED RESEARCH AND CURRICULUM DEVELOPMENT

CHAPTER 3

Combining Curriculum and Teacher Development through Design Research

Jan van den Akker and Nienke Nieveen

The focus of this chapter is the roles of teachers, and the way they interact with designers/developers and researchers, in design research for curriculum challenges. Such collaborative approaches are relevant as they increase chances on multiple valuable goals: (1) the professional development (PD) of teachers, (2) the development of high-quality curriculum products, and (3) the knowledge growth concerning curriculum design. In order to explain and justify this claim, we first present our notion of *curricular design research*, within the broader concept of design research. Then, we explain our understanding of curriculum and curriculum development, arguing how the success of curriculum development, in view of its design complexity and required teacher learning, can benefit from curricular design research. Next, we clarify such an approach with findings from an illustrative study on teacher design teams. In the closing section, we discuss implementation issues of design research, with special attention to the role of networks.

Introducing Curricular Design Research

Design research (as a generic label) is an increasingly applied approach in education that helps to underpin choices and build evidence in challenging design tasks (also see Chapter 1, this volume). Typically, in design research, design and research activities are interwoven: the design is, at least partially, based on research findings, and the research is design oriented. Roughly speaking, one may discern two relatively different emphases in design research approaches (Bakker, 2018; Plomp & Nieveen, 2013; van den Akker & Nieveen, 2017). In design-based research (DBR), the emphasis is on theoretical justification and explanation of the designed artifact, within specific, controlled research contexts, and focusing on student and teacher levels. In research-based design (RBD), the emphasis is on practical improvement or innovation, within realistic, natural contexts, and addressing various levels (student, teacher, organization).

As we shall explain, we consider research-based curriculum design, or shorter curricular design research (CDR; see van den Akker, 2013), as a particularly promising type of design research to contribute to a triple goal: PD of those involved, successful curriculum development, and more generic knowledge gains in the field of curriculum design.

Curriculum as Design for Learning

The concept of *curriculum* has been defined in the literature in many ways, as exemplified during recent decades in three major curriculum handbooks (Connelly, 2008; Jackson, 1992; Wyse, Hayward, & Pandya, 2016). Those usually long definitions often heavily depend on the specific contexts, roles and (ideological) perspectives of the authors (Jackson, 1992). For that reason, we prefer a short, more neutral and flexible definition to confront the complexity of the term and to facilitate its wider use (Kridel, 2010). As curricula for educational settings are not given by nature but represent artifacts that are deliberately created by humans (Simon, 1996), it is obvious that they represent a typical *design* challenge, with many choices to be made. Simon (1996) defined design as devising a course of action, which also captures the essence of curriculum work. For that purpose, the definition of curriculum as a *design for learning* suits well as a simple, open-ended, universal definition that allows for multiple specification to various contexts and perspectives. In the next paragraphs, we will outline those specifications.

Traditionally, curriculum is primarily associated with the aims, content, and organization of learning (Walker, 1990), but various authors (Klein, 1991; van den Akker, 2003) have expanded this list of components to include goals and objectives, content, materials and resources, learning activities, teaching strategies, assessment, grouping, time, and space. Especially when trying to redesign a curriculum and making it work in practice, it is wise to pay attention to the coherence of those components. The (normative) vision on the overarching, broader aims of learning and teaching serves as a central link, connecting all other curriculum components. A metaphor to illustrate this vision is a spider's web (van den Akker, 2003; see Figure 3.1). The curricular spider's web points out both the flexibility and vulnerability of curriculum, as every chain is as strong as its weakest element while all components are interrelated and interconnected.

Besides a visual representation of the challenging components, the curricular spider's web can serve as an analytic tool to explore and clarify the discrepancies between the existing and desired curriculum as well as a design tool that assists developers in prioritizing next steps in the process of getting to a coherent curriculum.

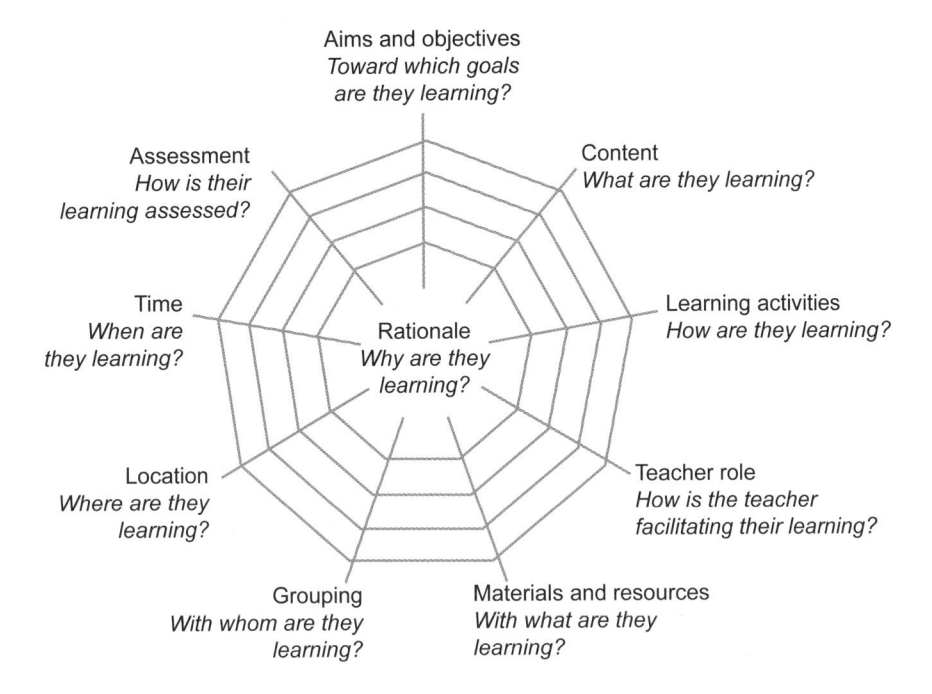

FIGURE 3.1. The curricular spider's web. Reprinted with permission from van den Akker (2013). Copyright © 2013 SLO.

Curriculum development refers to the (often lengthy and iterative) overall process of analyzing, designing, evaluating, and implementing curriculum change. Anticipation on implementation (actual use in the teaching and learning practice) is preferably kept in mind from the beginning and throughout the development process. To understand its complexity, it is important to bear in mind that curricula can exist at various levels of education:

- Supra (inter/transnational)
- Macro (national, regional)
- Meso (school, institution)
- Micro (classroom, group)
- Nano (individual, personal)

Thus, one should keep in mind that *the* curriculum does not exist. It is always necessary to specify the level of curriculum one is referring to, in order to support clarity in communication. At the same time, it is important to realize that curriculum change at scale will eventually have to relate to all those levels, thus implying much interaction between the various levels.

Moreover, curricula can be identified in various representations (Goodlad, 1979; van den Akker, 2003):

- *Visionary:* The ideas, ideals, and intentions for learning (and teaching), giving directions to or underpinning choices in the curriculum
- *Written:* How the intentions are elaborated and specified in documents/materials
- *Perceived:* How the intended curriculum is interpreted, in particular, by teachers
- *Operational:* How the curriculum is enacted in classroom practice
- *Experiential:* How the curriculum is experienced, in particular, by students
- *Learned:* The learner outcomes of the enacted curriculum

Often there are tremendous gaps between the aspirations of the intended curriculum (visionary and written), the realities of the implemented curriculum (perceived and operational), and the outcomes of the attained curriculum (experiential and learned). One can characterize the process of curriculum development as a comprehensive, systematic effort to transform ideas about desirable aims and contents for learning into documents and materials to stimulate instructional practices that foster learning activities and experiences leading toward intended learning outcomes.

Thus, curriculum development has both a product and a process dimension (see Priestley & Biesta, 2013). It can be portrayed as a mostly practical, but also sociopolitical and contextual endeavor with many uncertainties in making choices by many actors. Curriculum choices inevitably relate to (often conflicting) values and interests. Hence, curriculum is sometimes characterized as a war zone or battlefield (e.g., Carnochan, 1993). Although tensions will always remain in the process of designing curricula, it does help if participants in curriculum decision making do have a clear understanding of the different curriculum perspectives in levels, representations, and components. Context always matters, and notably in curriculum approaches. It is important to always keep in mind that one size does not fit all. Moreover, while grand visions may have an inspiring and mobilizing effect, *big bang* approaches to curriculum change should be avoided. Instead, it makes sense to start with relatively small steps in designing and piloting new parts of an envisaged curriculum, departing from an analysis of the current situation in school practice and aiming at the *zone of proximal development* of those involved. Essentially, at this point, the idea of CDR becomes relevant as it may help to address uncertainties on various quality issues (which will be elaborated in the next section) and to improve quality.

Curriculum Quality

It should be noted that curriculum design is not just a discourse about what needs to be learned by students and how to structure that learning. It is also about how to collaboratively bridge the gap between curriculum intentions and classroom practices throughout the multilayered curriculum domain. At each level, meaning-making is essential. Thus, curriculum design can be portrayed as social practice involving a lot of deliberation and negotiation (Walker, 2003), as social practice, not limited to developing products by external organizations that just need to be *delivered* by teachers (cf. Priestley, 2019). Instead of the fidelity perspective whereby teachers faithfully follow curricular prescriptions from external sources, an enactment perspective seems more helpful and appropriate. Teachers create their own curriculum realities, in interaction with their students (cf. Snyder, Bolin, & Zumwalt, 1992). For instance, teachers enact, refine, and/or adjust the curriculum based on their perceptions and aspirations, within the context of their school and classroom contexts (i.e., the perceived curriculum), and in relation to their students' characteristics. In all such (re)design activities, many quality aspects play a role. Although all actors usually express high ambitions about quality, "quality" appears to be a container concept that needs specification.

When thinking about how design research may underpin innovative curriculum (re)design, it is helpful to differentiate between the following, successive criteria of quality (elaborating on Nieveen, 1999; Nieveen & Folmer, 2013):

- *Relevance:* Is there a clear and shared rationale for the new curriculum?
- *Justification:* Is the curriculum supported by a credible knowledge base?
- *Consistency:* Are the various curriculum components (see our prior spider's web discussion) well aligned?
- *Practicality:* Is the curriculum feasible in practice (especially for teachers)?
- *Effectiveness:* Does the curriculum result in the intended learner outcomes?
- *Scalability:* Can the curriculum operate across various contexts?
- *Sustainability:* Is the curriculum change successful in traveling over time?

Of course, not all quality criteria can be met at once from the beginning of a curriculum change process. As Hargreaves and Fink (2006, p. 6) warned, "Change in education is easy to propose, hard to implement, and extraordinarily difficult to sustain." Actually, when thinking about curriculum change, this might even be an understatement of the complexity, as it immediately jumps from ideas to actual change in practice. Ample experience has shown that curriculum design and development, with the transformation of ideas into concrete plans and materials, are quite demanding and time-consuming tasks. However, when curriculum development includes design research features, it offers the potential to gradually meet those subsequent quality criteria. Before discussing how CDR, in collaborative approaches between teachers and researchers, may occur, we focus some attention on the teacher–curriculum interaction, leading toward the idea of teacher design teams.

Teachers and Curriculum (Re)Design

The history of curriculum change has taught us that teachers fulfill a key role in curriculum change (Cuban, 1992). Actually, one cannot expect serious curriculum change without teacher change (Stenhouse, 1975), as curriculum change is essentially what teachers do and think (Fullan, 2016), while they are mediating the (intended) curriculum to their students (the enacted curriculum). What counts most for students (the experiential and learned curriculum) is how their teachers behave in the classroom (operational curriculum). And for deep change, it matters most how teachers' beliefs about education evolve (perceived curriculum). Thus, the participation of teachers is key to any effort at curriculum change.

When teachers are overlooked in the design process, are not involved in the sense-making process, and are not placed in the position to bring their daily practices to the design table, the outcomes of any change efforts usually are disappointing (Fullan, 2008). Moreover, without the involvement of practitioners, it is impossible to gain clear insights into potential curriculum implementation problems and to generate measures to reduce those problems. Teachers need to be involved in curriculum development efforts at all levels, not only for social reasons (to build commitment and ownership of users), but also for technical benefits (to improve the fitness of the curriculum for survival in real-life contexts).

Powerful approaches for curriculum-related teacher professional learning and development require that teachers do not operate in isolation but work together (Pieters, Voogt, & Pareja Roblin, 2019). National curriculum frameworks may give directions for change, but real change in practice can only occur through the collaborative work of teachers in their own school situation. Especially promising appears to be the approach known as *teacher design teams* (TDTs), where small groups of teachers analyze, design, try out, and reflect on innovative parts of intended curriculum innovations (Handelzalts, Nieveen, & van den Akker, 2019).

Teacher Design Teams

TDTs can bridge the gap between curriculum intentions and classroom practices and make sustainable change happen with significant relevance for students (Handelzalts, 2009; Law & Nieveen, 2010). We define a TDT as a group of teachers of the same or adjacent subjects at the same school who cooperate in order to analyze, design, evaluate, and make sense of their common curriculum. When these teams take a RBD approach (preferably in cooperation with researchers), not only do they work toward a high-quality curriculum and contribute to increasing design knowledge, but they also have ample opportunities for teacher learning. As Skilbeck (1998) has also argued, active teacher participation in curriculum design helps improve the (local) relevance of what is taught, and at the same time strengthens teacher professionalism.

Much of the work around TDTs is informed by sociocultural theories about collaborative teacher learning and change. These theories are characterized by three elements: learning is mediated through activity; learning is social in nature; and learning is situated and culturally embedded (cf. Pieters et al., 2019). First of all, the learning in TDTs is mediated through design-related activities. The design of a curriculum needs an inquiring and reflective attitude, active discourse, and negotiation of all involved. While talking about, thinking through, trying out, evaluating, and negotiating the essence and attributes of their common curriculum, teachers will develop a relationship or sense of ownership with the intentions that are underlying the actual curriculum. Sense-making is a key aspect of this process. It involves the interpretation and construction of meaning of the curriculum intentions, aims, and demands in relation to existing beliefs, experiences, practices, and resources (Allen & Penuel, 2015; Century & Cassata, 2016; Honig & Hatch, 2004). These design-related discourses and sense-making activities are important ingredients for teacher learning (Brown, 2009; Remillard, 2005).

Second, studies on effective PD show the importance of collaboration for teacher learning (Greeno, 2011; Whitcomb, Borko, & Liston, 2009; also see Chapters 4, 11, and 12, this volume). In the setting of TDTs, teachers collaborate in the curriculum design process. While collaborating, they need to articulate their (often tacit) practical knowledge in order to develop a shared understanding of the intentions and nature and attributes of their common curriculum. This is an iterative process that can be expanded through interactions with experts who bring new experiences and knowledge (Voogt et al., 2011). Such joint activities lead to individual and collaborative learning. Moreover, the collaboration is indispensable for schools and teachers who are working toward more coherence in the overall school curriculum. For that purpose, teachers need to develop awareness and learn about the substance and pedagogical approaches in each other's subject areas (Handelzalts et al., 2019).

Finally, teacher learning is situated, meaning that what teachers think, do, and find relevant is rooted in the opportunities and demands of their school context (cf. Greeno, 2011; Janssen, Westbroek, Doyle, & van Driel, 2013). This situatedness also influences what teachers bring to the design table and want to work on. For relevant teacher learning to take place, it is important that it be embedded in the actual school and teaching practice (cf. Borko, 2004). When teachers of the same school are working together on their common curriculum, they will be urged:

- to make clear how the renewal fits with the overall school curriculum (aspirations of the school, pedagogical approaches, schedule, classroom organization, assessment practices, etc.);
- to explain what additional PD will be needed to support the renewal (i.e., regarding new pedagogies or assessment practices); and
- to clarify what they need from the school organization to make the renewal sustainable in the long run (i.e., coordination of the renewal and curriculum coherence by realizing crossover structures and supporting connections across curriculum initiatives).

Situating TDTs within the school brings the dynamics of the school into the design practices and prevents the teams from making isolated, nonsustainable changes.

Methodological Challenges of TDTs in the Context of CDR

It appears that TDTs often experience problems with *systematic* analysis, theoretical embedding, and formative evaluation (Huizinga, Handelzalts, Nieveen, & Voogt, 2014; Huizinga, Nieveen, & Handelzalts, 2019). When TDTs do cooperate with (external) researchers in CDR, chances increase that these teams strengthen the relationship of the new curriculum with theory, the systematic way they collect their data, and the articulation of their lessons learned with the help of design principles. The explicit performance of these research elements also distinguishes CDR from most curriculum development practices and from related teacher development approaches, such as action research, lesson study, and professional learning communities (PLCs). It has to be noted that such collaborative approaches require from both sides (teachers and researchers) an open-minded, curious attitude and willingness to invest in a joint agenda, with both practical and academic aspects.

Usually, the aim of CDR is to come to successive prototypes or drafts of the curriculum that increasingly meet the intentions and requirements of the curriculum change. This means that analysis, design, formative evaluation, and revision activities are iterated until a satisfying balance has been reached between the intended curriculum and the implemented and attained curriculum. These research-type activities characterize CDR, and even though they have some characteristics in common with typical or routine-like curriculum design and development approaches, they are more prominent and explicit in design research practices.

- *Preliminary investigation:* A more systematic, preliminary investigation of curriculum tasks, problems, and context is made, including searching for explicit connections of that analysis with state-of-the-art knowledge from the literature. Some typical activities include needs assessment of the intended target group of practitioners, literature review, consultation of experts, analysis of available promising curriculum examples for related purposes, and case studies of current practices to specify and better understand needs and problems in intended user contexts.

- *Theoretical embedding:* More systematic efforts are made to apply state-of-the-art knowledge in articulating the theoretical rationale for curriculum design choices. Moreover, explicit feedback to assertions in the design rationale about essential characteristics of the curriculum is gathered based on empirical testing of prototypes of the curriculum. Because of their specific focus, these theoretical notions are usually referred to as local theories (Bakker, 2018), although sometimes connections can also be made to middle-range theories defined with a somewhat broader scope.

- *Empirical testing:* Clear empirical evidence is delivered about the practicality and effectiveness of the curriculum for the intended target group in real user settings. In view of the wide variation of possible interventions and contexts, a broad range of (direct/indirect; intermediate/ultimate) indicators for success should be considered. The ultimate aim is not to test whether theory, when applied to practice, is a good predictor of events. The interrelation between theory and practice is more complex and dynamic: Is it possible to create a practical and effective curriculum for an existing problem or intended change in the real classroom practice?

- *Documentation, analysis, and reflection on process and outcomes:* Much attention is paid to systematic documentation, analysis, and reflection on the entire analysis, design, development, evaluation, and implementation process and on its outcomes in order to contribute to the expansion and specification of the methodology of curriculum design and development.

An *iterative* process of successive approximation or evolutionary prototyping of the intervention is desirable. Moreover, an *interactive* approach is needed, whereby teachers also reach out to peers, school leadership, other stakeholders within the school, and external experts and test workable prototypes in their classroom practices. Empirical testing of a mostly formative nature (improving rather than proving) is thus key in design research approaches. From the many methods and corresponding data collection activities, we here mention the following (Nieveen & Folmer, 2013):

- *Screening:* Members of the team check the curriculum themselves. Data could be collected by using a checklist containing the required characteristics of the curriculum.
- *Focus group* (also referred to as *expert appraisal*): A group of respondents (e.g., peers, experts, students) reacts to a prototype of the curriculum. Data could be collected by organizing group interviews.
- *Walkthroughs:* The design research team and representatives of the target group (usually peers) together go over the prototype (as in a theater play). Possible data collection activities include using a checklist, interviewing, and observing the respondents when they are running through the prototype.
- *Microevaluation:* A small group of target users (e.g., learners and/or teachers) uses parts of the curriculum outside its normal classroom setting. Possible data collection activities include interviewing, observing, administering a questionnaire, and assessing the performance of learners through a test, learner report, and/or portfolio.
- *Tryout:* The teachers and learners use the curriculum in practice. If the evaluation focuses on the practicality of the curriculum, the following evaluation activities are common: observation, interviewing, requesting logbooks, and administering questionnaires. If the evaluation focuses on the effectiveness of the curriculum, evaluators may decide to assess the performance of learners through a test, learner report, and/or portfolio.

In order to select an appropriate method, TDTs need to consider what kind of questions they have regarding the quality of the curriculum that they are working on. The previously mentioned list of quality criteria can be helpful to identify which criterion is at stake at that moment of the development trajectory. During the first stages of a design research trajectory, most attention will usually be given to the relevance, justification, and consistency of the prototypes. Literature review, screening, and focus group sessions are appropriate for this purpose. TDTs will be concerned about practicality when parts of the prototype are elaborated in detail. In order to collect data on the practicality of the prototype, usually the TDT will organize a walkthrough, microevaluation, or tryout. Effectiveness, scalability, and sustainability will become increasingly important in the latest stages. Here, data can be collected with case studies (in-depth) and surveys (for wider monitoring).

In the early stages of a design research study, it seems legitimate or even advisable that the teachers themselves in the TDTs play a prominent role in the formative evaluation of the prototype. Engaging in formative evaluation activities tends to lead the teachers toward important learning experiences. They will experience for themselves the problems that may occur and hear firsthand the suggestions for improvement that respondents come up with during their use of a prototype (e.g., by observing or interviewing teachers or students). This usually has stronger and more direct impact on their thinking and design activities than cases where external evaluators report the results to developers (Design-Based Research Collective, 2003; Plomp & Nieveen, 2013).

Of course, there are several pitfalls when TDTs are involved in the formative evaluation of the curriculum they are also designing (McKenney, Nieveen, & van den Akker, 2006; McKenney & Reeves, 2018; Plomp & Nieveen, 2013). For instance, they may easily become too attached to their prototype, which could lead to a less objective view of problems and comments from the respondents. In this respect, Scriven (1991) warns against what he calls (co-) authorship bias. On the other hand, the respondents could be biased during the evaluation. If they know how much effort the TDT has put into the design of the prototype, they may hesitate to be fully critical of it. This is another reason why it is important in a design research project to perform formative evaluations at an early stage in the design process and to apply various methods of triangulation. In the final stages of the development or prototyping stage, the design research team usually organizes tryouts with a larger group of representatives of the learners and teachers and with external evaluators responsible for data collection and reporting.

Embedding Teacher Design Research Teams in the School Context

The former sections provided insights into how teacher design teams can advance curriculum development as well as teacher development within the context of schools. In order to strengthen the design work of the teams and to improve the professional learning opportunities for team members, it was found that teacher design teams need to strengthen their research methodological basis. In case this kind of expertise is already available within a team or has been made available in the form of an external coach or researcher, one might consider changing the name of these TDTs into "teacher design research teams." Based on a study of 12 teacher design teams (some of which did receive research assistance) within the curriculum renewal processes at two schools for secondary education in the Netherlands (Handelzalts et al., 2019), we propose a set of seven recommendations regarding how these teacher design research teams may successfully operate within the context of secondary schools.

First and foremost, it is important that *the role of teachers as learners be taken seriously*. Teachers who were involved in the design activities of their team believed that their learning needs became increasingly apparent as soon as they started experimenting with their designs in daily practice and implementing them. In order to increase the chances of teachers having these strong learning experiences, they need to have ample opportunities for piloting "experimental" learning and teaching approaches in an early stage of development (instead of waiting until the next year for the implementation of a new or revised initiative). Moreover, given the fact that experimenting and reflecting are such central elements in learning, this process should gain specific attention, for instance, from external coaches who provide focusing questions before and after implementation. Taking the role of teachers as learners seriously calls for an iterative and evolutionary curriculum design approach with special attention paid to the reflection process based on experience with current and alternative practices.

A second recommendation leads back to our previous suggestion, that is, *look for pro-active external support for the teams in case research expertise is lacking*. These coaches can assist the teams in methodological and process-related issues, help them with embedding their curriculum work in the literature, and assist teachers in active orientation on alternative approaches and views, bringing in inspiring ideas that lead to discourse. For the coaches, a tension may arise between being too dominant and steering (pushing the team in a certain direction) and being reactive and somewhat passive (just following the teams and waiting for their initiatives and achievements). Proactive deliberation and articulation of the needs and wishes of the team and its coach appeared to lead to a better alignment of expectations and a more fruitful process of innovation.

Third, *meaning-making activities need to be in place*. In some instances, TDTs decided to divide their common design tasks among their team members. Although a great deal of cooperation was going on, it did not always lead to joint work and meaningful discussion of these individually conducted design tasks. In such cases, one may wonder how much collaborative learning was, in fact, occurring. This observation led to the suggestion that, although an approach of task division is understandable from a pragmatic perspective, teams need to pay special attention to stimulating meaningful interaction concerning their designs and to secure their collective learning process, for instance, by deliberating a common overall framework, by joint testing of the design, and by organizing reflection meetings.

Fourth, *a productive team composition needs to be encouraged.* As far as group composition is concerned, great variety in the teams did not yield unambiguous suggestions for the future. The larger teams (with about six members) showed more variation in personality and visions. There needs to be some variation within teams for inspiration and discourse to come about. However, when the intentions and motivations to work on renewal diverge too much, this may also lead to frictions. The smaller teams (with about three members) with less variation among their members were able to come to a common platform of ideas fairly quickly. However, the innovation process for them was sometimes hampered by a lack of inspiring ideas and discussions. In order to promote sufficient effective discourse, an external coach should be aware of such frictions in a team, make them explicit to the team, and have team members look together for ways to act on them. Especially in smaller teams (with sometimes limited horizons), attention should be given to the introduction of possible alternatives and new ideas.

Fifth, as the curriculum development activities carried out by the teams were rather unstructured and showed some imbalance, it is necessary to *help teams in curriculum coherence-making*. Most teams started working on the organizational or structural components of the renewal (timetable, sequence of the content) and put less effort into the implications for their own teaching roles and pedagogical changes. From a curricular perspective, it appeared fruitful to make use of the curricular spider's web to underscore the importance of consistency between the 10 components at a team and school level.

A sixth recommendation points to the importance of *working toward a collaborative school culture*. During the change process, culture change had not been high on the priority list of school leaders. However, it became clear that the school's professional culture had gradually transformed into a more collaborative one. On a regular basis, at school meetings and, maybe even more importantly, at informal meetings during breaks, teachers presented and discussed their joint work, shared experiences and information, asked colleagues for assistance, and commented on each other's work. Although more profound results may be accomplished when culture change is more explicitly emphasized during the process, it appears as if the work of TDTs together with regular schoolwide meetings has valuable potential in this direction.

Finally, as a seventh recommendation, we suggest facilitating *variation as well as cohesion*. The variety in the innovation process of the teams is related to a recurrent dilemma in the process. On the one hand, it is necessary to let teams work on a design that is relevant to them and in a way and speed that suit them. On the other hand, there is a need to arrive at a coordinated school framework that is coherent, practical, and realistic. Variation between participants (teachers, teams) should not be regarded as an obstacle, but rather as a normal feature of development processes. Differences in tasks, style, commitment, and support should be expected, sometimes perhaps even encouraged. In order to foster curricular cohesion, much emphasis should be placed on (both formal and informal) communication between all stakeholders in the process. All sorts of (ongoing) communication are helpful for stimulating the development process: personal/organizational; formal/informal; written/oral. The documentation of processes and active sharing of (preliminary) outcomes are beneficial for progress, although an overload of bureaucratic paperwork should be avoided. The school organization can facilitate collaborative development activities by creating smart crossover patterns, offering adequate working arrangements, and alert handling of emerging organizational and logistical problems. Leadership tasks and responsibilities should be distributed throughout the organization.

Design Principles as Knowledge Drivers

Next to curriculum and teacher development, CDR is aimed at knowledge production. The major knowledge outcome of design research is articulated in design principles to guide the actions of future designers. In the case of CDR, the principles usually refer to the design of curriculum programs and materials. They can vary from an emphasis on the characteristics of those products themselves (the substantive aspect) or on the methods/procedures of designing and implementing them (the procedural aspect). Sometimes the design principles can be precise (especially about recommended characteristics of materials, if strong empirical evidence is available); in other cases, they can be a bit more loosely formulated, in particular, in early design stages and for process-oriented principles where context always has a strong impact.

It is important to realize that CDR seldom occurs from scratch. Usually, it can build—at least partly—on previous research or related knowledge contributions. Ideally, the work is embedded in a programmatic approach of related and/or successive projects where cumulation of experiences, examples, and guiding principles can occur. The power of design principles will increase when their validity is tested through a variation of related artifacts/interventions, contexts, and sources, which will facilitate insight into essential versus adaptable design characteristics.

Crystallized design principles may have the following (formal) structure:

If you want to design intervention X [for purpose/function Y in context Z],
then you are best advised to give that intervention the characteristics $C_1, C_2, \ldots, C_m$ [substantive emphasis]
and to do that via procedures $P_1, P_2, \ldots, P_n$ [procedural emphasis]
because of theoretical arguments $T_1, T_2, \ldots, T_p$
and empirical arguments $E_1, E_2, \ldots, E_q$

Thus, although design principles are often concisely presented in one heading or short sentence, they preferably incorporate a full line of reasoning, including specification of (1) the intended intervention or artifact, with its purpose or function (what should it bring about?) and context of use; (2) the desirable characteristics of the intervention/artifact (how should it look and operate?), thus emphasizing the substance (or what); (3) the preferential approach/method/process to design and use the intervention, thus emphasizing the procedure (or how); (4) the theoretical explanation/justification of the reasons that underpin the recommended characteristics and procedures; and (5) the empirical arguments that evaluative research has to offer for the plausibility of the (various parts of) the design principle.

Not all these ingredients of design principles can be expected to be fully fledged at the early stages of design research. Often, at the beginning of new studies, the principles are still quite open and tentative, with only modest theoretical justification and an even more modest basis of empirical evidence. Then, iterative design and evaluation steps may offer findings that, on deliberate reflection, might result in more complete and sharper articulated design principles.

Generalization of knowledge contributions from design research is essential to consider. The more conventional statistical reasoning to make statements about effectiveness by generalizing from sample to population is usually inappropriate in design research, with its emphasis on qualitative methods with often limited, selective groups. Alternative, more natural, and built-in ways of generalization are needed. The approach to generalization is more analytic: readers/users make their own efforts to translate the findings to their own contexts. However, researchers/authors can facilitate those efforts by an articulate theoretical justification of the applied design principles, plus reflection on the findings. Such information can help readers make connections to their own design efforts. Moreover, researchers should offer a careful description of the evaluation procedures and results plus the context of implementation, in order to assist readers in relating findings to their own context. Transfer through built-in collaboration with various partners and networks may be helpful. We will elaborate on that issue in the next section.

Scaling of Results through Networking of Designers

Beside striving for broadly applicable insights, how can the results of CDR by TDTs contribute to wider improvement of practices in curriculum and teacher learning? In recent times, the scaling of change in education has become an increasingly relevant topic. Coburn (2003) sensitized many to the complexity of facing four different dimensions of scale: *depth* in the practice of teaching in schools; *sustainability* over longer periods of time; *spread* over more people and organizations; *shift* in ownership from original source to other people and contexts. Scale is definitely also a serious challenge for curriculum change (Fullan, 2008), for each of Coburn's dimensions. Does CDR, with the active roles of teachers in TDTs, also hold promise for curriculum change at scale? In this closing section, we will present some exploratory thoughts on this question.

For starters, the multilayered nature of curriculum may help. Just as teachers do not operate in a vacuum but within a school context, schools also operate in a wider system, usually a region or nation with its own specific curriculum policies. Whether curriculum policies are more or less centralized (see the overview by Kuiper & Berkvens, 2013, for variety in various countries), curriculum frameworks at the macro (national) level will inevitably define the playing field for the schools in their jurisdiction and may help create a common sense of direction for schools (meso) and teachers (micro), including other actors (such as teacher educators). Such a perspective may facilitate the (re)design activities of many actors.

In general, the most favorable implementation philosophy can be characterized as not aiming at the *high fidelity* of top-down or external prescriptions, but rather at an ongoing *mutual adaptation* between design and use. That implies sufficient space for and active encouragement of context-specific choices for local communities, parents, schools, teachers, and students. A clear example of such a localization approach (within the boundaries of the national framework) can be found in Finland (Halinen & Holappa, 2013), where local communities are expected and supported to make, translate, and add their own curriculum choices, together with the schools in their particular community. Moreover, a mutual adaptation approach requires that teachers, as the main curriculum enactors, have not only an appropriate degree of professional autonomy in the pedagogical and instructional domain, but also a sufficient degree of curricular capacity to recognize and utilize the potential of the curriculum. Such curricular capacity building of teachers individually and in teams, while also including school leaders, should be an important aim of PD strategies. Such an approach is furthered when the curriculum framework is not overloaded with aims and contents and not full of detailed prescriptions. Similarly, it is important that there not be undue emphasis on assessment and accountability.

Successful, deep curriculum change in classrooms, affecting both the use of teaching and learning materials as well the actions and thoughts of teachers (Fullan, 2016), requires lots of investments in bottom-up initiatives. TDTs constitute a promising vehicle for such school-based curriculum development, as they engage teams of teachers in collaborative curriculum analysis, design, and evaluation, stimulating joint action and reflection, potentially addressing all four of Coburn's dimensions.

Several aspects at the meso/school level can stimulate and support such joint teacher activities. Indispensable is active leadership to initiate and mobilize forces, to create favorable conditions for innovative design efforts, and to attend to coherence of various interventions through integral principles and planning (Mintrop, 2016). Such school leadership does not always or only have to come from the top; distributed approaches of leadership throughout the organization might even be more productive to stimulate wide involvement and ownership.

Joint vision building, a collaborative culture, and an interactive outlook to the environment are important school conditions for the work of TDTs, elaborating the school intentions within and across subjects and grades. Obviously (but often underestimated), such teams need realistic, thus ample facilities (in particular, development time) for teachers. Promising scenarios also include the sharing of good practices and offering adaptable exemplifications (e.g., educative lesson materials, digital portals). By the way, such scenarios and examples can also be the result of CDR through TDTs with the participation of teachers from different schools. The products of such heterogeneous networks might be less context-specific for the respective schools, but, on the other hand, more robust in use across various conditions. Moreover, collaborative work in such mixed teams may widen the professional horizon of the participants.

These more mixed collaboration approaches may also be extended through more interaction between not only teacher-designers and researcher-designers, but also school leaders, teacher educators, textbook developers, assessment developers, and the like. Practicing a design research approach in these *networked improvement communities* (Bryk, Gomez, Grunow, & LeMahieu, 2015) seems promising for professional capacity building and gradually coming to scale.

In all of this, we have to be aware of the differences between primary and upper secondary schools. In the latter, the role of subject-matter teachers is more dominant, asking for other collaboration patterns, than in the former, where usually more generic teachers are responsible for a wide range of domains. However, regardless of the specific education sector, the strong point of TDTs working along a CDR approach is that it matches the zone of proximal development of teachers. Lesson preparation and planning belong to the daily work of teachers. Expanding that basic repertoire of activities to more collaborative, curriculum-oriented, and research-supported patterns is beneficial for both teachers' learning and curriculum quality. Educational researchers who contribute to this work through supportive analysis, design, and evaluation activities may find the knowledge outcomes of their efforts highly relevant and rewarding.

REFERENCES

Allen, C., & Penuel, W. (2015). Studying teachers' sensemaking to investigate teachers' responses to professional development focused on new standards. *Journal of Teacher Education, 66*(2), 136–149.

Bakker, A. (2018). *Design research in education*. London: Routledge.

Borko, H. (2004). Professional development and teacher learning: Mapping the terrain. *Educational Researcher, 33*, 3–15.

Brown, M. (2009). The teacher–tool relationship: Theorizing the design and use of curriculum materials. In J. Remillard, B. Herbel-Eisenman, & G. Lloyd (Eds.), *Mathematics teachers at work: Connecting curriculum materials and classroom instruction* (pp. 17–36). New York: Routledge.

Bryk, A., Gomez, L., Grunow, A., & LeMahieu, P. (2015). *Learning to improve*. Cambridge, MA: Harvard Education Press.

Carnocahn, W. (1993). *The battleground of the curriculum*. Stanford, CA: Stanford University Press.

Century, J., & Cassata, A. (2016). Implementation research: Finding common ground on what, how, why, where, and who. *Review of Research in Education, 40*(1), 169–215.

Coburn, C. (2003). Rethinking scale: Moving beyond numbers to deep and lasting change. *Educational Researcher, 32*(6), 3–12.

Connelly, F. (Ed.). (2008). *The SAGE handbook of curriculum and instruction*. Los Angeles: SAGE.

Cuban, L. (1992). Curriculum stability and change. In P. Jackson (Ed.), *Handbook of research on curriculum* (pp. 216–247). New York: Macmillan.

Design-Based Research Collective. (2003). Design-based research: An emerging paradigm for educational inquiry. *Educational Researcher, 32*(1), 5–8, 35–37.

Fullan, M. (2008). Curriculum implementation and sustainability. In F. Connelly (Ed.), *The SAGE handbook of curriculum and instruction* (pp. 113–122). Los Angeles: SAGE.

Fullan, M. (2016). *The new meaning of educational change* (5th ed.). New York: Teachers College Press.

Goodlad, J. (Ed.). (1979). *Curriculum inquiry: The study of curriculum practice*. New York: McGraw-Hill.

Greeno, J. (2011). A situative perspective on cognition and learning in interaction. In T. Koschmann (Ed.), *Theories of learning and studies of instructional practice* (pp. 41–71). New York: Springer.

Halinen, I., & Holappa, A.-S. (2013). Curricular balance based on dialogue, cooperation and trust—The case of Finland. In W. Kuiper & J. Berkvens (Eds.), *Balancing curriculum regulation and freedom across Europe* (pp. 136–153). Enschede, the Netherlands: SLO (Netherlands Institute for Curriculum Development).

Handelzalts, A. (2009). *Collaborative curriculum development in teacher design teams*. Unpublished manuscript, University of Twente, Enschede, the Netherlands.

Handelzalts, A., Nieveen, N., & van den Akker, J. (2019). Teacher design teams for school-wide curriculum development: Reflections on an early study. In J. Pieters, J. Voogt, & N. Pareja Roblin, N. (Eds.), *Collaborative curriculum design for sustainable innovation and teacher learning* (pp. 55–82). Dordrecht, the Netherlands: Springer.

Hargreaves, A., & Fink, D. (2006). *Sustainable leadership*. San Francisco: Jossey-Bass.

Honig, M., & Hatch, T. (2004). Crafting coherence: How schools strategically manage multiple, external demands. *Educational Researcher, 33*(8), 16–30.

Huizinga, T., Handelzalts, A., Nieveen, N., & Voogt, J. (2014). Teacher involvement in curriculum design: Need for support to enhance teachers' design expertise. *Journal of Curriculum Studies, 46*(1), 33–57.

Huizinga, T., Nieveen, N. M., & Handelzalts, A. (2019). Identifying needs for support to enhance teachers' curriculum design expertise. In J. Pieters, J. Voogt, & N. Pareja Roblin (Eds.), *Collaborative curriculum design for sustainable innovation and teacher learning* (pp. 115–137). Dordrecht, the Netherlands: Springer.

Jackson, P. (1992). Conceptions of curriculum and curriculum specialists. In P. Jackson (Ed.), *Handbook of research on curriculum* (pp. 3–40). New York: Macmillan.

Janssen F., Westbroek, H., Doyle, W., & van Driel, J. (2013). How to make innovations practical. *Teachers College Record, 115*, 1–42.

Klein, F. (1991). *The politics of curriculum decision making*. Albany, NY: SUNY Press.

Kridel, C. (2010). *Encyclopedia of curriculum studies*. Los Angeles: SAGE

Kuiper, W., & Berkvens, J. (Eds.). (2013). *Balancing curriculum regulation and freedom across Europe* (CIDREE Yearbook 2013). Enschede, The Netherlands: Netherlands Institute for Curriculum Development.

Law, E., & Nieveen, N. (Eds.). (2010). *Schools as curriculum agencies: Asian and European perspectives on school-based curriculum development*. Rotterdam, the Netherlands: Sense.

McKenney, S., Nieveen, N., & van den Akker, J. (2006). Design research from a curriculum perspective. In J. van den Akker, K. Gravemeijer, S. McKenney, & N. Nieveen (Eds.), *Educational design research* (pp. 67–90). London: Routledge.

McKenney, S., & Reeves, T. (2018). *Conducting educational design research* (2nd ed.). London: Routledge.

Mintrop, R. (2016). *Design-based school improvement*. Cambridge, MA: Harvard Education Press.

Nieveen, N. (1999). Prototyping to reach product quality. In J. van den Akker, R. Branch, K. Gustafson, N. Nieveen, & T. Plomp (Eds.), *Design approaches and tools in education and training* (pp. 125–136). Dordrecht, the Netherlands: Kluwer Academic.

Nieveen, N., & Folmer, E. (2013). Formative evaluation in educational design research. In T. Plomp & N. Nieveen (Eds.), *Educational design research—Part A: An introduction* (pp. 152–169). Enschede, the Netherlands: SLO (Netherlands Institute for Curriculum Development).

Pieters, J., Voogt, J., & Pareja Roblin, N. (Eds.). (2019). *Collaborative curriculum design for sustainable innovation and teacher learning*. Dordrecht, the Netherlands: Springer.

Plomp, T., & Nieveen, N. (Eds.). (2013). *Educational design research*. Enschede, the Netherlands: SLO (Netherlands Institute for Curriculum Development).

Priestley, M. (2019). Curriculum: Concepts and approaches. *Impact Journal of the Chartered College of Teaching, 6*. Retrieved from https://impact.chartered.college/article/curriculum-concepts-approaches

Priestley, M., & Biesta, G. (2013). *Reinventing the curriculum: New trends in curriculum policy and practice*. London: Bloomsbury Academic.

Remillard, J. (2005). Examining key concepts in research on teachers' use of mathematics curricula. *Review of Educational Research, 75*(2), 211–246.

Scriven, M. (1991). Beyond formative and summative evaluation. In M. McLaughlin & D. Phillips (Eds.), *Evaluation and education: At quarter century* (pp. 19–64). Chicago: University of Chicago.

Simon, H. (1996). *The sciences of the artificial* (3rd ed.). Cambridge, MA: MIT Press.

Skilbeck, M. (1998). School-based curriculum development. In A. Hargreaves, A. Lieberman, M. Fullan, & D. Hopkins (Eds.), *International handbook of educational change* (pp. 121–144). Dordrecht, the Netherlands: Springer.

Snyder, J., Bolin, F., & Zumwalt, K. (1992). Curriculum implementation. In P. Jackson (Ed.), *Handbook of research on curriculum* (pp. 402–435). New York: Macmillan.

Stenhouse, L. (1975). *An introduction to curriculum research and development*. London: Heinemann.

van den Akker, J. (2003). Curriculum perspectives: An introduction. In J. van den Akker, U. Hameyer, & W. Kuiper (Eds.), *Curriculum landscapes and trends* (pp. 1–10). Dordrecht, the Netherlands: Kluwer Academic.

van den Akker, J. (2013). Curricular development research as a specimen of educational design research. In T. Plomp & N. Nieveen (Eds.), *Educational design research—Part A: An introduction* (pp. 52–71). Enschede, the Netherlands: SLO (Netherlands Institute for Curriculum Development).

van den Akker, J., & Nieveen, N. (2017). The role of teachers in design research in education. In S. Doff, & R. Komoss (Eds.), *Making change happen* (pp. 75–86). Wiesbaden, Germany: Springer.

Voogt, J., Westbroek, H., Handelzalts, A., Walraven, A., McKenney, S., & Pieters, J. (2011). Teacher learning in collaborative curriculum design. *Teaching and Teacher Education, 27*(8), 1235–1244.

Walker, D. (1990). *Fundamentals of curriculum*. San Diego: Harcourt, Brace, Jovanovich.

Walker, D. (2003). *Fundamentals of curriculum: Passion and professionalism* (2nd ed.). Mahwah, NJ: Erlbaum.

Whitcomb, J., Borko, H., & Liston, D. (2009). Growing talent: Promising professional development models and practices. *Journal of Teacher Education, 60*(3), 207–212.

Wyse, D., Hayward, L., & Pandya, J. (Eds.). (2016). *The SAGE handbook of curriculum, pedagogy and assessment*. London: SAGE.

CHAPTER 4

Curriculum Development in Science

Kalle Juuti and Jari Lavonen

There are two major challenges in science education: students have difficulties in making sense of phenomena and there is a need for more students to study science and technology and pursue related occupations (European Union [EU], 2004; Organisation for Economic Co-operation and Development [OECD], 2016). The European Commission's policy approach of responsible research and innovation is gaining momentum in European research planning and development as a strategy to align scientific and technological progress with socially desirable and acceptable ends. One of the responsible research and innovation agendas is science education, and the aim is to foster future generations' acquisition of the skills and values needed to responsibly engage in society. To this end, responsible research and innovation-based science education can benefit from more interdisciplinary methods, such as those based on the arts and digital technologies. Furthermore, science curricula must consider the wicked problems (e.g., global warming, mass extinction, pandemics, and digitalizing society) that currently challenge science education and society. In this chapter, we present two cases that show how these challenges—making sense of science phenomena and interest in science—can be addressed through the collaborative design-based research (DBR) efforts of researchers and teachers.

As noted in Chapter 1 of this volume, one of the major questions of DBR is "What could be learned about the world by changing it?" Curriculum can be seen as a way to make these changes in the world. Curriculum units, which are designed in accordance with the Finnish national-level core curriculum (*intended curriculum*), can be used to research how the curriculum is enacted and experienced (*achieved curriculum*). In addition to learning about science, the central objective of the national-level science curriculum is to support the development of interest in science and science-related tasks.

There are two levels of essential curriculum documents in Finland: the national-level core curriculum and the municipality-level local curriculum. In addition to subject-specific goals, content, and assessment criteria, the Finnish National Core Curriculum (2016) characterized the local curriculum-making process underlying the values of the education mission and the significance of school culture development, cooperation with parents, learning environments and assessments, organizing special needs education, and enhancing students' welfare. Municipalities have a great deal of autonomy in creating the local curriculum, and the national-level curriculum states that issues should be resolved at the municipality level.

Another important characteristic is that curriculum development is understood as a broad national- and local-level process that engages teachers in the translation of the national-level curriculum into the curriculum unit. The curriculum unit is co-designed by teachers and researchers in a DBR project. As such, teachers are considered curriculum-makers. During the translation process, the core concepts and skills in the national-level curriculum are elaborated to connect them with the experience, interests, and capacity of the students (Deng, 2020). This requires novel interpretation of the national-level curriculum documents and guidelines, detailed course objectives, and other curriculum materials. The curriculum unit describes in detail the kinds of knowledge, skills, and interests that students should learn and how they should learn them (Cuban, 1992; Deng, 2020; Schmidt, Raizen, Britton, Bianci, & Wolfe, 1997).

Meanwhile, the achieved curriculum refers to the learning outcomes of the students, including their level of interest in science learning; these outcomes are derived from the learning and teaching processes. To examine the effects of the achieved curriculum, we have researched students' interest in science and science learning, which is one of the important goals of the national-level curriculum.

In this chapter, we examine the curriculum unit development process, including the role of mutual action by teachers and researchers, and present two cases in which we co-designed a curriculum unit as part of our DBR work. In the following sections, we explain the theoretical frameworks that support curriculum unit design and their relation to DBR. Then we describe the Finnish context and comment on the curriculum unit design work in which we engaged with teachers.

Pragmatic Framework for DBR

DBR is about actions (see Chapter 1, this volume). The key is to design something that did not exist before, such as a curriculum unit related to a specific topic. There are two kinds of situations: indeterminate and problematic situations. According to Biesta and Burbules (2003), in an indeterminate situation, a teacher may feel uneasy since the normal flow of teaching is disrupted. When the teacher realizes that something needs to be done, the indeterminate situation becomes problematic. Such indeterminate situations stimulate DBR.

DBR is also pragmatic (see Chapter 1, this volume; Juuti & Lavonen, 2006). Although pragmatism has been considered a part of the history of philosophy, scholars outside of philosophy recently rediscovered pragmatism as a useful framework for analyzing the relationship between knowledge and action (Biesta & Burbules, 2003; Kilpinen, 2008). Biesta and Burbules (2003) noted that, in pragmatic thinking, problems emerge as a result of the identification of indeterminate situations. In this line of thinking, research is the transformation of the situation and is directed by reflection. Biesta and Burbules (2003) stressed that educational research will not result in rules for action, but it reveals possible connections between actions and consequences. Possible connections between theory, features of the designed environment, actions in these settings, and outcomes are conjectures that educational research aims to reveal (Sandoval, 2014).

When Dewey's view of knowledge as an organism–environment interaction (Biesta & Burbules, 2003) is applied to DBR in science education, the knowledge acquired during the research process can be seen as a construct located within the interactions of the teacher, the researcher, and the learning environment. In addition, curriculum units can be seen as constituting the environment. In this sense, the curriculum unit should consider the classroom setting; the social and psychological atmospheres; and pupils' motivations, affinity for and conceptions of the topic to be learned, and anticipations.

In pragmatism, knowledge and action are intimately connected. Knowledge about science teaching and learning, the design actions of teachers and researchers, and actions in the classroom are not separate. Knowledge about science teaching and learning emerges from the enactment of developed curriculum units in a classroom. Through reflection, knowledge is also gained from experiences in the classroom. In other words, the outcome of the experiences and the reflection is new knowledge (Dewey, 1984).

Activities in the classroom are directed according to national-level curriculum aims, and directed actions are reflected on in order to create knowledge about teaching and student learning, engagement, and interest. The reflection is a shared activity of the teachers and the researchers. In a shared activity situation, the teachers and researchers have a similar interest in optimal situations and want to share their ideas and emotions (Dewey, 1980). They design, enact, and evaluate curriculum units together. Shared activity requires communication between teachers and researchers. Biesta and Burbules (2003) characterized communication as the mutual coordination of action; therefore, it is not a process in which a teacher simply reacts to a researcher's movements, after which the researcher reacts to the teacher's reactions, and so on. Successful coordination requires that the teacher react to what the researcher intends to achieve with his or her activities, just as the researcher reacts to what the teacher intends to achieve with his or her activities. In other words, successful coordination requires that the partners in the interaction try to anticipate each other's actions (Biesta & Burbules, 2003).

Pragmatic DBR must start in a nebulous, indeterminate situation. Neither researchers nor teachers know what kind of curriculum unit might lead to a satisfactory situation (Juuti & Lavonen, 2006). The starting point could be to clarify the objectives of the national-level curriculum by asking the following questions: How should actions be directed and in which direction? What should happen in the enactment of a curriculum unit? What are the possibilities and constraints of action? By answering these questions, teachers and researchers can explicate the problem for which the curriculum unit is intended to be the solution. Based on the pragmatic frame (Biesta & Burbules, 2003), the shared curriculum unit development by the teachers and researchers directs the action in the classroom. Therefore, the designed curriculum unit creates novel educational phenomena for research. This is the core of DBR.

To better understand and foster learning, the objects of interest need to be designed in the appropriate educational setting. Thus, curriculum units that are co-developed with teachers are likely to be more authentic and answer the original demands of DBR (Brown, 1992). A researcher may acquire knowledge about teaching and learning by engaging in shared curriculum unit development, having similar experiences in the classroom, reflecting on the experiences together, and anticipating teachers' intentions concerning the curriculum unit (Juuti & Lavonen, 2006).

The Finnish Educational Context: The Value System

The educational context influences the objectives of the curriculum unit, the development process, the outcome, and the collaboration between the researchers and teachers. Therefore, the Finnish educational context is introduced below to help readers understand the development of the curriculum units.

Value of Equality and Decentralized Administration

In the Finnish educational context, equality is one of the most important values (Darling-Hammond, 2017). Free education is available at the primary, secondary, and tertiary levels. Moreover, free health care, counseling, tutoring (additional lessons), and library services are available to students at all levels. Although educational equality is emphasized in policy and in practice, indicators of equality have slightly decreased during the last 10 years (Vettenranta et al., 2016).

Since the 1990s, the quality of education has been promoted in all areas of governance in Finland through a decentralized approach. In collaboration with teachers, providers of education, typically municipalities, have been responsible for quality assurance, the preparation of local curricula, and the selection of textbooks (Niemi, Toom, & Kallioniemi, 2012). Teachers are responsible for student assessment and grading. Quality assurance procedures are based on self-assessment at all levels of education, on the collection and analysis of feedback, and, moreover, on national sample-based monitoring of student learning outcomes. As part of this decentralization, only basic guidelines are prepared at the national level, such as the national-level framework curricula (Finnish National Core Curriculum, 2016). Decentralization is possible because there is a culture of trust in Finnish education. Educational authorities and national-level policymakers trust that teachers, together with principals, headmasters, and parents, know how to provide the best education for children and youth in a particular district. Teachers are valued as autonomous professionals in curriculum development, teaching, and assessment at all levels (Chong, Huan, Wong, Klassen, & Allison, 2010).

Teachers as Professionals

The role of school principals and their leadership approaches, such as the sharing of responsibilities or shared leadership, influence teachers' collaboration and classroom operations. Principals in Finnish schools play an important role in facilitating a school culture that supports collaboration among teachers. This collaboration manifests itself in various school teams and networks, such as grade-level teams and multiprofessional teams.

Simola (2005) argues that the most important reason for Finnish students' relatively high success in the Programme for International Student Assessment (PISA) is the professionalism of teachers. This is supported by the 40-year-long tradition in Finland of educating primary and secondary school teachers at universities in 5-year master's-level programs. Since the 1960s, the objective of teacher education has been to educate professionals who are able to plan, implement, and assess their own teaching and their students' learning. Consequently, teachers are considered academic professionals just like other university degree holders. Furthermore, school-level operations support teachers' professionalism and collaboration.

Contrary to preservice teacher education, inservice education and the professional development (PD) of teachers are the responsibilities of municipalities in Finland. Teachers have to participate in inservice training for 2 days per year. However, several municipalities coordinate local development projects, and teachers take professional learning seriously. Thus, in addition to the required 2 days, teachers participate in various development projects at their schools. In fact, the DBR cases described here could be considered examples of municipality-level development projects.

National and Local Curricula Unit Development Processes in the Finnish Context

In Finland, the national-level science curriculum is revisited approximately every 10 years. The Ministry of Education and Culture (MEC) is responsible for the overall planning and legislation of education. The Finnish National Agency for Education (EDUFI) is responsible for developing comprehensive school and secondary education (high school and vocational school), creating the national-level curriculum for science. Lower secondary education (grades 7–9) is part of the nonselective

9-year basic Finnish education; it aims to support pupils' growth in terms of humanity and ethically responsible membership in society and to provide them with the knowledge and skills needed in life (Finnish National Core Curriculum, 2016). The Finnish National Core Curriculum for High School was finalized in 2019 (Finnish National Core Curriculum for High School, 2019). Municipalities are responsible for organizing lower and upper secondary education and preparing the local curriculum. Each school prepares an annual plan, and teachers are responsible for developing their curriculum units.

In Finland, it is common for the national-level science core curriculum to be planned in collaboration with national and local educational authorities. In addition to the authorities, researchers, teacher educators, teachers, and representatives from teacher unions and municipality unions participate in this consensus-seeking process. For example, national-level framework curricula for comprehensive schooling were prepared between 2012 and 2014 in close collaboration with teachers, teacher educators, and providers of education in the municipalities (Vahtivuori-Hänninen et al., 2014).

National-Level Science Curriculum in Middle and High Schools

In several countries, such as the United Kingdom, the United States, and Sweden, science is commonly taught in grades 7–9 as an integrated subject by science teachers who have, typically, not studied all science subjects. In Finland, science is divided into the separate subjects of physics, chemistry, geography, biology, and health education. This separation continues in high school, and students must take one compulsory course in each science subject and several optional courses.

A general description of the need for 21st-century competencies at all levels of education was included in the national-level science curriculum. The science curriculum emphasizes acquiring relevant competencies by familiarizing students with core scientific knowledge and science and engineering practices. These descriptions emphasize inquiry and problem-solving orientations in science learning and critical and creative thinking skills.

Learning is generally defined in the national-level curriculum (Finnish National Core Curriculum, 2016) as a goal-oriented behavior based on a student's prior knowledge, skills, feelings, and experiences. The student is considered an *agent* of her or his own learning who learns how to set goals and solve problems independently and with others. In addition, the student learns to reflect on the learning processes and his or her experiences and emotions while simultaneously developing new knowledge and skills. At its best, learning awakens positive emotional experiences and joy and is seen as a creative activity that inspires the development of the student's expertise. Moreover, learning is an integral part of an individual's comprehensive, lifelong growth as a person; it is the building material for a good life.

In Finland, descriptions of learning outcomes have not been used in the national-level curriculum to express the learning objectives. Instead, goals and subject-specific aims, as well as the core content of each school subject (syllabus), are described on a general level. For example, in the national-level physics curriculum for middle schools, there are six key content areas: scientific research, physics in daily life, physics in society, physics shaping the worldview, interaction and motion, and electricity. According to the national-level curriculum (Finnish National Core Curriculum, 2016, p. 390), "The contents are selected to support the achievement of objectives, and local possibilities are utilized in the selection." This leaves a lot of space for municipalities and teachers to decide not only teaching and learning methods but also the content of the curriculum unit. Local-level curricula may define the content, or it may be left to individual teachers to decide in their curriculum units. Thus, teachers have very broad autonomy in curriculum development.

Meanwhile, the national-level science curriculum emphasizes science and engineering practices through which students can identify, recognize, or observe scientific issues: design experiments, gather empirical data or use written sources of information, explain or interpret data or scientific phenomena, draw conclusions based on evidence, or formulate simple models or generalizations. The national-level science curriculum guides teachers to organize activities in which students make observations or collect data, present data as a graph, and give scientific explanations. Altogether, the science component of the national-level curriculum document is about 30 pages.

In summary, the national-level curriculum gives space for professional teachers to plan and implement curriculum units. Teachers' autonomous roles in local-level curriculum development and classroom-level curriculum unit development are also supported by teacher-led assessment and grading practices. Consequently, the Finnish education policy, curriculum practices, and teachers' professionalism offer an excellent starting point for teachers and researchers to participate in shared DBR projects.

The Curriculum Unit as an Artifact and an Outcome of the Shared Activity of Teachers and Researchers

Below, we describe two cases in which we have worked with teachers to develop curriculum units. These research projects aimed to better understand how to enhance students' science learning and interest in science. The projects were organized based on the general principles of DBR (see Chapter 1, this volume; Design-Based Research Collective, 2003; Juuti & Lavonen, 2006; Juuti, Lavonen, & Meisalo, 2016). Figure 4.1 illustrates the key features of our DBR projects.

The first step in developing curriculum units is understanding the context. This might require interviews with teachers and observations to understand the current practice, constraints, and affordances. For example, the national-level curriculum, the timetable, or available digital tools might be significant constraints or affordances. Naturally, it is necessary to familiarize oneself with learning science

	Practice	**Research**
Understanding the context	Indeterminate situation, stimulation of DBR	
	Sharing the same world	
	Teachers' understanding, current practices, beliefs, constraints, affordances, etc.	Literature review of current theoretical and empirical understanding of the situation
	Vision of the future learning, shared goals	
Design and iteration	Problematic situation, tentative strategies Better-justified strategies to orchestrate science learning	
	Artifact design	
	Classroom trials	Data gathering, analysis
	Reflection	
Outcomes	Theoretical and empirical understanding of the learning and design	
	Teachers' more intelligent actions (professional learning), materials for curriculum units to enhance future learning	More intertwined research and practice in teacher education (publications)

FIGURE 4.1. Key features of DBR for developing science curriculum units.

research on the topic. Based on the analysis of the context, it is possible to develop a vision of the future learning to be designed. Furthermore, teachers and researchers are able to share similar goals for DBR.

The second feature of DBR is the iterative process of artifact design, classroom trial, data gathering, data analysis, and reflection. The iterative part of a DBR project starts with the articulation of a tentative strategy to orchestrate future learning to realize shared goals in certain situations. During the iterative design and testing of the learning, teachers are positioned as members of the research group who plan, enact, and reflect on the developed curriculum units as well as participate in planning the data-gathering process.

Reflection is rigorous and systematic thinking (Rodgers, 2002). In DBR, reflection requires data gathering and analysis. This could include analysis of classroom video recordings, students' learning outcomes, discussions between teachers and researchers before and after piloting the curriculum unit, and students' experiences of learning in a new setting as well as measurements of situational interest. It is essential that teachers and researchers reflect on the experiences of the piloted educational innovation together. Teachers and researchers have different experiences, and something that is confusing to one person may be clear to another. Likewise, teachers and researchers may have different interpretations of what happened in the enacted curriculum in the classroom. Thus, several trials and reflection cycles are needed to achieve fruitful outcomes.

The third feature of DBR is building an understanding of learning and design. Through reflection, new knowledge concerning teaching and learning is constructed. The outcomes can be teachers' practical ability, curriculum unit plans, and materials for teachers and students. These practical outputs are essential for DBR to be useful and to support wider audiences, not just the teachers participating in a project. Furthermore, DBR not only addresses means but also emphasizes ends. Research may inform what kinds of ends are worth pursuing, even though science education research is often motivated by ends outside the practitioners' context, such as the societal need for more people in science and technology occupations. Finally, the empirical and theoretical understanding culminates in research reports published in academic forums.

Below, we describe two cases in which we developed curriculum units with teachers who were considered autonomous professionals.

Case 1: Booklet for Materials Science Learning and Engagement

Understanding the Context

DBR to bring materials science into the classroom was stimulated by the rapid development of new materials, such as nanomaterials, at the beginning of 21st century, enabling the development of new material properties related to increased strength, decreased friction, chemical reactivity, and conductivity. At the same time, there was discussion of the safety of the nanomaterials, and the EU supported the study of these new properties. We participated in the EU-funded Materials Science Project (Psillos & Kariotoglou, 2016), which aimed to bring materials science to different levels of science education. The project involved partnerships between teachers and researchers to design curriculum units (Psillos & Kariotoglou, 2016).

An essential aspect of understanding the macroscopic properties and behaviors of materials, including nanomaterials, is understanding their structural models. However, this relationship is one of the most challenging topics in school science (Margel, Eylon, & Scherz, 2008). At the beginning of the DBR effort, the role of models in the Finnish national-level core curriculum was not very clearly described. There was emphasis on the structure of matter, but the structure was used to describe the matter not as a model to explain certain macroscopic properties of the materials.

The vision of future learning on this topic was related to the idea of models in general. We understood models as tools used by people to cope with the problems they confront (Kivinen & Piiroinen, 2006). Thus, in science learning, students use models as tools to explain the observed properties of materials, and the behaviors of materials are predicted based on structural models. The aim of the unit was to better understand how to organize teaching in a situation where traditional chemistry and physics content are integrated in a materials science context and to learn about the properties, behaviors, production, and uses of materials in order to engage students in science learning or trigger interest.

Design and Iteration

Based on our experiences in science education, discussions with teachers, and the research literature (e.g., Kivinen & Piiroinen, 2006; Meijer, Bulte, & Pilot, 2009), we formulated the following tentative strategy to support learning about the properties and behaviors of materials: if students interact with different materials and models that describe the properties and behaviors of those materials in laboratory situations and are simultaneously exposed to the observable properties and behaviors of the materials and their models, they will be able to use the models as conceptual tools and, moreover, engage in materials science learning.

To embody the tentative strategy in the classroom, we needed to interpret the national-level curriculum to show that the curriculum unit would be designed in alignment with the national-level curriculum. We had planning sessions with teachers, and we selected metal, paper, and plastic materials and their properties and structures as the topic context for the curriculum unit. The core of the designed curriculum unit included new pedagogical models for the metal, paper, and plastic materials and laboratory activities in which students would predict and explain the properties and behaviors of the materials (White & Gunstone, 1992). During the planning sessions, the researchers introduced preliminary ideas about the pedagogical models, and the researchers and teacher evaluated preliminary ideas about the laboratory investigation based on the power of the pedagogical models to explain the properties and behaviors of aluminum foil, food wrap, and newsprint in certain investigation situations.

To better understand the problem of integrating materials science into middle school, we made several iterative trials of the curriculum unit and gathered various types of data during the trials. The first trial was organized with the teacher, who participated in designing the first version of the pedagogical model and the laboratory activities. The teacher had about 5 years of teaching experience and wrote his master's thesis on materials science. Students were asked to respond to a conceptual knowledge questionnaire before the trial lessons, and researchers observed and video-recorded the lessons and collected the students' laboratory activity sheets to ensure a detailed analysis of how students applied the models in the laboratory activities. After the trial lessons, the students were asked to fill out the conceptual knowledge questionnaire again to serve as a posttest.

After the trial lessons, we also had a reflective discussion with the teacher to share our views on what happened during the trial and the types of difficulties the students experienced. We found that students were willing to conduct laboratory activities in small groups. However, they rarely focused on explaining their findings, did not seem to use models in their explanations, and did not have enough time to conduct all designed laboratory activities. During the discussion, issues were also noted. For example, the teacher emphasized the use of the model at the beginning of the laboratory activities but not during the activities. Therefore, we concluded that more time was needed for activities, as was more guidance to encourage students to explain their findings. As such, we reduced the number of activities, modified the models, removed the thermoset plastics topic, and included the model in the laboratory activity sheets. The model of thermoset plastics (upper-right model in Figure 4.2) was removed from the second version (lower model in Figure 4.2). Even though we analyzed the students' pre- and postquestionnaires to determine their conceptual understanding (Juuti, 2009), the analysis results did not influence the major design conclusions. Revisions were made after a discussion with the teacher in which we solicited comments about the trial.

Based on the experiences of the trial, we organized a quasi-experiment. The 27 students in the experiment group used the redesigned curriculum materials; the control group consisted of 18 students and a teacher from the same school who followed the typical curriculum unit on the same topic, namely, chemical bonds (Karpin, Juuti, & Lavonen, 2014). The duration of the curriculum unit was three lessons (75 minutes each), and the control group used an equal amount of time for the topic. The students were asked to respond to the conceptual test before the curriculum unit. The test included four open-ended questions, such as "Explain the following situations, applying your chemical knowledge. An aluminum jar conducts electricity but a plastic bag does not." After the unit lessons, students filled out a posttest questionnaire. Finally, at the end of the course, 4 to 5 weeks later, the students were asked to respond to the test questions as part of the course assessment. In the pre- and posttests, the structure models were available; in the postponed test, the models were not available. The main result was that the experimental group's

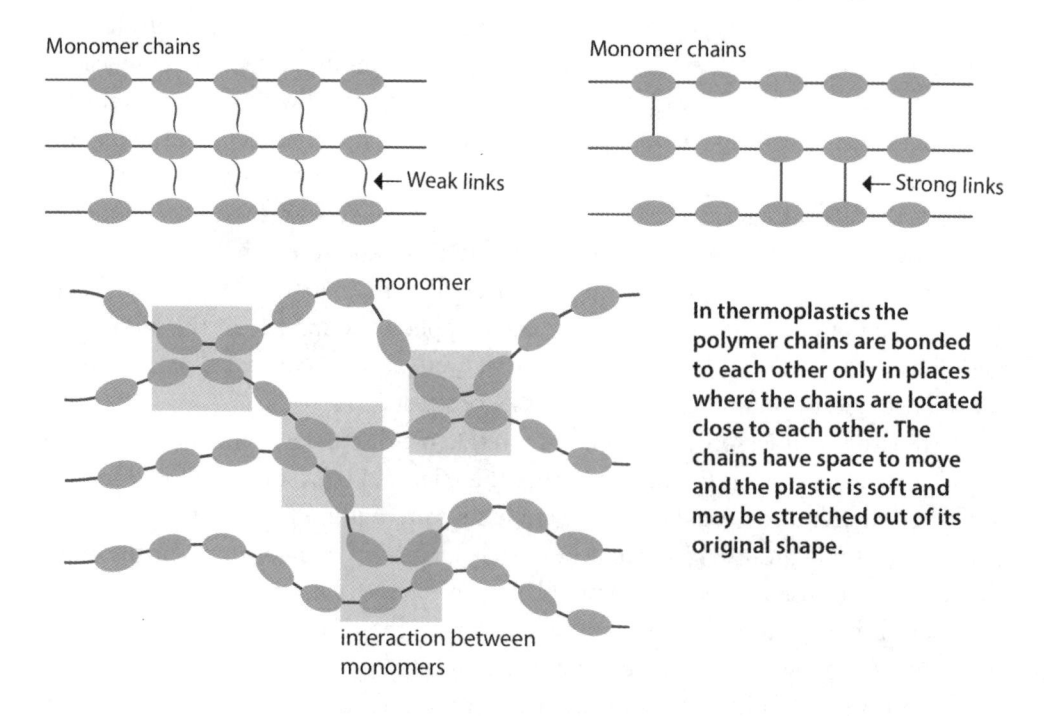

FIGURE 4.2. The first (upper) and second (lower) versions of the pedagogical model of plastics.

posttest and postponed test scores were statistically and significantly higher than those of the control group (Karpin et al., 2014).

Outcomes

The students learned to apply models that were simple, and they were guided to use the models during laboratory activities in which they predicted the behaviors of the materials in different situations and had to use different levels of structural models. The novelty in the curriculum unit was its use of models for metal, paper, and plastic in various experimental situations; traditionally, students become familiar with one material at a time. We argued (Karpin et al., 2014) that it is important to compare the behaviors of different materials in different situations and use various models to explain those behaviors. While designing the curriculum unit, we put a great deal of emphasis on the explanatory power of pedagogical models of materials and selected properties and behaviors that were possible to explain using those models.

This DBR effort was connected to variation theory (Marton & Tsui, 2004). In the curriculum unit, students examined several materials and structured models at the same time, bringing variation into the object of learning. Furthermore, we emphasized the role of models as tools, not as representations (Karpin et al., 2014). For learning, relying only on similarities is not enough; students also need to experience differences (Marton & Tsui, 2004). The practical outcomes were a co-designed student's booklet and a teacher guide on the curriculum unit (Loukomies et al., 2009a, 2009b).

Case 2: Inquiry-Based Teaching and Motivation

Understanding the Context

This project was stimulated by European-level support for inquiry-based science teaching as a means to increase students' motivation for and interest in science. Even though basic features of inquiry-based teaching and learning were emphasized in the national-level curriculum, they have not been very common in Finland (Lavonen & Laaksonen, 2009). Furthermore, there has been very little research-based evidence on motivational features of inquiry (Minner, Levy, & Century, 2010).

In the first case, the concrete outcomes of the project were published in the widely adoptable student booklet and the teacher guide for materials science. In this second case, we put more emphasis on the Finnish ethos of professional teachers. We invited teachers to participate in the project to design, enact, and reflect on inquiry-based curriculum units and positioned them as educational innovators (Loukomies, Juuti, & Lavonen, 2018). Furthermore, we argued that, instead of reading and following detailed lesson plan descriptions, the teachers and researchers should co-design the curriculum units, incorporating pedagogical approaches introduced in the science learning literature, and co-reflect on the units during the planning meetings.

Iteration

Our tentative strategy to understand how to design motivational inquiry-based science curriculum units was related to self-determination theory (Deci & Ryan, 2004). Specifically, our strategy was to ensure that the teaching fulfilled students' basic psychological needs in terms of feeling competence, autonomy, and relatedness.

During the first workshop with six participating teachers, we introduced the ideas of basic psychological needs, of inquiry-based science teaching and learning, and shared a mutual understanding with them about the loose structure of the motivating features of inquiry-based science. We asked the teachers to design, with our support, an inquiry-based science unit on any relevant and possible topic. There were no requirements regarding specific teaching methods, but the unit had to include features to support students' feelings of competence, autonomy, and relatedness; active thinking; students' responsibility for their own learning; and some aspects of the science investigative cycle, such as asking research questions, planning an investigation, or analyzing data.

During the workshop, the teachers initially planned in pairs, and then they planned their own one- to two-lesson-long curriculum units. At the end of the workshop day, the teachers presented their preliminary plans, and we engaged in constructive discussions that emphasized the motivating features of the plans. The leading idea was to identify motivating features from the preliminary plans and ask questions such as: How could students make more decisions on their own during the curriculum unit? How could the teacher show the significance of the topic? What could students do together?

After the teachers enacted the curriculum units, they presented their enactment during the second workshop. The goal was to support a mutual understanding of how to design motivating inquiry-based science teaching. We analyzed the motivating features of the teachers' curriculum units (Loukomies et al., 2018) based on the posters teachers created to communicate their curriculum unit for others and recordings of the reflection sessions. The analysis was based on the aforementioned theoretical ideas on inquiry-based science teaching and motivation and theory-driven content analysis (Patton, 2002). The analysis focused on revealing how the following features appeared in the units: motivation support (autonomy, competence, social relatedness, interest, significance, and utility value); students' responsibility; and possibility of active thinking.

The analysis revealed that the enacted curriculum units were quite traditional and teacher-centered. They included very little student responsibility for the process. However, students' active thinking was emphasized in all units, such as in the laboratory activities, concept mapping, making comics, or making presentations. The motivational features were mainly related to supporting students' feelings of autonomy by letting them make task-related decisions and supporting students' social relatedness by allowing them to work in pairs. The teachers did not include any support for feelings of competence. Building a mutual understanding of the motivating features of inquiry-based science teaching and learning made it possible for the teachers to include at least some elements of these features in their curriculum units. However, this analysis revealed only half of the story, namely, how the teachers described the units.

To evaluate the other half, namely, how the students experienced the motivating features of inquiry-based science learning, we interviewed 18 students who had participated in the teacher-designed curriculum units (Juuti, Loukomies, & Lavonen, 2013). High achievers, low achievers, and females and males with various motivations related to science were selected to provide a variety of student views. The students participated voluntarily during the school day. They were asked to describe their interests in science, typical science lessons, and how they would like to learn science. The main part of the interview focused on the developed units. The students were asked to describe the units and compare them with business-as-usual lessons in terms of the kinds of individual and group activities, how they participated, the decisions they were allowed to make, and whether they succeeded. Their responses were examined following the principles of deductive content analysis.

Compared to typical lessons, students liked that, in the curriculum unit, they could make more choices, the tasks were more open, and they were allowed to do more on their own. Students also shared that they learned more, and they were able to be creative, construct concrete products, and work with their friends to a greater degree. In addition, they noted that their teacher was more cheerful. However, they complained that the curriculum unit involved more work for them and believed that the teacher had not spent enough time teaching them. The curriculum unit was perceived to be more difficult, and some students stressed that they might have learned more if the teacher decided the student groupings instead of requiring them to select their own partners.

One limitation of the iteration was that the analysis relied on what the teachers and students remembered about the curriculum units. Thus, their actual feelings during the learning situations might have been different.

Outcomes

In this case, we emphasized the loose structure as a design principle in terms of the integration of the basic psychological needs introduced in self-determination theory with inquiry-based teaching. The analysis of the teachers' reports and the student interviews showed that the teachers were rather conservative while designing their curriculum units. The student interviews revealed that designing motivating inquiry-based science curriculum units is not straightforward. Some students found certain features to be positive, whereas others found the same features to be negative. This was an important message of the project: it highlighted that it is too ambitious to claim that a certain way of teaching would make all students more motivated. Furthermore, students may consider inquiry-based learning to be too difficult, and it may require too much independent work and advanced self-regulation skills.

The theoretical contribution of the project focused on showing how inquiry-based teaching might increase students' motivation to learn science. The practical output was Web-based introductory learning materials on motivation and inquiry-based science teaching (IBST; Inquiry-Based Science Teaching, n.d.-a, n.d.-b). The materials include short introductory videos and edited videos showing how motivating features appear in an actual classroom. This case also provided knowledge on collaboration with teachers. Even though Finnish teachers are considered autonomous professionals, they are still rather conservative; therefore, more intensive collaborative planning may be needed to achieve curriculum units that fulfill the visions of future learning.

Conclusions

In this chapter, we presented two cases of research projects in which the co-development of curriculum units by teachers and researchers was the central activity. Our aim was to show that, when positioning teachers as innovators and curriculum developers and co-developers in curriculum units, it is possible to change teaching practices and students' experiences. We also highlighted students' challenges in applying science knowledge and challenges designing motivating curriculum units.

The co-development of the curriculum units embedded the research in an authentic classroom context, as emphasized in early conceptualizations of DBR (Brown, 1992; Linn, 1996). Indeterminate situations, in which practitioners—in this case, teachers and researchers—do not know how to act, are emphasized or created in DBR because an indeterminate situation requires actions to define the problem to be solved. According to Biesta and Burbules (2003), research is not (only) a mental process, but it is the actual transformation of the situation. In fact, "educational knowledge, the 'product' of educational inquiry, reveals *possible* connections between actions and consequences" (Biesta & Burbules, 2003, p. 110, emphasis in original).

Even though organizations such as OECD, the World Bank, and UNESCO have raised international awareness of learning and education, education is still highly culturally dependent. In this chapter, we have argued that national curriculum and curriculum unit development is a means and an end. While teachers and researchers are designing, enacting, and evaluating curriculum units together and reflecting on the enactment, they are simultaneously transforming the educational situation and finding ways to regulate themselves. Through curriculum unit development, teachers are invited to participate in a process where teaching aims, visions of future learning, and strategies to embody features of future learning at school are critically reflected based on the research literature and practical experiences.

In Finland, teachers at all school levels have a master's degree, and they have a relatively large degree of autonomy in selecting teaching content. Furthermore, since the education system in Finland is decentralized, there is a great deal of freedom at the school level to organize special courses in various subjects. In addition, since teacher education is organized by research universities, a readiness exists to pursue ambitious shared activities where teachers are considered curriculum developers instead of curriculum adopters.

The world is changing, and educational needs are changing along with it. For example, new kinds of learning demands and societal issues, such as climate change adaptation and mitigation, preventing massive extinction, and avoiding pandemics, require continuous curriculum changes, and DBR is needed to understand and promote new learning. Instead of emphasizing certain methods in teacher education to achieve fixed aims, the focus should be placed on teachers' readiness to participate in curriculum development and DBR projects. Furthermore, Biesta and Burbules (2003, p. 111) emphasized the following:

> Finally, it is unlikely that educational reality will remain stable over time for the very practical reason that educators today are confronted with many problems that did not even exist in the past. This suggests that if educational research is to make a contribution to the improvement of education, it will be through the provision of new intellectual and practical resources for the day-to-day problem-solving of educators. Improvement of education is, in other words, to be found in the extent to which research enables educators to approach the problems they are faced with in a more intelligent way.

This realization that there is a need for change is crucial, especially for science education, as science provides students with conceptual tools to better understand and act in the world.

DBR is a future-oriented endeavor. Teachers and researchers design future learning for authentic settings. This requirement for research in authentic settings differentiates DBR from laboratory or intervention research (Brown, 1992; Design-Based Research Collective, 2003). To be authentic, practicing teachers need to have an active role in designing the curriculum units.

Curriculum unit design begins with sharing experiences and thoughts about phenomena of interest. In our cases, the phenomena were the role of models in explaining the properties and behaviors of materials and the role of basic psychological needs and inquiry approaches in motivating students to learn science. Based on a shared understanding of the context and the vision of future learning, teachers and researchers formulate a tentative strategy to achieve such learning.

The core of DBR is classroom trials, and the following questions should be considered: How and to what extent is it possible to achieve intended future learning? What is the role for learning of a certain feature in a designed curriculum? Since classroom trials of the curriculum units need to be connected to the theoretical understanding of learning, answers to why questions can also be proposed in certain settings.

In addition to theoretical understanding, DBR has practical outcomes. In our cases, along with academic publications, we published support materials for teachers on materials science and a framework to design motivating inquiry-based science curriculum units.

In Chapter 1 of this volume, Campanella and Penuel emphasize that DBR asks what could be learned about the world by changing it. In this chapter, we described two DBR cases where the teacher's role in curriculum unit design was central. By engaging in shared curriculum development, by obtaining similar experiences in the classroom, and by anticipating each other's intentions, researchers and teachers can come to a stage where they share the same world. Furthermore, through reflection, new knowledge concerning teaching and learning is constructed. Thus, DBR is not only about means but also emphasizes ends. Research can inform what kinds of ends are worth pursuing, the vision for future science learning, and how such learning can be orchestrated.

REFERENCES

Biesta, G. J. J., & Burbules, N. C. (2003). *Pragmatism and educational research.* Lanham, MD: Rowman & Littlefield.

Brown, A. L. (1992). Design experiments: Theoretical and methodological challenges in creating complex interventions in classroom settings. *Journal of the Learning Sciences, 2,* 141–178.

Chong, W. H., Huan, V. S., Wong, I., Klassen, R. M., & Allison, D. K. (2010). The relationships among school types, teacher efficacy beliefs, and academic climate: Perspective from Asian middle schools. *Journal of Educational Research, 103,* 183–190.

Cuban, L. (1992). Curriculum stability and change. In P. Jackson (Ed.), *Handbook of research on curriculum* (pp. 216–247). New York: Macmillan.

Darling-Hammond, L. (2017). Teacher education around the world: What can we learn from international practice? *European Journal of Teacher Education, 40,* 291–309.

Deci, E. L., & Ryan, R. M. (Eds.). (2004). *Handbook of self-determination research.* Rochester, NY: University of Rochester Press.

Deng, Z. (2020). *Knowledge, content, curriculum and didaktik.* New York: Routledge.

Design-Based Research Collective. (2003). Design-based research: An emerging paradigm for educational inquiry. *Educational Researcher, 32*(1), 5–8, 35–37.

Dewey, J. (1980). *Democracy and education. The middle works, 1899–1924: Vol. 9. 1916* (A. Boydston, Ed.). Carbondale: Southern Illinois University Press.

Dewey, J. (1984). The quest for certainty. *The later works, 1925–1953: Vol. 4. 1929* (A. Boydston, Ed.). Carbondale: Southern Illinois University Press.

European Union. (2004). *Europe needs more scientists: Report by the high level group on human resources for science and technology in Europe.* Brussels: European Commission, Directorate-General for Research.

Finnish National Core Curriculum. (2016). *The National Core Curriculum for basic education.* Helsinki: National Board of Education.

Finnish National Core Curriculum for High School. (2019). *Lukion opetussuunnitelman perusteet.* Helsinki: Finnish Educational Agency.

Inquiry-Based Science Teaching. (n.d.-a). *Motivaatio ja tutkivat työtavat fysiikan ja kemian opetuksessa* [Motivation and inquiry-based science teaching]. Retrieved from *www.edu.helsinki.fi/malu/inquiry*

Inquiry-Based Science Teaching. (n.d.-b). Motivation and inquiry-based science teaching. Retrieved from *www.edu.helsinki.fi/malu/inquiry/HTML/index%20EN.html*

Juuti, K. (2009, September 3). *Junior high school students' representations of the microstructure of material.* Paper presented at the meeting of the European Science Education Research Association, Istanbul, Turkey.

Juuti, K., & Lavonen, J. (2006). Design-based research in science education: One step towards methodology. *Nordina, 4,* 54–68.

Juuti, K., Lavonen, J., & Meisalo, V. (2016). Pragmatic design-based research—Designing as a shared activity of teachers and researchers. In D. Psillos & P. Kariotoglou (Eds.), *Iterative design of teaching-learning sequences: Introducing the science of materials in European schools* (pp. 35–46). Cham, Switzerland: Springer Science+Business Media.

Juuti, K., Loukomies, A., & Lavonen, J. (2013). Pupils' views on motivating features of inquiry based teaching. In M. Honerød Hoveid & P. Gray (Eds.), *Inquiry in science education and science teacher education.* Trondheim, Norway: Akademika forlag.

Karpin, T., Juuti, K., & Lavonen, J. (2014). Learning to apply models of materials while explaining their properties. *Research in Science & Technological Education, 32*(3), 340–351.

Kilpinen, E. (2008). John Dewey, George Herbert Mead ja Pragmatistisen yhteiskuntatieteen ongelmat. In E. Kilpinen, O. Kivinen, & S. Pihlström (Eds.), *Pragmatismi filosofiassa ja yhteiskuntatieteissä* (pp. 91–132). Helsinki: Gaudeamus.

Kivinen, O., & Piiroinen, T. (2006). Toward pragmatist methodological relationalism from philosophizing sociology to sociologizing philosophy. *Philosophy of the Social Sciences, 36*(3), 303–329.

Lavonen, J., & Laaksonen, S. (2009). Context of teaching and learning school science in Finland: Reflections on PISA 2006 results. *Journal of Research in Science Teaching, 46*(8), 922–944.

Linn, M. C. (1996). From separation to partnership in science education: Students, laboratories, and the curriculum. In R. F. Tinker (Ed.), *Microcomputer-based labs: Educational research and standards* (pp. 13–45). Berlin: Springer.

Loukomies, A., Juuti, K., & Lavonen, J. (2018). Teachers as educational innovators in inquiry-based science teaching and learning. In O. E. Tsivitanidou, P. Gray, E. Rybska, L. Louca, & C. P. Constantinou (Eds.), *Professional development for inquiry-based science teaching and learning* (pp. 185–201). Berlin: Springer.

Loukomies, A., Lavonen, J., Juuti, K., Lampiselkä, J., Meisalo, V., Ampuja, A., & Jansson, J. (2009a). *Materials around us: Metals, plastics and paper.* Economic Information Office. Retrieved from *www.edu.helsinki.fi/malu/materials/materials_around_us.pdf*

Loukomies, A., Lavonen, J., Juuti, K., Lampiselkä, J., Meisalo, V., Ampuja, A., & Jansson, J. (2009b). *Materials around us: Paper, metal and plastics: Teacher guide.* Economic

Information Office. Retrieved from *www.edu.helsinki.fi/malu/materials/materials_around_us_teacher.pdf*

Margel, H., Eylon, B.-S., & Scherz, Z. (2008). A longitudinal study of junior high school students' conceptions of the structure of materials. *Journal of Research in Science Teaching, 45*(1), 132–152.

Marton, F., & Tsui, A. B. M. (2004). *Classroom discourse and the space of learning.* Mahwah, NJ: Erlbaum.

Meijer, M. R., Bulte, A. M. W., & Pilot, A. (2009). Structure–property relations between macro and micro representations: Relevant meso-levels in authentic tasks. In J. K. Gilbert & D. Treagust (Eds.), *Multiple representations in chemical education* (pp. 195–213). Cham, Switzerland: Springer Science+Business Media.

Minner, D. D., Levy, A. J., & Century, J. (2010). Inquiry-based science instruction—What is it and does it matter? Results from a research synthesis years 1984 to 2002. *Journal of Research in Science Teaching, 47*(4), 474–496.

Niemi, H., Toom, A., & Kallioniemi, A. (2012). *Miracle of education: The principles and practices of teaching and learning in Finnish schools.* Rotterdam, the Netherlands: Sense.

Organisation for Economic Co-operation and Development. (2016). *PISA 2015 results: Vol. I. Excellence and equity in education.* Paris: OECD.

Patton, M. Q. (2002). *Qualitative research and evaluation methods* (3rd ed.). Thousand Oaks, CA: Sage.

Psillos, D., & P. Kariotoglou (Eds.). (2016). *Iterative design of teaching-learning sequences: Introducing the science of materials in European schools.* Cham, Switzerland: Springer Science+Business Media

Rodgers, C. (2002). Defining reflection: Another look at John Dewey and reflective thinking. *Teachers College Record, 104*(4), 842–866.

Sandoval, W. (2014). Conjecture mapping: An approach to systematic educational design research. *Journal of the Learning Sciences, 23*(1), 18–36.

Schmidt, W. H., Raizen, S., Britton, E., Bianchi, L. J., & Wolfe, R. G. (1997). *Many visions, many aims: A cross-national investigation of curricular intentions in school science* (Vol. 2). Dordrecht, the Netherlands: Kluwer Academic.

Simola, H. (2005). The Finnish miracle of PISA: Historical and sociological remarks on teaching and teacher education. *Comparative Education, 41*(4), 455–470.

Vahtivuori-Hänninen, S., Halinen, I., Niemi, H., Lavonen, J., Lipponen, L., & Multisilta, J. (2014). A new Finnish national core curriculum for basic education (2014) and technology as an integrated tool for learning. In H. Niemi, J. Multisilta, L. Lipponen, & M. Vivitsou (Eds.), *Finnish innovations and technologies in schools* (pp. 21–32). Rotterdam, the Netherlands: Sense.

Vettenranta, J., Välijärvi, J., Ahonen, A., Hautamäki, J., Hiltunen, J., Leino, K., . . . Vainikainen, M.-P. (2016). *PISA 15: ensituloksia. Huipulla pudotuksesta huolimatta* [PISA 15, First results. On top while dropping]. Helsinki: Opetus- ja kulttuuriministeriö.

White, R., & Gunstone, R. (1992). *Probing understanding.* New York: Falmer Press.

CHAPTER 5

Classroom Design-Based Research
Designing for Proportional Reasoning in Mathematics Education

Michelle Stephan

Design-based research (DBR) has gained prominence as a research methodology in mathematics and science education over the last two decades and varies in its purposes and educational settings (Cobb, Confrey, diSessa, Lehrer, & Schauble, 2003; Corcoran, Mosher, & Rogat, 2009; Daro, Mosher, & Cocoran, 2011; Penuel, Coburn, & Gallagher, 2013; see Chapters 3, 4, and 15, this volume). According to Cobb et al. (2003), DBR can take place in a variety of settings: classrooms, teacher professional development (PD) or preservice education (Simon, 2000), one or more school districts (Cobb & Jackson, 2011; Penuel et al., 2013), or across a state (Wilson, McCulloch, Curtis, Stephan, Mawhinney, & Webb, 2017). As an example of a statewide DBR, Wilson et al. (2017) describe a DBR project in which a digital infrastructure was created to support their state's K–12 mathematics teachers as they implemented new state standards. Data were collected to understand the supports and constraints of the infrastructure and resources as teachers adapted them in their classroom. As another example, Crabtree and Stephan (2021) conducted a DBR PD project with high school science teachers. Their goal was to design and implement a PD experience that leveraged science content to increase the teachers' awareness of the ways that science perpetuates racism in both the classroom and society.

One of the main differences between DBR and traditional research methodology is that, in DBR, some type of innovation is designed and tested in the very settings for which its use is intended (see Chapter 1, this volume). Thus, an analysis that utilizes a national database of ACT scores disaggregated by socioeconomic standing, for example, would not involve a DBR methodology since no innovation is created, nor is it tested within the sociocultural setting in which the data were captured. The appeal of DBR lies in the fact that, while much educational research is divorced from practical problems, DBR is necessarily located in the practical settings that it is designed to study. Furthermore, the main activity of researchers in this approach is highly interventionist in that they are proactively altering the research context and striving for change *as the implementation occurs*. The goal is not to test if the design worked, but rather to explore the implementation, to provide an analysis of the ways in which the design was realized and the means of supporting that realization for those who might wish to adapt the design in their own contexts (Cobb, 2003).

Since DBR involving teacher PD, district-, and statewide contexts has increased in number over the last decade, Stephan (2014) refers to design research in classroom settings as *classroom-DBR* (C-DBR). C-DBR differs from other types of DBR in the purpose and setting of the work. A newly designed resource typically consists of a set of instructional materials on a particular mathematics or science topic, as opposed to a set of PD materials for teachers or a digital resource for standards implementation. The purpose of C-DBR is to understand how the materials are implemented in the social setting of a classroom as well as document the mathematical learning of the students. Other DBR projects, as noted above, may design resources that are more appropriate for their setting, such as a PD experience to help teachers understand how to integrate technology meaningfully in their classrooms. The research may examine teachers' technology knowledge prior to the PD as well as their knowledge after implementation of the experience. Importantly, C-DBR is different from action research in that the goal is to generate a theory of instruction for a particular science or mathematics topic and communicate it in such a way that teachers can adapt it to their own settings. In action research, the goal is to study one's own classroom practices or materials for immediate improvement.

In all DBR cases, the research team typically conducts several cycles of design, implementation, and analysis, with revisions being made at the end of each cycle. For C-DBR, in particular, as the cycles come to a close, the outcome is a viable *instruction theory* that consists of the actual instructional materials as well as a description of the learning goals and means of supporting them. Examples of instruction theories that have been developed over the last 25 years in mathematics include three-digit place value (Bowers, Cobb, & McClain, 1999); small-number relations (Cobb, Gravemeijer, Yackel, McClain, & Whitenack, 1997); statistical reasoning (Cobb, McClain, & Gravemeijer, 2003); linear measurement (Stephan, Bowers, Cobb, & Gravemeijer, 2003); differential equations (Stephan & Rasmussen, 2002); and integer concepts and operations (Stephan & Akyuz, 2012). C-DBR involves a research team that typically includes a teacher who implements an instructional innovation that is analyzed and revised during the phases of DBR (Cobb, 2000; Confrey & Lachance, 2000). The teacher is considered a full member of the research team, with the primary responsibility of implementing instruction. In the C-DBR project reported here, I describe how a research team created, implemented, and analyzed/revised a ratio and proportion instructional sequence and the cycles that were conducted over a 4-year period. I begin by describing the C-DBR cycle and the activities conducted within it. I then use the ratio and proportion research project to illustrate each of these activities. I conclude with a discussion of the products of C-DBR and how they might be used.

Classroom-Based Design Research

Other chapters in this book go much deeper in the theoretical and practical aspects of DBR (see Chapter 1), so I use this chapter to illustrate these points with an example. To begin, it is worth revisiting the design research cycle in the context of C-DBR. A C-DBR cycle consists of three phases, each of which will be described in turn: design, implementation, and analysis/revision.

Design Phase of C-DBR

In the first phase, *design*, the researchers identify a practical and/or theoretical problem to explore. A literature review is conducted to find any research that may guide the design of the instructional innovation. For example, when the innovation is the design of an instructional sequence, relevant research could involve cognitive learning trajectories on the mathematics topic (i.e., how students reason about the mathematics concept and how it progresses). Other literature that could be helpful consists of descriptions of technology that may support students' learning of the concept, the historical development of that concept, and theoretical and practitioner articles on, say, the use of tools and inscriptions in supporting students' learning. The role of design team members is to read rich literature, adapt an instructional design theory (if available), and use the creativity and ingenuity of team members to sketch a possible learning trajectory and associated materials. A learning trajectory is a conjectured set of learning goals and tools, inscriptions, and activities to be used to support them (Clements & Sarama, 2004; Simon, 1995; Stephan, 2014). With this hypothetical learning trajectory (HLT), the designer or designers engage in a thought experiment to envision how the students may reason with the materials and tools/inscriptions and what type of conversations would be possible.

Implementation Phase

The second phase of the cycle, *implementation*, involves a full-time teacher, or one of the researchers in the role of a classroom teacher, implementing the HLT in a classroom setting. Sometimes, pre-interviews are conducted with only the students, both to determine whether the starting point of the HLT is reasonable for them and to collect baseline data on their mathematical understanding. Post-interviews can be also conducted to collect data on students' progress over time. During classroom enactment, typically video cameras capture all relevant student and teacher interactions for later analysis. Small groups can be selected as the focus of the video recordings as the students work together to solve problems. While formal analyses are not usually conducted during the classroom teaching experiment due to lack of time (Cobb, 2000), daily informal, yet formative, analyses are conducted in order to determine how the HLT is being realized by students and what changes should be made to the instruction for the subsequent day. Gravemeijer, Bowers, and Stephan (2003) referred to these as daily mini-cycles of implementation–informal analysis–revision that correlate nicely with the more formal design research cycle.

Analysis/Revision Phase

The final phase of the design research cycle, *analysis/revision*, consists of formal analysis of the data in order to document students' learning as well as revisions that should be made to the HLT. In this way, an *actual learning trajectory* is documented and can be compared to the hypothesized one. It is critical in these analyses that some type of theoretical perspective and associated framework be used. A theoretical perspective that was used in all of the C-DBR studies mentioned in the introduction was the *emergent perspective*, a version of social constructivism (Cobb & Yackel, 1996). The emergent perspective casts learning as both a social and individual accomplishment; thus, the formal analysis of learning documents classroom mathematical practices as well as individual students' ways of participating in and contributing to them (cf. Stephan et al., 2003). The formal analysis of classroom mathematical practices (i.e., learning of the community) and individual students' learning should shed light on any revisions that ought to be made to the emerging learning trajectory and materials.

Suggested revisions should then lead to the redesign and creation of a revised hypothetical learning trajectory and the start of a new cycle of C-DBR. These newly revised learning trajectory and materials go through the design, implementation, and analysis/revision cycle. At the end of several cycles of C-DBR, the results should be what Gravemeijer et al. (2003) call an "instruction theory" for ratio and proportion, or whatever concept has been targeted. It is referred to as an instruction theory, as opposed to an instructional sequence of activities, because the materials alone do not create the learning experience. Rather, someone who wants to adapt the materials to his or her own setting must know the learning goals, the tools/inscriptions, and the discourse topics that help support learning as students engage with those materials.

In the next section, I describe the process of developing an instruction theory for ratio and proportion that two teachers and I created when we taught middle school. I elaborate the activities we engaged in during each of the three phases of a full cycle. I then conclude with suggestions for how the products of this and other C-DBR projects are used.

Timeline of the Project

The formal C-DBR project was conducted over 4 years and can be described in the following timeline:

Year 1: Design phase (3 months)
- Identify a practical need.
- Perform literature review.
- Conduct and analyze student interviews.
- Design a hypothetical learning trajectory (see Table 5.1).

Year 1: Implementation phase (classroom teaching, 6 weeks)

Year 1: Analysis phase (daily and 2 weeks after implementation)

Years 2–4 (completed three more cycles, one per year)
- Yielded a stable instruction theory (see Table 5.2).

TABLE 5.1. Hypothetical Learning Trajectory for Ratio and Proportions

Learning goal	Tools/imagery	Possible topics of discourse
Linking composite units	Connecting pictures of aliens to food bars	If the rule is 1 food bar feeds 3 aliens, the rule can't be broken if we add more food bars.
Iterating linked composites	Informal symbolizing (e.g., tables, two columns of numbers, pictures of aliens and food bars)	How students keep track of two quantities while making them bigger
	Long ratio table (build-up method)	Keeping track of two linked quantities while they grow additively
Additive reasoning using addition and multiplication	Shortened ratio tables through multiplication and division with scale factors	Adding or multiplying to build up; efficient ways of curtailing long ratio tables
Creating equivalent ratios	Ratio tables with missing values; traditional proportion representation (two ratios separated with an equal sign)	Adding versus multiplying; how do we deal with scale factors that are decimals?
Comparing ratios	Ratio table; no ratio tables (standard proportion notation), but can use arrow notations	Finding common numerators or denominators; size of the scale factors; unit ratios
Comparing rates	Ratio table; arrow notation; standard proportion notation	Difference between a ratio and rate; unit rates; common denominator and numerators

TABLE 5.2. Stable Learning Trajectory for Ratio and Proportion

Learning goal	Tools/imagery	Possible topics of discourse
Linking composite units	Connecting pictures of aliens to food bars	If the rule is 1 food bar feeds 3 aliens, the rule can't be broken if we add more food bars.
Iterating linked composites	Informal symbolizing (e.g., tables, two columns of numbers, pictures of aliens and food bars)	How students keep track of two quantities while making them bigger
	Ratio table	Keeping track of two linked quantities while they grow additively
Additive versus multiplicative reasoning	Fold back to pictures; shortened ratio table	Adding or multiplying to build up
Structuring ratios multiplicatively	**Shortened ratio tables through multiplication and division with scale factors**	**Efficient ways of curtailing long ratio tables**
		What does the horizontal scale factor represent?
		What does the vertical scale factor represent?
Creating equivalent ratios	Ratio tables with missing values	Adding versus multiplying; meanings of scale factors; what do decimal scale factors mean?
	Traditional proportion representation (two ratios separated with equal sign)	
Change contexts		
	Ratio tables	Adding versus multiplying; horizontal and vertical scale factors
Analyzing equivalent ratios	**"Fraction" imagery**	**Reducing ratios;**
		vertical and horizontal scale factors
Comparing ratios	Ratio table	Finding common numerators or denominators; size of the scale factors; unit ratios
	No ratio tables, but can use arrow notations	
Comparing rates	Ratio table; arrow notation; standard proportion notation	Difference between a ratio and rate; unit rates; common denominator and numerators

Ratio and Proportion Design Phase

Identify a Practical and/or Theoretical Need

At the time of this particular C-DBR project, I was teaching full time in a middle school (12- to 14-year-olds) in Florida. I had informally partnered with two other teachers, one who was a second-year teacher (Sean) and the other a veteran, special education teacher (Jenny; the names of all teachers and students given here are pseudonyms). The special education teacher and I were co-teachers in an inclusion classroom (i.e., a classroom setting with regular and special needs students combined). Since I had experience conducting C-DBR, my role can be described as a researcher-teacher in that I led the design of the instructional materials, data collection, literature search, and other research activities. The teachers, for their part, participated as teacher-researchers by reading literature, assessing designed instructional activities, implementing the innovation in their classrooms, and participating in all team meetings. To begin, the three of us were dissatisfied with our district-adopted textbook's approach to teaching ratios and proportions. The first problems involved comparing ratios and percentages, without developing students' understanding of those ideas first. Additionally, the textbook's use of ratio tables as an inscriptional support came halfway through the unit, whereas we believed it could be better utilized much earlier. From a designer's perspective, it was difficult for me to find a learning trajectory (i.e., a coherent learning route) supported in the materials. Knowing that ratio and proportions are the crux of middle school mathematics (Lesh, Post, & Behr, 1988), we decided to create our own instructional materials that would better support our students' development of ratio and proportion at a more meaningful level. Thus, our first collaborative research project was born. It should be noted here that the two teachers were interested in C-DBR only for its practical output, while I was interested in both the practical and research products.

Literature Review

To begin work on the design process, I did a literature search for studies that described students' cognitive understanding of ratios and proportions as well as anything that resembled a possible learning trajectory. Students' understanding of ratio and proportions has been well researched, and my search yielded dozens of relevant articles. What was missing at that time was any classroom-based studies of ratio instruction. However, a couple of articles served to develop the first draft of a hypothetical learning trajectory as well as helpful interview tasks. In particular, Lamon (1990) and Battista and Borrow (1995) gave us the most useful tasks (described in the next section) that we adapted for interviews with our students. The purpose of conducting cognitive interviews in classroom DBR is threefold: (1) Results can inform designers whether their hypothesized starting point for instruction is reasonable, (2) students' strategies can lend insight into possible discussion topics for the hypothetical learning trajectory, and (3) pre- and post-interviews can document the mathematical development of students over the course of the classroom teaching experiment.

Prework: Cognitive Pre-Interviews

In consultation with my team of teachers, we developed a set of five interview questions from the literature, three of which are shown below. Questions 1 and 2 assessed if students can link together two quantities, such as $2 and 3 balloons, and scale up to find larger equivalent ratios. Question 3 assessed if students could find equivalent ratios when the scale factor was not a whole number or if they would revert to additive reasoning.

- Question 1: (*Shows a picture of 3 balloons costing $2.*) Ellen, Jim, and Steve bought 3 helium-filled balloons and paid $2 for all 3. They decided to go back to the store and get enough balloons for everyone in their class. How much did they have to pay for 24 balloons? (Lamon, 1990)
- Question 2: (*A picture of 3 aliens and 1 food pellet is shown to students.*) How many aliens would be fed with 15 food pellets? How many aliens would be fed with 16 food pellets? How many food pellets are needed for 63 aliens? (Lamon, 1990)
- Question 3: Lisa and Rachel drove equally fast along a country road. It took Lisa 6 minutes to drive 4 miles. How long did it take Rachel to drive 6 miles? (Battista & Borrow, 1995)

We decided to interview a total of six students: three from Sean's roster and three from ours. We chose a diverse group of students including low-, middle-, and high-performing students; students with special needs; and students whose first language was not English. We hoped that this diversity would reveal a range of different strategies and thinking processes about ratios, especially since the topic had not been introduced formally in an educational setting yet. Students' solutions to these three questions provided insight into starting points for the instructional sequence. For example, consider three solutions that were common for Question 1, the balloon problem (Figure 5.1). In Figure 5.1a, Nadia drew sets of 3 balloons, labeling as she went, and stopped when she reached 24 balloons. She then counted the number of $2 to reach a total of $16. We knew from Nadia's solution that many students would naturally draw pictures to keep track of both quantities in the "ratio"; this could thus serve as a productive starting point for the instructional sequence. We learned from Brian, a student with a formally diagnosed learning disability, that some students would try to keep track of the two quantities simultaneously *without* pictures, yet would need some organizational support (Figure 5.1b). Finally, a student like Arthur, who was not proficient as determined by his score on the state's

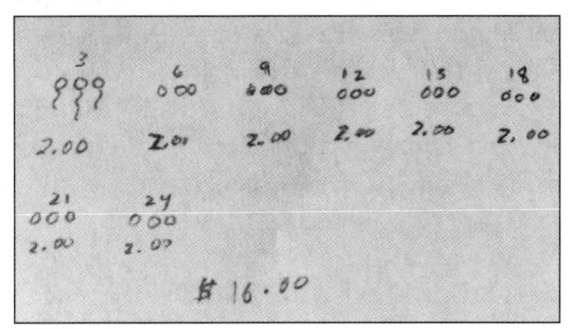

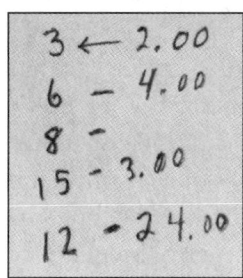

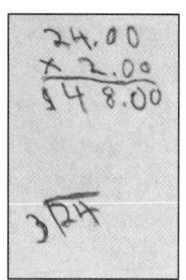

Classroom DBR

(a) Nadia's solution (b) Brian's solution (c) Arthur's solution

FIGURE 5.1. Three students' solutions to the balloon interview task.

end-of-grade assessment, might not have a way to organize the quantities in the problem (Figure 5.1c).

We also learned that almost all of the students reasoned additively for Question 3, the country road question. To solve this, students noticed that the difference between miles and minutes for Lisa was 2, so they added 2 to the number of miles Rachel drove (i.e., 6) to get 8 minutes. This did not surprise us, yet highlighted the need for the learning trajectory to support structuring ratios multiplicatively, not just additively. Finally, the ease with which students solved Question 2, the alien question, led us to decide that the alien scenario could serve as a reasonable context for the instructional materials. With these data in mind, and a possible learning trajectory suggested by Battista and Borrow (1995), we now sketched the first hypothetical learning trajectory.

Sketch an HLT and Supporting Materials

There are several instructional design theories that can be used by designers to create an HLT and associated instructional materials for mathematics, namely, Realistic Mathematics Education (RME; Streefland, 1991), variation theory (Koichu, Zaslavsky, & Dolev, 2013), anthropological theory of the didactics (Artigue & WinslØw, 2010), and frameworks from the Shell Centre in England (Burkhardt & Swan, 2013). We use RME because it is compatible with our theory of learning (social constructivism) and commitment to the fact that mathematics is a human activity. The underlying metaphor from Freudenthal (1973) is that mathematical ideas invented over long periods of time can and should be reinvented by students through problem solving. Freudenthal (1991) refined the metaphor as *guided* reinvention in that students need supports to be able to reconstruct difficult, abstract ideas in shortened periods of time. These supports come in the form of physical tools, symbols, mathematical discourse, and instructional sequences that promote abstraction from concrete situations.

There are several tenets of RME that guide the design of the materials. First, the materials should pose problems that are *sequenced* to support students moving from concrete situations to more abstract mathematical reasoning. Second, the starting points for the instructional sequence should be experientially real in that the students can imagine themselves interacting in the context, even if they have not actually done so in their daily life. Third, activities should be designed to engage students in modeling their activity with a variety of inscriptions and symbols (Gravemeijer & Stephan, 2003). For the ratio sequence discussed here, we used the research of Battista and Borrow (1995) to sketch a set of possible learning goals. The cognitive interviews described above led us to use the aliens and food bar context as the starting point for instruction. Research from Middleton and van den Heuvel-Panhuizen (1995) convinced us that students' reasoning with a ratio table could serve as the overarching model for the instructional sequence.

The Learning Trajectory

According to Battista and Borrow (1995), a possible learning route for proportional reasoning begins with iterating linked composites. Take, for instance, Nadia's diagram of the cost of 3 balloons (Figure 5.1a). To complete this task, Nadia formed 3 balloons as a composite unit (a unit of 3 singles) and a composite unit of $2. Furthermore, she linked these two composite units together and iterated them proportionally, that is, for every 3 balloons there must be $2. Battista and Borrow refer to Nadia's reasoning as a critical first step in reasoning about ratios, *forming* and *iterating linked composites*. The two composite units must grow in the same coordinated manner as they are iterated simultaneously. In other words, understanding that the ratio 2:3 is equivalent to 10:15 means that students can iterate a composite unit of 2 *five* times *and* 3 *five* times. Iterating by adding the numerator to itself and the denominator to itself the same number of times is called the *build-up strategy* by Kaput and West (1994). Simply stated, students who use the build-up method use repeated addition with both the numerator and denominator to find an equivalent ratio. When the targeted ratio is too high, however, students may invent an *abbreviated build-up strategy* in which they shorten the addition method by multiplication (Kaput & West, 1994). For example, if there are 2 girls for every 3 boys and we want to know how many boys there are when there are 58 girls, instead of repeatedly adding 2's and 3's to get to the target, an abbreviated strategy might involve multiplying 2 by 29 to get 58 girls and 3 by 29 to get 87 boys, the answer.

The next step might be *extending linked composites sequences by whole numbers*. Battista and Borrow noticed that when the target ratio did not yield a whole number scale factor, students began to reason additively. For example, consider the problem in which there are 3 utensils for every 4 plates. How many utensils are there for 30 plates? The multiplier (i.e., scale factor) from 4 to 30 is a decimal that can cause students to revert back to additive reasoning. A student might argue that there is 1 utensil less than plates, so if there are 30 plates, there must be 1 less utensil, 29. Or, a different student might decide that, since you add 26 more plates to get to 30, you must add 26 utensils to get to 29. In either case, unknown to the student, the link has been broken between the original two composite units. Thus, instruction must introduce nonwhole number scale factors to revisit the meaning of the linkage between the two composites in a ratio. A final step in the potential learning route may be proportional reasoning in which students abstract the meaning of the link—that the scale factor is what each composite number grows by simultaneously. We drew on Battista and Borrow's (1995) research as well as the results of our interviews to draw a sketch of a possible hypothetical learning trajectory (see Table 5.1).

Initial instructional activities would provoke students to form linked composites and determine what it means to "link" them together. We would pose initial questions in the context of alien invaders who can only be pacified by food (see the Ratio Instructional Unit given at *www.nc2ml.org/6-8-teachers/6-2*). For example, the first page presents a picture of 1 food bar and 3 aliens as the *rule*. Then, the first two problems show a picture of 9 aliens and 2 food bars, with the second showing 9 aliens and 4 food bars. The question for each was: *Is there enough food to feed the aliens?* We hypothesized that creating a strong link, further enforced by the context (if aliens don't get fed enough, there will be an intergalactic war), would be important for future mathematical tasks. If students circle a set of 3 aliens and draw a line to a food bar, we would highlight that particular inscription and ask students to explain what the line signified, that is, the linkage. The problems on the next few pages would prompt students to find the number of food bars it would take to feed 36 aliens, or how many aliens could be fed by 9 food bars. We expected students to draw pictures like Nadia did in Figure 5.1a, make a list like Brian in Figure 5.1b, or use some multiplication or division number sentences. For students who created a vertical or horizontal list, we would capitalize on the inscription and reorganize it as a ratio table.

Strategies using pictures, lists, and long ratio tables (as the students came to call them) illustrate students' use of the *build-up strategy* by iterating linked composites. We conjectured that possible topics of conversation would involve the reasons for iterating by two different numbers and knowing when to stop. We thought students might notice patterns in the long ratio table, such as the difference between the top and bottom number increases or that the bottom number is always 3 times bigger than the top (the unit rate/constant of proportionality interpretation). If those topics emerged from students, we would encourage them to notice that one is additive (difference) and the other is multiplicative (unit ratio), something not highlighted by Battista and Borrow (1995).

As the learning trajectory progresses, we would pose different scenarios, particularly those that had high target ratios, to encourage students to invent more efficient strategies. We would introduce the short ratio table that supports students curtailing their build-up strategies and create an abbreviated one that capitalizes on multiplication or division (see Figure 5.2 for a sample task).

| # of food bars | 1 | 2 | | | | | | 33 |
| # aliens | 3 | 6 | | | | | | x |

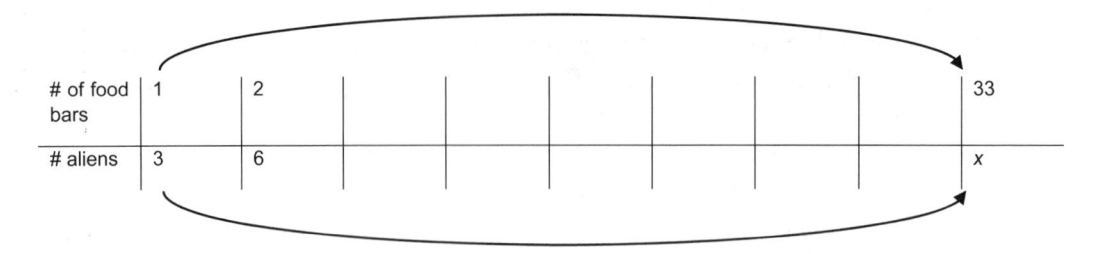

Who can figure out a short way to determine how many aliens 33 food bars will feed?

FIGURE 5.2. Task that encourages moving from a long to short ratio table.

After students solve problems within the alien context, utilizing various methods and inscriptions (i.e., pictures, long and short ratio tables), we would introduce problems with nonwhole number scale factors. We expected to have conversations about the meaning of the decimal scale factor as well as which method would be easier: the scale factor (horizontal relationship) or constant of proportionality (vertical relationship).

Next, we posed problems in a variety of new contexts to encourage students to reason proportionally in new situations. We gave students an actual day care pamphlet from a local business and asked them to notice the general requirements, such as *Maintain minimum staff-to-child ratios 1:11 for 2-year-old classrooms*. Again, the consequences for *breaking the link* between the ratios were high stakes, that is, a day care center can lose its license. Other contextual situations we used included recipes, prices of a variety of calculators, and seventh and eighth graders' preference for a certain rock band.

The final part of the hypothetical learning trajectory involved supporting students to make meaningful comparisons between and among ratios. While our district-adopted textbook began with comparisons among percent and ratios, we decided to develop students' meaning for ratios first and then have them make comparisons. We conjectured that their creation of ratios and linked composites and invented strategies for finding equivalent ratios using a ratio table would support meaningful strategies for comparing different ratios. An example of an initial task for comparing ratios concerned a Halloween problem (presented in pictorial form):

> The Band wants to make fake blood for their Halloween party. They found a recipe online that uses corn syrup and red food dye to make blood. Three Band students decided to experiment with the recipe to see who could make the darkest shade of red blood. Michelle's recipe contains 8 ounces of corn syrup and 32 drops of red dye, Julianna's recipe contains 12 ounces of corn syrup and 24 drops of red dye, and Kyle's recipe contains 6 ounces of corn syrup and 18 drops of red dye. Whose recipe makes the darkest red color? Explain.

We anticipated that students would make equivalent ratios to compare recipes by creating unit ratios for each, finding common numerators across pairs of ratios or across all three, and finding common denominators. Other students may simply notice that the drops for each recipe are 4, 2, and 3 times larger than the amount of corn syrup, respectively, and decide that Michelle's recipe will result in the strongest red color. The most important conversations around these comparison problems would involve interpreting the equivalent ratios in terms of the context to decide whether to use the largest or smallest quantity. For example, if each of the ratios are converted to unit ratios, ¼, ½, and ⅓, Michelle's recipe is the reddest due to the corn syrup (clear liquid) being the same across all three and the quantity of red should be as large as possible. However, if students found a common denominator, they should choose the smallest numerator to get the least amount of clear liquid to dilute the red dye. Thus, interpreting the ratios in terms of the context is a critical component of this part of the HLT.

Ratio and Proportion Implementation Phase

With a hypothetical learning trajectory and associated instructional materials in hand, a classroom teaching experiment (Cobb, 2000) was performed. Since we were employed as teachers, not researchers, the resources to run a formal classroom teaching experiment were not available. The only formal data we could collect were our own personal field notes and records of teacher team meetings. However, we managed to implement the same instructional materials in all sections of our mathematics classes for a total of five different sets of students, including an inclusion class. The three of us met on an almost daily basis to *lesson image* (Stephan, Pugalee, Cline, & Cline, 2016), which consisted of reflecting on the students' strategies, adjusting the instructional materials for the following day, and hypothesizing the types of strategies students might invent as well as questions we would ask to facilitate the learning goal from the HLT.

Although we were unable to collect video data from the ratios classroom teaching experiment, we were able to make copies of students' assessments and daily work. We also kept track of changes to the instructional sequences made during the daily debriefing sessions as well as the rationale. Additionally, we video-recorded post-interviews of the same six students in order to determine the ways in which their proportional reasoning had changed during the instruction. It was through our daily notes and interview analyses that we were able to engage in the next phase of C-DBR.

Ratio and Proportion Analysis/Revision Phase

To conduct a formal analysis of classroom implementation data, researchers utilize their theoretical framework and analysis technique to document the learning of the classroom as well as the ways individuals participated in and contributed to that learning. In other C-DBR projects, we have used the emergent perspective and its theoretical constructs (Cobb & Yackel, 1996) as the lens for the data and an analytical tool created by Rasmussen and Stephan (2008) to document classroom mathematical practices. Since we were unable to collect formal data during the ratio work, we refer the reader to Stephan and Akyuz (2012) as an example of rigorous, data-based analysis. We began our analysis with the post-interview results. To analyze the interviews, we watched all the students' videos, listened to their explanations for the solutions they used, and checked our interpretations against their written work. The students' reasoning indicated that all six could reason proportionally using a variety of strategies, but most used a shortened ratio table or proportions. For example, for the balloon problem, Nadia immediately drew a short ratio table with money on the top and number of balloons on the bottom. Knowing she wanted to find the price for 24 balloons, she divided 24 by 3 to find the scale factor of 8 and completed the multiplication to get $16 (Figure 5.3a). Brian, for his part, began by writing down some calculations that started to not make sense to him. At one point, he exclaimed, "Oh!" and drew a shortened ratio table like Nadia did (Figure 5.3b). Finally, Arthur, a student who had historically underperformed in mathematics, created a short ratio table that resembled a long one with the middle ratios missing (Figure 5.3c). Arthur found the scale factor that brought 3 balloons to 24, and then multiplied $2 times the scale factor to create the equivalent ratio 24:16. Every student also solved Question 3, the country road problem, by making a ratio table containing each person's miles and time and scaling up with a 1.5 scale factor determining the constant of proportionality by finding the vertical relationship of 1.5 times greater or scaling down to create a unit rate.

We also analyzed the results of a common summative assessment (i.e., the unit test) to determine the reasoning of the whole class. Each teacher created a summary of students' solutions for each problem. For example, one problem involved students deciding which recipe, among three, was sweetest when given the amount of blueberries and sugar. Our records indicate the most common solutions involved comparing tastes by (1) finding common numerators; (2) finding common denominators; and

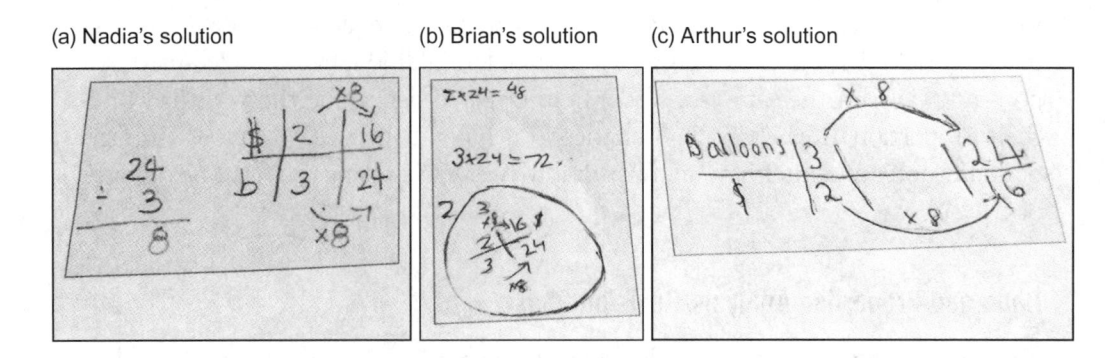

(a) Nadia's solution   (b) Brian's solution   (c) Arthur's solution

FIGURE 5.3. Students' solutions to the balloon problem in the post-interview.

(3) creating unit ratios, with a 1 in either the numerator or denominator. The most common error occurred when students concluded incorrectly that the food item with the bigger number always had the sweetest taste (i.e., choosing 6 cups of blueberries to 2 cups of sugar over 4 cups of blueberries to 2 cups of sugar). We brought our analytic summaries to a meeting and compared the results to determine if there were patterns in students' solutions. Both sets of data revealed that students across the five classrooms were able to solve ratio and proportion problems with great success. However, both these data and our daily teacher/research meetings suggested three major revisions for the next cycle of design research: (1) calculational reasoning, (2) structuring a ratio multiplicatively, and (3) analyzing equivalent ratios.

Calculational Reasoning

Although students could solve ratio and proportion problems given in a variety of contexts, their reasoning was very procedural. In other words, the ratio table became a procedural device with shaky conceptual understanding underlying the calculations. We wondered, in retrospect, what students would say if we asked them what the ×8 stood for in the balloons problem. In fact, several of us asked students informally after the unit test and learned that the ×8 unanimously stood for *the number you multiply by to get up to $16*.

Students' calculational orientation to the ratio table, while reasonable, was not the meaning we hoped the inscription would hold for most students. Thompson, Philipp, Thompson, and Boyd (1994) had convinced us that the teacher and students should hold a conceptual orientation to mathematics, a perspective that mathematics is not just about calculating to obtain correct answers. Rather, mathematical procedures should have meaning within the context of the problem. For example, we hoped that the ×8 would stand for the number of groups of 3 balloons and the number of groups of $2 it would take to create a 24 balloons to $16 ratio. The fact that it did not mean this for most students led us to make our first major revision to the instructional sequence.

In order to support students' interpreting the result of multiplying both units in the ratio by the same number, we added tasks that focused explicitly on this idea. For example, we would show a picture of three students' strategies to the same problem: one that used a short ratio table, one that drew pictures, and one that wrote a long ratio table. We asked students to explain what the scale factor in the short table stood for using the picture and long ratio table solutions. The teachers, for their part, also pressed students to explain why they multiplied by the same number during discussion. Typical questions that contained contextual press (Reinke, Stephan, Ayan, & Casto, submitted for publication) were "Why did you multiply both the top and bottom by 6?" "What does that ×6 stand for in the picture?" "What does the ×6 stand for on the long ratio table?" "Why can't you just add 15 to the top and 15 to the bottom?"

Structuring a Ratio Multiplicatively

The second adjustment we made to the learning trajectory involved adding more tasks that emphasized the vertical relationship between ratios on a long or short table and helping students relate this constant of proportionality to the unit ratio. In this way, we were attempting to support students to structure a ratio multiplicatively. In other words, 3 food bars to 6 aliens is proportional to 18:36 because both denominators are 2 times larger than their numerator. More contextually, there are always twice as many aliens than food bars for both quantities. Alternatively, there are always half as many food bars as aliens. The teachers asked questions about the relationship between the numerator and denominator in the table as well as the difference between a horizontal scale factor and vertical multiplier. We hoped students would notice that the vertical multiplier stayed constant throughout a long table while the horizontal scale factor changed depending on the target ratio. We also hoped that students would relate the constant vertical multiplier (what we call the constant of proportionality) to the unit ratio 1:2.

Analyzing Equivalent Ratios

As students structured ratios multiplicatively, we introduced one more learning goal that was a short extension of the previous one. We posed problems in the day care context again by giving them a variety of ratios from different day care classrooms (2:16, 4:20, 80:400, 2:10, 8:64, 6:48, 7:35, and 7:56). The students were to determine if the ratio of teachers to students represented a toddler classroom (1:8) or an infant classroom (1:5). We expected students to use flexible strategies based on their diverse ways of structuring ratios to this point. Some students might reduce each ratio to a unit ratio to determine the type of classroom while others may simply see that 16, for example, is 8 times as big as 2, so anything whose denominator is 8 times as big as its numerator is a toddler room. Some students might just assume that any denominator that is a factor of 5 is a toddler room. All of these strategies would allow teachers an opportunity to revisit what the vertical multiplier means and how it can be used to determine equivalent ratios/proportional relationships.

Stable Instruction Learning Theory

Recall that one of the main products of several cycles of C-DBR is an instruction learning theory that can be adapted by teachers in other social contexts. The ratio and proportion instruction theory that resulted from 4 years of design experiments is summarized by Table 5.2. The three revisions that resulted from the implementation and analysis of several different classroom sites are highlighted and bolded in the table.

The stable learning trajectory, coupled with the proposed instructional sequence, constitute the *instruction theory for ratio and proportion*. As can be seen in the table, an instruction theory is not equivalent to only the instructional materials that are to be used in a classroom. Gravemeijer et al. (2003) argued that there is no reason to expect that the materials themselves should reproduce the same results in other teachers' classrooms; they are not a recipe that can be followed to produce a homogeneous product. The reason for this discrepancy is that classroom cultures are diverse in their students, reasoning, and experiences. Rather, it is the instruction theory, that is, the materials, potential learning goals, discourse, and tools, that are generalizable, and it is the responsibility of teachers to adapt the materials, forming their own hypothetical learning trajectory, for his or her particular context. When creating an HLT for their own classroom, teachers should consider (1) how students may reason with the tools and inscriptions, (2) how this reasoning relates to their previous activity, and (3) how the learning goals and students' conceptual reasoning relate to the tools and inscriptions. In this way, the teachers may alter some of the activities as they enact the instruction theory to better support their students.

Conclusion

In this chapter, I have described the process of enacting the three phases of a C-DBR project. At the macro level, the designers/teachers engaged in cycles of C-DBR as a way to understand how their proposed learning trajectory was actualized in social context. After multiple cycles of C-DBR, a stable instruction theory for the mathematical concept resulted and was ready to be adapted to other classrooms. The ratio and proportion instruction theory has been adapted by at least a dozen middle school teachers with whom I have worked and is currently listed on a public website developed for North Carolina mathematics teachers (*www.nc2ml.org*). In terms of adaptation, one teacher from Turkey has adapted it for her students, and a formal analysis is being conducted to document the learning of the students as well as the ways in which the instruction theory was changed as a consequence of being utilized in another country. For example, the teacher did not think that aliens and food bars would be a context that connected with her students, so she changed it to fish and food pellets. She also added a new learning goal that supports students' reasoning with ratios qualitatively, not just quantitatively. Such adaptations do not mean that the instruction theory was flawed, but rather that it is dynamic and adaptable to states or countries where mathematical standards for K–12 may differ. The power of the instruction theory is that it documents the rationale, expected learning, and possible support so that adaptations can be made more easily.

One unexpected outcome of conducting C-DBR with my teacher colleagues was that they traveled with me to numerous conferences to disseminate findings from our work. Sean commented to me at the time that he was not really interested in research because, in his view, it was not useful for teaching. His impression of educational research was that it was full of t-tests and ANOVAs that told him some intervention worked, but he did not envision a way to integrate it into his practice. Both Sean and Jenny revealed that being included as a contributing member of a C-DBR team helped them see how our research immediately impacted their classroom practice as well as their students' learning. To this day, Sean continues to read research, searches for learning trajectories in textbook materials, and analyzes the diversity of student reasoning for revisions to instruction, and Jenny became a mathematics coach for her district. Future research might focus on the role that engaging in C-DBR plays in teachers' feelings of empowerment as teacher-researchers as well as what residue remains with teachers after a design researcher has left the school setting.

REFERENCES

Artigue, M., & Winsløw, C (2010). International comparative studies on mathematics education: A viewpoint from the anthropological theory of didactics. *Recherches en Didactique des Mathématiques, 30*(1), 47–82.

Battista, M. T., & Borrow, C. V. A. (1995). *A proposed constructive itinerary from iterating composite units to ratio and proportion concepts.* Paper presented at the annual meeting of the North American Chapter of the International Group for the Psychology of Mathematics Education, Columbus, OH.

Bowers, J., Cobb, P., & McClain, K. (1999). The evolution of mathematical practices: A case study. *Cognition and Instruction, 17*(1), 25–66.

Burkhardt, H., & Swan, M. (2013). Task design for systemic improvement: Principles and frameworks. In C. Margolinas (Ed.), *Task design in mathematics education: Proceedings of the International Commission on Mathematical Instruction* (Vol. 22, pp. 431–440). Oxford: Oxford University Press.

Clements, D., & Sarama, J. (2004). Learning trajectories in mathematics education. *Mathematical Thinking and Learning, 6*(2), 81–89.

Cobb, P. (2000). Conducting teaching experiments in collaboration with teachers. In A. E. Kelly & R. A. Lesh (Eds.), *Handbook of research design in mathematics and science education* (pp. 307–334). Mahwah, NJ: Erlbaum.

Cobb, P. (2003). Investigating students' reasoning about linear measurement as a paradigm case of design research. In N. Pateman (Series Ed.), M. Stephan, J. Bowers, & P. Cobb (with K. Gravemeijer) (Vol. Eds.), *Journal for Research in Mathematics Education Monograph Series: Vol. 12. Supporting students' development of measuring conceptions: Analyzing students' learning in social context* (pp. 1–16). Reston, VA: National Council of Teachers of Mathematics.

Cobb, P., Confrey, J., diSessa, A., Lehrer, R., & Schauble, L. (2003). Design experiments in educational research. *Educational Researcher, 32*(1), 9–13.

Cobb, P., Gravemeijer, K., Yackel, E., McClain, K., & Whitenack, J. (1997). Mathematizing and symbolizing: The emergence of chains of signification in one first-grade classroom. In D. Kirshner & J. A. Whitson (Eds.), *Situated cognition: Social, semiotic, and psychological perspectives* (pp. 151–233). Mahwah, NJ: Erlbaum.

Cobb, P., & Jackson, K. (2011). Toward an empirically grounded theory of action for improving the quality of mathematics at scale. *Mathematics Teacher Education and Development, 13*(1), 6–33.

Cobb, P., McClain, K., & Gravemeijer, K. (2003). Learning about statistical covariation. *Cognition and Instruction, 21*(1), 1–78.

Cobb, P., & Yackel, E. (1996). Constructivist, emergent, and sociocultural perspectives in the context of developmental research. *Educational Psychologist, 31*, 175–190.

Confrey, J., & Lachance, A. (2000). Transformative reading experiments through conjecture-driven research design. In A. E. Kelly & A. Lesh (Eds.), *Handbook of research design in mathematics and science education* (pp. 231–266). Mahwah, NJ: Erlbaum.

Corcoran, T., Mosher, F., & Rogat, A. (2009). *Learning progressions in science: An evidence-based approach to reform.* Philadelphia: Consortium for Policy Research in Education.

Crabtree, L., & Stephan, M. (2021). Using critical case studies to cultivate in-service teachers' critical science consciousness. *Innovations in Science Teacher Education, 6*(1). Retrieved from https://innovations.theaste.org/using-critical-case-studies-to-cultivate-inservice-teachers-critical-science-consciousness

Daro, P., Mosher, F., & Cocoran, T. (2011). *Learning trajectories in mathematics: A foundation for standards, curriculum, assessment, and instruction.* Philadelphia: Consortium for Policy Research in Education.

Freudenthal, H. (1973). *Mathematics as an educational task.* Dordrecht, the Netherlands: Reidel.

Freudenthal, H. (1991). *Revisiting mathematics education.* Dordrecht, the Netherlands: Kluwer.

Gravemeijer, K., Bowers, J., & Stephan, M. (2003). Continuing the design research cycle: A revised measurement and arithmetic instructional sequence. In N. Pateman (Series Ed.), M. Stephan, J. Bowers, & P. Cobb (with K. Gravemeijer) (Vol. Eds.), *Journal for Research in Mathematics Education Monograph Series No. 12* (pp. 103–122). Reston, VA: National Council of Teachers of Mathematics.

Gravemeijer, K., & Stephan, M. (2003). Emergent models as an instructional design heuristic. In K. Gravemeijer, R. Lehrer, B. van Oers, & L. Verschaffel (Eds.), *Symbolizing, modeling and tool use in mathematics education* (pp. 145–169). Dordrecht, the Netherlands: Springer.

Kaput, J. J., & West, M. M. (1994). Missing-value proportional reasoning problems: Factors affecting informal reasoning patterns. In G. Harel & J. Confrey (Eds.), *The development of multiplicative reasoning in the Learning of mathematics* (pp. 235–287). Reform in Mathematics Education Series. Albany, NY: SUNY Press.

Koichu, B., Zaslavsky, O., & Dolev, L. (2013). Effects of variations in task design using different representations of mathematical objects on learning: A case of a sorting task. In C. Margolinas (Ed.), *Task design in mathematics education: Proceedings of the International Commission on Mathematical Instruction* (Vol. 22, pp. 461–470). Oxford: Oxford University Press.

Lamon, S. (1990). *Ratio and proportion: Cognitive foundations in unitizing and norming.* Paper presented at the annual meeting of the American Educational Research Association, Boston.

Lesh, R., Post, T. R., & Behr, M. (1988). Proportional reasoning. In M. Behr & J. Hiebert (Eds.), *Number concepts and operations in the middle grades* (Vol. 2, pp. 93–118). Reston, VA: National Council of Teachers of Mathematics; Hillsdale, NJ: Erlbaum.

Middleton, J. A., & van den Heuvel-Panhuizen, M. (1995). The ratio table: Helping students understand rational number. *Mathematics Teaching in the Middle School, 1*(4), 282–288.

Penuel, W. R., Coburn, C. E., & Gallagher, D. J. (2013). Negotiating problems of practice in research–practice design partnerships. *National Society for the Study of Education Yearbook, 112*(2), 237–255.

Rasmussen, C., & Stephan, M. (2008). A methodology for documenting collective activity. In A. E. Kelly, R. A. Lesh, & J. Y. Baek (Eds.), *Handbook of design research methods in education: Innovations in science, technology, engineering and mathematics learning and teaching* (pp. 195–215). New York: Routledge.

Reinke, L., Stephan, M., Ayan, R., & Casto, A. R. (submitted for publication). Teachers' use of contextual problems to ground students' mathematical understanding, *Journal of Mathematics Teacher Educators*.

Simon, M. (2000). Research on mathematics teacher development: The teacher development experiment. In A. E. Kelly & A. Lesh (Eds.), *Handbook of research design in mathematics and science education* (pp. 335–359). Mahwah, NJ: Erlbaum.

Simon, M. A. (1995). Reconstructing mathematics pedagogy from a constructivist perspective. *Journal for Research in Mathematics Education, 26*(2), 114–145.

Stephan, M. (2014). Conducting classroom design research with teachers. *ZDM, The International Journal of Mathematics Education, 47*(6), 905–917.

Stephan, M., & Akyuz, D. (2012). A proposed instructional theory for integer addition and subtraction. *Journal for Research in Mathematics Education, 43*(4), 428–464.

Stephan, M., Bowers, J., Cobb, P., & Gravemeijer K. (Eds.). (2003). *Journal for Research in Mathematics Education Monograph Series: Vol. 12. Supporting students' development of measuring conceptions: Analyzing students' learning in social context* (N. Pateman, Series Ed.). Reston, VA: National Council of Teachers of Mathematics.

Stephan, M., Pugalee, D., Cline, J., & Cline, C. (2016). *Lesson imaging in math and science: Anticipating student ideas and questions for deeper STEM learning*. Alexandria, VA: Association of Supervisors and Curriculum Designers.

Stephan, M., & Rasmussen, C. (2002). Classroom mathematical practices in differential equations. *Journal of Mathematical Behavior, 21*(4), 459–490.

Streefland, L. (1991). *Fractions in realistic mathematics education. A paradigm of developmental research*. Dordrecht, the Netherlands: Kluwer.

Thompson, A., Philipp, R., Thompson, P., & Boyd, B. (1994). Calculational and conceptual orientations in teaching mathematics. In D. Aichele & A. Coxford (Eds.), *Professional Development for Teachers of Mathematics, 1994 Yearbook of the National Council of Teachers of Mathematics* (pp. 79–92). Reston, VA: National Council of Teachers of Mathematics.

Wilson, P., McCulloch, A., Curtis, J., Stephan, M., Mawhinney, K., & Webb, J. (2017). Partnering for professional development at scale. In E. Galindo & J. Newton, (Eds.), *Proceedings of the 39th Annual Meeting of the North American Chapter of the International Group for the Psychology of Mathematics Education* (pp. 1431–1434). Indianapolis: Hoosier Association of Mathematics Teacher Educators.

CHAPTER 6

Curriculum Development of Reading and Writing in the Middle Grades

Zoi A. Philippakos and Charles A. MacArthur

The recent reading results of the National Assessment of Educational Progress (NAEP; McFarland et al., 2017) found an unchanged performance among middle and high school students. Despite policy changes on literacy acquisition, standards, and instruction (see Common Core State Standards [CCSS; National Governors Association Center for Best Practices & Council of Chief State School Officers, 2010]; Every Student Succeeds Act [ESSA]), underperformance persists. The results of students' writing performance on NAEP have not yet been released, but there is a concern that they may mirror the results in reading, confirming a replicable underperformance among U.S. students (National Center for Education Statistics, 2017). Internationally, the Programme for International Student Assessment (OECD, 2019) showed that U.S. students performed above the average (U.S. average score 505) of the Organisation for Economic Co-operation and Development (OECD; average score 497), but there has not been a statistically significant change in performance since 2000.

To make progress in literacy achievement within the United States, there is a need to redouble efforts to apply evidence-based methodologies. Research has indeed provided a range of evidence-based practices for reading and writing instruction (e.g., Shanahan, 2016), but these practices are not widely used in schools (Dockrell, Marshall, & Wyse, 2016; Gillespie, Graham, Kiuhara, & Hebert, 2014). The research–practice gap is a substantial problem. In this problem space, the use of design-based research (DBR) allows the closer examination of contexts, practices, and development of approaches that can be later tested for their efficacy as appropriate. DBR has the potential to contribute to improved application of effective practices because of its focus on examining and improving instructional practices in authentic settings. In this chapter, we will report our work with middle school students on the design and modification of writing and reading processes using genre-based strategy instruction.

What Works in Secondary Education

Despite the often circulated opinion that writing instruction methods do not have adequate research support, there is plenty of research conducted with elementary and secondary learners on evidence-based practices. Those practices can be located in the practice guides that the Institute of Education Sciences has shared (*www.ies.gov*). Based on Graham et al. (2016), for example, writing instruction in the secondary classrooms should (1) explicitly teach appropriate writing strategies using a model–practice–reflect instructional cycle; (2) integrate writing and reading to emphasize key writing features, and (3) use assessments of student writing to inform instruction and feedback to students. According to those guidelines and relevant research, writing instruction should first support students' understanding about the audience, writing purpose, and writing process and explicitly teach students how to set goals and navigate the writing process to complete those goals. Strategies need to be modeled and practiced with feedback, and learners should be supported in reflecting on their use of strategies, on their writing, and on their peers' writing. Second, writing and reading should not be viewed as separate entities, but instruction should support both and connections between them. Furthermore, instruction should incorporate the use of exemplars or mentor texts to highlight the text features and better understand them for their own writing. Finally, formative assessment can support the identification of specific instructional needs in order to effectively design instruction and monitor students' progress. Overall, these recommendations address instruction, pedagogy, and assessment.

Argumentation

Argumentation is a common academic type of writing that is challenging for learners (Knudson, 1992; Kuhn, Shaw, & Felton, 1997; Midgette, Haria, & MacArthur, 2008; Newell, Bloome, Kim, & Gof, 2019; Voss & Van Dyke, 2001). Its challenge lies in its dialogic nature, learners' lack of an accurate schema about the genre and its requirements, learners' difficulty developing and including convincing reasons, and their challenge to effectively address and rebut the opposing position. Argumentation is dialogic in nature (Ferretti & Fan, 2016) and requires critical thinking and judgment of ideas (Walton, 1989). Students may find it challenging to respond to an opposing position and may weaken it; they may favor specific ideas and support a specific view without being able to develop an opposing position or respond to one (Kuhn & Udell, 2007).

The Common Core standards emphasize instruction to address persuasion and argumentation (National Governors Association Center for Best Practices

& Council of Chief State School Officers, 2010). Across kindergarten to grade 6, students should be able to provide a clear position, reasons with evidentiary support (drawn from their knowledge and readings), and a closure. After grade 6, they should be able to address the opposing position, arguing that their position is stronger. Across middle school grades, students are expected to write papers that present their claim, that are clear, and that include accurate evidence. Students are expected to write arguments in response to readings and also participate in conversations in which they present their points and support them with evidence. Overall, there is an expected synchrony between reading, writing, speaking, and listening for students to function as critical readers, writers, and thinkers.

Instructional Approaches: Strategy Instruction

Several approaches support argumentative writing that draw from social and cognitive theories (for a review, see Ferretti & Graham, 2019). A cognitive approach that has led to positive changes on writing quality is *strategy instruction* (Graham, 2006; Graham, Harris, & Chambers, 2016). Strategy instruction addresses both cognitive and metacognitive strategies, their explicit and systematic instruction, and their gradual application through systematic scaffolds provided by the teacher. In general, strategy instruction responds to three questions: (1) what strategies to teach, (2) how to teach them, and (3) how to support their independent use (MacArthur, 2011; Philippakos, MacArthur, & Coker, 2015).

Decisions about *what strategies to teach* are based on extensive research on the cognitive processes of proficient writers. The work of Hayes (1996), Hayes and Flower (1980), Bereiter and Scardamalia (1987), and McCutchen (2006) revealed the complex strategies used by experienced writers for planning and revision. *How to teach* is guided by research on pedagogical approaches that help students master strategies. Specifically, in strategy instruction, teachers model by using live think-alouds that demonstrate how to complete challenging tasks and how to overcome anticipated challenges. Modeling is followed by collaborative practice in which teachers and students practice together, but teachers scaffold and guide the appropriate application of taught strategies. Through this gradual release of responsibility, students observe the teacher model how to use the strategies, explain in their own words why to use them, and work to memorize them before they proceed to guided practice. In guided practice, teachers support students as needed through individual conferences or small-group instruction. Finally, the question about *how to support* independence is answered with explicit instruction on self-regulation strategies to identify goals, select strategies for managing factors such as time and space of work, monitor progress toward goals and strategy use, and reflect on strategy use and writing progress. Teachers model and apply this process of self-regulation throughout the writing tasks and support students to break goals into smaller, manageable ones, monitor their progress, and cumulatively expand their goals, and repertoire of strategies.

In this current work, we provided instruction on genre-based strategy instruction that coordinates theories and approaches while it connects critical reading, writing, and thinking.

Genre-Based Strategy Instruction

Genre-based strategy instruction draws from several theories and instructionally sound methodologies. The instructional components draw from an effective model of strategy instruction with self-regulation, the self-regulated strategy development (SRSD) model (Harris & Graham, 1999, 2009). This model has been studied across many grades and contexts, and has been found to positively improve students' writing performance as well as their motivation to write (Graham, 2006; Graham et al., 2016; Graham, Harris, & Santangelo, 2015; Graham, McKeown, Kiuhara, & Harris, 2012). SRSD includes specific instructional stages that address activation of background knowledge, teacher modeling, guided practice, and independent application. Most importantly, SRSD includes self-regulation strategies for goal setting, task management, self-evaluation, and maintenance of motivation. Strategy instruction combined with self-regulation leads to higher gains in writing quality (Graham, McKeown, et al., 2015; Harris & Graham, 2009). In the current project, self-regulation strategies are embedded across writing and reading tasks.

Instructional components in this project, Developing Strategic Writers, also draw from the work of Englert and colleagues (1991) on cognitive strategy instruction in writing (CSIW); they were the first to integrate text structure, or genre elements, into planning and revising strategies. In CSIW, planning strategies began with rhetorical analysis of the writing assignment to select an appropriate text structure or genre; then genre elements were used to generate and organize content using graphic organizers. Revision in CSIW was based on evaluation criteria specific to those genres. In the current project, we extended the use of genre features to support reading comprehension as well as planning and revising.

Furthermore, the instructional components draw on work on genre-based literacy pedagogy (Martin & Rose, 2012; Rose, 2016). Genre includes more than text structure and a focus on the organization of a type of writing (Martin & Rose, 2012). In Developing Strategic Writers, genre refers to discourse as it relates to text structure and linguistic and syntactic characteristics that characterize the discourse. Thus, genres are text forms developed to meet particular social purposes and communicate with readers. As a result, there are multiple genres within the general categories of narrative, argumentative, and informative texts. Genre includes the linguistic features of text in addition to the organizational elements of text structure (McCutchen, 1986, 2006). In the current project, instruction begins with explicit explanations about the writing purposes, discussion of the specific writing purpose that will be the basis of instruction and elements of the targeted genre; text analysis follows in which learners deconstruct a text, and examine its language features and specific text and genre characteristics (e.g., the use of an opposing position and a rebuttal). Instruction introduces genre and linguistic features through the use of mentor texts, model student texts, and sentence frames.

Critical reading is incorporated in the instructional sequence to support the development of self-evaluation. An emphasis is placed on evaluation and on the role of critical reading using genre-specific evaluation criteria for revision that connect with the elements of the genre and the planning elements. Before students plan and write their own papers, they learn genre-specific evaluation criteria and apply them collaboratively to evaluate both good and weak examples of writing by unknown students. Also, prior to peer review, teachers model how to evaluate using genre-specific criteria and other linguistic features, and students practice with partners evaluating the work of unknown others before they self-evaluate and peer-review their papers. Several studies have found that teaching genre-specific evaluation criteria has a positive impact on revision and writing (for a review, see MacArthur, 2011; MacArthur, Graham, & Harris, 2004). In our own experimental work with fourth and fifth graders (Philippakos & MacArthur, 2016), students who learned genre-specific criteria and applied them to give feedback on papers written by unknown peers improved the quality of their own revised essays.

Instructional research also supports reading and writing connections. Research on reading and writing connections has found that the two are connected on pragmatic, cognitive, and procedural levels (Shanahan, 1984; Tierney & Shanahan, 1991). Both are used for communication purposes and are reciprocal as writers are authors who write for readers, and readers process the work of authors. Also, they share common cognitive processes and knowledge, such as knowledge of pragmatics, text attributes, domain knowledge, and procedural knowledge (Fitzgerald & Shanahan, 2000; Shanahan, 2006, 2009, 2016, 2018). Proficient readers use knowledge of genre to extract the gist of text information and to respond with their own perspectives. As a writing strategy, summarization as well as note taking supports reading comprehension (Graham & Hiebert, 2010). In the current project, genre-based strategies were used both to take notes and comprehend information from reading and then to write about that information by consulting those notes.

This genre-based approach to writing coincides with the recommendations provided by Graham et al. (2016) on writing instruction for secondary learners. Specifically, it has a strong emphasis on genre as this relates to purposes, audiences, and discourse. Also, it provides explicit and systematic instruction on the writing process but also develops a predictable relationship between planning and revision on the basis of text structure. It promotes instruction that supports a gradual release of responsibility and promotes evaluation for self-reflection.

Using this instructional approach, we developed lessons on the genres of opinion, procedural, story, report writing for grades K–2 (e.g., Philippakos & MacArthur, 2020; Traga Philippakos, 2019; Traga Philippakos & MacArthur, 2020; Traga Philippakos, MacArthur, & Munsell, 2018) and compare–contrast, story, and opinion writing in grades 3–5 (Philippakos & MacArthur, 2016; Philippakos et al., 2015; Traga Philippakos, 2020a). In the meantime, we also worked with schools to examine the obstacles teachers faced in the implementation of genre-based strategy instruction and the pedagogical and content knowledge needs teachers had (Traga Philippakos, 2020a). This information was used to design professional development (PD) practices and a model for PD (see Chapter 11, this volume) (Traga Philippakos, 2020b).

Current DBR Work: Purposes and Rationale

Historically, in our work on genre-based strategy instruction, DBR has been a working methodology for the development of instructional procedures and PD practices across the K–5 Developing Strategic Writers curricula. This current work with middle grades arose naturally from our prior work with elementary schools. Teachers and principals of middle schools contacted us asking for instructional suggestions that addressed genre-based pedagogy. They shared that students who attended schools that had taught using this approach were better prepared in the sixth grade. Furthermore, districts that had committed to a K–5 genre-based strategy instruction requested continuity for their curriculum, for students' instructional performance, and for teachers' confidence and professional growth. Considering that our goal was to expand the work from K–5 and examine its application in the middle grades, we initiated a research collaboration with two middle school sites that included students from K–5 elementary schools that had applied the Developing Strategic Writers curriculum. The following research questions guided this current project:

- Is the strategy for teaching strategies applicable in grades 6–8?
- What revisions are needed based on teachers' feedback and on students' performance?

Methods

Participants and Setting

Participants in this work were the social studies, science, and English language arts (ELA) teachers across two middle schools ($n = 32$) (Traga Philippakos & MacArthur, in press) and their students as well as the school principals. Both sites were located in a rural section of the southern United States, and one of them was a Title I school.

Instructional Process: Writing

The instructional process and components are based on strategy instruction (Graham, 2006; Graham & Perin, 2007; MacArthur, Philippakos, & Ianetta, 2015;

Traga Philippakos, 2019). Drawing from the work with K–5 students (Philippakos & MacArthur, 2019; Philippakos et al., 2015) and postsecondary learners (MacArthur et al., 2015), an instructional sequence called *Strategy for Teaching Strategies* (STS) was applied:

- *Explanation of the writing purposes:* Teachers explain that writing involves three purposes: to persuade, inform, and entertain or convey experience. Teachers explain to students that every time they read an assignment, they need to carefully consider what Form they are asked to produce, what the Topic is, who the Audience would be, who the Author is and whether students write from a specific point of view (i.e., assume the persona of someone else), and finally what the writing Purpose is (FTAAP). For the latter, students are asked to imagine the writing purposes as represented in a pie, with the different purposes each taking a piece (Philippakos, 2018). This process of completing a careful reading and analysis of an assignment is called a *rhetorical task analysis*.

- *Explanation of the genre and its purpose:* Teachers explain that within each of the pieces of the purposes pie, there are several genres representing types of writing. Teachers discuss with students the specific genre they will be working in and develop through discussion needed background knowledge. In addition, they address misconceptions that students may have (e.g., the perception of argumentation as fighting). Furthermore, teachers discuss with students the importance of the genre, its application in real life, its organizational elements, and linguistic, syntactic characteristics.

- *Introduction of genre via read-alouds:* Genre elements as well as specific linguistic and vocabulary characteristics are further explained through a read-aloud of a mentor text. Using a graphic organizer based on the genre elements, students and teachers draw information from the text, retell the information, and write a summary, sometimes with a response. The value of introducing the genres through reading is twofold: (1) The process of using the genre elements to outline the information from a book can support reading comprehension and demonstrate the value of note taking to record essential information from the text; and (2) it connects reading and writing by showing that authors who are writers also plan, and their work can be represented on the same graphic organizer that students will use to plan their own work. A graphic organizer with a clear outline translates to a paper that readers are able to follow and understand.

- *Evaluation of model samples and weak examples:* Teachers proceed with the evaluation of writing samples for that genre that vary on the clarity of their organization and meanings. The strong and weak model examples are student essays, like those students will be asked to write. The evaluation is done using genre-specific criteria and a scoring system that allows learners to easily detect the presence of the element and its clarity for readers. For this work, critical reading is introduced, with the teacher first modeling the process of evaluation and understanding of the modeled papers, students practicing with the teacher, and then students evaluating their own baseline papers and setting specific writing goals. The same process of evaluation is used later in preparation for self-evaluation and peer review.

- *Explicit explanation and think-aloud modeling with problem solving:* At the modeling stage, the teacher explains the writing process and the behaviors of good writers. Teachers conduct a think-aloud in order for students to see how to use the strategies for planning, drafting, evaluating to revise, and editing. Modeling addresses both cognitive and metacognitive strategies. Through the use of coping models, teachers think aloud about the task, solve problems, and model how to maintain motivation even when the task is challenging. The use of coping models has the ability to change participants' beliefs in their ability to complete a challenging task (Schunk & Hanson, 1989). During the modeling session, teachers plan, draft, evaluate to revise, make one revision, and edit their work (see Figures 6.1, 6.2, and 6.3 for planning materials, sentence frames, and evaluation rubric, respectively).

- *Addressing self-regulation:* At the end of modeling, teachers reflect on the process and strategies they used and discuss with students observed behaviors and comments the teachers made (e.g., "I should not skip the graphic organizer because it will help me outline my ideas"). They explain how the strategies can support students' completion of the writing task to avoid negative talk and feelings toward writing.

- *Collaborative practice:* Teacher and students work together to complete a paper on a new topic. The teacher guides students to use the strategies and records students' responses, but students provide all the content. In case students find the use of the strategies challenging and if a lot of students were absent during modeling, teachers are encouraged to revert to modeling. This collaborative application of the strategies is a part of the gradual release of responsibility (Pearson & Gallagher, 1983).

- *Guided practice:* Teachers support students as they work on a paper using the steps of the writing strategy. Teachers may conference with students individually or in small groups. Teachers may also assist them with a specific challenge they face (e.g., how to begin a paper) and differentiate their instruction.

- *Preparation for peer review, self-evaluation, and peer review:* Peer review is challenging to students who often do not find it to be valuable (Topping, 1998), so training on peer review is necessary. The training is based on critical reading, evaluation using genre-specific criteria, generating comments, and giving feedback using those elements. Students self-evaluate, identify their progress toward their goal, reflect on their use of strategies, and set a new goal for improvement. This process of goal setting will be ongoing, with students reflecting across cycles of application and reflection.

- *Continuous practice to mastery and independence:* Students work through the steps of the writing strategy producing papers in the same genre. During continuous

PLAN

Form: What is it that I am writing?   Essay   Paragraph   Letter   Other _____

Topic/task:

Audience:

Author:

Purpose (What piece of the purposes pie?):

What genre?

What elements?

IDEAS

In Favor (YES . . .)	Against (NO . . .)

Graphic Organizer

Beginning	Topic/Issue/Problem Space:
	Position:
Middle — ME	Reason 1 Evidence 1 Reason 2 Evidence 2 Reason 3 Evidence 3
Middle — OTHERS	Opposing Position:
	Reasons and Evidence:
	Rebuttal:
End	Restate Position:
	Message to Think/Expand the Issue:

FIGURE 6.1. Planning materials for argumentative writing. Adapted by permission from Philippakos, MacArthur, and Coker (2015). Copyright © 2015 The Guilford Press.

```
┌─────────────────────────────────────────┐
│                                         │
│       Middle for Opposing Position      │
│                                         │
└─────────────────────────────────────────┘

- On the other hand, _____
- Others suggest/claim/assert/think/believe that _____
- On the other side of the controversy, X suggest that _____

┌─────────────────────────────────────────┐
│                                         │
│        Middle for Opposing Reason       │
│                                         │
└─────────────────────────────────────────┘

- A first reason _____
- One reason _____

┌─────────────────────────────────────────┐
│                                         │
│           Middle for Rebuttal           │
│                                         │
└─────────────────────────────────────────┘

- Even though X is _____, this suggestion is not _____, because _____
- This is an interesting/important perspective/idea/suggestion; however, it is _____
```

FIGURE 6.2. Transition words for opposing position. Adapted by permission from Philippakos, MacArthur, and Coker (2015). Copyright © 2015 The Guilford Press.

practice, teachers could continue supporting individuals and smaller groups by differentiating their instruction.

Instructional Process: Reading

Teachers were asked to first support students in writing a paper without sources and to then go through a process of modeling, collaborative practice, and guided practice using sources. We acknowledged that reading comprehension can be a challenge and wanted to make sure that students were initially aware of the writing strategies before learning to read and incorporate information from sources into their writing. For reading, students were taught to analyze a text using a similar rhetorical-analysis process as with the writing assignments (see FTAAP), determine the genre and its organization, and use that information to take notes to comprehend the text, and later utilize that information to write a draft. Then they

			Score of 0–1–2
Beginning		**Topic/Issue/Problem Space:** Is the topic clearly stated and analyzed for the reader to understand the controversy or issue?	
		Position: Is the writer's position clearly stated?	
Middle	ME	*For reasons: Are the reasons connected to the opinion. and are they clear and convincing to the reader?	
		**For evidence: Is there sufficient evidence to support the reasons? Is the evidence explained?	
		Reason 1 Evidence 1	
		Reason 2 Evidence 2	
		Reason 3 Evidence 3	
	OTHERS	**Opposing Position:** Is there a clear opposing position that states what others who do not agree with the writer think?	
		Reasons and Evidence: Are the reasons connected with the opposing position, and are they clear and sufficient?	
		Rebuttal: Does the rebuttal **prove that what others say is wrong** and the writer is right?	
End		**Restate Position:** Did the writer restate the position?	
		Message to Think/Expand the Issue: Did the writer leave the reader with a message to further think about the topic and issue and/or take action?	
Other considerations		**Tone:** Is the tone appropriate to the audience?	
		Sources: When sources were used, were they used accurately?	
		Sources: When sources were used, were they cited and referenced appropriately?	
		Sentence frames: Did the writer use sentence frames to guide the reader?	

REVIEWER/WRITER AS A READER
- Was the paper overall convincing? Why?
- What revisions should be made?

GOALS
- What should be the writer's current and future goals?

FIGURE 6.3. Evaluation rubric for argumentative writing. Adapted by permission from Philippakos, MacArthur, and Coker (2015). Copyright © 2015 The Guilford Press.

were supported in summarizing the information in order to make meaning across the text they processed and/or use their notes to respond to a writing prompt. The process used for reading was the following:

- *Application of FTAAP to determine the purpose and genre:* Teachers asked what the Form, Title, Audience, Author, and Purpose of an article or reading selection were. When asking about the form, they considered whether it was an article in response to a previous paper, an opinion, a book chapter, a book, and so on. When reading the title, they examined unknown vocabulary or content-related terms/phrases. If terms were unknown, they looked for their definition and for an example. When examining the author, they asked about other types of work by that same author, the credibility the author had, how reliable the information he or she shared was, and whether the author had a specific bias that would lead him or her to present information in a specific manner. When they reached the P in FTAAP, teachers asked what the purpose was (the piece of the pie to be obtained).

- *Identification of the genre:* If teachers were not able to identify the purpose and genre from the title, they read the *first* few paragraphs and wondered aloud what genre the author presented. Based on this information, they began taking notes on the article and/or recording notes on the brainstorm sheet that represented ideas in favor or against the topic.

- *Note taking:* Teachers continued with the reading and at the end of each paragraph asked, "What did the author say in this paragraph? What did I learn? What is this paragraph about? Does this information offer a reason? Or, is it general information about the topic? What did I learn about the topic?"

- *Oral summary using the notes or written summary:* At the end of the reading, teachers reviewed their notes and verbally provided a summary using them, or they modeled how to write a summary by using information from the FTAAP (e.g., In (Form) written by (Author), _____ is shared).

- *Use of notes to compose:* Since students were aware of the strategy for planning, drafting, evaluating to revise, and editing, teachers modeled how to draft and cite information (e.g., according to _____, based on the information shared by _____, etc.).

Procedures

ELA teachers at the two sites participated in a half-day workshop, and teachers of science and social studies took part in another half-day session as there was no additional time for meetings. In each of the half-day sessions, the researcher explained the theoretical basis for the instruction, modeled instruction, answered questions, and invited teachers to participate in research. Teachers in science and social studies were presented with the standards and discussed with the researcher the differences between the types of reasons students might develop (from text, experimentation, observation). Once teachers agreed to participate, written samples were collected from students on opinion and argumentative writing. In ELA, students responded to controversial topics that did not require readings, and students used their prior knowledge. In science and social studies, students were provided with two articles on controversial topics. Students responded to different topics at the beginning of the study and, after 2 weeks of instruction, typed their responses and uploaded them to Google Drive, where they were de-identified and shared by the administrative team with the researcher.

Measures

In order to examine changes in students' writing performance, we developed writing assignments that (1) combined reading and writing, and (2) focused only on writing. The rationale was to examine how students applied the strategies taught in ELA without the need to cite sources and how they utilized this knowledge in the subject areas where they learned about content and cited sources. The selection of reading sources was based on the following criteria: (1) readings that related to content and standards teachers needed to teach and (2) readings that were on grade level. The latter became a challenge as teachers shared concerns about students' low reading levels. This was a negotiation between them and the researcher, who explained that if students were to be evaluated on grade-level standards, students had to practice and work using grade-level resources. Eventually, teachers agreed to use the provided texts. In addition to the writing resources, the district and schools used the Measures of Academic Progress (MAP; North West Evaluation Association) to examine reading growth.

To better understand instructional challenges and to examine teachers' views on the feasibility of the approach, we interviewed participating teachers at the end of the project and conducted live observations and video observations. Not all teachers were comfortable with video observations, and in those instances, the first researcher observed their instruction in person. The interview questions used were drawn from previous studies (Traga Philippakos & MacArthur, 2020b; Traga Philippakos, MacArthur, & Munsell, 2018).

Analysis and Findings

Students completed writing samples at pretest and posttest in ELA, science, and social studies; in ELA, the writing prompts did not require readings, but the science and social studies tasks did. The papers in ELA were scored using a 7-point holistic rubric that examined ideas, organization, sentence formation and variety, tone, and punctuation. The papers in science were also scored using a 7-point rubric that also included the use of sources. We did not analyze the social studies papers as not all teachers completed the posttest assessments due to concerns about preparing for the state tests.

The results showed that students' papers improved on quality from pretest to posttest (Traga Philippakos & MacArthur, in press). Furthermore, teachers' comments and overall feedback were positive as teachers spoke with enthusiasm about the opportunity to receive support on their writing and learn how to support their students. Principals also verified teachers' comments and shared the need for consistency within the district, with a focus on reading and writing and consistent support. Based on information the district shared, there was growth in students' reading scores on MAP and on science. This was also confirmed in interviews with teachers, who enthusiastically attributed this growth to students learning how to critically think about what they read.

Learning Points and Future Research in DBR

In this project, the quantitative and qualitative data as well as observations of classroom instruction led to specific revisions. Because we applied DBR methodologies, we were able to utilize quantitative and qualitative data to better determine revisions that would support teachers' instructional delivery. Without the use of teachers' interviews, instructional observations, and students' writing samples, we would not have been able to determine what works, what does not work, and what needs to be revised. Their feedback and critical comments and, in general, the combination of quantitative and qualitative data sources allowed us to make significant rewrites and revisions in the argumentative unit in response to the linguistic, background knowledge, and vocabulary needs of rural learners. The DBR learning points and identification of inhibiting factors provided guidance for revisions to be applied in the next cycle of implementation.

Modeling and Collaborative Practice Challenges

Even though teachers appreciated the modeling process and were able to explain the importance of thinking aloud in front of their students, they seemed to have the tendency to transform the modeling process into a collaborative practice. Thus, instead of using "I" and talking about their thinking process, use of strategies, and retrieval of ideas from their long-term memory, teachers tended to use "we" and ask students to provide ideas about the topic. Some of the teachers also asked students to copy the work teachers produced during modeling as they followed along. When asked about this, some shared their concern that a full think-aloud and modeling would disengage students. This information helped us reexamine the explanations provided for think-aloud modeling.

In modeling, teachers spent considerable time developing their papers and working at a fairly high level. Thus, in the second cycle, we plan to explain that the think-aloud should represent the quality and level that students are expected to produce and should be conducted in a timely manner (up to 30 minutes). Students are less likely to disengage if the process is conducted in a prompt manner. When working on writing from sources, students could be asked to read the articles in small groups, review the content, and then participate in larger conversations to collaboratively complete planning. The pace does not need to be slow to ensure comprehension.

Background Knowledge: Inclusion of Read-Alouds and Shared Readings

A general challenge that teachers shared, and which we also observed during the project, was students' struggles to express themselves. Students lacked background knowledge, which affected their ability to make connections, identify main and secondary ideas, and participate in classroom discussions. Perhaps this lack of background knowledge also affected their confidence to express their thoughts about what they were reading. Thus, we plan to incorporate the use of read-alouds to introduce concepts and support conversations. Furthermore, we plan to suggest the inclusion of short clips and videos to support students in developing needed knowledge (e.g., about a historical period). Noticeable was that teachers avoided the use of read-alouds. We also noticed that in certain instances, because of students' low reading performance (up to five grade levels below their grade-level placement), some teachers purchased lessons through online teacher sites, using those resources instead. In the next cycle and in preparation for the academic year, we will better explain the importance of grade-level instruction and assure that teachers use grade-level texts with read-alouds and shared readings, and we will provide such sources for both assessment and instruction.

Reading Selections

A related challenge was the variety of reading choices teachers used. Teachers would consult the state's curriculum that outlines the standards to be addressed in an academic year and select materials from various sources (e.g., NewsELA, chapters, books, blogs, other websites). However, this wide variety of resources resulted in a wide variety of understanding among students. In one case, a social studies instructor used novels to teach historical events and limited the number of informative texts and primary sources to cover those events; in another case, a science teacher watched videos with students on live experiments, while another only read the information. In our revisions, the goal will be to develop a curriculum map (in collaboration with the district) to identify the specific standards to be taught across the year and select resources that all faculty will have access to and to which they may add.

Reading Comprehension

Comprehension was a challenge. To address this, possibly before even working on summarization, students should develop their own questions about the content they read, answer them (orally even), and then proceed with the summary and composition. Critical questions can support students' argumentative reasoning (Nussbaum et al., 2018). Perhaps the incorporation of those can support students' understanding about information as they read and consider their arguments.

Incorporation of Dialogic Principles of Argumentation

In order to further support students' oral language, and drawing from work on collaborative argumentation, we plan to include oral argumentation as part of book reading. Also, we will include debate as part of idea generation to support students' understanding of content and expression of ideas. The use of collaborative argumentation is a common practice applied in dialogic pedagogy that we have additionally incorporated in our K–2 work (e.g., Traga Philippakos et al., 2018; Traga Philippakos & MacArthur, 2020). Through this practice, students engage in arguments about the text, while the teacher facilitates the process and supports them in using sentence frames and language related to the genre. Then once students are taught the writing strategy, they can apply knowledge they have acquired about sentence construction and syntax. This process of oral argumentation also helps students consider the audience and alternative views to their own. In the next cycle, we will incorporate this process in a debate for the development of ideas. Teachers will explain the principles of debate and then support students to engage in an oral debate on a topic while tending to the syntactic and linguistic expectations of argument. This process of idea exchange could further support students' understanding of the value of a strong position and of a rebuttal that enhances a writer's position.

Mini-Lessons on Opposing Position

Although we advised teachers to first teach writing essays without including the opposing position, only later adding it, due to time restrictions, teachers immediately worked on essays that incorporated the opposition position. However, students found it challenging to develop a rebuttal. Therefore, in the next cycle, we will include mini-lessons on opposing position as well as examples and nonexamples of effective rebuttals.

Citations and Their Accurate Use

A challenge that was evident in students' writing was the appropriate citation of sources. When referring to a source, students would state, for example, "The article says . . . ," but then not name the title or the author. As a result, it was difficult for readers to understand the origin of comments. In addition, students did not accurately use sources, sometimes copying sections. We plan to include lessons on what plagiarism is and how to avoid it. Teachers also requested this clarification and shared that it would be helpful for students to know how to cite information and develop a reference list before they enter middle school.

Inclusion of Evidence from Graphs

Something that was observed when students completed their responses in science was the absence of evidence from a bar graph or, in general, a graph that represented data. Students treated such information like a picture and did not comment on its information, but rather restated information about the graph as it was phrased in the text. In the next cycle, we plan to explicitly explain data from graphs and statistical representations of information as well as observational data to structure reasons and evidence. Furthermore, we will set the expectation for science teachers who also teach mathematics and for social studies teachers to explain how to analyze a graph, instead of assuming that students enter middle school with this information. It could be argued that graph analysis is its own genre. Thus, we will develop mini-lessons only on the analysis of graphs and on the use of that information to support a claim.

Author Bias, Reader Bias, and Evaluation of Sources

When working on social studies, some of the teachers used primary sources and discussed with students the authors' point of view and biases. Students were challenged by the idea of a bias and seemed to want to accept information that was published as the truth. They also seemed to think that bias was something that existed outside of them, that they were free of. Bias and point of view, though, are important concepts to understand in order to be a critical reader. A critical reader will consider the origin of information and attempt to discern the motive/biases that an author may have. At the same time, critical readers need to be able to assess their own bias when reading a text, a goal we need to address. This is a challenge many students face because of their lack of background knowledge on historical contexts. For instance, when reading about Cuba, without understanding the Cold War and communism, they will be less likely to understand the adversarial relationship between the United States and Cuba. Considering that librarians often provide workshops to students about plagiarism, evaluation of sources, and source validity, perhaps we could collaborate with librarians to provide additional practice and further enhance students' critical thinking.

Addressing Self-Regulation and Explanations of Metacognitive Strategies

Teachers shared that the process of explaining their thinking process, modeling, reflecting on goals, and holding discussions about use of strategies was challenging to them. This could have resulted because of the limited initial time the researcher had with teachers. Perhaps the focus was more on the "what to teach and how" and not on ways to support self-regulation. Some of the teachers were better able to address self-regulation after they received feedback from the researcher, but still this remained a challenge. Therefore, in the next cycle, self-regulation procedures as well as specific tasks for goal setting, progress monitoring, and reflection will be included, such as journal responses and sharing procedures (Traga Philippakos, 2020b).

Differentiation Needs due to the Vast Differences on Students' Levels

Without a doubt, one of the main challenges that teachers faced and continuously expressed in their communications with the researcher was the variety of students' reading levels. Teachers wanted to support them, but not all were aware of ways to differentiate their instruction, and some struggled with how to develop groups for differentiation. In some instances, teachers with backgrounds in elementary education were more effective in scaffolding instruction. In general, though, the tendency was to use less challenging material, teach the whole group, and try to support each student in individual conferences, but they were not able to meet with everyone. We were pleasantly surprised by one of the social studies teachers who developed rotating groups (at the different stages of the writing process) in which students would respond to content-based questions. The incorporation of suggestions for differentiation would be a goal for the next cycle.

Assessments

Teachers were accustomed to reading assessments and the district used a norm-referenced test for reading, math, and science. However, they were not accustomed to writing assessments and expressed a challenge in grading those. Even though teachers used the same rubric that students used to examine their performance, teachers were concerned about their scores and objectivity. Therefore, in the next stage, we will spend time assessing writing and also provide teachers with a matrix to map students' performance (or for students to add to themselves). In addition, we are exploring the possibility of incorporating automated essay scoring (AES) procedures for the screening and progress monitoring measures (at the beginning, middle, and end of the year) and providing the genre-based evaluation ones as progress monitoring for the genres taught (Traga Philippakos & FitzPatrick, 2018).

Closing Thoughts

This project began because of a pragmatic need that was shared by schools to expand our work on Developing Strategic Writers with K–5 students into middle school. The information we collected in this project with middle school teachers and students helped us see that we need to further explore reading comprehension and support students in meaning-making prior to writing. DBR allows researchers to work in a real setting and actively collaborate with participants. In this work, we engaged in observations of classroom instruction, solicited teacher feedback on the instructional design, and analyzed students' writing. Without this information and by only using student data, we might have missed the opportunity to make comprehensive revisions that could address the needs of a larger group of teacher and student learners. Because of DBR, we were able to listen to the voices of our collaborators and redesign the instruction to serve those needs. Teachers appreciated the opportunity to contribute, and this collaboration supports a cohesive program of study embedded within a true educational setting.

REFERENCES

Bereiter, C., & Scardamalia, M. (1987). *The psychology of written composition*. Hillsdale, NJ: Erlbaum.

Dockrell, J., Marshall, C., & Wyse, D. (2016). Teachers' reported practices for teaching writing in England. *Reading & Writing: An Interdisciplinary Journal, 29*(1), 409–434.

Englert, C. S., Raphael, T. E., Anderson, L. M., Anthony, H. M., & Stevens, D. D. (1991). Making strategies and self-talk visible: Writing instruction in regular and special education classrooms. *American Educational Research Journal, 28*, 337–372.

Ferretti, R., & Graham, S. (2019). Argumentative writing: Theory, assessment, and instruction. *Reading and Writing, 32*, 1345–1357.

Ferretti, R. P., & Fan, Y. (2016). Argumentative writing. In C. A. MacArthur, S. Graham, & J. Fitzgerald (Eds.), *Handbook of writing research* (2nd ed., pp. 301–315). New York: Guilford Press.

Fitzgerald, J., & Shanahan, T. (2000). Reading and writing relations and their development. *Educational Psychologist, 35*(1), 39–50.

Gillespie A., Graham, S., Kiuhara, S., & Hebert, M. (2014). High school teachers' use of writing to support students' learning: A national survey. *Reading and Writing: An Interdisciplinary Journal, 27*(2), 1043–1072.

Graham, S. (2006). Strategy instruction and the teaching of writing: A meta-analysis. In C. A. MacArthur, S. Graham, & J. Fitzgerald (Eds.), *Handbook of writing research* (pp. 187–207). New York: Guilford Press.

Graham, S., Bruch, J., Fitzgerald, J., Friedrich, L., Furgeson, J., Greene, K., . . . Smither Wulsin, C. (2016). *Teaching secondary students to write effectively* (NCEE 2017-4002). Washington, DC: National Center for Education Evaluation and Regional Assistance (NCEE), Institute of Education Sciences, U.S. Department of Education. Retrieved from *http://whatworks.ed.gov*.

Graham, S., Harris, K. R., & Chambers, A. B. (2016). Evidence-based practice and writing instruction: A review of reviews. In C. A. MacArthur, S. Graham, & J. Fitzgerald (Eds.), *Handbook of writing research* (2nd ed., pp. 211–226). New York: Guilford Press.

Graham, S., Harris, K., & Santangelo, T. (2015). Research-based writing practices and the Common Core: Meta-analysis and meta-synthesis. *Elementary School Journal, 115*(4), 498–522.

Graham, S., & Hiebert, M. (2010). Writing to read: A meta-analysis of the impact of writing and writing instruction on reading. *Harvard Educational Review, 81,* 710–744.

Graham, S., McKeown, D., Kiuhara, S., & Harris, K. R. (2012). A meta-analysis of writing instruction for students in the elementary grades. *Journal of Educational Psychology, 104,* 879–896.

Graham, S., & Perin, D. (2007). What we know, what we still need to know: Teaching adolescents to write. *Scientific Studies of Reading, 11,* 313–335.

Harris, K. R., & Graham, S. (1999). Problematic intervention research: Illustrations from the evolution of self-regulated strategy development. *Learning Disability Quarterly, 22,* 251–262.

Harris, K. R., & Graham, S. (2009). Self-regulated strategy development in writing: Premises, evolution, and the future. *British Journal of Educational Psychology Monograph Series II, 6,* 113–135.

Hayes, J. R. (1996). A new framework for understanding cognition and affect in writing. In C. M. Levy & S. Ransdell (Eds.), *The science of writing* (pp. 1–27). Mahwah, NJ: Erlbaum.

Hayes, J. R., & Flower, L. (1980). Identifying the organization of writing processes. In L. Gregg & E. R. Steinberg (Eds.), *Cognitive processes in writing* (pp. 3–30). Hillsdale, NJ: Erlbaum.

Knudson, R. (1992). Analysis of argumentative writing at two grade levels. *Journal of Educational Research, 85*(1), 169–179.

Kuhn, D., Shaw, V., & Felton, M. (1997). Effects of dyadic interaction on argumentative reasoning. *Cognition and Instruction, 15*(3), 287–315.

Kuhn, D., & Udell, W. (2007). Coordinating own and other perspectives in argument. *Thinking & Reasoning, 13*(2), 90–104.

MacArthur, C., Graham, S., & Harris, K. R. (2004). Insights from instructional research on revision with struggling writers. In L. Allal, L. Chanquoy, & P. Largy (Eds.), *Revision: Cognitive and instructional processes* (pp. 125–137). Boston: Kluwer Academic.

MacArthur, C. A. (2011). Strategies instruction. In K. R. Harris, S. Graham, & T. Urdan (Eds.), *Educational psychology handbook: Vol. 3. Applications of educational psychology to learning and teaching* (pp. 379–401). Washington, DC: American Psychological Association.

MacArthur, C. A., Philippakos, Z. A., & Ianetta, M. (2015). Self-regulated strategy instruction in college developmental writing. *Journal of Educational Psychology, 107,* 855–867.

Martin, J. R., & Rose, D. (2012). *Learning to write, reading to learn: Genre, knowledge and pedagogy in the Sydney School.* Sheffield, UK: Equinox.

McCutchen, D. (1986). Domain knowledge and linguistic knowledge in the development of writing ability. *Journal of Memory and Language, 25,* 431–444.

McCutchen, D. (2006). Cognitive factors in the development of children's writing. In C. A. MacArthur, S. Graham, & J. Fitzgerald (Eds.), *Handbook of writing research* (pp. 115–130). New York: Guilford Press.

McFarland, J., Hussar, B., de Brey, C., Snyder, T., Wang, X., Wilkinson-Flicker, S., . . . Hinz, S. (2017). *The condition of education 2017* (NCES 2017-144). Washington, DC: National Center for Education Statistics.

Midgette, E., Haria, P., & MacArthur, C. (2008). The effects of content and audience awareness goals for revision on the persuasive essays of fifth- and eighth-grade students. *Reading and Writing, 21*(1–2), 131–151.

National Center for Education Statistics. (2011). *National Assessment of Educational Progress*. Retrieved from *http://nces.ed.gov/nationsreportcard/naepdata*

National Center for Education Statistics. (2012). *National Assessment of Educational Progress*. Retrieved from *http://nces.ed.gov/nationsreportcard/naepdata*

National Governors Association Center for Best Practices & Council of Chief State School Officers. (2010). *Common Core State Standards for English language arts & literacy in history/social studies, science, and technical subjects*. Retrieved from *www.corestandards.org/assets/CCSSI_ELA%20Standards.pdf*

Newell, G., Bloome, D., Kim, M.-Y., & Gof, B. (2019). Shifting epistemologies during instructional conversations about "good" argumentative writing in a high school English language arts classroom. *Reading and Writing: An Interdisciplinary Journal, 32*, 1359–1382.

Northwest Evaluation Association. (2005). *RIT scale norms for use with achievement level tests and measures of academic progress*. Lake Oswego, OR: Author.

Nussbaum, E. M., Dove, I., Slife, N., Kardash, C. M., Turgut, R., & Vallett, D. B. (2018). Using critical questions to evaluate written and oral arguments in an undergraduate general education seminar: A quasi-experimental study. *Reading and Writing: An Interdisciplinary Journal, 32*(2), 1531–1522.

OECD. (2019). *PISA 2018 Assessment and Analytical Framework, PISA*. Paris: OECD Publishing.

Pearson, P. D., & Gallagher, M. C. (1983). The instruction of reading comprehension. *Contemporary Educational Psychology, 8*(3), 317–344.

Philippakos, Z. (2018). Using a task analysis process for reading and writing assignments. *Reading Teacher, 72*(1), 107–114.

Philippakos, Z. A., & MacArthur, C. A. (2016). The effects of giving feedback on the persuasive writing of fourth- and fifth-grade students. *Reading Research Quarterly, 51*(4), 419–433.

Philippakos, Z. A., & MacArthur, C. A. (2020). *Developing strategic, young writers through genre instruction: Resources for grades K–2*. New York: Guilford Press.

Philippakos. Z. A., MacArthur, C. A., & Coker, D. L. (2015). *Developing strategic writers through genre instruction: Resources for grades 3–5*. New York: Guilford Press.

Rose, D. (2016). New developments in genre-based literacy pedagogy. In C. A. MacArthur, S. Graham, & J. Fitzgerald (Eds.), *Handbook of writing research* (pp. 227–242). New York: Guilford Press.

Schunk, D. H., & Hanson, A. R. (1989). Self-modeling and children's cognitive skill learning. *Journal of Educational Psychology, 81*(1), 155–163.

Shanahan, T. (1984). The nature of the reading-writing relations: An exploratory multivariate analysis. *Journal of Educational Psychology, 76*, 466–477.

Shanahan, T. (2006). Relations among oral language, reading, and writing development. In C. A. MacArthur & J. Fitzgerald (Eds.), *Handbook of writing research* (pp. 171–183). New York: Guilford Press.

Shanahan, T. (2009). Connecting reading and writing instruction for struggling learners. In G. A. Troia (Ed.), *Instruction and assessment for struggling writers: Evidence-based practices* (pp. 113–131). New York: Guilford Press.

Shanahan, T. (2016). Relationships between reading and writing development. In C. A. MacArthur, S. Graham, & J. Fitzgerald (Eds.), *Handbook of writing research* (2nd ed., pp. 194–207). New York: Guilford Press.

Shanahan, T. (2018). Reading-writing connections. In S. Graham., C. A. MacArthur, & M. Hebert (Eds.), *Best practices in writing instruction* (3rd ed., pp. 309–332). New York: Guilford Press.

Tierney, R. J., & Shanahan, T. (1991). Research on the reading-writing relationship: Interactions, transactions, and outcomes. In R. Barr, M. L. Kamil, P. Mosenthal, & P. D. Pearson (Eds.), *Handbook of reading research* (Vol. II, pp. 246–280). New York: Longman.

Topping, K. (1998). Peer assessment between students in colleges and universities. *Review of Educational Research, 68*(3), 249–276.

Traga Philippakos, Z. (2019). Effects of strategy instruction with an emphasis on oral language and dramatization on the quality of first graders' procedural writing. *Reading & Writing Quarterly, 35*(5), 409–426.

Traga Philippakos, Z. A. (2020a). A yearlong, professional development model on genre-based strategy instruction on writing. *Journal of Educational Research, 113*(2), 1–14.

Traga Philippakos, Z. A. (2020b). Developing strategic learners: Supporting self-efficacy through goal setting and reflection. *The Language and Literacy Spectrum, 30*(1), 1–24.

Traga Philippakos, Z. A., & FitzPatrick, E. (2018). A proposed tiered model of assessment in writing instruction: Supporting all student-writers. *Insights into Learning Disabilities: From Prevailing Theories to Validated Approaches, 55*(2), 149–174.

Traga Philippakos, Z. A., & MacArthur, C. A. (in press). Examination of genre-based strategy instruction in middle school English language arts and science. *The Clearing House: A Journal of Educational Strategies, Issues and Ideas.*

Traga Philippakos, Z. A., & MacArthur, C. A. (2020). Integrating collaborative reasoning and strategy instruction to improve second graders' opinion writing. *Reading & Writing Quarterly, 36*(4), 379–395.

Traga Philippakos, Z., MacArthur, C., & Munsell, S. (2018). Collaborative reasoning with strategy instruction for opinion writing in primary grades: Two cycles of design research. *Reading & Writing Quarterly, 34*(6), 485–504.

Voss, J. F., & Van Dyke, J. A. (2001). Argumentation in psychology: Background comments. *Discourse Processes, 32*(1), 89–111.

Walton, D. N. (1989). Dialogue theory for critical thinking. *Argumentation, 3*, 169–184.

PART III
DESIGN-BASED RESEARCH AND SPECIFIC APPLICATIONS

CHAPTER 7

Literacy Is Transformative
Secondary Reading Interventions Using Design-Based Research

Alejandro Gonzalez Ojeda, Nancy Frey,
Douglas Fisher, and Diane Lapp

The National Assessment of Educational Progress (NAEP) results for reading paint a discouraging picture: Scores for eighth-grade students have actually declined since the last administration in 2017. The decline is not evenly distributed. Categories of individuals who identify as Black, Hispanic, Native American/Alaska Native, or Two or More Races youth experience a more precipitous decline. More specifically when compared with their white and Asian peers, those who identified as Black, Native American, and Two or More Races declined 5 points, and students identifying as Hispanic declined 4 points. Similar declines among the same student groups were evidenced on the Trial Urban District Assessment (TUDA). Of the 11 districts in the trial, 10 reported lower reading scores for eighth graders (the District of Columbia was the only one with gains). Both the NAEP and TUDA reaffirm what many secondary educators already know—too many adolescents struggle with reading. More specifically, all students of color scored lower than their white counterparts who also showed a decline in their scores. Only Asian students showed a growth of 1 point. Furthermore, low literacy rates negatively impact knowledge acquisition as core subjects from history, science, and mathematics require significant reading skills, even while there is little literacy instruction available in those courses (Heller & Greenleaf, 2007).

Health Sciences High and Middle College in San Diego was the site of this intervention, and where we all work. We observed through assessment of daily in-class and homework performance that several students, within each grade, were exhibiting below-grade-level literacy skills. These literacy needs were being exhibited by students, especially those who were learning English as an additional language. These insights were first noted by classroom teachers in the form of concerns addressed to school coaches suggesting that within each class several students were unable to read the texts and assigned articles. Like many adolescents, they did not want to be exposed to their peers, so instead they acted out in class in order to refocus attention from their inabilities to read the subject-related materials to their clowning around in class. Once these concerns were identified, we met to determine the validity of the claims and to design a plan of action that would support these students in gaining the needed literacy skills.

A result of continued low literacy levels in adolescence and low progress in academic achievement is decreasing motivation in schooling in general and reading in particular. Klauda and Guthrie (2015) discussed three elements of motivation in reading: devaluing, perceived difficulty, and peer devaluing. The first, *devaluing*, is the belief that reading is not important, and therefore it is not worth pursuing. *Perceived difficulty* is the added perception that reading is too hard and therefore not within a learner's realm of accomplishment. The third, *peer devaluing*, is the conviction that classmates do not respect a learner's reading ability. The researchers noted that "students' negative perceptions of their peers' goals for them (such as telling them to leave school as soon as possible) relate negatively to both elementary and high school students' GPA" (2014, p. 242). The damage caused by low reading skills is not only academic; it is also emotional and psychological. Literacy levels are associated with employment, lifetime earnings, and involvement in civic life (Kutner et al., 2007). Turning around learning for students not able to read at grade level is crucial as those identified as struggling readers in third grade rarely catch up. In fact, students not proficient in reading by the end of third grade are 4 times more likely to drop out of high school than proficient readers (Casey Foundation, 2010).

Unlocking Adolescent Reading Skills and Challenges

Students who fail to make progress in reading do so for a variety of reasons, and together these factors amplify their stagnation. One contributing factor is the background knowledge and inherent vocabulary students lack, which are needed to comprehend increasingly complex texts. Readers draw on their knowledge of the topic to understand, and vocabulary in particular is a strong predictor of reading comprehension (e.g., Cromley & Azevedo, 2007; Suggate, Schaughency, McAnally, & Reese, 2018). However, the inability to comprehend grade-level texts interferes with the learner's ability to acquire knowledge, thus creating a downward spiral—as knowledge lags, so do reading comprehension and vocabulary acquisition.

For adolescents reading far below grade level, generally defined as 4 or more years below expected proficiency, sound-and-word- and sentence-level difficulties abound. Many of these students fail to acquire the necessary decoding and fluency skills needed for basic comprehension as emergent or early readers in elementary school (Catts, Compton, Tomblin, & Bridges, 2012; Verhoeven & van Leeuwe, 2008). However, their reading profiles present a more checkered array of strengths and gaps. Some may have relative language or knowledge skills that are idiosyncratic to the topic, such as knowing quite a bit about World War II, which can somewhat obscure (at least temporarily) their reading deficiencies. Other students may have experienced interrupted schooling and missed crucial instruction. Still others may be learning English as a subsequent language, learning English while learning *in* English and thus facing double the work (Short & Fitzsimmons, 2007).

Addressing Challenges in Designing a Reading Intervention for Adolescents

We identified three main challenges in designing reading interventions for adolescents who perform far below grade level. The first challenge has to do with reading skills. Adolescent readers need to possess the skills of decoding and fluency needed for basic comprehension. Reader profile variance between students is essential for understanding the unique nature of intervention for struggling adolescent readers. Unlike their younger counterparts who struggle in ways that are more similar to one another, older poor readers often present a more scattered array of strengths and gaps. Therefore, ongoing reading and language assessment data, both quantitative and qualitative, would be crucial for progress monitoring. However, for those who struggle there exists continued study and debate regarding causes and scientifically based reading supports (Lyon & Chhabra, 2004; National Institute of Child Health and Human Development, 2000; Shaywitz & Shaywitz, 2003; Snowling & Hulme, 2008). Chief among these has been the science of reading (Dehaene, 2009; Seidenberg, 2017; Willingham, 2017) and related best instructional practices (Foorman et al., 2016; Mesmer, 2020; Seidenberg, 2013).

The second challenge lies in ensuring that knowledge building continued during intervention sessions that maintained relevance to subject-matter courses. Intervention often advances the idiom of *rob Peter to pay Paul* conundrum, which involves students missing subject-matter instruction while working with a reading interventionist. It would be essential to design an intervention process that can be aligned to the academic knowledge students would be using in their courses, rather than relying on more generic intervention materials developed to focus on general reading skills.

A third challenge was to remain mindful of the emotional and psychological ramifications of an intervention. On the one hand, formally identifying students as being in need of intensive reading intervention supports could have an unintended negative effect on their social emotional learning especially if their peers become aware of it. Reading motivation among adolescent struggling readers is undermined by devaluing and perceived difficulty (Klauda & Guthrie, 2015) and the effort they are willing to expend (Cantrell, Rintamaa, Anderman, & Anderman, 2018). On the other hand, we were hopeful that students would welcome receiving much needed support and intervention. We were well aware that balancing the academic press needed to continue to gain knowledge, while at the same time addressing reading skills associated with younger readers, would require careful balance. Kim et al. (2017) aptly summarized these challenges:

> Although there are engagement-focused approaches to adolescent literacy instruction ... struggling readers also need instruction in word- and sentence-level processes that underlie skilled reading. Multicomponent reading interventions often include isolated practice on basic reading skills but rarely embed basic skills work in more cognitively challenging and engaging literacy activities. As a consequence, students may fail to see the relevance of skills work and may lack adequate opportunities for applying new skills in meaningful and cognitively demanding contexts. (p. 358)

To blend the identification of the needs with instruction that was very explicit but not exposing, we developed the Literacy Is Transformative Lab (LIT Lab), a reading intervention program designed to provide struggling high school readers with one-to-one intensive intervention for 6-week cycles of 30-minute sessions, between 2 to 4 times per week.

Using Design-Based Research to Design the Intervention

The LIT Lab was designed as a response to concerns about students struggling with reading and how to best support them. Modeled as a formative experiment (Reinking & Bradley, 2008; see also Chapters 8 and 12, this volume), the LIT Lab is an intervention purposefully designed so that data and results from the process and student outcomes would inform revisions to the intervention using an iterative approach to future modifications to the intervention (Reinking & Watkins, 1998). To ensure that a method of data collection and analysis was embedded in the intervention, the following sequential framework was used to guide the development, monitoring, and evaluation of the intervention (Reinking & Watkins, 1998):

1. Identify and justify a valued pedagogical goal.
2. Specify an instructional intervention and provide a rationale for why it might potentially be effective.
3. Collect data to determine which factors in the educational environment enhance or inhibit the specified intervention's effectiveness.
4. Use data to modify the intervention to achieve the pedagogical goal more efficiently and effectively.
5. Consider what positive or negative effects the intervention is producing beyond those associated with the pedagogical goal.
6. Consider the extent to which the educational environment has changed as a result of the intervention.

Quantitative and qualitative data were used to help identify students who would best benefit from the one-on-one support that this intervention will provide, focusing specifically on improving their reading, language, writing, and content comprehension skills. Immediate considerations were made by reviewing students' Lexile scores, a quantitative measure of reading ability, as well as state English language arts test scores, and teacher recommendations based on student work and observations of progress across their courses. Based on these initial and continuing assessments, instruction was designed, implemented, and monitored. The intent for each student was to bridge the chasm between his or her existing and grade-level literacy skills so that the student could function successfully and independently in each of his or her subject-specific classes. In doing so, we continually assessed the occurrences at the Literacy Lab by the five constructs of design-based research (DBR) identified by Wang and Hannafin (2005) as "pragmatic, grounded, iterative and flexible, integrative, and contextual" (p. 7). The intervention was both pragmatic and grounded because we took a practical approach to support the learning of students within the context of their learning site. Scheduling was flexible to accommodate their preexisting class participation. Because we had identified grade-level skill development for each student, we were able to implement a process that was iterative and flexible enough to be continually redesigned within an existing school context. Each student remained central in the design-based assessment and planning of instructional interventions that had the goal of ensuring literacy skill development.

School Profile

The school featured in this study, Health Sciences High and Middle College (HSHMC), is a Title I school located in an urban area of San Diego, which serves over 600 students in grades 9–12, 75% of which qualify for free and reduced-price meals. The school's student population reflects that of the city of San Diego, with the majority of the student body being Hispanic (54%). The next largest population are African American students, at 20.70%. The most recent reported graduation rate for the school is 98.70%, an indication that students enrolled at the school persevere at high levels. In the most recent state testing, 36.72% of students met and 20.31% exceeded the ELA standards for California's annual summative assessment, the California Assessment of Student Performance and Progress (CAASPP). California schools also report College and Career Indicators (CCI) for post-high school readiness. In the 2018–2019 school year, HSHMC reported 76% of students prepared under CCI indicator criteria.

Similar to many schools in the community, a large percentage of HSHMC's student population come from households where the primary language is a language other than English. A total of 68% of students at the school speak a language other than English. Spanish is the predominant language at 54%, followed by 8%

speaking Somali and 5% identifying another non-English language. Although most of the students speak another language at home, only 90 students were identified as being English learners in the most recent reporting year. This number reflects the school's long-term efforts at supporting English learners through development of targeted program and curriculum supports. Most recently, the school's work on supporting English learners has shown an increase in redesignated fluent English-proficient students, up from 232 three years ago to 294 in the last school year.

Since the school opened its doors, it has adopted and maintained an inclusive education model to support special education students. Part of the school's vision is to provide access and opportunities for all students to rigorous education curriculum. The percentage of students at the school who qualified for special education services under an individualized education program (IEP) is 17%. The school actively recruits students with disabilities to better represent and support the larger community, and those currently reflect 13 of the 14 federal eligibility criteria. This inclusive model includes comprehensive supports across all grade levels, content areas, clubs, sports, and other school organizations. Collaboration between content-area teachers and educational specialists is a key component of the school's inclusive model. Education specialists are assigned to support a single content area across all grade levels. This allows for cross-grade-level alignment as students matriculate through their high school years. Opportunities for immediate and long-term instructional planning in support of student learning are part of the model, as content-area teachers and education specialists work closely to synchronize curriculum supports, as well as to increase readiness for a student's next steps in achieving set goals.

Intervention Participants

The LIT Lab has provided intervention services to 57 high school students since its inception in the 2018–2019 school year, 30 ninth- and 27 tenth-grade students in total. These numbers fluctuate as students cycle in and out of the intervention based on their progress during and monitoring that takes place after a student's intervention cycle. In its most recent roster, the intervention served 8 ninth-grade and 33 tenth-grade students. In the ninth-grade roster, 3 students were female and 5 were male. The tenth-grade roster consisted of 20 female and 14 male students. Each of the ninth-grade students also qualified for an IEP, while none of the tenth-grade students had an IEP.

Phase 1: The Initial Intervention

The first iteration of the LIT Lab involved two intervention teachers, and a smaller group of students than the second, much larger, present version. In the fall of 2018, there were nine students who participated in a one-to-one literacy intervention. Students for this first iteration were identified through analysis of Lexile scores, which are collected for all students through the online, independent, and adaptive reading program called Achieve3000. The first students had the lowest Lexile scores in their grade levels. The number of students to be served was based on the daily capacity of a single reading intervention teacher. Sessions were 30 minutes in length, utilized materials from existing reading intervention programs, and were supplemented with some teacher-created lessons. There was no end-date identified; these students wound up being served for 19 weeks.

An initial concern of ours was how the intervention was being perceived by students and by classroom teachers. The reading intervention teacher had students write their impressions of the intervention as part of their exit ticket at the end of each intervention session. An analysis of responses from all nine participating students proved to be generally favorable. The exit tickets were analyzed by intervention teachers to identify any concerns or problems that could be addressed with practical solutions within processes in an intervention session and inform the intervention. The analysis of data informed the iterative design of the intervention, as it provided insights to evaluate learner progress as well as components of the intervention and the overall design. A ninth-grade student provided a response in the fourth week that was illustrative of this sentiment: "I like that I get help for reading. I am getting to be a better reader." Despite our misgivings, we discovered that once the routines were established, students showed a positive outlook and participated in the intervention. As noted by the intervention teacher at the time,

"Kids were kind of stiff when I would go get them out of their class. But they relaxed and got more talkative pretty quickly. We talk while we're walking down the hall and, by the time we get to the LIT Lab, they'd be smiling."

Scheduling with the teacher, however, was more of a problem. One teacher's humanities class was identified as being the point of contact. There was a surface logic to this, as the course involved both ELA and social studies, which seemed to make it an ideal location for mirroring subject-matter content. In addition, we believed that it would work better to coordinate the intervention with a single teacher, who was supportive of the initiative. In practice, however, it became burdensome for the humanities teacher, as students were constantly in and out of her room. In an interview, she said, "It's hard to keep track of who is present for an activity and who isn't. Lots of interruptions are making it tough for me to make sure they are all getting what they need from my class." This challenge intensified as the weeks went by, as we realized that we had not put an endpoint on the intervention. There were students who were making progress, as measured by their Lexile scores, writing and reading fluency scores, and decoding skills. But, the reading intervention teacher was unsure about when or if to end or continue the intervention support with individual students. As the spring semester began, we recognized that we needed to revise the intervention to include data-based decision making (DBDM; see Filderman, Toste, Didion, Peng, & Clemens, 2018, for a meta-analysis on the use of DBDM in reading interventions), and to rethink how and when students would receive intervention services. In doing so, we returned to our experiences with a short-burst interval reading intervention we had designed and implemented with primary students (Frey, Lapp, & Fisher, 2009).

Phase 2: Modifying the Intervention

While we had some preliminary evidence that there was a positive impact on students' reading skills and dispositions, we also needed to confront the length and intensity of the intervention. We decided to deploy a short-cycle reading intervention schedule similar to the one we had used at an elementary school in the same community. Based on the success we had with that model and the evidence that the effects endured over a 3-year time span, we reconceived this intervention as a 6-week cycle. Students would now receive reading intervention support for 6 weeks, then monitored for an additional 6 weeks by tracking their Lexile scores, course grades, and soliciting classroom teacher reports about motivation and engagement. In the meantime, a new cohort of students would be receiving reading intervention during this second cycle. At the end of the second 6-week cycle, any students from the first cycle who failed to make progress would be re-enrolled in the third cycle. We referred to this approach as "academic booster shots" that could be delivered as needed for those who did not sustain the initial momentum generated by the intervention (Frey et al., 2009, p. 39).

Of primary concern was monitoring the intervention's effectiveness by examining student progress. A majority of students who were on track, based on assessment information, participated in a single 6-week cycle. But for students who showed little growth during the 6-week cycle, there had been a modification to the length of the cycle in which they participated. Slightly less than half (44%) of the high school students who participated in the intervention had their cycles modified to go beyond 6-week cycles. As a result, a change was implemented to further support students who continued to struggle and may require ongoing, rather than short-term, one-to-one intervention. Thus, students who had not seen a significant increase in their growth to be on track for meeting their projected goals participated in an additional intervention cycle for a total of 12 weeks. Extended time in a reading intervention has not historically proven to increase an older struggling student's progress (Scammacca, Roberts, Vaughn, & Stuebing, 2015), including those identified as English learners (Ludwig, Guo, & Georgiou, 2019). However, the increased emphasis on DBDM in this intervention has been done in order to increase its precision, not only in terms of the individualized content, but also who the individual is (Filderman et al., 2018). Based on the learning and instructional insights we continue to gain through DBR, we encourage that every classroom teacher use a similar framework to identify students' strengths and needs and continually scaffold the next steps of instruction. Using this model invites teachers to view grade-level expectations for students as competencies and then continually assess attainment while providing needed scaffolds to ensure success.

Monitoring Impact on Student Progress

Understanding as much as possible about students is imperative to best support their learning. If teachers are persistent in their efforts to get to know as much as possible about their students as learners and as people, then they are better prepared to connect with their students and support their needs (Lee, 2012). Considering the plethora of data that can be collected through assessments, the intervention was designed to allow for intervention teachers to be informed about their students with as much quantitative and qualitative data as could be gathered through intervention cycles.

To facilitate data collection, an intervention monitoring tool was developed to help collect and monitor student progress across four metrics: reading level, fluency in oral reading, writing, and vocabulary scores. Throughout the school year, monthly assessments were administered and the data were collected in individual student monitoring templates and then compiled into a master spreadsheet database, which provided the intervention team with a broader look at trends and patterns in student progress (see Figure 7.1).

The first metric documented in the monitoring tool was the reading level. Along with the reported Lexile level, the reading intervention teacher also recorded the expected Lexile level of the student, based on his or her grade level. Because all students in the school used this program as part of their science and history literacy curricula, these data were readily obtained and proved to be a convenient way to gauge progress during and after intervention cycles. The availability of this data to both content-area and intervention teachers was a key part of facilitating conversations, as all supporting teachers were working with the same metric.

Oral reading fluency was the second area of assessment on the monitoring tool. Fluency is measured by assessing three factors: a qualitative measure of prosody, the number of words read correctly per minute (WCPM), and answers to comprehension questions. The intervention team used a digital tool that facilitated this process by having students read text aloud on a computer. The tool captured the student's reading as an audio recording and used an algorithm to measure a student's fluency. The tool provided a report on each metric and produced a running record that was accessible digitally.

Digital tools and algorithms did some of the heavy lifting in the analytical processing of the work students produce. By leveraging two digital tools to help with scoring and reporting growth in their respective metrics, intervention teachers were able to focus their attention on other forms of supportive instruction and assessments during the sessions. Writing and vocabulary were two areas that were assessed and monitored manually by intervention teachers. Instructional materials and multiple assessments for writing and vocabulary were developed and curated by each intervention teacher to provide the individualized support each student needed. In assessing a student's level of writing, intervention teachers guided students through timed writing exercises. The number of words per minute a student

Name						Grade				
	Sep	Oct	Nov	Dec	Jan	Feb	Mar	Apr	May	Jun
Reading (Expected Lexile level ___)										
Level										
Oral Reading (Expected text level ___)										
Level										
WCPM										
Comprehension										
Writing										
WPM										
Score										
Errors										
Vocabulary										
% correct out of 20										

FIGURE 7.1. Intervention monitoring.

writes during an exercise was tracked by the intervention teacher and recorded. While a student composed a response, the intervention teacher observed for timing, composition, and errors. Writing prompts were developed from a variety of sources, including those relative to what students were learning in their courses.

Similarly, comprehension of vocabulary was assessed through a collection of word banks developed in collaboration with content-area teachers. Using a curriculum-based measurement approach for secondary students developed by Espin, Shin, and Busch (2005), reading interventionists collaborated with content teachers to identify vocabulary terms currently being used in their classes. Performance on vocabulary matching tasks provided them with a progress monitoring metric to gauge whether reading comprehension skills learned during intervention were being transferred to content-area learning.

Results of Intervention

The results from the data collected through the monitoring tool span from initial recording in September 2019 through February 2020. This time roughly spans shortly after the beginning of the school year to near the end of the first semester grading period. The intervention was suspended for the remainder of the 2019–2020 school year due to the COVID-19 pandemic that forced the school's closure. Ninth-grade intervention participants averaged Lexile growth of +108.78. The highest gain experienced by an individual ninth-grade student was 490 Lexile points. Growth was maintained for this student after the initial 6-week cycle, as he continued to make gains from an initial 190L pre-intervention score to a current level of 680L, including an additional 30-point increase between the time the intervention cycle ended and the school closed. His early progress post-intervention is a hopeful sign that he will continue to benefit from the initial momentum gained during the intervention.

Results from the tenth-grade group of students indicated an average growth of 92.5 Lexile points. This group consisted of 33 students, 50% of whom showed a triple-digit increase in Lexile over time. The highest increase was 290 Lexile points for a student who had a baseline of 765 in September 2019 and gradually grew to 1055L through February 2020.

Results for oral reading in the same timeline showed more fluctuation in certain areas, particularly in oral reading level. Both ninth- and tenth-grade students showcased a trend in assessing at a higher oral reading level initially, and then dropping a level or two in the next two monthly assessments, before trending up again in the late January assessment. A consistent frequency of assessments is needed to help capture student progress and inform next steps. It was also observed that WCPM and comprehension tended to follow this same trend as the student achieved, experienced a dip midway, and then scored a little higher in the most recent assessment. Data on comprehension showed that 75% of the ninth-grade participants reported above 60%. In the tenth-grade group, 69% of students reported comprehension at

60% or above. In addition, 21 of the 33 tenth-grade students achieved 100% on the most recent vocabulary assessments in February 2020. One student had reported 40%, though the data fluctuated over the previous two assessments, ranging from 80 to 100%. It is important to note that these data points are snapshots in time, and although they indicate a student's performance, it is within the context of the content being used to assess. It is not possible to know the extent to which knowledge informed growth in reading, and vice versa.

Data Are Only Half the Story

There was a synergy that resulted from the partnership between reading intervention and grade-level teachers, and the connections that were created with students through the multifaceted approach in supporting their growth in the intervention. Each session offered opportunities for students to be vulnerable, more so than in a larger class setting. Intervention teachers expressed the value of connecting with students beyond simply teaching and assessing, and attributed much of what they knew about their students from having deeper conversations with them on who they were as learners and individuals. By creating a time and place where students felt safe, students were willing to let down their guard and practice skills they had been reluctant to use in a larger class setting, such as reading aloud or participating in discussions. The trust that intervention teachers built with students also benefited other grade-level teachers, as all the teachers were then able to learn more about the students and how to support them through the collaborative opportunities in professional learning community (PLC) sessions. Reading intervention teachers attended part of the weekly grade-level meetings to provide updates on student progress and highlight possible support steps to use in classes. The goal of these efforts was that the literacy instruction being shared by the LIT Lab teachers became familiar enough to classroom teachers to apply in their own classes.

Impact on Student Confidence

Students acknowledged their growth, as well as their areas for improvement, as an outcome of their participation in the intervention cycles. All students who participated in a cycle identified personal next steps to apply their skills within their content-area classes. What truly stood out was the level of self-confidence that students now exhibited when they recognized their growth. In some cases, students expressed their confidence by acknowledging an increase in class participation or completion of class readings. One student said that the LIT Lab helped her "because I feel more confident in my reading and writing. I can read faster and write more too." Another student stated, "I volunteer more in class and read more books by myself," and attributed his motivation to read to being more confident in his abilities. Finally, one student was quoted as saying, "The LIT Lab taught me to never give up!"

Literacy Is Transformative

The LIT Lab intervention was designed to increase student literacy skills to benefit not only their academics, but also their confidence as learners. In designing this intervention, we gave strategic considerations to design questions that guided our planning. We used and adapted a set of design inquiry questions to determine logistics, practices, supports, and evaluative measures to address implementation of the intervention. See Figure 7.2 for a detailed look at the design questions (Frey et al., 2009).

Learning Points

Throughout the DBR and the cycles of design, implementation, analysis, and iterations, we have attempted to chronicle our decision-making processes and how we made adjustments using the quantitative and qualitative data gathered from

Elements of Intervention Design	Design Questions
Before the intervention: communication and logistics	• Who will coordinate? • How will stakeholders (teachers, administrators, families) be consulted? • How will interventionists be identified? • What materials will be used? How will they be obtained? • What are the space requirements? • What are the scheduling requirements? • What is the budget for the intervention?
Before the intervention: establishing practices	• What is the intent of the intervention? • What is the method of delivery? • What lesson framework fits the intent? • What are the duration and frequency of the intervention? • What formative assessments will be used? • How will data be collected?
During the intervention: ongoing support	• How will interventionists be trained? • How will they be coached? • How will they access professional development? • How will they communicate with classroom teachers? • How will ongoing assessments be utilized to make instructional decisions?
After the intervention: making decisions about next steps	• What do the collected data, both qualitative and quantitative, reflect about the intervention? • What improvements can be made for the next intervention? • How will students gain access to the next intervention?
After the intervention: academic booster shots	• At what interval will subsequent interventions occur? • How will continuity from one intervention cycle to the next be assured?

FIGURE 7.2. Design questions for reading interventions. Adapted with permission from Frey, Lapp, and Fisher (2009). Copyright © 2009 International Literacy Association.

students and staff. We reached specific learning points that were identified and informed through practice (see Noyes, 2008, regarding addressing how rather than why change occurs) and were manifested across three dimensions: how the intervention team worked internally; how the intervention team worked in the larger context of the school; and how we strengthened the intervention through DBR by involving the wider school community, including content-area teachers and the instructional technology team.

The Reading Intervention Team

The reading intervention team consisted of five members: a lead intervention advisor, two full-time reading intervention teachers, and two part-time reading intervention teachers. The make-up of this team was strategic in both teacher expertise and the emphasis of their work with the specific students they support. The lead advisor (Diane), was an experienced educator with deep knowledge and experience in the field of early and adolescent literacy. The role of the lead advisor was to help guide the design of the intervention based on academic achievement gaps in reading and writing, oversee the implementation of the designated intervention strategies, and provide guidance to the reading intervention teachers in relation to the practices implemented and the modification of these practices based on evaluation of student progress.

The four reading intervention teachers implemented the intervention cycles with their respective student groups. Two were full-time, meaning they were solely dedicated to this intervention program, and two other teachers were part-time, splitting their time with the intervention program and other duties at the school site. One part-time reading intervention teacher focused on supporting a small group of ninth-grade students who also had an IEP. This group of students received additional dedicated one-on-one literacy support through this intervention. The second part-time reading intervention teacher focused on supporting tenth-grade students who had also been identified as English learners. Each teacher collected data for their respective students, which informed progress and modifications of the intervention approaches as needed.

Professional Learning for Reading Intervention Teachers

Ongoing support is a crucial component of DBR. In this case, the professional learning of each reading intervention teacher was an important investment made to improve the learning experience of the students and the overall impact of the intervention effort. There were professional learning opportunities that were scheduled each week and were specifically designed for reading intervention teachers to learn, share their findings with grade-level teachers, and gather feedback to inform the intervention program itself.

Literacy Is Transformative

Formal in-house professional learning sessions were led by the lead advisor. During these sessions, the facilitator guided the reading intervention team through an analysis of quantitative and qualitative data to measure student growth, introducing or revisiting a specific strategy, and reviewing instructional materials. Datasets were sourced from multiple instruments and analytic services. These included the intervention monitoring tool, which was specifically designed for the LIT Lab; student reports on progress from the digital Lexile development tool; reports measuring fluency and comprehension scores produced by the audio recording tool; and student observation notes from the reading intervention teacher collected during sessions. Analysis of multiple data sources was an important practice as it helped the team determine what was working and what needed to be addressed strategically. Using data to inform next steps is a critical component of the team's collaboration in evaluating the intervention process and making modifications as needed to its design.

The success of the team as a whole required that each intervention teacher have a foundational understanding of the literacy strategies that were part of the intervention's design, that each can properly implement a strategy and monitor student progress. To this end, the in-house professional learning sessions offered the lead advisor opportunities to facilitate introducing and modeling a new strategy, as well as returning to a strategy that had been in place. In a similar fashion, instructional materials were introduced or revisited as needed during these dedicated intervention team sessions. Throughout intervention cycles, conversations also addressed ways of making appropriate accommodations and modifications for students that would benefit them or identify accommodations in IEP that provide such supports to be in place.

Partnerships with Instructional Technology

Reading intervention teachers must also be familiar with and confident in using the digital resources that are adopted to help students develop skills as well as provide metrics on student growth. To support the team's understanding of the mechanics of the tool from a teacher's and a student's perspective, representatives from each tool's development company provided initial trainings to the team members and the school site's technology support team early at the start of the school year. Product-specific training took place over the summer, and follow-up sessions were scheduled during the school year to provide ongoing support to the intervention teachers. School site technology team supports were also available to help the intervention team with the technical aspects of the digital tools. Both the product and school site technology supports were good partnerships to have in helping address the custom setup of tool environments, rosters, complexity levels, and such, as each tool may have components and information that are necessary to function properly, and often can be unique for each student.

Involvement in the Broader School Context

Once a week throughout the study, a PLC session took place for an hour and a half. During these sessions, the reading intervention team became part of a larger group of school site educator teams. This larger schoolwide intervention PLC involved educators working in other teams that support intervention efforts not specific to literacy development. The group consisted of a student advancement and reteaching team, an independent study program, the educational technology support team, and special education support teachers. These weekly PLC sessions created a time and space for the intervention teams to come together and review data specific to their programs, discuss trending issues regarding learning interventions, and possible strategies that can benefit a concerted effort from each program. In addition to the reading intervention team, a student was also receiving supports from one or more of these PLC intervention teams. Therefore, these PLC sessions offered each member opportunities to share further insight on students, and also allowed for each PLC member to learn from one another additional strategies and tools that could be used to support their respective efforts. This PLC shared a common challenge, supporting the growth of struggling students across grade levels. By participating in this type of PLC, the reading intervention teachers gained a deeper knowledge of what was taking place in other academic efforts that several reading intervention students may also experience. Having another connection to the learner, outside of a single intervention session, expanded the lens into what approaches a student responded to or which ones had not yielded results in academic growth. Through this PLC, all participating educators were able to gather a more well-rounded understanding of intervention efforts, determine areas of need and resources to assist, and inform their own practices.

Communication with Content-Area Teachers

In addition to the intervention PLC sessions, reading intervention teachers also participated in a weekly combined ninth- and tenth-grade-level meeting with content-area teachers. The connection between content-area and reading intervention teachers helped form a relationship through which a two-way dialogue took place. This feedback loop informed the instruction of struggling readers on two fronts. First, reading intervention teachers had the opportunity to highlight a student and provide an update on that student's progress. This brief snapshot of a student opened the floor for conversations regarding the student, what the content teachers were observing from student work samples, and further insight on student successes and needs within their classrooms. Second, these insights were then taken into consideration by the reading intervention teachers to further refine the student's support during individualized sessions, and also curated content to integrate what was being used within content courses to further support knowledge building and reading skills. Learning more about the student allowed for intervention and grade-level teachers alike to develop a more in-depth understanding of the student and the types of supports required to help him or her succeed. If a content teacher is not aware of the student's reading, fluency, writing, or vocabulary abilities, then they may not be able to properly support the student. On the other hand, if the intervention team does not know what content is being covered, and how the student is performing in classes, then it is more difficult to help provide the student with contextualized instruction that will be relevant to his or her learning. The relationship between content and intervention teachers provided incredible value to the intervention effort and informs best approaches to support the student.

Conclusion

Professional learning is important for all educators, and in our DBR, we integrated opportunities for LIT Lab teachers to receive, participate in, and contribute to their professional growth and that of their educator peers to create a strong collective effort based on shared knowledge and skills. These PLC partnerships across intervention teams and grade-level teachers allowed for reading intervention teachers to raise awareness of student literacy abilities and communicate their needs. For example, a grade-level teacher may express concerns regarding a specific student, though not have the proper knowledge on how to best support the student without an assessment, or an understanding of the literacy strategies that can be strategically implemented to support this student. Creating a communication loop is key to share information about the student and his or her learning needs, as well as to inform intervention teachers of content that was relevant to use in an intervention cycle. In addition, content-area teachers became more familiar with literacy building strategies that they could use in their classrooms to extend supports.

We identified three challenges for this reading intervention that have informed our approach. The first is to enhance the reading skills of adolescents, and our early results appeared to show success in this realm. We were heartened that a slight majority of students (56%) maintained and increased their reading proficiency after the 6-week cycle ended. Our monitoring of the students who received a second consecutive intervention cycle continued until school closure. As we continue to participate in distance learning, we will examine both the trajectory of growth and its association with the individualized session content. This is a question that remains unanswered and will require more time to do so.

The second challenge identified is content knowledge building. There is a tension between providing individualized supports yet decreasing the time in quality core instruction. We addressed this in several ways. The first was in staying apprised of the topics currently being taught in content courses in order to align materials to contribute to the student's knowledge in meaningful ways. This required that reading intervention teachers and content teachers communicate regularly about student progress and subject-matter demands. In addition, otherwise well-intentioned interventions (not just reading interventions) can be undermined when the student experiences them as fractured events that are not related to one another. We have learned that in a busy high school, coordinated efforts cannot be left to chance. Teachers needed scheduled time to have these conversations, and grade-level meetings and professional learning communities made that possible.

The third challenge we identified was understanding and responding to the psychological and emotional needs of struggling adolescent readers. Reading motivation and poor self-concept are linked (e.g., Cantrell et al., 2018). Failure to attend to relationship building, goal setting, and the student's monitoring of his or her progress can dim the otherwise positive gains made in terms of skills and knowledge. It is difficult to capture on a data monitoring sheet the increased smiles, the bounce in the step, and the openness of students to talk about their reading. Our observations, however, told us that we were moving in the right direction.

As mentioned earlier, data provide but one part of the story. By bringing together intervention teachers, content teachers, and the wider school community, there are opportunities to further develop the understanding of who a student is, what his or her literacy needs are, and what strategies to put into practice to maximize the impact on that student's learning and in reaching his or her potential.

REFERENCES

Cantrell, S. C., Rintamaa, M., Anderman, E. M., & Anderman, L. H. (2018). Rural adolescents' reading motivation, achievement and behavior across transition to high school. *Journal of Educational Research, 111*(4), 417–428.

Casey Foundation. (2010). *Early warning! Why reading by the end of third grade matters.* Baltimore: Author.

Catts, H. W., Compton, D., Tomblin, J. B., & Bridges, M. S. (2012). Prevalence and nature of late-emerging poor readers. *Journal of Educational Psychology, 104*(1), 166–181.

Cromley, J. G., & Azevedo, R. (2007). Testing and refining the direct and inferential mediation model of reading comprehension. *Journal of Educational Psychology, 99*(2), 311–325.

Dehaene, S. (2009). *Reading in the brain: The new science of how we read.* New York: Penguin.

Espin, C. A., Shin, J., & Busch, T. W. (2005). Curriculum-based measurement in the content areas: Vocabulary matching as an indicator of progress in social studies learning. *Journal of Learning Disabilities, 38*(4), 353–363.

Filderman, M. J., Toste, J. R., Didion, L. A., Peng, P., & Clemens, N. H. (2018). Data-based decision making in reading interventions: A synthesis and meta-analysis of the effects for struggling readers. *Journal of Special Education, 52*(3), 174–187.

Foorman, B., Coyne, M., Denton, C., Dimino, J., Hayes, L., Justice, L., . . . Wagner, R. (2016). *Foundational skills to support reading for understanding in kindergarten through 3rd grade.* What Works Clearinghouse [NCEE 2016-4008]. Washington, DC: U.S. Department of Education.

Frey, N., Lapp, D., & Fisher, D. (2009). The academic booster shot: In-school tutoring to prevent grade-level retention. In J. Richards & C. Lassonde (Eds.), *Literacy tutoring that works: A look at successful in-school, after-school, and summer programs* (pp. 32–45). Newark, DE: International Reading Association.

Heller, R., & Greenleaf, C. (2007). *Literacy instruction in the content areas: Getting to the core of middle and high school improvement.* Washington, DC: Alliance for Excellent Education.

Kim, J. S., Hemphill, L., Troyer, M., Thomson, J. M., Jones, S. M., LaRusso, M. D., & Donovan, S. (2017). Engaging struggling adolescent readers to improve reading skills. *Reading Research Quarterly, 52*(3), 357–382.

Klauda, S., & Guthrie, J. (2015). Comparing relations of motivation, engagement, and achievement among struggling and advanced adolescent readers. *Reading & Writing, 28*(2), 239–269.

Kutner, M., Greenberg, E., Jin, Y., Boyle, B., Hsu, Y.-C., & Dunleavy, E. (2007). *Literacy in everyday life: Results from the 2003 National Assessment of Adult Literacy* (NCES 2007-480). Washington, DC: National Center for Education Statistics, U.S. Department of Education.

Lee, J.-S. (2012). The effects of the teacher–student relationship and academic press on student engagement and academic performance. *International Journal of Educational Research, 53*, 330–340.

Ludwig, C., Guo, K., & Georgiou, G. K. (2019). Are reading interventions for English language learners effective? A meta-analysis. *Journal of Learning Disabilities, 52*(3), 220–231.

Lyon, G. R., & Chhabra, V. (2004). The science of reading research. *Educational Leadership, 61*(6), 12–17.

Mesmer, H. A. E. (2020). Phonics is just one part of a whole. *Education Week, 39*(21), 23.

National Institute of Child Health and Human Development. (2000). *Report of the National Reading Panel: Teaching children to read: An evidence-based assessment of the scientific research literature on reading and its implications for reading instruction: Reports of the subgroups.* National Institute of Child Health and Human Development, National Institutes of Health. Rockville, MD: Author.

Noyes, D. (2008). Humble theory. *Journal of Folklore Research, 45*(1), 37–43.

Reinking, D., & Bradley, B. A. (2008). *On formative and design experiments: Approaches to language and literacy research.* New York: Teachers College Press.

Reinking, D., & Watkins, J. (1998). Balancing change and understanding in literacy research through formative experiments. *National Reading Conference Yearbook, 47*, 461–471.

Scammacca, N. K., Roberts, G., Vaughn, S., & Stuebing, K. K. (2015). A meta-analysis of interventions for struggling readers in grades 4–12: 1980–2011. *Journal of Learning Disabilities, 48*(4), 369–390.

Seidenberg, M. S. (2013). The science of reading and its educational implications. *Language Learning and Development, 9*(4), 331–360.

Seidenberg, M. S. (2017). *Language at the speed of sight.* New York: Basic Books.

Shaywitz, S. E., & Shaywitz, B. A. (2003). The science of reading and dyslexia. *Journal of American Association for Pediatric Ophthalmology and Strabismus, 7*(3), 158–166.

Short, D. J., & Fitzsimmons, S. (2007). *Double the work: Challenges and solutions to acquiring language and academic literacy for adolescent English language learners.* New York: Carnegie Corporation of New York.

Snowling, M. J., & Hulme, C. (Eds.). (2008). *The science of reading: A handbook* (Vol. 9). Hoboken, NJ: Wiley.

Suggate, S., Schaughency, E., McAnally, H., & Reese, E. (2018). From infancy to adolescence: The longitudinal links between vocabulary, early literacy skills, oral narrative, and reading comprehension. *Cognitive Development, 47*, 82–95.

Verhoeven, L., & van Leeuwe, J. (2008). Prediction of the development of reading comprehension: A longitudinal study. *Applied Cognitive Psychology, 22*(3), 407–423.

Wang, F., & Hannafin, M. (2005). Design-based research and technology-enhanced learning environments. *Educational Technology Research and Development, 53*(4), 5–23.

Willingham, D. T. (2017). *The reading mind: A cognitive approach to understanding how the mind reads.* Hoboken, NJ: Wiley.

CHAPTER 8

Collaborative Design to Support Digital Literacies across the Curriculum

Kelly Chandler-Olcott, Sharon Dotger, Kathleen A. Hinchman,
Heather Waymouth, and Keith O. Newvine

It's July 5, Day 2, of a graduate literacy course required for teacher candidates in English, mathematics, science, and social studies education. The course is located on-site in the Leroy school district, which is partnering with Etna University to offer Camp Questions, a voluntary summer enrichment program, to Leroy's middle schoolers.[1] Candidates are in the midst of a week of intensive coursework about literacy, inquiry, and instructional planning, to be followed by 3 weeks of daily teaching in Camp Questions with university instructors and Leroy teachers.

Kelly and her co-instructor Mike are teaching candidates how to construct online surveys so they can help Leroy students generate data for use in written arguments. Candidates discuss a reading about surveys, construct and refine questions about school recess and physical activity (the programwide inquiry topic) using Google Forms on Leroy's Chromebooks, and answer each other's questions to test their effectiveness and clarity. Mike and Kelly co-lead a debriefing, focusing on what candidates think they need to consider when using Forms themselves and with students. The lesson represents a significant change from the first iteration of the program 2 years prior when instructors had similar expectations for candidates but provided less scaffolding.

This chapter shares findings from a multiyear formative experiment (Reinking & Bradley, 2008) investigating the design, implementation, and adjustment of Camp Questions (see Chapters 7 and 12, this volume, for further discussion of design-based research [DBR] as formative experiment). We focus on the intervention's role in preparing teacher candidates to address digital literacies, defined in this chapter

---

[1] All research participants, organizations, and locations have been assigned pseudonyms to protect confidentiality. Real names are used for course instructors and researchers coauthoring this piece.

as "the use of digital tools to consume and produce knowledge" (Manderino & Castek, 2016, p. 79). The opening vignette introduces key ideas we explore later in the chapter, including the blurring of print and digital literacies in the intervention, its evolution across multiple years of data analysis, and the collaborative nature of our work.

In the first part of the chapter, we describe the project's context, including its grounding in the literature and its relationship to an existing research–practice partnership (Penuel & Gallagher, 2017). Next, we describe the intervention and our methods for studying and improving it. We then share findings, describing three key adjustments related to digital literacies. We conclude with a discussion of what we learned about managing trade-offs associated with designing literacy interventions to address digital literacies.

What Issues Stimulated the DBR?

Scholars agree that definitions of literacy should encompass the multiplicity of purposes and practices in today's world, including digital literacies (Cope & Kalantzis, 2015; Manderino & Castek, 2016; Mills, 2015; Rhodes & Robnolt, 2009). Use of digital tools for self-expression, information sharing, commerce, and collaboration is embedded in daily life for many individuals, prompting revision of older, print-based practices and invention of new ones (Lankshear & Knobel, 2008). These practices are about more than skill deployment; they also involve "the mind-set and competencies needed to make choices, interact, and engage in an open, networked society" (Manderino & Castek, 2016, p. 79). For candidates preparing to teach secondary subjects such as science and social studies, digital literacies are nearly inextricable from disciplinary literacies—the ways of reading, writing, and communicating associated with participation in a disciplinary domain—because contemporary disciplinary practice almost always involves the use of digital tools (Castek & Manderino, 2017).

Many K–12 schools struggle to address digital literacies robustly for varied reasons (Colwell, Hunt-Barron, & Reinking, 2013; Howell, Perez, & Abraham, 2021; Johnson, 2016; Leu et al., 2011). In the United States, two decades of test-based accountability have pressured teachers and school leaders to align curriculum and instruction with high-stakes tests, few of which address digital literacies explicitly (Leu et al., 2011). This omission creates the impression that attention to digital literacies is less crucial. New standards such as the Common Core State Standards (CCSS) and the Next Generation Science Standards (NGSS) are compatible with promoting digital literacies, but the documents are also not explicit about what this might look like in classrooms (Drew, 2012). For example, science standards' emphasis on developing and using models could be achieved by students' composing with multimodal digital tools, but performance indicators leave tool selection up to teachers. The situation is complicated further by equity issues plaguing schools, such as funding differences that reduce access to digital tools for students in urban and rural settings (Gorski, 2017; Henry, 2009).

These issues present opportunities and challenges for literacy teacher educators. Their role in preparing practitioners to address discipline-specific digital literacies is likely more important than ever (Mirra, 2019). Yet, they must do this work with teacher candidates who have not uniformly experienced digitally mediated instruction themselves and thus may lack crucial sensibilities. Even if teacher educators can address this variation among candidates in campus-based courses, candidates need situated experience in enacting both print and digital literacy pedagogies with young people (Zenkov & Pytash, 2018). These experiences can be difficult to provide, however, because of the inconsistent attention to digital literacies in K–12 schools already discussed and the variability associated with fieldwork in most teacher preparation programs. That the bulk of supervision and coaching is done by school personnel off-campus means that university teacher educators often struggle to access and mediate their own students' learning (Grossman, 2018). Regarding digital literacies, candidates' field placement assignments introduce new variability and potential inequities, as under-resourced schools tend to use digital tools more for remediation and test preparation and less for multimodal composition and collaboration than their better-funded and often less accountability-driven counterparts (Leu et al., 2011). Candidates assigned to high-needs settings may have few opportunities to practice digital literacy pedagogies and may be skeptical about the appropriateness of such pedagogies in such contexts.

Our team embraced DBR because the approach acknowledges complexities like these as the starting point for innovation and inquiry, rather than treating complexities as separable from an intervention. Aware that literacy researchers' recommendations have not always been fully responsive to realities in K–12 settings (Hinchman & O'Brien, 2019), we were keen to take a collaborative approach to DBR with our school partners. We describe those efforts in the next section.

How Did DBR Work within the Setting?

Our study was a formative experiment—an approach to research intended to "bring about positive change in education environments through creative, innovative, instructional interventions grounded in theory and guided by systematic data collection and analysis" (Reinking & Bradley, 2008, p. 6). The emphasis in a formative experiment on adaptive and iterative work in authentic contexts was a good fit for a program we hoped to offer, study, and improve over multiple summers. We also viewed that approach as compatible with the idea of a "design-based research–practice partnership" (Penuel & Gallagher, 2017, p. 27), where researchers and educators collaboratively design solutions to problems of shared interest—a description that encapsulates the work that Etna faculty and Leroy personnel sought to do together.

The Partnership Context

Leroy is a small public school district in the northeast United States. Etna is a midsized private research university located nearby. The Leroy–Etna partnership originated in 2013, when district leaders asked university faculty to collaborate on improving access for students to cutting-edge pedagogy and college-readiness support—an invitation that aligned with faculty's growing interest in field-based teacher education. At the time, Etna placed a handful of student teachers in Leroy annually, and several Etna graduates worked in the district. Hoping to deepen the collaboration, a steering committee of representatives from both institutions established a three-pronged agenda, including (1) enrichment for K–12 students, (2) field placements for teacher candidates, and (3) professional learning for adults from both organizations. The steering committee continues to meet monthly.

The summer program was the first partnership initiative to implicate all three prongs simultaneously. Leroy staff hoped to bolster literacy engagement for youth, boost low test scores, and provide opportunities for participating teachers to develop leadership skills. Etna faculty wanted to address state certification mandates around literacy content and pre-practicum field hours and challenge traditional discourses about the campus–field divide (Zeichner, 2010).

Designing the Intervention

Once a summer 2015 launch date was selected, the steering committee charged a subgroup of literacy faculty from Etna and central and building leaders from Leroy with developing the intervention. The subgroup began by sharing insights from prior initiatives the district and the university had sponsored independently, such as a summer camp at Leroy Elementary, discontinued when its funding expired, and a graduate literacy course featuring campus-based tutoring for adolescents that presented recruitment challenges for instructors and transportation difficulties for families. These discussions were key to establishing what Reinking and Bradley (2008) call "baseline conditions" prior to implementing a new intervention.

The group then moved to identifying pedagogical goals for the intervention for its varied constituencies (see Table 8.1) and determining what features had the best chance of supporting those goals in light of existing theory and research.

TABLE 8.1. Pedagogical Goals of the Intervention

Middle school students	Teacher candidates	Leroy teachers
Use literacy as a tool for thinking and communicating learning during inquiry	Build capacity to teach literacy as part of inquiry-based instruction	Build capacity to support early-career colleagues in teaching literacy as part of inquiry-based instruction

They decided, for instance, that *Teaching Argument Writing* (Hillocks, 2011), which informed Common Core implementation for many in the region, offered an example of what instruction might look like in the new program. Subgroup members were intrigued by Hillocks's emphasis on organizing inquiry around what Kelly described as "real kid-generated questions and data sets, rather than around traditional [curricular] content." Leroy representatives believed that the district's ample supply of Chromebooks would support students to construct and distribute surveys they developed to address current events and topics of interest, tabulate and analyze data, access multimodal texts, and communicate their findings. Faculty believed that candidates' facilitation of such work would meet many literacy course objectives and align well with disciplinary agendas to develop argumentation and evidence-based explanations. They also believed that candidates would benefit from using Chromebooks and Google tools, which were available in many schools but used mostly for word processing and information searching.

Table 8.2 describes the five elements the group came to view as most essential (Colwell et al., 2013) to achieving the project's pedagogical goals. Our focus on digital literacies for this chapter sits primarily at the intersections of essential elements 3 (literacy as multimodal communication) and 4 (support for student inquiry), although the other three elements play roles as well. Lesson study (no. 5) is implicated in our analysis because it helped to reveal how members of the heterogeneous student population (no. 1) used (or did not use) those digital tools. Adult collaboration across roles and experience levels (no. 2) was also important as instructors and teachers supported candidate teams' planning and instruction.

Intervention Implementation

The program took place each year at Leroy Middle School during July. What came to be known as Week 0 because of the presence of adults but not youth was organized as a traditional graduate course in literacy, albeit in a compressed format requiring 6 hours of class per day. One of those days brought together candidates for joint planning with Leroy teachers. During Weeks 1–3, Leroy students were on site for 3 hours daily, Monday through Thursday, and the schedule was as follows:

- 8:30–9:00 A.M.: Candidate teams meet with instructors and teachers.
- 9:00 A.M.–12:00 P.M.: Teams work with youth, supported by teachers and instructors.
- 12:00–12:30 P.M.: Lunch break.
- 12:30–1:15 P.M.: Candidates, teachers, and instructors debrief instruction.
- 1:15–2:30 P.M.: Instructors lead class for candidates.

Candidates and instructors spent full days on Fridays exploring new content related to literacy instruction and planning for the next week.

TABLE 8.2. Essential Elements of the Intervention

Element	Description	Research support
Enrichment for a heterogeneous population of students	The district advertises the program as enrichment for all students, rather than remediation for some. Instructional groupings are multiage and balanced by gender, race/ethnicity, and language to support candidates in problematizing grade-level norms and leveraging diversity in culturally proactive ways.	Chandler-Olcott (2019); Garcia & O'Donnell-Allen (2015)
Collaboration in shared space by adults across experience levels and roles	Instructors and teachers design and deliver lessons collaboratively to model research-based practices. Candidate teams co-plan and co-teach lessons with teachers.	Friend & Cook (2013); Zenkov & Pytash (2018)
Literacy conceptualized as multimodal communication across contexts	Leroy students read, write, view, and represent ideas across print and digital platforms. They use writer's notebooks, Chromebooks, and Google tools to construct texts in various genres. Teachers from multiple subject areas help candidates envision how attention to literacy supports disciplinary priorities.	Cope & Kalantzis (2015); Manderino & Castek (2016)
Support for student inquiry	Objectives focus on helping Leroy students frame researchable questions about problems and controversies linkable to their lives.	Hillocks (2011); Janks (2014)
Lesson study	Each team plans and delivers two hour-long public research lessons. Candidates, teachers, instructors, and partnership guests observe the lessons and discuss evidence of student learning. Teams revise the lessons for re-teaching or portfolio inclusion.	Leavy & Hourigan (2016); Lewis & Hurd (2011)

The schedule reflected an intentional gradual release of responsibility (Pearson & Gallagher, 1983) over 4 weeks from instructors and teachers to candidates. Week 1 required all teams to address the programwide inquiry topic using the same instructor-created plans. During Week 2, each team planned and taught a different 4-day unit for 1 hour a day, then worked with its Leroy partner for another hour. Drawing on instructor feedback and data from the first round of public research lessons, teams taught a revised version of this unit to a new group of students in Week 3.

Study Participants

Participants across the four iterations (2015–2018) of the program analyzed here included 25 to 40 Leroy middle schoolers a year (98 of 130 consented for the study, with some returning for multiple years), 4 to 6 Leroy teachers a year (all 14 consented for the study, with many returning for multiple iterations), and 9 to 18 teacher candidates a year (51 of 53 consented for the study).

According to public data when the study began, 78% of Leroy Middle School students were white, 10% multiracial, 7% Latino, and 3% Black, with 1% each for Asian and Native American students. The gender ratio was 53% female and 47% male. Sixty-two percent of students were identified as economically disadvantaged, the second highest rate in the region. Leroy employed about 250 teachers serving 1,400 PreK to grade 12 students. Nearly all staff were white, with inexperienced teacher and turnover rates approximately equal to the state average. Etna served 22,000 students, with about 1,200 enrolled in the School of Education. As in many U.S. teacher education programs, its candidates were predominantly female (78%) and white (76%). Within the program, we did not ask youth, candidates, or teachers to self-identify in categories such as gender or race, and we are wary of inferring such identifications from physical characteristics or casual interactions, given contemporary discussions about the shifting, constructed nature of identity. We have no reason to believe that program demographics differed dramatically from the information about both organizations included above, but our lack of verified individual data means that we do not share participant-related percentages here or use particular descriptors when discussing individuals in our findings.

Researchers

Because of the longitudinal, collaborative nature of the project, our research team is large. To honor varied contributions while allowing for shifting commitments and availability, individuals, including key Leroy partners and local adjuncts serving as instructional staff, make decisions about their level of involvement for each proposed publication. We include two professors of literacy education (Kelly and Kathy), one associate professor of science education (Sharon), and two PhD students in literacy education (Heather and Keith), all of whom identify as white. Although Kelly took the lead on crafting our findings, all five of us were involved with data analysis, drafting, and revising.

Data Sources and Analysis

As is typical of formative experiments, the study had multiple goals for data collection and drew on various qualitative sources. Fieldnotes and handouts from partnership planning meetings documented the instructional context in both organizations and documented "conditions prior to introducing the intervention" (Reinking & Bradley, 2008, p. 49). Correspondence among instructors, transcripts from Leroy teacher and candidate interviews, and instructional materials from the graduate course captured evidence of "the factors that enhanced or inhibited movement"

(p. 49) toward the pedagogical goal, as well as adjustments made to capitalize on or ameliorate those factors. Lesson study observation notes, candidate unit plans, and samples of Leroy student work from the Chromebooks documented intervention outcomes on candidates' learning to teach digital literacies, both before and after the adjustments.

As recommended for design research (Gravemeijer & Cobb, 2006), our analysis involved multiple layers. The first layer occurred within each program iteration, as instructors made and documented fine-grained instructional adjustments to benefit current participants, often through collaboration with Leroy teachers. In the middle of Year 3, for example, we offered several options for constructing infographics when observational data revealed that the middle schoolers were struggling to compose collaboratively in the Piktochart tool. Between program iterations, the instructional staff, aided by other members of the partnership, reviewed data from the previous year to make and document larger-scale instructional adjustments while beginning to construct an instructional theory. An example of this kind of adjustment took place between Years 1 and 2 when we began to specify topics for inquiry because of an emerging conjecture that new candidates lacked enough experience with youth to select them independently in a compressed time frame.

The most comprehensive layer, retrospective analysis (Gravemeijer & Cobb, 2006), took place longitudinally, across multiple iterations, in order to refine instructional theory and author reports for an external audience. In this phase, we limited the dataset to the first 4 years of the ongoing project, and we identified data sources particularly relevant to candidates' learning to teach digital literacies, as opposed to literacy more broadly defined. We coded this subset of data using formative-experiment categories drawn from Reinking and Bradley (2008), such as enhancing factors, inhibiting factors, outcomes, and adjustments.

Once the data were coded, we identified patterns within and across coding categories. We noted, for example, that many factors inhibiting capacity-building around teaching digital literacies were linked to candidates' inexperience as professionals. We constructed assertions about the intervention over time that linked ideas from one coding category to another. For instance, we identified Leroy leadership's willingness to deploy Chromebooks for all adults and students connected to the program as a key enhancing factor. A related enhancing factor was Leroy teachers' knowledge of Chromebooks, Google tools, and Leroy students. The positive impact of this knowledge was blunted a bit, however, by an inhibiting factor: a Year 1 pay schedule that reduced teachers' time to coach candidates when the middle schoolers were not present and limited their access to literacy recommendations made by instructors. Adjustments to teachers' schedules in Year 2 made it easier for instructors and Leroy teachers to coordinate work with candidates, including (1) teacher participation in 45 minutes of instructor-led debriefing with candidates each afternoon, and (2) a standing weekly meeting of teachers and instructors for data sharing and problem solving.

What Were the Results of the DBR?

Since we have implemented multiple program iterations, we decided to organize results around the coding category that speaks to that longitudinal quality most directly: data-driven adjustments. In this section, we describe three adjustments our analysis suggested had the most impact on our pedagogical goal related to teacher candidates' capacity to support students' digital literacies: (1) instructor-determined topics for inquiry, (2) construction and use of high-level curriculum organizers, and (3) selection and implementation of a small set of high-leverage, focal literacy practices. Attention to other coding categories, such as outcomes, inhibiting factors, and enhancing factors, is threaded through each section as appropriate.

Instructor-Determined Topics for Inquiry (Years 2–4)

The curricular openness of summer enrichment compared to academic-year instruction enhanced and inhibited the program's pedagogical goals. Freedom from content mandates allowed candidates to tailor topics to student interests, potentially increasing students' motivation. Yet, the lack of an established curriculum made that tailoring challenging for candidates with limited knowledge of young adolescents, middle-grade priorities, and academic use of digital literacies. That Leroy teachers were embedded on candidate teams mitigated lack of experience as an inhibiting factor, but the teachers were not always present when teams planned.

In Year 1, the planning group sought to address topical challenges in two ways. First, with Janks (2014) as inspiration, we selected issues related to bottled water for programwide exploration during Week 1. According to Kelly's email summary of a planning meeting, that topic allowed Leroy kids to consider their families' "consumption of bottled water to create a data set" and had "a real-world application" for making hydration recommendations for the camp itself. Second, we assigned candidate teams to design units for Weeks 2 and 3 with a broad science or social studies focus, to capitalize on those being the most common undergraduate majors in the candidate cohort and thus a source of content knowledge. We envisioned that candidates would learn to facilitate literacy skills during the water unit they would then integrate into their own units, providing additional skill practice for youth and facilitation experience for candidates. But, lesson study observations and post-lesson discussions revealed considerable variation in how generative these topics were. A few teams' selections supported student-driven exploration with varied sources and survey data, but most funneled learners into more predictable, constrained responses, reducing opportunities for literacy.

To avoid these pitfalls in Year 2, we specified a programwide topic (proposed changes to U.S. currency, then in the news) and three more topics for team exploration—school lunch, growth mind-set, and drones in everyday life—that we thought would better support student inquiry. We brainstormed and selected these topics with the partnership steering committee to access insider knowledge of the students and community resources. In response to another Year 2 change—the need to accommodate one-to-one tutoring for some Leroy students by literacy master's students completing their practica—we divided the team topics into two foci: one inquiring with multimodal texts and another with online survey construction and data analysis This division made it easier to keep track of what tutees missed during tutoring pullouts, as well as ensured that every student experienced both foci over the program. We used information from a precourse questionnaire about candidates' interests and backgrounds to assign them to teams with a particular topic and focus (e.g., School Lunch Survey). These moves led to team-constructed units that instructors and returning Leroy teachers judged as more literacy-infused than those the previous year, but concerns remained that some teams' interpretation of the topics led them, in Leroy teacher Kaitlyn's words, in "a completely different direction" than what instructors envisioned, an outcome that "took away from some of the literacy aspects."

This between-iteration analysis led to two adjustments of the topic-selection process for Year 3. First, in May, we vetted proposed topics with Leroy middle schoolers during lunchtime pizza parties that adjusted our priority list while recruiting camp participants. We also generated explicit selection criteria that remain in use, including topics' potential for analysis from multiple perspectives rather than binaries; limited overlap with required school curricula; and availability of free, multimodal, and accessible resources on the topic (see Chandler-Olcott et al., 2018, for more on this). These adjustments yielded a programwide inquiry topic around increasing recess and physical activity in schools and team topics focusing on the influence of music in teens' lives and ways to welcome refugees into new communities.

Because all three topics appeared to be successful judging by within- and between-iteration analysis, we expected to use the same processes again in Year 4. We made additional adjustments, however, due to a serendipitous occurrence: The Leroy mayor announced his desire to involve youth more deeply in the community, and Kara, the camp's long-time librarian, proposed addressing his invitation as our programwide focus for Week 1. This topic met our recently articulated selection criteria and also presented numerous subtopics that could be explored by teams in Weeks 2 and 3. Leroy kids helped us brainstorm and rank these subtopics during the pizza parties, generating several ideas (e.g., ways that youth might connect with seniors in the community) that neither instructors nor veteran Leroy teachers anticipated. The Year 4 program thus began with a Week 1 interview of the mayor before shifting to community-related subtopics in Weeks 2 and 3. This increased coherence across the program and allowed us to assign multimodal text and survey foci to topics that best fit those foci. Topics like improving the local youth center, which many camp participants had frequented, worked well with a survey focus, while the seniors' topic was better explored through multimodal texts about initiatives in other communities that suggested new possibilities for Leroy.

Reducing candidate time and energy spent on topic selection left them more time to plan for print and digital literacy. As Leroy teacher Noelle noted, preset topics addressed the "struggle" she witnessed when candidates lacked enough "real direction on where to go." Such direction helped them "work cohesively" through their varying ideas about instruction. Strong preselected topics also meant that teachers and instructors spent more time coaching teams around facilitating student learning with the Chromebooks and Google tools, rather than helping teams navigate differences in how they viewed topics' potential or dimensions.

Another benefit of preselected topics was time to identify multimodal texts that were accessible for kids with varying literacy profiles. While the graduate course had a learning objective related to text selection, most candidates needed the full course to develop that skills set—a lag that threatened instructional quality for the middle schoolers, especially early on. To address this issue, instructors established a routine over multiple iterations that involved instructors and Leroy teachers sharing text suggestions and rationales via email. Kara posted links to these texts on a website, with some texts designated as required and others as optional. Aware of many teams' preference for distributing traditional print to students in Year 1, we subsequently chose texts with clear digital affordances. As part of the mayor's challenge in Year 4, for instance, programwide plans drew on an online article, "15 Ways That Teens Are Changing the World," that candidates dubbed a "listicle," an online genre blending aspects of feature articles and lists. This example was selected because of its nonsequential text structure, headings, and mechanisms for directing readers to related multimedia—all features that could support better online reading by youth. Given the rapid pace and long days associated with the program's compressed format (an enhancing factor for Leroy teacher and student participation but more challenging for teacher candidates and instructors), it was difficult to locate and select texts with those affordances without the lead time of preselected topics.

Four-Day Curriculum Organizers (Years 2–3)

A second set of adjustments with implications for candidates' teaching of digital literacies was associated with what we called 4-day organizers, instructor-constructed graphic organizers specifying learning objectives, texts, and recommended activities for a weeklong (4-day) unit. This represented a shift from Year 1, when we wrote full lesson plans with some limited candidate input for the bottled water inquiry but then required candidates to write their own plans for the topics they selected for Weeks 2 and 3. As hinted in the previous section, the Year 1 approach yielded multiple problems. Following lengthy plans authored by someone else was a struggle for candidates, particularly given their inexperience, and the practice appeared to have limited transfer for their own planning, judging by the weakness of their team-written lessons.

Even more troubling given the graduate course focus was the reduced attention to reading and writing in the team-authored plans for Weeks 2 and 3, as compared with instructor-authored ones for Week 1. Candidates seemed to view student talk or even more generic hands-on activities as more engaging to students than print or digital literacies. More specifically, we observed limited carryover into Weeks 2 and 3 of the Chromebook-supported approaches we encouraged candidates to employ in Week 1. Despite the emphasis on constructing and analyzing data from surveys in the bottled water unit and our ongoing feedback to reuse those approaches in subsequent units, only one of 24 lessons authored by the six teams included any attention to Google Forms or Sheets. Candidates did ask Leroy students to glean information from multimodal texts, including video clips and online articles. But, they tended to structure those text interactions with teacher-directed graphic organizers that had not been introduced in either the Week 0 graduate course sessions or the bottled water unit itself. The organizers' appearance in the team-authored plans suggested that Leroy partners drew on their own experience to support candidates in the absence of more clearly articulated alternatives from instructors. Although we did not realize it at the time, retrospective analysis revealed that team substitutions also tended to be less digitally mediated than the approaches in the instructor-authored plans.

To address this set of issues in Year 2, we produced a 4-day organizer for the programwide topic for Week 1—U.S. currency changes—rather than full-blown lesson plans. We asked team members to develop detailed daily plans from the bulleted recommendations in the organizer to guide instruction for their assigned students' needs as well as direct their collaboration as co-teachers. The organizer reduced the cognitive load for novices while retaining some crucial aspects for them to puzzle through with help from Leroy partners. Our intention was to find the sweet spot between past approaches offering too little direction and Mike's warning to fellow instructors that being "too prescriptive" would cause candidates to "lose ownership." The adoption of the organizer, and the shift to predetermined topics for teams described in the previous section, led to overall improvement in candidates' lessons as instructors observed and then evaluated them on paper.

At the same time, our lesson-study efforts revealed that some candidates continued to struggle to write manageable learning objectives and align them with appropriate learning activities in the team units. Furthermore, interview data from Jamie and other Leroy staff suggested that it could be challenging to mediate that process, particularly if all parties on a team were not clear about who should be doing what. Consequently, we decided to construct 4-day organizers for all units across the program in Year 3, as well as plan more explicit instructional support to help candidates and teachers learn to use the organizers more effectively in the camp context. By Year 4, we devoted an hour during the first meeting of candidates and teachers to learning how to create executable lesson plans from bulleted organizer content like the following:

Survey, Day 1

- Discuss why it will be valuable to supplement proposals to [school] leaders with survey data from adults and students participating in Camp Questions [5 minutes].
- Have students brainstorm questions pertaining to recess that they see as answerable with surveys [15 minutes].
- Sort questions into three or four categories (e.g., personal preferences, knowledge about recess, awareness of others' perspectives) and assign pairs or trios to those categories [10 minutes].
- Give groups time to begin drafting questions in Google Forms for their assigned survey sections [25 minutes].

Some of the best evidence of organizers as an enabling factor came from Mike's running notes during a weekly meeting between instructors and Leroy teachers. The meeting took place after candidates had planned with two organizers, one for the programwide topic and another for their team topic. When Kelly asked what was working in the classrooms, teachers described the organizers' positive impact on planning. Cynthia shared that candidates were "less reliant on the Leroy partners and more willing to take risks." Jamie concurred, claiming that his candidates knew "where they are going," in contrast with the previous year, when, without an organizer to guide them, his team had sometimes enacted its assigned topic in surprising, not always helpful, ways. Kaitlyn believed the organizer supported her group's division of labor as co-teachers, and Noelle thought that hers had a greater sense of urgency around converting the organizer directions into fully realized lessons: "They are not putting off planning or neglecting it." The exchange represented a positive convergence of perspectives from teachers with considerable knowledge of the program (each were 2- or 3-year veterans).

From a digital literacies perspective, adherence to the organizers also reduced candidates' and teachers' inclination to sidestep digitally mediated approaches in favor of print-based ones. Instructors could stipulate, for instance, whether students should be reading in print or online, taking notes in their hard-copy writer's notebooks or an online document shared with group mates, or providing peer feedback with sticky notes or Google comments.

In addition, the organizers specified the form of writing students would use to communicate learning at unit's end. This component reinforced the course's *Understanding by Design*-influenced message (Wiggins & McTighe, 2005), that candidates' plans should support students in developing the knowledge and skills aligned with a culminating product chosen in advance, not after the fact. It offered more genre variety to the middle schoolers than was the case in Year 1, when three of six teams asked their students to compose petitions, a genre worthy of study but perhaps not with so much emphasis. And, most relevant to digital literacies, it helped to ensure student opportunities to compose multimodal texts with digital tools. Candidates themselves began to recognize these opportunities as valuable. For instance, Madeline, a future mathematics teacher, shared this: "Seeing my students create infographics and presenting them was a heartwarming experience." By Year 4, the relevant culminating product was clearly labeled at the top of each 4-day organizer, with planned genres ranging from written proposals and cover letters to visual maps and slides to accompany oral presentations, each tailored to the particular needs of audiences such as the mayor, parks and recreation supervisor, and middle school principal. If the product was not explicitly digital, students were guaranteed to have experienced multimodal or online reading and writing at other points in the 4-day sequence.

Focal Instructional Practices (Years 3–4)

A final adjustment with implications for digital literacies was the adoption of three focal instructional practices in Year 3 simultaneously with our decision to construct curriculum organizers for all units. For months, instructors had discussed growing concerns that candidates were juggling too much in the course. Discussions of the pedagogical approaches described in assigned readings were often short and shallow, and candidates had few opportunities to test them with students more than once. Like a growing segment of other teacher educators (Grossman, 2018), we conjectured that in-depth understanding of a few versatile, important core practices would be better for candidates than the scattershot consideration of many. As a team, we brainstormed evidence-based instructional practices to support the program's inquiry focus and align with disciplinary priorities (Castek & Manderino, 2017). Eventually, we narrowed our list to three: eliciting student talk, writing to capture thinking, and facilitating student interaction with multimodal text.

That we envisioned these practices as applying, with appropriate adaptation, to both digital and print contexts was clear from the team's earliest exchanges. When Mike proposed recasting "text-based discussion" as "facilitating students' interaction with text," Kelly agreed, offering a list of multimodal texts ("a video clip, a set of survey data, an informational article"), while noting that their use would open up space for instructional modeling about "how to identify important info or how to organize info into your own written product." Other team members concurred, allowing us to unveil the finalized focal practices to Leroy teachers at the staff orientation held later that week, where they, too, endorsed the idea. By the program's July start, all unit organizers were labeled with consistent abbreviations for each practice—eliciting student talk (EST), writing to capture thinking (WCT), and facilitating student interaction with text (FSIT)—as shown in Figure 8.1.

Once we settled on practices, we adjusted various course aspects to address them. We listed the practices on the first page of the Year 3 syllabus, where they were hard to miss, and we revised the order and relative emphasis of lessons in Week 0 to ensure in-depth discussion of all three. When work with Leroy students

Multimodal Texts: Product	Survey: Product
Memos proposing actions school leaders can take to leverage the benefits of recess for middle school students	Groupwide slide deck summarizing survey data to accompany memo

EST—Eliciting student talk   WCT—Writing to capture thinking   FSIT—Facilitating student interaction with text

Day 1, Morning Meeting

- Introduce overall goals of program, provide overview of weekly/daily schedule
- Introduce personnel (by roles and in groups, not by individual name) and bio page on Weebly
- Introduce recess as shared inquiry topic and view/discuss two short video clips for background (FSIT, EST)
- Introduce writer's notebook as key tool for work and facilitate first entry (WCT)

Multimodal Texts: *Reading, viewing, and writing about informational text*	Survey: *Constructing researchable questions, identifying patterns in data, supporting claims with evidence*
Day 1: Multimodal Texts Objective: Draw on texts to consider multiple points of view on topic Objective: Determine important information from text	Day 1: Survey Objective: Frame questions about topic that can be addressed by gathering and interpreting data
• Play a getting-to-know-you game with recess-related content (5) • Explore multiple perspectives on recess by discussing a sampling of cartoons on Weebly (15; FSIT, EST) • Model how to annotate informational text with inquiry questions with this article: *http://teens.lovetoknow.com/Middle_School_Recess* (10; FSIT) • Have student pair finish article (15) • Brainstorm questions about recess that can be answered using Internet-based text, first individually in notebook and then on chart as group (10; WCT, EST)	• Discuss why it will be valuable to supplement proposals with survey data from adults and students participating in Camp Questions (5) • Brainstorm questions about recess that can be answered with surveys (15; EST) • Sort questions into three or four categories (e.g., personal preferences, knowledge about recess, awareness of others' perspectives) and assign pairs or trios to address categories (10) • Groups draft questions in Google Forms for their survey sections (25)

Day 2, Morning Meeting

- Share infographics about recess statistics, including at least one that raises equity questions (FSIT)
- Ask students to write about what they notice about patterns and to speculate about possible causes (WCT)
- Invite students to share their thinking in small group conversations (EST)

Day 2: Multimodal Text Objective: Frame questions about topic that can be answered by gathering and interpreting textual evidence Objective: Determine important information from text to address topics	Day 2: Survey Objective: Evaluate and refine questions to make them more researchable
• Invite students to select one or more texts in Weebly to gather and record information about topic in notebooks (15; WCT)	• Conduct mini-lesson on typical issues with survey questions using categories from *https://owl.english.purdue.edu/owl/resource/559/06* (15; FSIT)

FIGURE 8.1. Overview of Week 1 unit: recess.

commenced, we regularly asked candidates and teachers to reflect on the practices during afternoon debriefing. These changes, combined with the topic- and organizer-related adjustments already described, led us to identify what course assistant Molly, an alumna who was a literacy specialist in a nearby district, called an "uptick" in the quality of the instruction and the quantity of reading and writing opportunities for students. In that same conversation, however, we discussed continuing concerns about missed opportunities for student-to-student talk as well as unclear purposes for students' text transactions. These concerns led us to further adjustments in Year 4, most notably, an overhaul of the session when candidates first met and planned with Leroy teachers. In Years 1 and 2, that session focused primarily on models of inquiry and strategies for co-teaching, with an additional focus in Year 3 on learning to navigate the 4-day organizer. By Year 4, however, we highlighted focal practices more clearly within the organizer exploration, using instructions like the following to guide discussion by candidates and teachers within their teams:

- Review the Week 1 organizer for all references to FSIT.
- Make a list of various texts you will explore with students (are there others we might consider?).
- Make a list of key principles about this focal practice that you can infer from how it is used across the organizer.

This joint activity helped to build shared understandings of the focal practices, making it easier for instructors and teachers to coach candidates consistently toward instructional coherence for students.

To further cement the focal practices, we also made adjustments in Year 3 to a major course assignment: the discipline-specific application project. This multicomponent assignment, dating back to Year 1, asked candidates to (1) consider the literacy implications of disciplinary standards, (2) respond to discipline-specific articles about teaching literacy, and (3) locate and evaluate multimodal texts appropriate for high school units in their subject area. After completing these components, candidates wrote about how they intended to support literacy in their teaching beyond Camp Questions. In Years 3 and 4, we asked them to discuss specifically how they would use the focal practices "to support students in achieving disciplinary outcomes." This adjustment made the project a better assessment of candidates' understanding of the practices. It also supported more explicit connections between coursework and subsequent teaching—an outcome instructors sometimes found challenging when candidates took a narrow view of their future subject-specific teaching. Analysis revealed that while candidates' memos in Years 3 and 4 varied in thoroughness and nuance, nearly all could identify subject-specific applications for the practices that cut across print and digital platforms. For example, Rich, a social studies education major, proposed to elicit student talk through in-person jigsaw groups as well as voice memos shared online; his ideas about facilitating student interaction with texts involved the investigation of print-based historical documents alongside content from "digital archives and databases." Data like Rich's suggested some emerging candidate awareness of the practices' malleability for disciplinary purposes.

From a digital literacies perspective, the adoption of focal practices made it easier to address candidate needs that could otherwise remain in tension—tension exacerbated by the pace of the Camp Questions experience. Some candidates demonstrated strong instincts for use of digital tools, either from previous schooling, work, or extracurricular experiences. Others, however, required additional instructional support in such areas as searching library databases and sharing Google Docs to uploading images to an online discussion thread. Focusing most of our attention on just three practices exposed candidates to fewer instructional options from which to choose, but it provided time to shore up gaps in knowledge and skills that would otherwise have inhibited their ability to enact the practices well. Like the adjustments we made with preselected topics and instructor-designed organizers, adoption of the practices reflected a calculated trade-off, constraining some aspects of candidate practice, such as unit design from scratch, to improve opportunities for learning in others, such as the support of digital literacies.

How Did the DBR Influence Participant and Researcher Learning?

The formative experiment, particularly the retrospective analysis reported here, revealed how interconnected the various adjustments were on candidates' capacity to support digital literacies during Camp Questions and within their disciplines. Analyzing those adjustments separately was valuable, particularly in terms of our research team members' ability to identify fine-grained changes in our approaches over time. But, treating the adjustments discretely did not reveal the degree to which they influenced each other: establishing workable topics for inquiry made it easier to bound the 4-day organizer; having a 4-day organizer made it clearer how focal practices could be embedded.

Longitudinal analysis revealed that we paid more attention to digital literacies in the program than we realized from within- and between-iteration analysis. Opportunities for candidates and youth to learn about and use digital tools were threaded throughout the program, but in service of inquiry rather than as the focus. Closer scrutiny of candidate data from discipline-specific application projects has convinced us that the intervention will be better served in future iterations by explaining more explicitly to candidates how they were learning to facilitate such functional use of digital literacies.

What are the learning points for design-based researchers? Some might see the intricate relationships of our intervention components as confounding factors— undesirable complications. However, we see them as central to the intervention's responsiveness to the complexities of teaching and learning. Longitudinal collaborative analysis helped us enhance the impact of these reciprocal design features in concert with one another.

Another impact of the project was keener understanding of design-research affordances of close collaboration with school partners. This included enhanced documentation quality. The need to communicate across a sizable and varied implementation team helped preserve the intervention's twists and turns—including rationales for adjustments—with detail atypical for us when working on smaller, less diverse teams. Collaborative analysis also ameliorated some limitations associated with teacher educators studying their own practice. Because Leroy partners drew on different lenses and experiences than instructor-researchers, their contributions steered us away from seeing what we wanted to see. Such triangulation seemed especially helpful with digital literacies, which can tempt early adopting researchers to take advocacy positions rather than offer clear-eyed analyses.

These findings also contribute to research on the benefits of teacher educators, teachers, and candidates working with youth in shared community space, as opposed to more typical decontextualized approaches (Zeichner, 2010; Zenkov & Pytash, 2018). For instance, when all adults shared observations during afternoon debriefings about middle schoolers' technology-mediated reading and writing, discussion was grounded in common experiences involving youth known to all. The influence of collaboration was multidirectional: teachers gained access to recent pedagogical scholarship, instructors gained insights about candidate preparation, and candidates were less likely to reject digital literacies because both teachers and instructors endorsed their potential. Common tools like the 4-day organizer and focal practices provided important shared language.

The preceding suggests that digital literacies researchers consider formulating the kind of rich, long-term partnerships that we have been able to establish with our partners. These relationships allowed us to identify and promote high-leverage digital literacies practices as credible, practices we had not been as able to promote in previous work. These relationships also allowed us to implement community-based inquiry topics and candidates' use of curriculum organizers. Digital literacies researchers may also want to consider longitudinal design-based projects to develop the specifics of instructional frameworks over time in ways that allow them to recognize interactions among their model components.

REFERENCES

Castek, J., & Manderino, M. (2017). A planning framework for integrating digital literacies for disciplinary learning. *Journal of Adolescent & Adult Literacy, 60*, 697–700.

Chandler-Olcott, K. (2019). *A good fit for all kids: Collaborating to teach writing in diverse, inclusive settings.* Cambridge, MA: Harvard Education Press.

Chandler-Olcott, K., Dotger, S., Waymouth, H., Crosby, M., Lahr, M., Hinchman, K., . . . Nieroda, J. (2018). Teacher candidates learn to enact curriculum in a partnership-sponsored literacy enrichment program for youth. *New Educator, 14*(3), 192–211.

Colwell, J., Hunt-Barron, S., & Reinking, D. (2013). Obstacles to developing digital literacy on the internet in middle school science instruction. *Journal of Literacy Research, 45*(3), 295–324.

Cope, B., & Kalantzis, M. (2015). *A pedagogy of multiliteracies: Learning by design*. New York: Palgrave Macmillan.

Drew, S. (2012). Open up the ceiling on the Common Core State Standards: Preparing students for 21st century literacy—now. *Journal of Adolescent & Adult Literacy, 56*, 331–340.

Friend, M., & Cook, L. (2013). *Interactions: Collaboration skills for school professionals* (7th ed.). New York: Pearson.

Garcia, A., & O'Donnell-Allen, C. (2015). *Pose, wobble, flow: A culturally proactive approach to literacy instruction*. New York: Teachers College Press.

Gorski, P. (2017). *Reaching and teaching students in poverty: Erasing the achievement gap*. New York: Teachers College Press.

Gravemeijer, K., & Cobb, P. (2006). Design research from a learning design perspective. In J. van den Akker, K. Gravemeijer, S. McKenney, & N. Nieveen (Eds.), *Educational design research* (pp. 17–51). New York: Routledge.

Grossman, P. (2018). *Teaching core practices in teacher education*. Cambridge, MA: Harvard Education Press.

Henry, L. (2009). Unpacking social inequalities: Lack of technology integration may impede the development of multiliteracies among middle school students in the United States. In D. Pullen, C. Gitsaki, & M. Baguley (Eds.), *Technoliteracy, discourse, and social practice: Frameworks and applications* (pp. 55–79). Hershey, PA: IGI Global.

Hillocks, G. (2011). *Teaching argument writing, grades 6–12*. Portsmouth, NH: Heinemann.

Hinchman, K., & O'Brien, D. (2019). Disciplinary literacy: From infusion to hybridity. *Journal of Literacy Research, 51*(4), 521–536.

Howell, E., Perez, S., & Abraham, W. T. (2021). Toward a professional development model for writing as a digital, participatory process. *Reading Research Quarterly, 56*(1), 95–117.

Janks, H. (2014). Critical literacy's ongoing importance for education. *Journal of Adolescent & Adult Literacy, 57*, 349–356.

Johnson, L. L. (2016). Writing 2.0: How English teachers conceptualize writing with digital technologies. *English Education, 49*(1), 28–62.

Lankshear, C., & Knobel, M. (2008). *Digital literacies: Concepts, policies, and practices*. New York: Peter Lang.

Leavy, A., & Hourigan, M. (2016). Using lesson study to support knowledge development in initial teacher education: Insights from early number classrooms. *Teaching and Teacher Education, 57*, 161–175.

Leu, D. J., McVerry, J. G., O'Byrne, W. I., Kiili, C., Zawilinski, L., Everett-Cacopado, H., . . . Forzani, E. (2011). The new literacies of online reading comprehension: Expanding the literacy and learning curriculum. *Journal of Adolescent & Adult Literacy, 55*(1), 5–14.

Lewis, C., & Hurd, J. (2011). *Lesson study step by step: A guide to instructional improvement*. Portsmouth: NH: Heinemann.

Manderino, M., & Castek, J. (2016). Digital literacies for digital learning: A call for action. *Journal of Adolescent & Adult Literacy, 60*(1), 79–81.

Mills, K. (2015). *Literacy theories for the digital age: Social, critical, multimodal, spatial, material, and sensory lenses*. Bristol, UK: Multilingual Matters.

Mirra, N. (2019). From connected learning to connected teaching: Reimagining digital literacy pedagogy in English education. *English Education, 51*(3), 261–291.

Pearson, P. D., & Gallagher, M. (1983). The instruction of reading comprehension. *Contemporary Educational Psychology, 8*, 317–344.

Penuel, W. R., & Gallagher, D. (2017). *Creating research–practice partnerships in education.* Cambridge, MA: Harvard Education Press.

Reinking, D., & Bradley, B. (2008). *On formative and design experiments.* New York: Teachers College Press/NCRLL.

Rhodes, J. A., & Robnolt, V. (2009). Digital literacies in the classroom. In L. Christenbury, R. Bomer, & P. Smagorinsky (Eds.), *Handbook of adolescent literacy research* (pp. 153–169). New York: Guilford Press.

Wiggins, G., & McTighe, J. (2005). *Understanding by design* (2nd ed.). Alexandria, VA: ASCD.

Zeichner, K. (2010). Rethinking the connections between campus courses and field experiences in college and university-based teacher education. *Journal of Teacher Education, 61*(1–2), 79–99.

Zenkov, K., & Pytash, K. (2018). Critical, project-based clinical experiences: Their origins and their elements. In K. Zenkov & K. Pytash (Eds.), *Clinical experiences in teacher education: Critical, project-based interventions in diverse classrooms* (pp. 1–14). New York: Routledge.

CHAPTER 9

Multilingual Students and Design-Based Research
Developing Opportunities in Partnerships

Ryan McCarty, Tim Pappageorge, and Claudia Rueda-Alvarez

Design-based research (DBR) is a powerful tool to address authentic pedagogical problems facing schools (Reinking, 2011; Reinking & Bradley, 2008). This chapter examines the use of DBR within partnerships to address the learning needs of multilingual students. In this chapter, we use the term emergent bilinguals to describe students who speak another language and are learning English because it implies a continuum of language learning. This term encourages a shift toward higher expectations and developmentally appropriate instruction and assessment practices (García, 2009). Such a change is essential because emergent bilinguals are the fastest growing group of children in grades K–12 (U.S. Department of Education, 2012). We also use the broader term *multilingual students*, which includes both emergent bilinguals and students who have already learned English and speak one or more additional languages (Kieffer & Thompson, 2018; National Council of Teachers of English, 2020). This inclusive term is appropriate because the students in our research are by no means a monolithic group.

Latinx students comprise a large proportion of multilingual students, and Spanish is the home language of nearly three-quarters of English learners nationwide (Batalova & McHugh, 2010). As with any group, family structures and socioeconomic status vary widely. Some Latinx students in the district where our research occurs were born in the United States, with families who have lived here for generations, while others are recent immigrants. Regionally, Latinx students often have familial ties to Mexico, Puerto Rico, Guatemala, Ecuador, Cuba, or other countries and speak different varieties of Spanish. We avoid binary categories such as *second-language students* because they can become permanent labels. In addition, English may be a student's third language, they may have learned English and another language simultaneously, or they may lack formal education or literacy skills in a home language.

This chapter will first review research perspectives for work with multilingual students and present the advantages of DBR. It will next introduce our own DBR on helping Latinx students write effective arguments and excel in Advanced Placement (AP) coursework. Principles and guiding questions for research with multilingual students will then be presented, framed around Reinking and Bradley's six phases for conducting DBR (2008), and followed by extended examples from our own research. The chapter concludes by discussing new opportunities for research partnerships to serve multilingual students. Readers may refer to Chapter 1 of this volume for an overview of DBR and Chapter 2 for more examples of research utilizing DBR methodologies.

Challenges Facing Multilingual Students

Learning a new language is an ongoing process that is both rewarding and challenging. Understanding a given linguistic register, or how language varies according to a particular discipline or context, adds to the complexity (Fang & Park, 2020). While the Common Core State Standards institute ambitious learning goals for emergent bilinguals (Graham & Harris, 2015), their knowledge of other languages and cultures are rich resources for meaning-making and can powerfully support learning with complex texts and concepts (e.g., García & Wei, 2014). However, schools often fail to help students build on linguistic and cultural assets, treating multilingualism as a detriment and even prohibiting students from using other languages (Jimenez, 1997; Paris & Alim, 2017). The so-called *achievement gap* is often a manifestation of systems narrowly defining whose literacy and language matter (Madrid, 2011). Indeed, emergent bilinguals are more likely to attend underfunded schools, taught by adults inexperienced or underprepared to teach culturally and linguistically diverse youth (García, 2009).

Deficit thinking has plagued literacy research in general (Dudley-Marling & Lucas, 2009) and research with Latinx and multilingual students in particular (e.g., Paris & Alim, 2017). Myths that Latinx students are apathetic about education intersect with damaging narratives that deficits in language, values, culture, and parental support largely explain apparent gaps in achievement (Madrid, 2011). The omnipresent term *English language learner* (ELL) is problematic, setting up a false binary of knowing or not knowing a language and defining students entirely by their status as learners of English, rather than their knowledge of other languages (e.g., García, 2009). Students designated as *long-term English language learners* (LTELs) may languish in ESL classrooms for 6 or more years with little exposure to academic language or challenging texts (Olsen, 2010). The term *limited English proficient* (LEP) is even worse, ascribing limits in English knowledge without recognizing strengths in other languages.

Embracing Asset-Based Views of Multilingual Students

In contrast, asset-based pedagogical approaches view diversity in language, culture, and thinking as a strength. For example, through translanguaging, multilingual students can use their whole linguistic repertoire as an "integrated system" (Canagarajah, 2011, p. 403) to learn English content (García & Wei, 2014). Writers use *envoicing* strategies, making intentional choices to reference cultural practices or include words or phrases from languages other than English (introduced, for instance, through dialogue or quotations from multilingual texts) in order to convey their own unique voice or achieve rhetorical goals (Canagarajah, 2013).

Multilingual students often serve important roles as *language brokers:* helping navigate their families' health and financial concerns and translating complex documents in meetings at hospitals, banks, and government offices (e.g., Alvarez, 2014). Many Latinx high school students in our research are wage earners, caregivers, and decision makers, yet feel treated as *just a student* in school, when given worksheets and low-level tasks (Fieldnotes, Cycle 2).

The constellation of culturally responsive teaching (CRT) practices (e.g., Moll & Diaz, 1987; Paris & Alim, 2017) continue to gain prominence, providing rich possibilities for DBR with multilingual students. While the 2017 International Literacy Association Standards for the Preparation of Literacy Professionals spotlight CRT, the 2010 standards only mention the importance of diversity (International Literacy Association, 2018). We emphasize cooperation and interdependence over classroom cultures of competition and individualism (Au, 2007), and foster *personalismo*, a cultural value prioritizing meaningful, personal connections and trusting relationships believed to be important within Latinx communities (e.g., Ayon & Aisenberg, 2010). We build these relationships through one-on-one writing coaching sessions, individualized academic planning, and whole-group meaning-making within agentive roles (McCarty, Pappageorge, & Rueda-Alvarez, 2018).

Argument Writing and Multilingual Students

Our own research emphasizes argument writing, an essential yet underdeveloped area of research with multilingual students (Canagarajah, 2011). Though crucial for college, career, and civic engagement (Graff & Birkenstein, 2007), argument writing instruction often consists of formulaic or fill-in-the-blank tasks (e.g., Applebee & Langer, 2011). Philosopher Stephen Toulmin (1958) determined that effective arguments contain an assertion or claim, supported by evidence or data, and a warrant or explanation of how the evidence supports the claim. Tools such as argument templates (Graff & Birkenstein, 2007) help scaffold key rhetorical moves utilizing these elements. Analyzing warrants helps students unearth tacit cultural assumptions that vary across cultural groups and academic disciplines. Deconstructing divisive media rhetoric can help students craft and warrant counter-arguments to advocate for themselves and their communities (Warren, 2010).

Self-efficacy is another important consideration for instruction with multilingual students. Writers with greater self-efficacy or belief in their own writing ability value writing, set clearer goals, and persevere amidst difficulty (Pajares, Johnson, & Usher, 2007). Three key sources of self-efficacy beliefs include *mastery experiences* or success with challenging writing tasks, *vicarious experiences* or observing others complete tasks, and *social persuasions* or interactions with others and the judgments they provide (Bandura, 1997; Pajares et al., 2007).

Academic language is often emphasized within writing instruction for multilingual students. Academic language represents cultural capital, providing tools for knowledge building, social positioning, and career advancement (Imbrenda, 2018a). While difficulties for emergent bilinguals are often attributed to differences between oral and academic language (e.g., Snow & Uccelli, 2009), creating such binaries is problematic (Flores, 2019) because elevating academic language positions dominant white perspectives above the discourse practices of culturally and linguistically diverse students (Fang & Park, 2020). Our work addresses these criticisms by encouraging multilingual students to use academic registers flexibly through codemeshing and hybrid language practices (e.g., Canagarajah, 2011, 2013).

Dialogic instruction is particularly suited to argumentative writing given the emphasis on influencing one's audience (Newell & Bloome, 2017), yet meaningful discussion opportunities are sorely lacking for Latinx students (Kong & Pearson, 2003). In dialogic classrooms, students and teachers co-construct meaning by discussing challenging texts and ideas (Bakhtin, 1981; Reznitskaya, 2012). Organizing dialogic teaching as inquiry into essential questions supports higher levels of literacy learning (e.g., Nachowitz & Wilcox, 2018).

Advantages of DBR with Multilingual Students

In DBR, an intervention is tested and refined in a real-world setting through cycles of implementation, data collection, analysis, and redesign to build theory and progress toward a pedagogical goal (Gravemeijer & Cobb, 2006; Reinking & Bradley, 2008). DBR begins with collecting data to provide a thick description of the instructional context. This ecological perspective illuminates how structural factors, such as tracking and language education policies, impact multilingual student achievement (e.g., Conchas, 2001). Given the marginal outcomes of so-called *gold standard*, large-scale experimental research (e.g., Kim, 2019), there is growing interest in what works *here*, *why*, and *under what circumstances* (Reinking & Bradley, 2008). A simultaneously descriptive and iterative approach, DBR encourages combining methods to track qualitative factors (e.g., degree of interaction or forms of discourse) in combination with pre–post measures, providing insight into linguistic processes and learning development.

DBR and related methods have an established history of use with multilingual students. For example, Luis Moll and colleagues used tools from ethnography and case study in ways now associated with DBR to examine the *funds of knowledge* of Spanish-speaking students in bilingual programs, identifying enhancing and inhibiting factors in their education (e.g., Moll & Diaz, 1987, as cited in Reinking & Bradley, 2008). Some of the earliest design-based or formative experiments in top literacy journals involved work with emergent bilinguals (e.g., Jimenez, 1997).

DBR with multilingual students may begin with a broad theoretical framework, such as dialogic teaching (e.g., Bakhtin, 1981; Reznitskaya, 2012), that was not specifically designed for multilingual students. Cycles of teaching, data collection, and analysis can distill a *humble theory* to better inform instruction in similar contexts (Gravemeijer & Cobb, 2006; Howell, Butler, & Reinking, 2017). DBR with multilingual students covers a range of purposes, from exploring a general premise (e.g., Ivey & Broaddus, 2007) to refining specific interventions (e.g., Schleppegrell, 2013). It often examines the learning of multilingual students in heterogeneous settings by using *focal students* (Colwell, Hunt-Barron, & Reinking, 2013; Reinking & Bradley, 2008). For example, Chandler-Olcott and Nieroda (2016) studied the instruction of emergent bilingual students from African or Middle Eastern countries with limited or interrupted prior formal education within a heterogeneous summer writing institute.

In critiques of "linear and top-down notions of design experiments" (Gutierrez & Vossoughi, 2010, p. 102), researchers recently have argued for more agentive roles for school-based partners as *co-designers* (e.g., Fowler-Amato & Warrington, 2017). Given that "few design studies have been conducted that focus explicitly on equity" (Cobb, Jackson, & Dunlap, 2016, p. 228), increasing the agency of partners and multilingual students within DBR is clearly warranted.

The Ascend Program: A DBR Partnership

This chapter shares information on a collaborative DBR project conducted at a diverse high school adjoining a major midwestern city, where 40% of students are Latinx and over 40% of all students are eligible for free and reduced lunch (Illinois State Board of Education, 2017). In 2014, leaders identified a difference of 30 points between Latinx students and white students on the Prairie State Achievement Exam (Illinois State Board of Education, 2014), along with comparatively lower grade point averages and college enrollment and completion rates. Rather than assume a deficit within the learners themselves, they identified an *opportunity gap* underlying this pattern (da Silva, Huguley, Kakli, & Rao, 2007). Opportunity gaps exist when students have less access to educational opportunities such as advanced coursework. In this instance, Latinx students (many of whom are multilingual) made up 40% of the student body, but only 17% of AP students. Similar trends persist nationwide (Theokas & Saaris, 2013).

Opportunity gaps are often symptomatic of a pernicious view of multilingual students as less capable of advanced work (García, 2009). School leaders suspected that policies perpetuated patterns of unequal access, despite their best intentions. This is troubling because access to challenging coursework is the strongest predictor of college success (Adelman, 2006). Attempting AP classes may positively impact a student's academic future by increasing engagement with rigorous content and emphasizing matriculation to college (Bowen et al., 2009; Jackson, 2010).

Therefore, we sought to understand why so few multilingual students were enrolled in AP coursework and to design interventions to disrupt this pattern. Over a 2-year period, we used DBR to help multilingual students join and successfully complete AP courses. The pedagogical goal was to improve students' mastery of writing evidence-based arguments warranted by original reasoning, a key skill for AP success and civic engagement (Graff & Birkenstein, 2007). We were not alone on this journey. We brought in the experts: the students themselves. Centering student experiences strengthens DBR by honoring the assets and insights of multilingual learners.

The partnership began in the fall of 2016 when two school-based leaders (Tim and Claudia) contacted their university partner (Ryan) for help supporting Latinx student enrollment and success in AP coursework. The team first designed and co-led an extracurricular group, named *Ascend* to convey a sense of growth and possibility. We intended to encourage Latinx students not previously viewed as AP candidates to choose to enroll in advanced classes. In Year 1, our DBR centered on the Ascend group, which emphasized developing a growth mindset (Dweck, 2006) and improving academic self-concept through experiences that included interviewing current AP students and successful Latinx alums, meeting AP teachers, and collectively completing AP-style essays. In Year 2, we transitioned to one AP Language and Composition classroom, where Ascend students and their classmates learned to write arguments warranted with original reasoning. Over the 2-year period, Ascend students became consultants and leaders, helping us understand and address the causes and consequences of unequal AP access (McCarty et al., 2018).

Our intersectional identities are important to acknowledge. Tim is a white male English Department Chair and AP Language and Composition teacher at the research site. Claudia is the Associate Principal for Student Services who is a Latinx female with extensive experience supporting Latinx students and families as a counselor and administrator. Ryan, the university partner, is a white male who previously served in similar contexts as a literacy coordinator, a coach of principals and teachers, and a secondary teacher. Claudia's linguistic and cultural knowledge as a Colombian immigrant was an essential asset to our research, while Tim's expertise in literary theory and dialogic teaching was invaluable in analyzing AP literacy demands and designing classroom-based interventions. Ryan's knowledge of

DBR methods and experience guiding change efforts helped trace the enhancing and inhibiting factors of our interventions. Our personal and professional identities both influenced and limited how we interpreted our students' schooled lives.

Principles for DBR with Multilingual Students

Critical DBR principles informed our research, which, in turn, shaped practice and policy changes in the school. We argue that researchers should take specific actions to maximize the full potential of DBR partnerships with multilingual students. To that end, we offer guiding questions for research teams to ask themselves at each phase of DBR (Reinking & Bradley, 2008). These questions emerged from a synthesis of research and theory and were refined through our DBR partnership (see Table 9.1). We will now briefly describe how these questions guide research within each phase.

Phase 1: Forming a Research Partnership

Phase 1 typically includes recruiting schools and teachers, discussing project goals, and negotiating research plans and responsibilities (Reinking & Bradley, 2008). In practice, the university partner commonly *pitches* different involvement opportunities to potential research partners, which can be problematic if partners do not feel empowered to propose alternatives. Each party's priorities should be stated, and any competing priorities should be addressed. In our research, Tim and Claudia identified the pedagogical problem and initiated our partnership, engendering mutual ownership that sustained and strengthened our research. A sense of reciprocity (Harrison, MacGibbon, & Morton, 2001) should be a guiding principle, ensuring direct benefits to partners and multilingual students.

Given the multidimensional challenges facing multilingual students, research teams should include members with direct knowledge of their experiences. Representation matters, and team members who share common cultural and linguistic characteristics with multilingual students can help ensure that assets are recognized and students are not essentialized. If university-based researchers are outsiders to the groups being studied, they should proceed with humility and curiosity, learning from and with key informants with direct knowledge of participants' assets and needs.

Phase 2: Collecting Information to Understand the Context

In Phase 2, Reinking and Bradley (2008) recommend using ethnographic and interview methods to collect contextual and demographic information and create a thick description of the context. Our school-based research team had helpful knowledge of district policies governing multilingual students, including hypotheses

TABLE 9.1. Guiding Questions for Design-Based Research with Multilingual Students

DBR phase[a]	Guiding questions for design-based research with multilingual students
Phase 1: Forming a Research Partnership	• Does your research team include partners with insider knowledge of the pedagogical problem as experienced by multilingual students? • Does your team have the cultural and linguistic knowledge to capture nuanced student language use?
Phase 2: Collecting Information to Understand the Context	• Does your analysis include the prior learning experiences of multilingual students? • Do you consider structural and systemic factors that may contribute to differences in achievement? • Have you chosen a research design that provides direct access to the thinking of multilingual students? • Are you avoiding a deficit mindset when examining demographic data that may indicate differences in student achievement?
Phase 3: Gathering Baseline Data Prior to the Intervention	• Do your baseline data capture what multilingual students can already do, as well as where they may need support? • Do your baseline data include multiple measures of student learning? • Do your data include information about multilingual students as learners (e.g., language histories)?
Phase 4: Implementing and Refining the Intervention through Design Cycles	• Are you offering multilingual students active and agentive roles in their own learning? • Are design changes informed by both empirical data and affective experiences of multilingual students and their teachers? • Have you created trusting relationships and contexts that invite multilingual students to share openly and honestly?
Phase 5: Administering a Post-Assessment	• Are your data collection tools sensitive enough to capture developmental and uneven changes in learning? • Are you assessing what multilingual students can do as well as what they cannot yet do? • Are you using multiple measures of student learning, such as degree of interaction or forms of discourse? • Are you examining the ways in which modifications may have influenced how students feel about themselves as learners?
Phase 6: Consolidating Data and Refining Theory	• Do your implications include recommendations to build upon multilingual students' assets? • Do your conclusions avoid essentializing the experiences of multilingual students? • Have you shared your conclusions with multilingual students and faculty and gotten their input? • Do your implications acknowledge structural or systemic factors that may limit the effectiveness of your intervention, and suggest ways to overcome or eliminate them?

[a]Adapted from Reinking and Bradley (2008).

about structural barriers and messages students might receive about what classes are, and are not, meant for them.

However, if teachers and researchers aspire to teach for social justice by working to critique and dismantle systems of privilege and oppression, they must acknowledge how their own privilege and implicit biases shape their interpretations of multilingual student learning (Dyches & Boyd, 2017). In this manner, the rigor of DBR methods (e.g., ongoing data collection, triangulation from multiple sources, participant validation of findings) helps ensure that researchers confirm and refine initial impressions to honor students' lived experiences.

A key decision in Phase 2 is whether to examine multilingual student learning in homogeneous or heterogeneous settings. Chandler-Olcott and Nieroda (2016) caution that using multilingual status as the only factor in DBR can create reductionist views of students and their needs. That being said, creating Ascend, the school's first academically focused Latinx extracurricular group, offered several affordances. While multilingual students typically had monolingual teachers and classmates, convening a critical mass of multilingual students encouraged codemeshing (Canagarajah, 2011, 2013). In Cycle 1, Claudia often combined English and Spanish with humor and warmth, incorporating idioms and insights from her immigrant experience and inviting students to interpret and remix technical concepts like growth mindset (Canagarajah, 2011). A heterogeneous setting with a balance of multilingual and monolingual students was appropriate for Cycle 2, given the makeup of many AP classes.

Phase 3: Gathering Baseline Data Prior to Intervention

In Phase 3, the research team conducts a baseline assessment, determining performance in relation to the pedagogical goal. Any assessment of multilingual students should provide information about both what students *can* and *cannot yet* do. In the Cycle 1 Ascend group intervention, baseline data included surveys of growth mindset and academic self-concept. In Cycle 2 within the AP classroom, baseline data included self-efficacy surveys (Pajares et al., 2007), interviews, reading achievement test scores, and writing samples. We later realized that since our argument writing task (adapted from a released AP Language and Composition exam) required a cold read of several challenging texts on unfamiliar topics, it was difficult for multilingual students to demonstrate their full range of synthesis and argument skills.

Phases 4 and 5: Enacting, Refining, and Determining Intervention Impact

In Phase 4, the intervention is enacted and refined as researchers gather and analyze data in iterative cycles, tracing preliminary enhancing and inhibiting features (Reinking & Bradley, 2008). Building trusting relationships where students share openly and honestly in their languages of choice strengthens research validity, while offering students active and agentive roles improves the potential for transfer of skills. In Phase 5, researchers administer assessments, comparing post data and baseline performance to determine progress toward the pedagogical goal. Capturing multiple dimensions of language learning, such as oral discourse, planning documents, revisions, and written products, helps ensure that researchers document both what students *can* do, and leading edges of growth.

Phase 6: Consolidating Data and Refining Theory

Phase 6 often includes conducting a retrospective analysis (Gravemeijer & Cobb, 2006) where findings are consolidated by examining patterns across cycles and data sources. Researchers then draw conclusions, proposing pedagogical assertions or a humble theory to inform work in similar contexts (Gravemeijer & Cobb, 2006; Reinking & Bradley, 2008). While it is essential to examine the role of structural or systemic factors that may limit opportunities for multilingual students, it is also important not to essentialize their experiences.

We will present our research to illustrate these principles in practice. To be clear, our own work did not initially exemplify each principle; it was often through the failure inherent within the design process (Sloane & Gorard, 2003) that their importance came to light. Our DBR consisted of three long-term macrocycles (Table 9.2) that were made up of shorter minicycles of design and analysis (Gravemeijer & Cobb, 2006). Our pedagogical goal was to improve Latinx students' mastery of writing evidence-based arguments warranted by original reasoning.

The designs in each cycle contained three essential characteristics: (1) an emphasis on writing warranted arguments (e.g., Toulmin, 1958; Warren, 2010); (2) dialogic teaching (e.g., Bakhtin, 1981; Reznitskaya, 2012); and (3) academic self-efficacy (e.g., Bandura, 1997; Pajares et al., 2007). These characteristics are justified because although an argument's effectiveness hinges on the warrant (Toulmin, 1958), adolescent writers often do not use them, overlooking their usefulness for one's audience (Crammond, 1998; VanDerHeide, Juzwik, & Dunn, 2016). Emphasizing warrants within dialogic teaching where multilingual students debate controversial issues positions them in agentive roles, reinforcing the structure and purpose of warranting arguments, and encouraging critical thinking about the arguments they encounter in their daily lives. Finally, promoting self-efficacy through examining models of effective warranted arguments and receiving extensive peer and teacher feedback generates mastery experiences, helping multilingual students persevere with challenging writing tasks (Pajares et al., 2007).

In Cycle 1 (2016–2017 school year), we formed the Ascend group, recruiting Latinx sophomores who fell within the 30th and 50th percentile on a standardized screening assessment or who were recommended by their teachers. The group participated in 12 hour-long workshops that emphasized developing a growth mindset (Dweck, 2006) and promoting self-efficacy (e.g., Bandura, 1997) by offering students agentive roles as expert consultants to the school principal on increasing Latinx AP enrollment. In later sessions, students collaboratively completed modified AP

TABLE 9.2. Cycles of the Ascend Program, a DBR Partnership

Essential element	Practices enacting the essential element in Cycle 1: Ascend Group SY 2016–2017 (24 students)	Practices enacting the essential element in Cycle 2: AP Class First Semester SY 2017–2018 (30 students/4 focal students)	Practices enacting the essential element in Cycle 3: AP Class Second Semester SY 2017–2018 (30 students/4 focal students)
Writing warranted arguments	Collectively unpacking and writing AP synthesis essay prompts	Providing argument templates for structuring warrants (Graff & Birkenstein, 2007)	Explicitly teaching types of reasoning to warrant an argument (Brockriede & Ehninger, 1967)
Dialogic teaching	Whole-class and small-group discussions of growth mindset and overcoming obstacles to AP enrollment	Structured Academic Controversy (SAC) discussions and role-play on issues including fracking and gun control (Johnson & Johnson, 2009)	Partner peer critique dialogues and discussion of ways to strengthen reasoning within warrants (Reznitskaya, 2012)
Enhancing self-efficacy	Positive mastery experience of serving as consultants to the principal (Pajares et al., 2007)	Social persuasions of peers within SAC discussions	Vicarious experiences of teacher modeling warrant types and sharing mentor texts (Bandura, 1997)

argument writing tasks and interviewed panels of AP students and successful Latinx alums. At the close of Cycle 1, 54% of Ascend students enrolled in AP, a promising trend given that only 17% of all AP students were Latinx (McCarty et al., 2018).

Having made modest progress in increasing Latinx AP enrollment, our next two design macrocycles (Cycles 2 and 3) shifted to Tim's particularly diverse junior-level AP Language and Composition course, which was nearly 50% Latinx and included four Ascend students. This shift occurred because on the Cycle 1 post survey, students implored us to continue the Ascend group, and because further support with evidence-based argument writing was warranted based on Cycle 1 findings.

The dialogic approach within Cycle 2 emphasized crafting arguments about controversial issues through Structured Academic Controversy (SAC) discussions (Johnson & Johnson, 2009) and role-play prior to writing. Cycle 3 added an emphasis on explicitly teaching types of warrants (Brockriede & Ehninger, 1960) through exercises of increasing cognitive complexity, including teacher modeling, mentor texts, and peer feedback (Anderson, Krathwohl, & Bloom, 2001).

Enacting, Refining, and Determining Impact

Phases 4 and 5 of DBR, where the intervention is enacted and refined through a series of iterations and the impact on student learning is determined (Reinking & Bradley, 2008), are when the bulk of essential design work occurs. Therefore, we will discuss our iterations from each DBR cycle separately, highlighting connections to the guiding questions that illustrate principles for DBR with multilingual students (Table 9.1). We then close this section by sharing our Phase 6 retrospective analysis of patterns across all three macrocycles.

Cycle 1: The Ascend Group (2016–2017)

We began Phase 4 in the Ascend group with carefully designed lesson plans, which we co-taught. While there were brief, structured opportunities for peer collaboration, the overall approach was teacher-centered. When we examined initial field notes and student work, it was clear that instructors were doing most of the talking—from unpacking the content (excerpts from Carol Dweck's 2006 book *Mindset*), to debriefing exit tickets.

Claudia pointed out that we mistakenly assumed we knew the right interventions, when, in fact, the students themselves were the true experts on why they and their peers were not enrolling in AP. Acknowledging their expertise and affirming the value of their experiences made our project more asset-based, providing insights that accelerated progress toward our pedagogical goal. We modified our intervention, telling students we needed their insights as consultants to the principal, and expanded discussion of student-selected topics.

Offering students agentive roles also made space for powerful translanguaging practices (e.g., Canagarajah, 2013; García & Wei, 2014). After analyzing survey data from their peers, students coined the phrase *más o menos mindset* (literally translated as "more or less"). They explained that many multilingual students had a *más o menos* mindset, falling somewhere between Dweck's (2006) binary descriptions of fixed or growth mindsets. They are hesitant to fully commit to AP due to mixed messages from teachers and peers about their readiness for advanced work. Ascend students presented these findings to the school principal, who took notes and asked thoughtful questions (McCarty et al., 2018). They also collectively unpacked and answered a released AP essay prompt on honor codes, contrasting school-based and family notions of honor. We believe these positive mastery experiences supported writing self-efficacy (Pajares et al., 2007).

In Phase 5, we conducted post surveys and student interviews, coding transcripts from Ascend group discussions and interviews, and triangulating these with survey data to understand conditions that encourage or inhibit participation in advanced coursework. One student named Miguel (all student names are pseudonyms) stated, "I'm doing AP next year. And sooner or later you're going to have to start talking. You can't just sit there and nod at everything. You have to get out of your comfort zone" (Student Interview, Cycle 1). By refining our intervention to offer agentive roles to multilingual students, we created a virtuous cycle whereby elevating student voices elevated our understanding of enhancing and inhibiting factors, which, in turn, elevated the quality of our intervention designs for Cycles 2 and 3.

Cycle 2: Dialogic Teaching in the AP Classroom
(First Semester, SY, 2017–2018)

Based on insights from Cycle 1, in Phase 4 of Cycle 2, we knew we wanted to offer multilingual students agentive roles within the AP classroom. We chose a modified approach to Structured Academic Controversy (SAC) discussions (Johnson & Johnson, 2009) to examine controversial issues (i.e., fracking and gun control). After a whole-class inquiry dialogue introducing the issue (Reznitskaya & Gregory, 2013), students examined a series of challenging texts, gathering evidence for both sides of their arguments. They then negotiated the specific inquiry question and were assigned a side of the issue, working with a partner to craft and rehearse arguments before forming a group of four with another pair who argued the opposite side. For the discussion of fracking, students debated while playing a role (e.g., as a state representative or an energy executive), arguing from their chosen perspective before eventually conceding points of agreement and reaching consensus on a mutually beneficial resolution (Pappageorge, 2013). Field notes of small-group interactions provided insight into how focal Ascend students collaboratively constructed their arguments. We believe these SAC dialogues provided social persuasions that supported writing self-efficacy. Following these discussions, they wrote essays using argument templates (Graff & Birkenstein, 2007) utilizing Google Docs to scaffold key rhetorical moves (McCarty et al., 2018).

We initially hypothesized that taking on agentive roles while discussing controversial topics would be sufficient to foster warranted arguments. Our primary Cycle 2, Phase 5 outcome measure was an AP Synthesis writing task (focused on whether or not college was worth the expense), along with interview data. Since the holistic AP Synthesis Essay rubric provided by the College Board provided little insight into the quality of reasoning within students' warrants, we developed a rubric to measure original reasoning within warrant attempts (McCarty et al., 2018). Though direct causal claims cannot be made, students wrote longer essays with more idea units ($m = 2.75$ pre vs. $m = 7.5$ post) devoted to warrant attempts. However, students tended to merely restate or summarize arguments found within the accompanying text sets, as illustrated in the following response: "These reasons mentioned show that even though unemployment rates might be rising, high school students will still have a greater possibility to earn more income" (Cycle 2, Student Essay). While dialogic teaching appeared to help students recognize the need for warrants, we hypothesized that more explicit instruction in reasoning to warrant a claim was needed.

Cycle 3: Adding Explicit Instruction and Feedback
(Second Semester, SY, 2017–2018)

To help students include more original reasoning in their warrants, we provided explicit instruction in four common reasoning approaches to warrant a claim, namely, cause and effect, comparison and contrast, sign, and analogy. These approaches indicate beliefs about evidence reliability due to relationships between ideas (Brockriede & Ehninger, 1960). We explicitly taught these approaches using tasks of increasing cognitive complexity (Anderson, Krathwohl, & Bloom, 2001), emphasizing modeling with a mentor text and peer feedback. Tim wrote the mentor text, an essay about the possibilities and pitfalls of language, from an ongoing argument synthesis inquiry unit that included over a dozen suggested informational texts and novels. The mentor text included evidence from articles about the Arab Spring uprising, Black Lives Matter, and the #MeToo movement. Tim modeled his thinking as he shared his essay and then proposed several potential warrants. Students helped him refine and strengthen his writing. This modeling and mentor text use provided students with vicarious experiences of effective argument writing (Pajares et al., 2007). Students then practiced writing each warrant type within a sample paragraph the teacher had begun, analyzing their effectiveness with peers before applying them in their own essays.

Though multilingual students often only receive feedback on the superficial features of their writing (e.g., Ferris, 2009), these students engaged in peer critique dialogues, providing targeted feedback on reasoning within warrant attempts using both the researcher-created warrant rubric from Cycle 2 and the warrant types. These dialogues offered students active roles and emphasized providing peers with honest and helpful critiques as they co-constructed arguments (Reznitskaya, 2012). They audio-recorded these dialogues on their Chromebooks, submitting the audio files to the teacher using Google Classroom for a formative grade.

In Phase 5 of Cycle 3, Writing Self-Efficacy Scale (WSES) data (Pajares et al., 2007) showed an increase in confidence of just over 10 points from 71.28 to 81.50 (100-point scale), surpassing the gains of the rest of the class by approximately 5 points. A selective sample of students interviewed following Phase 3 revealed that both Ascend and non-Ascend students valued the interventions, particularly the SAC discussions in Cycle 2 and the peer and teacher feedback on warrant attempts in Cycle 3. On the post unit writing task (a released AP Synthesis essay about whether or not certain texts should be required reading), the results were mixed, though some focal students successfully applied the warrant types introduced in the unit. For example, one wrote, "If a student is assigned to read a specific piece of text and has no say in it they might feel less compelled to completed [sic] the task" (Student Essay, Phase 3). This example shows the student hedging their thinking and includes linguistic markers of cause–effect reasoning.

Retrospective Analysis: Consolidating Data and Refining Theory

While our researcher-created warrant rubric provided a metalanguage to discuss reasoning, it did not capture developmental changes in student writing. Therefore, in our retrospective analysis, we turned to the work of researcher Jon-Philip Imbrenda (e.g., Imbrenda, 2018a, 2018b), who designed and tested semantic differential scales to capture important developmental dimensions of high school student writing in urban schools. Dimensions include reciprocity (inviting the reader into the conversation and making an arguable claim; Nystrand, 1986) and indexicality (using conventional forms of academic reasoning in contextually appropriate ways; Chafe, 1986). Analyzing focal student writing with these tools across cycles enabled us to recognize new strengths (McCarty, 2020). For example, the focal student María demonstrated a high level of reciprocity in her essay about whether or not college is worth the expense. To initiate her argument, she wrote:

> Picture parents yelling at you every day, telling you that you have to be better than them, that they want you to have a better life than they had, that they didn't come to America so you could just lay around all day and do nothing. Parents like these most likely never went to college, so that you could have a better life than them and not have to work as hard as they do. (Student Essay, Cycle 2)

This essay invited the reader into the perspective of a multilingual student by citing a vivid example, both particular to the immigrant experience and connected to the universal challenge of meeting parental expectations. Such reciprocity is often a leading edge of growth toward further academic reasoning (Imbrenda, 2018b). This excerpt also used hedges and employed inventive sentence structure to suggest a nagging parent, assets overlooked in our initial Cycle 2 analysis.

Multilingual students are rarely included as partners in understanding, researching, and shaping education practice and policy (Paris & Alim, 2017), a pattern we aspire to disrupt in our research. In Cycle 1, students served as consultants, highly influencing our decision to expand Ascend and extend our research to the AP classroom. In Cycle 2, students debated real-world issues such as fracking and gun control, advocating for new legislation and greater gun manufacturer accountability. In Cycle 3, students learned powerful new tools for warranting arguments, applying them in peer critique dialogues using evidence from contemporary and culturally responsive texts.

Our work began with a broad theory of dialogic instruction to support the argumentative writing of multilingual students. We initially believed that creating a dialogic space through SAC discussions and role-play alone would improve student mastery of warranting arguments with original reasoning. While the number of warrants did seem to increase, we needed to further refine our interventions to progress toward our pedagogical goal. Due to its iterative nature, DBR is amenable to such changes, an important quality given the complexity of academic writing in another language. Each DBR cycle with multilingual students generates powerful insights into pedagogical problems, student assets, and needed supports.

Our *humble theory* is that mastery of argumentative writing warranted by original reasoning for multilingual students can be strengthened by dialogic writing instruction that offers opportunities to take on agentive roles and discuss controversial issues. This should include explicit instruction in writing specific types of warrants. Situating these cognitive moves within authentic, collaborative inquiry and peer critique helps students build an understanding of arguments as ongoing conversations. Formative assessment tools should measure multiple dimensions of student learning and classroom interaction in order to capture developmental changes in writing, including strengths to build on and areas for support.

Impact and Opportunities for Future DBR Partnerships

What began with a group of 24 Ascend sophomores over 3 years ago has expanded to currently include more than 100 students who attend bi-weekly meetings, forming an emerging network of multilingual students who are successfully navigating advanced classes. We have broadened the criteria for AP enrollment beyond test scores to include student interest, teacher and peer recommendations, and class performance. Though the opportunity gap has not closed completely, Latinx students have comprised close to 30% of all AP enrollment. As one Ascend student stated,

> "I finally feel like I'm kind of on the same level as everyone else (in AP) . . . like if we are in the group and we're having a discussion, I feel like I can add to that discussion. I'm actually helping others." (Student Interview, Cycle 2)

Ascend students have also taken on greater leadership roles within the school, having spoken to the school board, organized a *Familias en Educación* parent night in partnership with an area university, and mentored Latinx underclassmen.

In future design cycles, we will continue to refine interventions guided by our humble theory. We are expanding students' choices in selecting controversies and texts reflective of their lived realities, balancing explicit instruction into ways of warranting an argument with opportunities to leverage their own linguistic and cultural knowledge through translanguaging practices. We are increasing student agency and moving beyond writing for AP tests and toward crafting digital and multimodal arguments to address social justice issues affecting their communities.

There is currently a renewed emphasis on educational equity in response to police brutality and the resulting Black Lives Matter movement, along with the disproportionate impact of COVID-19 on Black and Brown communities. Educators are eager to examine antiracist and culturally sustaining practices (Paris & Alim, 2017). DBR is an ideal method for such work, and the methodology would benefit from the greater involvement of multilingual researchers, teachers, students, and families as co-designers of educational futures (Fowler-Amato & Warrington, 2017). For example, translanguaging has been strongly theorized and would benefit from DBR to test and refine models of instruction to support codemeshing practices (Canagarajah, 2013; García & Wei, 2014). With the emphasis on digital literacy amidst remote learning, DBR should be used to examine the affordances of digital technologies to co-construct and warrant arguments, including semiotic resources beyond language (Canagarajah, 2013).

Now more than ever, DBR is needed to develop and refine new theories and practices to support the learning of multilingual students—when used as part of a principled approach building on their linguistic and cultural assets. By spotlighting important and often inconvenient truths including inhibiting factors and unintended consequences, DBR methods empower educators and school leaders to critically examine their own practice in order to enhance learning opportunities for multilingual students.

REFERENCES

Adelman, C. (2006). *The toolbox revisited: Paths to degree completion from high school through college.* Washington, DC: U.S. Department of Education.

Alvarez, S. (2014). Emergent bilingual youth as language brokers for homework in immigrant families. *Language Arts, 91,* 326–339.

Anderson, L. W., Krathwohl, D. R., & Bloom, B. S. (2001). *A taxonomy for learning, teaching, and assessing: A revision of Bloom's taxonomy of educational objectives.* New York: Longman.

Applebee, A. N., & Langer, J. A. (2011). EJ extra: A snapshot of writing instruction in middle schools and high schools. *The English Journal, 100*(6), 14–27.

Au, K. (2007). Culturally responsive instruction: Application to multiethnic classrooms. *Pedagogies: An International Journal, 2*(1), 1–18.

Ayon, C., & Aisenberg, E. (2010). Negotiating cultural values and expectations within the public child welfare system: A look at *familismo* and *personalismo*. *Child & Family Social Work, 15*(3), 335–344.

Bakhtin, M. M. (1981). *The dialogic imagination: Four essays* (M. Holquist, Ed.). Austin: University of Texas Press.

Bandura, A. (1997). *Self-efficacy: The exercise of control.* New York: Freeman.

Batalova, J., & McHugh, M. (2010). *Top languages spoken by English language learners nationally and by state.* Washington, DC: Migration Policy Institute.

Bowen, W. G., Chingos, M. M., & McPherson, M. S. (2009). *Crossing the finishing line: Completing college at America's public universities.* Princeton, NJ: Princeton University Press.

Brockriede, W., & Ehninger, D. (1960). Toulmin on argument: An interpretation and application. *Quarterly Journal of Speech, 46*(1), 44–53.

Canagarajah, S. (2011). Codemeshing in academic writing: Identifying teachable strategies of translanguaging. *The Modern Language Journal, 95,* 401–417.

Canagarajah, S. A. (2013). Negotiating translingual literacy: An enactment. *Research in the Teaching of English, 48,* 40–67.

Chafe, W. (1986). Evidentiality in English conversation and academic writing. In W. Chafe & J. Nichols (Eds.), *Evidentiality: The linguistic coding of epistemology* (pp. 261–272). Norwood, NJ: Ablex.

Chandler-Olcott, K., & Nieroda, J. (2016). The creation and evolution of a co-teaching community: How teachers learned to address adolescent English language learners' needs as writers. *Equity & Excellence in Education, 49*(2), 170–182.

Cobb, P., Jackson, K., & Dunlap, C. (2016). Design research: An analysis and critique. In L. English & D. Kirshner (Eds.), *Handbook of international research in mathematics education* (3rd ed., pp. 481–503). New York: Routledge.

Colwell, J., Hunt-Barron, S., & Reinking, D. (2013). Obstacles to developing digital literacy on the Internet in middle school science instruction. *Journal of Literacy Research, 45*(3), 295–324.

Conchas, G. (2001). Structuring failure and success: Understanding the variability in Latino school engagement. *Harvard Educational Review, 71*, 475–505.

Crammond, J. G. (1998). The uses and complexity of argument structures in expert and student persuasive writing. *Written Communication, 15*, 230–268.

da Silva, C. D., Huguley, J. P., Kakli, Z., & Rao, R. (2007). *The opportunity gap: Achievement and inequality in education.* Cambridge, MA: Harvard Education Press.

Dudley-Marling, C., & Lucas K. (2009). Pathologizing the language and culture of poor children. *Language Arts, 86*, 362–370.

Dweck, C. S. (2006). *Mindset: The new psychology of success.* New York: Random House.

Dyches, J., & Boyd, A. (2017). Foregrounding equity in teacher education: Toward a model of social justice pedagogical and content knowledge. *Journal of Teacher Education, 68*(5), 476–490.

Fang, Z., & Park, J. (2020). Adolescents' use of academic language in informational writing. *Reading and Writing, 33*(1), 97–119.

Ferris, D. (2009). *Teaching college writing to diverse student populations.* Ann Arbor: University of Michigan Press.

Flores, N. (2019). From academic language to language architecture: Challenging raciolinguistic ideologies in research and practice. *Theory into Practice, 59*, 22–31.

Fowler-Amato, M., & Warrington, A. (2017). Teachers as designers: Social design experiments as vehicles for developing antideficit English education. *Literacy Research: Theory, Method, and Practice, 66*, 358–372.

García, O. (2009). Emergent bilinguals and TESOL: What's in a name? *TESOL Quarterly, 43*(2), 322–326.

García, O., & Wei, L. (2014). Translanguaging and education. In *Translanguaging: Language, bilingualism and education* (pp. 63–77). London: Palgrave Macmillan.

Graff, G., & Birkenstein, C. (2007). *"They say/I say": The moves that matter in persuasive writing.* New York: Norton.

Graham S., & Harris, K. (2015). Common Core State Standards and writing: Introduction to the special issue. *The Elementary School Journal, 115*, 457–463.

Gravemeijer, K., & Cobb, P. (2006). Design research from a learning design perspective. In J. van den Akker, K. Gravemeijer, S. McKenney, & N. Nieveen (Eds.), *Educational design research* (pp. 45–58). London: Routledge.

Gutierrez, K. D., & Vossoughi, S. (2010). Lifting off the ground to return anew: Mediated praxis, transformative learning, and social design experiments. *Journal of Teacher Education, 61*(1–2), 100–117.

Harrison, J., MacGibbon, L., & Morton, M. (2001). Regimes of trustworthiness in qualitative research: The rigors of reciprocity. *Qualitative Inquiry, 7*(3), 323–345.

Howell, E., Butler, T., & Reinking, D. (2017). Integrating multimodal arguments into high school writing instruction. *Journal of Literacy Research, 49*(2), 181–209.

Illinois State Board of Education. (2014). Illinois School Report Card 2014. Retrieved from *www.illinoisreportcard.com/Default.aspx*

Illinois State Board of Education. (2017). Illinois School Report Card 2017. Retrieved from *www.illinoisreportcard.com/Default.aspx*

Imbrenda, J. P. (2018a). Developing academic literacy: Breakthroughs and barriers in a college-access intervention. *Research in the Teaching of English, 52*(3), 317–341.

Imbrenda, J. P. (2018b). "No facts equals unconvincing": Fact and opinion as conceptual tools in high school students' written arguments. *Written Communication, 35*(3), 315–343.

International Literacy Association. (2018). *Standards for the preparation of literacy professionals 2017.* Newark, DE: Author.

Ivey, G., & Broaddus, K. (2007). A formative experiment investigating literacy engagement among adolescent Latina/o students beginning to read, write and speak English. *Reading Research Quarterly, 42,* 512–545.

Jackson, C. K. (2010). A little now for a lot later: An evaluation of a Texas Advanced Placement incentive program. *Journal of Human Resources, 45,* 591–639.

Jimenez, R. T. (1997). The strategic reading abilities and potential of five low-literacy Latina/o readers in middle school. *Reading Research Quarterly, 32,* 224–243.

Johnson, D. W., & Johnson, R. T. (2009). Energizing learning: The instructional power of conflict. *Educational Researcher, 38*(1), 37–51.

Kieffer, M. J., & Thompson, K. D. (2018). Hidden progress of multilingual students on NAEP. *Educational Researcher, 47*(6), 391–398.

Kim, J. S. (2019). Making every study count: Learning from replication failure to improve intervention research. *Educational Researcher, 48,* 599–607.

Kong, A., & Pearson, P. D. (2003). The road to participation: The construction of a literacy practice in a learning community of linguistically diverse learners. *Research in the Teaching of English, 38*(1), 85–124.

Madrid, E. M. (2011) The Latino achievement gap. *Multicultural Education, 19*(3), 7–12.

McCarty, R. (2020). "High schoolers want to be challenged": Helping Latinx students excel in advanced classes though design-based research on writing effective warrants. In *American Reading Forum Annual Yearbook* (Vol. 39). Retrieved from www.researchgate.net/profile/Robert-Griffin-16/publication/343920956_Teachers_as_writers_Engaging_in_a_writing_marathon_to_reclaim_the_neglected_R/links/5f47f7c6458515a88b75cf45/Teachers-as-writers-Engaging-in-a-writing-marathon-to-reclaim-the-neglected-R.pdf

McCarty, R., Pappageorge, T., & Rueda-Alvarez, C. (2018). Resisting the *"más o menos"* mindset: Design-based research to boost Latinx success in advanced coursework through dialogically organized instruction. In M. Nachowitz & K. C. Wilcox (Eds.), *High literacy in secondary English/language arts classrooms: Bridging the gap to college and career* (pp. 185–209). Lanham, MD: Rowman & Littlefield.

Moll, L., & Diaz, S. (1987). Change as the goal of educational research. *Anthropology & Education Quarterly, 18,* 300–311.

Nachowitz, M., & Wilcox, K. C. (2018). Conceptualizing high literacy. In M. Nachowitz & K. C. Wilcox (pp. 3–21). *High literacy in secondary English language arts: Bridging the gap to college and career.* Langham, MD: Rowman & Littlefield.

National Council of Teachers of English. (2020). NCTE position paper on the role of English teachers in educating English language learners (ELLs). Retrieved from *https://ncte.org/statement/teaching-english-ells*

Newell, G. E., & Bloome, D. (2017). Teaching and learning literary argumentation in high school English language arts classrooms. In K. Hinchman & D. Appleman (Eds.), *Adolescent literacy: A handbook of practice-based research* (pp. 379–397). New York: Guilford Press.

Nystrand, M. (1986). *The structure of written communication: Studies in reciprocity between writers and readers.* Norwood, NJ: Ablex.

Olsen, L. (2010). *Reparable harm: Fulfilling the unkept promise of educational opportunity for California's long term English learners.* Long Beach: Californians Together.

Pajares, F., Johnson, M. J., & Usher, E. L. (2007). Sources of writing self-efficacy beliefs of elementary, middle, and high school students. *Research in the Teaching of English, 42,* 104–120.

Pappageorge, T. (2013). *Roles of engagement: Examining the use of role-playing controversy in the teaching and learning of argument writing among 9th grade students.* PhD diss., University of Illinois at Chicago. Retrieved from *https://indigo.uic.edu/bitstream/handle/10027/11297/Pappageorge_Tim.pdf?sequence=1*

Paris, D., & Alim, H. S. (Eds.). (2017). *Culturally sustaining pedagogies: Teaching and learning for justice in a changing world.* New York: Teachers College Press.

Reinking, D. (2011). Beyond the laboratory and the lens: New metaphors for literacy research. In P. J. Dunston, L. B. Gambrell, K. Headley, S. K. Fullerton, P. M. Stecker, V. R. Gillis, & C. C. Bates (Eds.), *60th Yearbook of the Literacy Research Association* (pp. 1–17). Oak Creek, WI: Literacy Research Association.

Reinking, D., & Bradley, B. A. (2008). *On formative and design experiments: Approaches to language and literacy research.* New York: Teachers College Press.

Reznitskaya, A. (2012). Dialogic teaching: Rethinking language use during literature discussions. *Reading Teacher, 65,* 446–456.

Reznitskaya, A., & Gregory, M. (2013). Student thought and classroom language: Examining the mechanisms of change in dialogic teaching. *Educational Psychologist, 48*(2), 114–133.

Schleppegrell, M. J. (2013). The role of metalanguage in supporting academic language development. *Language Learning, 63*(1), 153–170.

Sloane, F. C., & Gorard, S. (2003). Exploring modeling aspects of design research. *Educational Researcher, 32*(1), 29–31.

Snow, C. E., & Uccelli, P. (2009). The challenge of academic language. In D. R. Olson & N. Torrance (Eds.), *The Cambridge handbook of literacy* (pp. 112–133). New York: Cambridge University Press.

Theokas, C., & Saaris, R. (2013). *Finding America's missing AP and IB students.* Washington, DC: The Education Trust.

Toulmin, S. (1958). *The uses of argument.* Cambridge, UK: Cambridge University Press.

U.S. Department of Education, Institute of Education Sciences, National Center for Education Statistics (2012). Digest of education statistics 2012. Retrieved from *nces.ed.gov/programs/digest/d12/tables/dt12_047.asp*

VanDerHeide, J., Juzwik, M., & Dunn, M. (2016). Teaching and learning argumentation in English: A dialogic approach. *Theory into Practice, 55*(4), 287–293.

Warren, J. E. (2010). Taming the warrant in Toulmin's model of argument. *English Journal, 99*(6), 41–46.

CHAPTER 10

Using Design-Based Research to Develop a Formative Assessment Tool

Kristi Tamte Bergeson

Comprehension is a massive and active multivariable process (Hoffman, 2017; Pressley & Afflerbach, 1995). To comprehend means that a reader engages with a text, for a purpose, situated in a setting, at a particular point in time (Rosenblatt, 1978). The many variables that contribute to a reader's comprehension include the reader's purpose for reading, motivation, goals, executive skills, strategies, knowledge, decoding, fluency, vocabulary, language, and culture (Duke & Cartwright, 2019). These variables interact with one another in self-perpetuating ways (Paris, 2005). As an example, a reader's purpose for reading influences the strategies that a reader may use while reading, and this impacts the knowledge and understanding a reader gains from texts (van den Broek, Bohn-Gettler, Kendeou, Carlson, & White, 2011).

The Challenge of Assessing Comprehension

The complexity in this active, multivariable reading process can lead to unclear views of comprehension instruction in schools and even greater perplexity in knowing how to support students who may be struggling in this area of their schoolwork (see also Chapter 7, on adolescent reading, and Chapter 9, on second-language learners, this volume). Students experiencing difficulty with comprehension do not fit a single cognitive profile (Karlsson et al., 2018). Some readers, for example, may have difficulty identifying central information in texts (van den Broek, Helder, & van Leijenhorst, 2013), while other readers differ between their difficulty with higher-order processes and word- or sentence-level processes (Oakhill & Cain, 2012). Sometimes readers activate background knowledge that is not relevant to the text, and this can lead to inaccurate inferences (Kendeou & van den Broek, 2007). Still other readers may have difficulty holding onto a central idea in the text while considering important connections and details across the text (Budd, Whitney, & Turley, 1995).

Though comprehension is a dynamic, multivariable process, it is often assessed in schools as a product or an outcome of reading (Leslie & Caldwell, 2017; Pearson & Hamm, 2005). Product assessments, such as multiple-choice tests, question–response, and retell are used to assess comprehension after a student has finished reading a text. This limits the teacher's instructional approach because product assessments do not show how individual readers are thinking about texts while they are reading (van den Broek & Espin, 2012). Product assessments make it hard for practitioners to know why a student may be experiencing difficulty and when in the reading process this difficulty has occurred. Comprehension is an unconstrained skill, and this necessitates assessments that can take into account cognitive flexibility and contextual variation (Paris, 2005). Recently, comprehension researchers have highlighted the need for comprehension assessments that can guide instruction (Leslie & Caldwell, 2017) and support the individual student's reading process (Kendeou, van den Broek, Helder, & Karlsson, 2014). When practitioners pay close attention to the processes students use as they read, they have the opportunity to adjust instruction to better support readers. This is critically important when working with students who are experiencing difficulty.

Why Design-Based Research in the Context of Reading Comprehension Assessment?

I became interested in design-based research (DBR; McKenney & Reeves, 2012; Reinking & Bradley, 2008) related to this vexation of comprehension assessment for several reasons. DBR creates a bridge between research and practice; it is firmly grounded in theory while seeking a solution to a complex problem; it allows for formative decisions to be made as part of the research process and draws on the expertise of practitioners (see Chapter 1, this volume, for an overview of DBR). In the following section, I describe each of these attributes of DBR that led me to approach the development of a comprehension assessment through a DBR study.

A Bridge between Research and Practice

DBR (McKenney & Reeves, 2012; Reinking & Bradley, 2008) allowed me to seek a solution to a complex problem by creating a bridge between research and practice. As a classroom teacher and reading specialist, I struggled to understand the challenges many of my students faced with reading comprehension. Available comprehension assessments in schools provided only a partial view of my students' difficulty. With my colleagues, we wondered if students' difficulty was related to interest in texts, reader identity, decoding, fluency, vocabulary knowledge, or the match of background knowledge with a text. Without a strong understanding of the reason/s individual readers struggled with comprehension, it was difficult for me—as their teacher—to know how to provide instructional support in the school setting.

As a researcher, I strived to provide an answer. Thus, through my readings of the literature, I discovered laboratory studies that investigated complex comprehension processes through the use of verbal protocols. Verbal protocols reveal thinking (Ericsson & Simon, 1993; Pressley & Afflerbach, 1995). They have been used since the beginning of psychology to study mental processes (Pressley & Hilden, 2004). Ericcson and Simon (1993) explain that verbal protocols allow readers to *think aloud* without needing to practice, and this dramatically increases the amount of observable behavior. Verbal protocols have been used in laboratory settings to reveal differences among readers who are struggling with comprehension, and these differences are often undetected by more traditional measures (Israel, 2015). Based on my emergent understanding, I began to wonder if verbal protocols could be used in schools to better understand individual reader's challenges with comprehension.

In DBR, scholars move their research from laboratory settings to naturalistic contexts in order to create usable knowledge and ecological validity (Barab & Squire, 2004; Brown, 1992). I wondered if moving verbal protocols from a laboratory setting to the school setting would support practitioners in being able to better understand their individual student's comprehension processes. In addition, I wondered how the naturalistic setting of a school might influence the usability or validity of verbal protocols. Verbal protocols are time-intensive because they generally require a researcher (or in this case, practitioner) to focus on one student at a time. I wondered if this would put too much of a demand on practitioner time to be useful. Also, I wanted to understand how knowledge about cognitive processes would be used by practitioners to locate information from verbal protocols. Furthermore, I wondered how verbal protocols might be used with preset curriculum and whether the social context of classrooms might impact students' verbal reports.

I selected the reading specialist setting as the most natural and relevant place to design this study. Reading specialists often work with one to six students at a time, and this would create less strain on teacher time than a classroom setting. In addition, reading specialists generally have advanced training with reading development, processes, and instruction, and I believed this advanced training would be useful in forming a collaborative partnership. Moreover, reading specialists are focused on better understanding the challenges individual students face in order to support students with their reading development. The idea of working to reveal a deeper understanding of individual student's comprehension processes seemed relevant to the reading specialist's role in a school.

Grounded in Theory

The DBR goal of developing usable knowledge is firmly grounded in theory (Bell, 2004; Brown, 1992). I believed theory would be fundamental to my study for several reasons. First, theory could provide a foundation to understand cognitive processes involved with comprehension. Second, though verbal protocols have been promoted as an instructional practice in schools, not a lot of work has been done in those settings to interpret think-aloud statements based on a theoretical understanding of comprehension processes. Without this theoretical understanding, practitioners are left to interpret verbal protocol statements based on their own unique perspectives and prior knowledge. Third, comprehension researchers and measurement experts have articulated the importance of, and need for, theory-guided comprehension assessments (Kintsch, 2012; Leslie & Caldwell, 2017). By approaching the design of assessments through a theoretical lens of comprehension processes, we could watch for indicators of the reader's comprehension processes and hopefully gain diagnostic information about a reader's difficulty. Fourth, by attaching theory to assessments, we could increase validity of the measurement tool (van den Broek & Espin, 2012), avoiding misleading information from verbal reports, such as focusing on a unidimensional indicator of comprehension. Fifth, an important goal for DBR is to develop and better understand theory by applying it to authentic contexts of learning. Without testing the boundaries of theory in different contexts, or studying the application of theory to practice, the benefits of theory are limited. This study would put theory to work within the natural contexts of learning in schools.

Innovative and Solution-Oriented

DBR is solution oriented through the development of an intervention (Cobb, Confrey, diSessa, Lehrer, & Schauble, 2003). My goal in this study was to create a solution to the challenge of comprehension assessment in schools by developing a way for practitioners to better understand how individual readers process texts. Reinking and Bradley (2008) suggest that DBR researchers ask the question "What could be?" This fit my inquiry and allowed me to explore, design, and test possibilities for educational improvement. The question I wanted to address in this project was: In what ways does a group of reading specialists use information from verbal protocols for their instruction?

Formative Design Decisions

In order to develop verbal protocols as an assessment tool to be used in schools, I wanted to make formative decisions with the reading specialists, based on the ongoing collection of data throughout the study. DBR is open-ended and guided by an inference that is based on theory (Confrey & Lachance, 2000; Reinking & Bradley, 2008). The open-ended nature of the inquiry sustains a posture of continual design, implementation, analysis, and reflection, and this provides opportunities for adjustments, adaptations, and modifications to be made throughout the study. I structured this study in weekly microcycles of enactment that would allow us to respond to unforeseen needs revealed during planned phases of data collection and also during the daily implementation of verbal protocols in the reading specialist setting.

Collaborative Partnerships

DBR is intentionally collaborative and conducted with practitioners whose practical knowledge, expertise, and understanding of the problem at hand are valued and used to design solutions (Wagner, 1997). Indeed, there are several reasons that a collaborative partnership with reading specialists in schools was critical to my study. Importantly, I wanted to develop a fuller understanding of the problem that practitioners faced with comprehension assessments because a shared understanding of the problem could lead to a better innovative product. Furthermore, I believed the expertise, unique perspectives, and knowledge the reading specialists would bring to this study could enhance the intervention design. Additionally, reading specialists had access to important and valuable information for this study. For example, they could let me know if verbal protocols provided new and useful information about their individual student's comprehension processes that had not previously been known through other comprehension assessments. Moreover, by forming a collaborative partnership, the reading specialists and I could alternate in the role of researcher and practitioner. This would allow each of us the opportunity to implement verbal protocols as an assessment tool in the reading specialist setting and also observe and take fieldnotes. Though I planned to spend more time than reading specialists analyzing data between the three schools, I valued the role of reading specialists, not only as practitioners, but also as researchers who could observe, take fieldnotes, analyze their fieldnotes, and share their analysis with me.

Study Explanation and Design

According to McKenney and Reeves (2012), DBR has three main phases. I planned the timeline of my study with these three phases in mind (see Table 10.1 on the project timeline).

Phase 1: Analysis and Exploration

DBR often begins with a preliminary examination of a problem (McKenney & Reeves, 2012). As a researcher, I joined six reading specialists within one midwestern

TABLE 10.1. Timeline for Project

Phase 1: analysis and exploration (6 months)	Phase 2: design and construction (2 months)	Phase 3: evaluation and reflection (2 months)
• Collaborative analysis of problem • Establish theoretical framework and methods • Develop the initial design	• Iterative cycles of testing and refinement of the design • Investigate theoretically principled ideas in practice	• Evaluate the effectiveness of the design • Reflect to produce design principles

public school district for their professional learning community (PLC) meetings for 6 months to inquire about the challenges they faced in their teaching of reading and to ask for their feedback on the design of a formative assessment tool for comprehension. During these months, each of the six reading specialists explored and analyzed with me: (1) current understandings about comprehension processes, (2) approaches that were being used to support students with comprehension in the intervention setting, and (3) strengths and challenges of these approaches.

As part of the preliminary examination of the problem, I also conducted a literature review and shared highlights of this review at the reading specialists' PLC meetings. Specifically, I communicated information about the use of verbal protocols as a research tool used in laboratory settings to study comprehension processes, and I described two theories of comprehension. The first theory I described was constructively responsive reading (Pressley & Afflerbach, 1995). I explained that this theory was created by synthesizing 40 verbal protocol studies and could be used to measure reading comprehension. The second theory that I described to reading specialists was the landscape model of reading (van den Broek, Young, Tzeng, & Linderholm, 1999). The landscape model describes reading comprehension as a cognitive process that involves a parallel activation of information in the text along with related prior knowledge in memory. In the landscape model, readers move through a text in cycles, and for each cycle concepts associated with the text are activated in the reader's mind to various degrees based on four factors: text input in the current sentence, carryover from the previous sentence, the current representation of the text in memory, and a reader's background knowledge. When information is activated, it spreads across a network and links to related concepts. This strengthens understanding and memory of the text. The landscape model describes comprehension as a dynamic interaction between memory-based processes that activate automatically during reading and constructionist processes that are intentional and goal-directed. By the end of Phase 1, I had completed a literature review and established the theoretical framework for the study in consultation with the reading specialists.

The feedback I received from reading specialists during the exploratory phase of DBR helped establish the direction of the project. Based on our initial collaboration, I presented a research proposition to the reading specialists that included the exploration of the use of verbal protocols as a formative assessment tool in the reading specialist setting. In addition, I described DBR as a methodology and invited reading specialists to join me as collaborators in the project. A discussion of the participants, data sources, and findings follows.

Reading Specialists

The primary role of the reading specialists at the time of this study was to work with students in a Tier 2 intervention setting, though reading specialists also provided leadership to the reading programs at their schools. Each of the reading specialists held an elementary education license, had experience as a classroom teacher, received advanced training in reading, held a reading specialist license, and worked at his or her school for at least 5 years in his or her current role.

Three of these reading specialists agreed to become co-learners (Wagner, 1997) for this study. In co-learning agreements, both researchers and practitioners engage as colleagues in collaborative and reflexive inquiry, with the shared goal of contributing knowledge to instructional practice in schools and also contributing knowledge beyond the classroom. The reading specialists and I collaborated on the majority of the project, including developing a shared understanding of the issue, designing the intervention, taking turns teaching and observing, writing fieldnotes, refining the design, contributing to theoretical understanding, and establishing design principles.

The reading specialists' experience and knowledge were critical to the implementation and outcomes of this project. Their extensive knowledge about reading development provided valuable information on the usefulness of verbal protocols as an assessment tool in relation to previous comprehension assessments they had used in their practice. As collaborative colleagues, reading specialists and I alternated between the practitioner role of teaching the students and the researcher role of observing and taking fieldnotes. This opportunity to use verbal protocols with students and also observe the use of verbal protocols in the intervention setting allowed us to combine our understanding, and we discussed both the practical and theoretical implications of verbal protocols as a formative assessment tool.

Students

Eleven students (nine fourth-grade students and two fifth-grade students) from three separate reading groups at three different schools participated in the study. All of the student participants were eligible for intervention services based on district guidelines and their performance on standardized tests. Specifically, students qualified for Tier 2 intervention support based on scores that fell below the 40th percentile on the Measures of Academic Progress (MAP) assessment (Northwest Evaluation Association, 2003). In addition, data from the Qualitative Reading Inventory IV (Leslie & Caldwell, 2006) and a teacher recommendation were used in the selection process. Furthermore, according to district guidelines, students were not pulled from the classroom for multiple intervention programs, so none of the students in the reading intervention sessions also qualified for special education or English language support. Students had been working with the reading specialists for a minimum of 4 months at the start of the study.

Materials

I selected eight trade books and a website about raptors for students' reading materials and presented these materials to reading specialists for feedback. To accommodate the content requirement and standards of the district, one of the texts came from the school district's intervention curriculum. This text was about falcons and led to the choice of raptors as a reading topic. The reading specialists and I valued content grouped texts for reading materials because we recognized the role knowledge played in the reading process (Kendeou & van den Broek, 2007). Furthermore, we wanted students to view reading as an opportunity to learn, rather than a set of isolated skills. Three of the trade books were about eagles, three were about owls, and two were about falcons. Texts ranged from a 2.9 grade level to a 5.2 grade level according to Co-metrix (Graesser, McNamara, & Kulikowich, 2011). This is equivalent to a text range of 525 and 860 Lexile.

Intervention Sessions

Students met in a small-group, pullout setting 5 days a week for 30 minutes at a time for 8 weeks. There were four students in two groups and three students in one group. The reading specialists and I took turns in the role of instructor for these sessions. During these 30 minutes, the instructor provided a purpose statement for the lesson, introduced the text, modeled thinking processes, and then moved around the room listening to students read and think out load. Students also talked with one another about their reading, and on some of the days students wrote a reflection of their learning. During the final week of the study, students created a book about raptors, and they gave this book to the University of Minnesota Raptor Center. In response, each student received a free family pass to visit the Center.

Phase 2: Design and Construction

The implementation phase of DBR is systematic problem solving, while also flexibly iterative to allow for formative decisions about the design to be made throughout the project (McKenney & Reeves, 2012). The reading specialists and I made instructional and design decisions across microcycles of enactment throughout the study. Table 10.2 displays a timeline for Phase 2 implementation of the intervention.

Week 1: Using Verbal Protocols as a Pre-Instruction Assessment

One week before we began the small-group lessons, I met with each of the 11 students independently in a quiet room and asked them to read a text about raptors and share their thinking as they read. I followed the methodological recommendations of Ericsson and Simon (1993) for collecting these data. Specifically, I explained to students, "Strong readers think a lot as they read. It's like a conversation in our heads. When you are aware that you are thinking something about your reading, I want you to say what you are thinking out loud." Then I modeled my own thinking for students while reading the first couple of lines of the text. After this,

TABLE 10.2. Timeline for Phase 2: The Implementation of the Intervention

Week	Micro-cycles of enactment	Output
1	*Exploration* Researcher met with each student independently to gather data using verbal protocols.	Initial view of comprehension challenges for individual readers
1	*Analysis and reflection* Researcher and reading specialists met to analyze and reflect on initial data.	Shared understanding of readers' verbal protocol data
2–3	*Exploration* Students read about eagles (Week 1) and owls (Week 2), while the researcher and reading specialists implemented verbal protocols as a formative assessment tool.	Discovered verbal protocols were easy to implement and revealed points of difficulty in students' reading process.
2–3	*Evaluation and reflection* Reading specialist and researcher engaged in conversations and written reflections about verbal protocols as an assessment tool.	Enthusiasm about verbal protocols in providing new and useful information about students
3	*Design and construction* Refer to the landscape model of reading in relation to verbal protocol data to consider instructional support	Created a table that listed indicators of student difficulty along with coaching prompts.
3	*Evaluation and reflection* Reading specialists and researcher engaged in emails, conversations, written reflections, and sharing of fieldnotes.	Enthusiasm about the table for accurately summarizing different observations and providing a common language to prompt students
4	*Exploration* Students read about falcons, while the researcher and reading specialists coached student processing.	Usefulness of the table to coach students at an identified point of difficulty
4	*Evaluation and analysis* Audiorecorded a reading specialist coaching students based on prompts from the coaching table	Evidence of effective coaching Usefulness of the landscape model as a theoretical model
5–6	*Exploration and analysis* Students read about raptors, wrote about their learning, and created a book about raptors, while the researcher and reading specialists continued to use verbal protocols as a formative assessment tool.	Ongoing data collection and analysis of verbal protocols Refine coaching prompts
7	*Exploration and analysis* Researcher met with each student independently to gather post-intervention data using verbal protocols.	Comparison of pre- and post-intervention verbal protocol statements
8	*Analysis and reflection* Researcher and reading specialists analyzed and reflected on final verbal protocol statements.	View of impact of the study Collaborative insight regarding the ongoing successes and challenges with comprehension assessment

students began reading the raptor text out loud and shared their thinking as they read. If students did not volunteer thinking statements after a paragraph of reading, I prompted students to think out loud with the open-ended prompt "What are you thinking?" I selected this prompt because open-ended prompts are conducive to theoretical understanding (Ericsson & Simon, 1993). Additionally, open-ended prompts provide students with a freedom of response, which is useful in considering formative assessment. Equally important, I prompted readers to share *what* they are thinking, rather than explain their thinking. This activates information in the reader's short-term memory, and short-term memory is a more accurate reflection of processing than long-term memory (Ericsson & Simon, 1993). Furthermore, by activating students' current thinking at different points of the text, this reveals a view of readers' processing as they move through the text.

I audio-recorded 196 minutes of reading and verbal protocol statements and transcribed this information. Then I examined and categorized each think-aloud statement based on Pressley and Afflerbach's (1995) theory of constructively responsive reading. I differentiated between thinking statements that were text-based (paraphrase, ask a question about text content, monitor) and thinking statements that integrated information (relate the text to prior knowledge, make an inference, make a prediction, substantiate a prediction based on new information, critical/evaluative stance). Previous verbal protocol research demonstrated that readers with strong comprehension integrate information during reading, while readers experiencing difficulty with comprehension stay close to the text in their verbal protocol statements (Rapp, van den Broek, McMaster, Kendeou, & Espin, 2007). I added a third category of inaccurate or unclear statements made by students.

At the end of Week 1, I met with each reading specialist individually and shared the verbal protocol statements of their individual readers aligned to categories of thinking. Based on this initial analysis of pre-instruction verbal protocol data, we adjusted our plan for instruction by focusing less on intentional support for reader engagement and motivation during our lessons. This change occurred because of the enthusiasm readers shared during their verbal protocol statements. Frequent comments, such as "Wow that's creepy" and "It's really interesting that . . . ," displayed readers' enthusiasm about reading books on raptors and being part of this study.

We also determined that the readers in this study fit the profile of a student who is struggling with comprehension based on a cognitive view of the reading process. Students' verbal protocol statements revealed a majority of text-based (51%) statements, rather than integration statements (25%). In addition, verbal protocols revealed that when students did integrate information from their background knowledge or the text, many of these statements were inaccurate and uncovered student difficulty understanding how ideas were connected across the text (24%). Based on this finding, we believed an important goal of our sessions would be supporting the integration of information while reading.

Weeks 2–3: Implementing Verbal Protocols in the Reading Specialist Setting

Our initial analysis of verbal protocol data provided insights into the challenges that students may be experiencing. Our next step was to move verbal protocols to the reading specialist classroom. During the next couple of weeks, the reading specialists and I took turns using verbal protocols in the intervention setting while students independently read about eagles (Week 1) and owls (Week 2). We worked as co-learners during this time, taking turns teaching students and observing and taking fieldnotes. In the meantime, we communicated our observations and reflection notes with one another through face-to-face conversations and email.

The data collected and analyzed across these 2 weeks revealed several important findings. First, reading specialists and I discovered that verbal protocols were easy to implement in the intervention setting. During independent reading, the reading specialists and I simply moved around the table to sit next to a student and asked the student to read and think out loud. If students did not share any thinking by the end of a page, we provided the prompt "What are you thinking?" and students shared. Other students in the intervention setting continued reading independently and seemed undistracted by the activity of students reading out loud and sharing verbal protocol statements.

Second, reading specialists reported learning new and useful information about some of the challenges their individual students faced based on verbal protocols. This included being able to identify moments in the processing of texts that their students were experiencing difficulty. Following are examples of the reading specialists' written reflection notes that show initial thinking about verbal protocols:

> "Think-alouds have given me the best insight I've had at where each student's comprehension is breaking down."
>
> "I feel like, just asking the open-ended question of 'What are you thinking?' while a student is reading opens up huge insights into the thought processes that lead to understanding a text. When we wait until after the entire text has been read to ask about the story, we may find out what they remember, but not the processes that they are using to pick out the information." (Bergeson, 2019, p. 188; quotes used with permission from *The Reading Teacher*)

In all three schools reading specialists reported similar findings, and this led me to have confidence that verbal protocols provided new and useful information for practitioners to better understand the challenges their students faced. Based on this conclusion, I referred to the landscape model of reading (van den Broek et al., 1999) to consider our students' verbal protocol statements in relation to this model of cognitive processing. According to the landscape model, there are four sources of information activated during reading. These sources include (1) text input in the current sentence, (2) carryover from the preceding sentence, (3) current understanding of the text as a whole, and (4) readers' background knowledge. I organized our thinking into a table based on these four sources of information with input and feedback from reading specialists. On the left-hand side, I listed indications of difficulty students displayed through verbal protocols for each of the sources of information, and on the right-hand side, I listed coaching prompts that the reading specialists and I believed could support students' processing based on an identified point of difficulty (see Table 10.3).

We created this table to capture significant understandings and to serve the practical goal of coaching students at a point of difficulty. In addition, through this process, we put theory to work and discovered that student's verbal protocol statements aligned to the four sources of information described in the landscape model of reading.

Week 4: Coaching Students at an Identified Point of Difficulty

Each of the reading specialists began using these coaching prompts with their students, and they shared their enthusiasm with me through emails, conversations, and written summaries. One reading specialist wrote in an email:

> "I LOVE THIS!!! This sums up the different observations we have seen and gives us a common language to follow-up with to prompt or redirect the type of thinking needed to understand what is happening at that moment in time in the text, and in their processing. I am already starting to use this language in working with other groups of students too. They really give great insight into what the child is thinking and how to help them move forward in their comprehension development." (Bergeson, 2019, p. 191; quote used with permission from *The Reading Teacher*)

During this fourth week of our project, I audio-recorded and transcribed two 20-minute coaching sessions to analyze the effectiveness of our coaching. Through the transcription, I discovered that the reading specialist coached multiple students with each of the four sources of information based on indicators of student difficulty from our table. Following are examples of the coaching that originated from verbal protocol statements for each of these identified points of difficulty.

- *Source 1: Text input in the current sentence.* By listening to the student read and think out loud, the reading specialist noticed that this student didn't understand the meaning of an important word (*eyases*) in the sentence. The specialist recognized that the placement of commas was keeping the student from using context clues to understand this word. In response, the reading specialist modeled how to read the sentence with commas and then asked, "What do you think 'eyases' means?" The student responded, "A baby falcon?" The reading specialist and student talked about how the commas interrupted the sentence to describe another

TABLE 10.3. Coaching Table

1. If students show difficulty processing text input in the current sentence

Students may . . .	*Teacher prompt:*
Have difficulty pronouncing a word.	"Read that sentence again, think about what's happening in the story, and see if you can figure out what _____ means."
Skip or misread an important word.	"Read that sentence again and be careful to read each word. What are you thinking?"
Ask a question about something that is literal and can be found in the text.	"Read that sentence again and see if you can find your answer in the text."

2. If students show difficulty integrating information from one sentence into the next

Students may . . .	*Teacher prompt:*
Have difficulty with pronouns.	"What is _____ referring to? How do you know?"
Show they are missing important information from a previous sentence.	"Read these two sentences, and look for clues in the sentences that tell you more about _____."
Get stuck on a thought and not pay attention to important new text information.	"Read this sentence again, and look for clues to tell you more about _____."

3. If students show difficulty integrating current representation of text

Students may . . .	*Teacher prompt:*
Show evidence that they are not aware of the big idea in the text.	"How does your thinking connect with what you already know about _____?"
Paraphrase details in the text.	"What do you think is the main message so far in the text? How does _____ fit that main message"
	"How does your thinking connect with the heading '_____' in this informational text?"
	"What's the author trying to tell us?"
	"What do you think is the main problem, and how does what you just read connect to that main problem?"

4. If students show difficulty integrating prior knowledge

Students may . . .	*Teacher prompt:*
Consistently only paraphrase the words they just read and not draw on prior knowledge.	"What do you know about that? Have you ever experienced anything like that? How does that help you understand what's happening in the text?"
	"How does this part of the text connect with something in your life?"
Draw on prior knowledge that takes students away from the meaning in the text.	"Reread this sentence. How does what you know help you understand this sentence?"
	"How does what you know about _____ fit with what this sentence says or is happening in the story?"
	"What do you know now about _____ that you didn't know before?"

Note. Reprinted with permission from Bergeson (2019). Copyright © International Literacy Association.

word for *eyases*. This coaching supported the student in understanding an important word for the story.

- *Source 2: Integrating information from one sentence into the next.* In this example, the reading specialist recognized that a student paraphrased the text in the form of a question because he was missing important information from the previous sentence in the text. The specialist provided the coaching prompt to reread a couple of sentences and look for the answer to his question. In doing so, the student answered his own question and reached an understanding of this portion of text.

- *Source 3: Difficulty integrating current representation of text.* In this example, the reading specialist recognized through verbal protocols that a student was struggling to connect what was happening near the end of the story with the big idea in the text. In addition, she recognized the student was relying on pictures, rather than words, to gain meaning from the text. The reading specialist coached the student to reread a portion of the text and connect his thinking to what was happening in the story. The specialist explained that the author gives clues to show why something is important. Through this coaching, the student made an accurate inference and connected it to the big idea in the text.

- *Source 4: Integrating prior knowledge.* In this example, the reading specialist noticed that a student's activated background knowledge was taking the reader away from the text. The specialist affirmed the student for drawing on background knowledge and prompted him to think about what else the words in the text were revealing. Based on this prompt, the student elaborated on relevant background knowledge about raptors and reached deeper connections and understandings with the text.

In each of these identified points of difficulty, the reading specialist coached and prompted, and the student reached understanding. During this time, one of the reading specialists reminded me about the importance of explicit coaching for students who are experiencing difficulty with reading. Explicit explanations help students internalize the processes they are using, and this carries learning from the reading specialist setting to the student's reading at home and in the classroom.

Weeks 5–7: Refining the Use of Verbal Protocols as a Formative Assessment Tool

The reading specialists and I continued to listen to students read and think out loud. During the seventh week of this project, reading specialists sent me their field and summary notes from the project and shared the ways in which they were working to individualize instruction based on verbal protocol reports. They wrote:

> "Prompt Mary to expand her thinking to understand the big idea of the passage. She doesn't connect to prior knowledge often."

"Ian gets lost in his thoughts and loses focus easily. He needs to be prompted to stay connected with the text. Maybe asking him to think aloud after shorter pieces of text can help him focus. When he stays focused he generally understands what he has read."

"Nancy needs extra time to process before answering questions, and she can give unrelated answers. Does language impact her comprehension?"

"Darleen is able to understand text better than I previously thought. Listening to her think aloud showed that she usually grasps the big idea, but her struggle comes from her difficulties with unknown words." (Bergeson, 2019, p. 191; quotes used with permission from *The Reading Teacher*)

These data showed that reading specialists used verbal protocols to better understand the unique challenges their individual students faced. Furthermore, reading specialists used this information to identify an instructional approach for each of their students. The data revealed that verbal protocols provided insight into the ways individual readers were processing texts. In just a few weeks, all three reading specialists reported learning a lot of information about their students. This led me to have confidence that our findings were more than just a local interaction with the intervention.

During this seventh week, I again met with each of the 11 students independently in a quiet room and asked the students to read a text about raptors out loud and share their thinking as they read. I followed the same procedure to collect post-instruction assessments as I did for the pre-instruction assessments. I transcribed the verbal protocol data and analyzed each statement based on the three categories developed at the beginning of the study. These categories included (1) text-based statements, (2) integration statements, and (3) unclear or inaccurate statements.

Week 8: Impact of Our Work with Students

Findings from the post-instruction assessments showed a positive response to our work with students. I met with the reading specialists and shared the following data.

Increased Words Spoken during Verbal Protocols. Students spoke an average of 147 words during the pre-instruction verbal protocol data collection. After instruction, the average number of words spoken increased to 251 words for the same passage. Previous research demonstrates that strong readers think a lot as they read (Pressley & Afflerbach, 1995), and we viewed this increase in words spoken as a positive response to our work with the students.

Shift in Types of Thinking Statements. There was also change in how the verbal protocol statements aligned to categories established during the pre-instruction analysis. During post-instruction think-aloud statements, students shared more inferences, related text content to prior knowledge more often, made more predictions, and substantiated on these predictions. The percentage of integration statements shifted from 25% in the pre-instruction assessments to 54% in the post-instruction assessments. Adding to the significance of this change, all 11 students increased the number of integration statements made during the post-instruction assessments. In addition, during the pre-instruction assessments, 24% of the statements represented an inaccurate understanding of the text, and this number fell to 7% in the post-instruction assessments.

I believe there are two reasons for this change between pre- and post-instruction verbal protocol statements. First, students were more familiar with the content they were reading by the post-instruction assessments, and this made it easier to activate background knowledge, integrate such knowledge with the text, and form a mental representation of the text. Second, our data suggest that coaching students with reading processes, based on information gained from verbal protocols, increased students' cognitive processing related to inferences, predictions, and background knowledge.

Phase 3: Evaluation and Reflection

The reflection and evaluation phase of DBR involves active and thoughtful consideration of what has occurred during the implementation phase of the study (McKenney & Reeves, 2012). This process is conducted with the goal of finding new understandings. The aim of this phase is both practical in seeking design principles and theoretical in reflecting on the implementation of the design.

Reading specialists and I continued to meet for the next 2 months to review our data and discuss the implications of our study. As we reflected, we were able to conclude that verbal protocols did provide valuable information about individual student's comprehension processes, they were easy to implement in the reading specialist setting, and they led to coaching opportunities for students at an identified point of difficulty. We also recognized that verbal protocols do not only provide information about errors students make as they process texts; they also illuminate students' successes. By making these processes visible and explicit to students, reading specialists can affirm students' processing of text and support students in using these processes outside the intervention setting.

Practical Output

As a practical output of this study, the six reading specialists and I identified design principles of a prescriptive nature to support the development of a formative approach to assessment by reading specialists to be used with students who are struggling with comprehension. The principles illustrate that reading specialists can:

- become familiar with processes of comprehension described in models of cognitive processing.
- listen to students read and think out loud using the prompt "What are you thinking?"
- coach students with their processing of texts based on an individualized understanding of each student.
- make processes visible and explicit to students in order to illuminate their successes and support metacognition.

Future Iterations

During the process of reflection, we also determined that more work is needed to refine verbal protocols as a formative assessment tool. DBR allows for iterative testing over time. We determined that future iterations might address the following questions:

- What length of passage provides reading specialists with useful information about the comprehension processes of individual students?
- How does text difficulty influence the value of the information from verbal protocols?
- What level of expertise about reading comprehension processes is needed to use verbal protocols effectively as a formative assessment tool in schools?
- How can verbal protocol data be easily recorded for further analysis?

Research in these areas is still needed.

Impact and Spread: Learning Points

Reading without understanding widens the achievement gap in schools (Duke & Carlisle, 2011). Program and curriculum changes in schools work to address this achievement gap over time, but DBR is a form of professional development that can have an immediate impact on participants in a study. At a local level, reading specialists and I were able to consider the instructional needs of individual students from a cognitive processing perspective during this study. By listening to students think out loud, reading specialists and I grew in our understanding of cognitive theories in the context of practice. In addition, throughout this study, reading specialists learned new information about their students, and they shared this information with classroom teachers, parents, specialists, and principles.

Student participants were also impacted by this study. When considering the pre- to post-data of verbal protocols, our students shifted their thinking toward more integration statements. These integration statements are consistent with the research of strong readers (Rapp et al., 2007) and demonstrate positive learning from this study. We found that our students were enthusiastic participants in this study. They knew that their work was valued, and they engaged with us in many rounds of metacognition throughout our study. Research often takes years to influence practice, but the impact of a DBR study can be immediate on both students and teachers (Confrey & Lachance, 2000).

The flexibility and iterative nature of DBR led to the development of useful knowledge. DBR allowed us to make adjustments throughout the study based on our ongoing data collection, analysis, and the unique contexts for our study. As an example, data from verbal protocols showed that students in our study had difficulty with higher-order processes, and this led us to reconsider the landscape model (van den Broek et al., 1999) as a theoretical framework. While revisiting the landscape model, we recognized students' verbal protocol statements aligned to the four sources of information, and we could see indicators of student difficulty with (1) processing text input in the current sentence, (2) integrating information from one sentence into the next, (3) integrating current representation of the text, and (4) integrating prior knowledge. After this discovery, we wanted to develop a way to support students at this identified point of difficulty and referred back to the landscape model to create a table that compiled our observations. This sequence of decisions and events demonstrates how our design was based on a flexible, iterative, formative approach to research. We also discovered through this process that the landscape model transfers well from a lab to a school setting, and it is particularly useful for describing comprehension processes from a cognitive perspective. The DBR goal of putting theory to work (Reinking & Bradley, 2008) helped us interpret our data and also led to a theoretically guided formative assessment tool.

There is evidence of spread beyond the local level as teachers across states read about our study and seek to better understand their individual student's unique comprehension processes while reading texts. This study adds to existing literature that displays the difference between process and product assessments for comprehension. Additionally, this study describes an approach for reading specialists to better understand the challenges their readers face with comprehension. The act of creating meaning with texts is complex, but our understanding of individual student's cognitive processes, and not just comprehension outcomes, provides valuable information for supporting students with reading comprehension.

REFERENCES

Barab, S., & Squire, K. (2004). Design-based research: Putting a stake in the ground. *Journal of the Learning Sciences, 13*(1), 1–14.

Bell, P. (2004). On the theoretical breadth of design-based research in education. *Educational Psychologist, 39*(4), 243–253.

Bergeson, K. (2019). Reading specialists use verbal protocols as a formative assessment tool. *The Reading Teacher, 73*(2), 185–193.

Brown, A. L. (1992). Design experiments: Theoretical and methodological challenges in creating complex interventions in classroom settings. *Journal of the Learning Sciences, 2*(2), 141–178.

Budd, D., Whitney, P., & Turley, K. (1995). Individual differences in working memory strategies for reading expository text. *Memory and Cognition, 23*, 735–748.

Cobb, P., Confrey, J., diSessa, A., Lehrer, R., & Schauble, L. (2003). Design experiments in educational research. *Educational Researcher, 32*(1), 9–13.

Confrey, L., & Lachance, A. (2000). Transformative teaching experiments through conjecture driven research design. In A. E. Kelly & R. A. Lesh (Eds.), *Handbook of research design in mathematics and science education* (pp. 231–265). Mahwah, NJ: Erlbaum Associates.

Duke, N., & Carlisle, J. (2011). The development of comprehension. In M. Kamil, D. Pearson, E. Moje, & P. Afflerbach (Eds.), *Handbook of reading research* (Vol. IV, pp. 199–228). New York: Routledge.

Duke, N., & Cartwright, K. B. (2019). The DRIVE model of reading: Deploying reading in varied environments. In D. E. Alvermann, N. J. Unrau, M. Sailros, & R. B. Ruddell (Eds.), *Theoretical models and processes of literacy* (7th ed., pp. 118–135). New York: Routledge.

Ericsson, K. A., & Simon, H. A. (1993). *Protocol analysis: Verbal reports as data*. Cambridge, MA: MIT Press.

Graesser, A. C., McNamara, D. S., & Kulikowich, J. M. (2011). Coh-Metrix: Providing multilevel analyses of text characteristics. *Educational Researcher, 40*(5), 223–234.

Hoffman, L. (2017). Comprehension is not simple. In S. E. Israel (Ed.), *Handbook of research on reading comprehension* (pp. 57–69). New York: Guilford Press.

Israel, S. (2015). *Verbal protocols in literacy research: The nature of global reading development*. New York: Routledge.

Karlsson, J., van den Broek, P., Helder, A., Hichendorff, M., Koornneef, L., & van Leijenhorst, L. (2018). Profiles of young readers: Evidence from thinking aloud while reading narrative and expository texts. *Learning and Individual Differences, 67*, 105–116.

Kendeou, P., & van den Broek, P. (2007). The effects of prior knowledge and text structure on comprehension processes during reading of scientific texts. *Memory & Cognition, 35*, 1567–1577.

Kendeou, P., van den Broek, P., Helder, A., & Karlsson, J. (2014). A cognitive view of reading comprehension: Implications for reading difficulties. *Learning Disabilities Research and Practice, 29*(1), 10–16.

Kintsch, W. (2012). Psychological models of reading comprehension and their implications for assessment. In J. P. Sabatini, E. Albro, & T. O'Reilly (Eds.), *Measuring up: Advances in how to assess reading ability* (pp. 21–39). Lanham, MD: Rowman & Littlefield.

Leslie, L., & Caldwell, J. (2006). *Qualitative Reading Inventory IV*. Boston: Pearson.

Leslie, L., & Caldwell, J. (2017). Assessments of reading comprehension. In S. E. Israel (Ed.), *Handbook of research on reading comprehension* (pp. 57–69). New York: Guilford Press.

McKenney, S., & Reeves, T. C. (2012). *Conducting educational design research*. New York: Routledge.

Northwest Evaluation Association. (2003). *Measures of academic progress*. Portland, OR: Author.

Oakhill, J., & Cain, K. (2012). The precursors of reading ability in young readers: Evidence from a four-year longitudinal study. *Scientific Studies of Reading, 16*(2), 91–121.

Paris, S. G. (2005). Reinterpreting the development of reading skills. *Reading Research Quarterly, 40*(2), 184–202.

Pearson, P. D., & Hamm, D. N. (2005). The assessment of reading comprehension: A review of practices past, present, and future. In S. G. Paris & S. A. Stahl (Eds.), *Children's reading comprehension and assessment* (pp. 13–69). Mahwah NJ: Erlbaum.

Pressley, M., & Afflerbach, P. (1995). *Verbal protocols of reading: The nature of constructively responsive reading.* Hillsdale, NJ: Erlbaum.

Pressley, M., & Hilden, K. (2004). Verbal protocols in reading. In N. K. Duke & M. H. Mallette (Eds.), *Literacy research methodologies* (pp. 308–321). New York: Guilford Press.

Rapp, D. N., van den Broek, P., McMaster, K. L., Kendeou, P., & Espin, C. A. (2007). Higher order comprehension processes in struggling readers: A perspective for research and intervention. *Scientific Studies of Reading, 11*(4), 289–312.

Reinking, D., & Bradley, B. A. (2008). *On formative and design experiments.* New York: Teachers College Press.

Rosenblatt, L. M. (1978). *The reader, the text, the poem: The transactional theory of the literary work.* Carbondale: Southern Illinois University Press.

van den Broek, P., Bohn-Gettler, C., Kendeou, P., Carlson, S., & White, M. J. (2011). When a reader meets a text.: The role of standards of coherence in reading comprehension. In M. T. McCrudden, J. P. Magliano, & G. Schraw (Eds.), *Text relevance and learning from text* (pp. 123–139). Greenwich, CT: Information Age Publishing.

van den Broek, P., & Espin, C. A. (2012). Connecting cognitive theory and assessment: Measuring individual differences in reading comprehension. *School Psychology Review, 41*(3), 315–325.

van den Broek, P., Helder, A., & van Leijenhorst, L. (2013). Sensitivity to structural centrality: Developmental and individual differences in reading comprehension skills. In M. A. Britt, S. R. Goldman, & J. F. Rouet (Eds.), *Reading: From words to multiple texts* (pp. 132–146). New York: Routledge, Taylor & Francis Group.

van den Broek, P., Young, M., Tzeng, Y., & Linderholm, T. (1999). The landscape model of reading. In H. van Oostendorp & S. R. Golmann (Eds.), *The construction of mental representations during reading* (pp. 71–98). Mahwah, NJ: Erlbaum.

Wagner, J. (1997). The unavoidable intervention of educational research: A framework for reconsidering researcher–practitioner cooperation. *Educational Researcher, 26*(7), 13–22.

PART IV
DESIGN-BASED RESEARCH AND TEACHER-RESEARCHERS

CHAPTER 11

Professional Development on Genre-Based Strategy Instruction on Writing

Zoi A. Philippakos

After college graduation, teachers are expected to continue growing as professionals, acquiring best practices, and engaging in evidence-based pedagogical approaches. In addition to teachers' own attempts to identify effective practices and methods, schools and districts often support teachers' professional development. Professional development (PD) often takes the form of in-house sessions and workshops, and sometimes schools support teachers' attendance at professional conferences. The potential benefits of PD are substantial for teachers, who enhance their understanding about *what works* to better prepare students for college, careers, and citizenship. Despite the positive effects of PD on learning (Yoon, Duncan, Lee, Scarloss, & Shapley, 2007), PD on writing is not as developed and supported in educational settings, especially when compared to PD on reading. Furthermore, even though in reading there is an emphasis on the design, identification, and delivery of instruction in a whole group (Tier 1), such practice is not as clearly applicable in writing. In the following section, I discuss the need for PD on writing and review recent research. I then introduce a study on PD in which design-based research (DBR) was employed (see Chapter 1, this volume, for the principles of DBR) to better identify ways to develop a sustainable and feasible PD model on genre-based writing for whole-group (Tier 1) instruction and suggestions for scaffolded, differentiated instruction.

State of Writing: Reform Policies and Writing

Writing has often been characterized as the neglected "R" (see National Commission on Writing Report, 2003), and this neglect was evident across time in policies that addressed school reform. For instance, in the United States, reform efforts, such as No Child Left Behind Act of 2001 (2002), the Individuals with Disabilities Education Act (IDEA, 2004), and Race to the Top (2005), emphasized improvements in reading instruction and later in mathematics. This lack of attention to writing at a policy level resulted in a gradual decrease of writing instruction and various writing times and applications in classrooms (Cutler & Graham, 2008; Gilbert & Graham, 2010). This decrease did not result because teachers did not understand or appreciate the value of writing. On the contrary, I argue that teachers acknowledge and are aware of the value of reading and writing as integral literacy tasks. However, when accountability shifted focus to improvement of reading scores, it should have been expected that an instructional shift would take place in favor of reading at the cost of writing. I should note that concerns about writing performance and instruction are not a phenomenon limited to the United States; such concerns are shared across the globe (Graham & Rijlaarsdam, 2016; Hsiang, Graham, & Yang, 2020).

Specifically, in the United States, the Common Core State Standards Initiative (National Governors Association Center for Best Practices & Council of Chief State School Officers, 2010) led to a change in policy because it focused more attention on writing and supported a writing-across-the-curriculum approach for students to think critically about information they read and respond to in writing. These standards set expectations about writing purposes, development processes, research, and duration of engagement on writing tasks. Based on the standards' guidelines, students would write in order to argue, inform, and entertain. In their writing, they would follow the writing process to plan, draft, evaluate to revise, and edit, and throughout they would thoughtfully develop ideas and organize them based on the needs of the audience, the specific task, and genre requirements. Students would also conduct research to enhance their knowledge about a topic or learn about a topic and then write by integrating that information in their writing and acknowledging the source of information. Finally, students would write with time allocations dependent on the purpose and task; thus, they would write short responses to information read and compose longer papers after conducting research across time. This policy shift brought renewed attention to writing and the need for teachers to return to the connection of reading and writing in their instructional day. This policy shift required instructional revisions to incorporate writing and also promote reading and writing in the instructional data.

State of Writing: Research on Evidence-Based Practices

Around the same time that policy brought attention to writing, the Institute of Education Sciences (IES) released practice guides that addressed guiding principles for writing instruction across grades K–5 (Graham, Bolinger, et al., 2012) and 6–12 (Graham, Bruch, et al., 2016). The authors of the practice guides provided recommendations and indicated whether the recommendations were supported with strong, moderate, or weak evidence. The authors of the elementary practice guide share the following recommendations for writing instruction: (1) provide daily time for students to write (minimal evidence); (2) teach students to use the writing process for a variety of purposes (strong evidence); (3) teach students to become fluent with handwriting, spelling, sentence construction, typing, and word processing (moderate evidence); and (4) create an engaged community of writers (minimal evidence).

Regarding the first recommendation, the authors of the practice guides propose an hour of writing instruction and practice daily, including writing during content-area learning. Writing across subject areas can support students' content learning and knowledge of academic writing. Also, writing about information they read can improve their reading comprehension (Graham et al., 2016).

In reference to the second recommendation, writing instruction should address the writing process and multiple purposes. Instruction should help students understand different writing purposes and their relationships to genres and discourse, expand students' understanding about audience, and expose them to features of good writing. Instruction should also include explicit explanations and modeling of strategies for planning, revision, and editing with gradual release of responsibility from teachers to students.

Regarding foundational skills, the practice guide addresses the importance of fluent transcription skills. Evidence supports the value of instruction in spelling, handwriting, word processing, and sentence construction (Graham et al., 2016). Finally, engagement is of great importance in writing instruction. Students should be encouraged to collaborate through the stages of the writing process, give and receive feedback on their writing, write on topics of choice, and publish their work for audiences other than the classroom peers and teacher.

The practice guide for secondary learners echoes the recommendations for the elementary grades. According to Graham, Bruch, et al. (2016, p. 2), writing instruction in secondary classrooms should (1) explicitly teach appropriate writing strategies using a model–practice–reflect instructional cycle; (2) integrate writing and reading to emphasize key writing features; and (3) use assessments of student writing to inform instruction and feedback. Thus, instruction should support students' understanding about the audience, writing purpose, and writing process and explicitly teach them how to set goals and navigate through the writing process to complete those goals. Strategies need to be modeled and practiced with feedback, and learners should be supported in reflecting on their use of strategies, their writing, and their peers' writing. Instruction on what writing is, what good writing looks like, and how it can be achieved affects students' self-efficacy and motivation to write (Graham et al., 2019; Grenner, Johansson, van de Weijer, & Sahlén, 2020).

Writing and reading should not be viewed as separate entities, but rather instruction should support the identification of commonalities in use of strategies between reading and writing. Instruction on writing can support reading comprehension, and instruction in reading can support writing. Furthermore, instruction should incorporate the use of exemplars or mentor texts to highlight text features and help writers to better understand the genres and their characteristics (as those relate to syntax, vocabulary, and text structure) and use them in their own writing (Philippakos, 2021). Finally, formative assessment supports instructional goal setting and allows for the identification of specific instructional needs. Teachers can use data to guide their instructional design and delivery and also monitor students' progress. In addition, formative assessment can support students' goal setting, so they can monitor their own progress toward specific learning goals.

Overall, the recommendations from the practice guides could be used to develop a system of instruction and assessment and to best teach writing while addressing standards.

State of Writing Instruction: A Paradox

Even with the focus on writing instruction and an expectation for students to develop as writers, and despite the fact that there are research-based recommendations about the best ways to support writers, instruction using evidence-based practices is not consistently evident in classrooms (Drew, Olinghouse, Luby-Faggella, & Welsh, 2017; Graham, 2019; Hertzberg & Roe, 2016; Kennedy, 2005). One example is the application of strategy instruction, an approach with strong research support (Graham, 2006). Strategy instruction acknowledges that writing is a challenging and cognitive demanding task that requires the learner to juggle several cognitive demands; therefore, strategy instruction provides explicit and systematic instruction of cognitive skills and processes in an effort to support learners in understanding how to complete those challenging tasks. Students are taught through a gradual release of responsibility how to complete a specific process, such as planning of narrative writing (for an example, see Zumbrunn & Brunning, 2013), revision (see MacArthur, Schwartz, & Graham, 1991; Philippakos & MacArthur, 2016a, 2016b; Philippakos, 2017), or how to complete the planning, drafting, evaluation to revise, and editing for a specific genre (e.g., see Philippakos, 2019; Philippakos & MacArthur, 2020; Traga Philippakos & MacArthur, 2020). In strategy instruction, students are also taught metacognitive strategies that support them in managing the task and their effort, space, and overall behavior. Research shows that strategy instruction addressing self-regulation supports learners to manage the writing tasks and demands of good writing (Graham et al., 2016), while the benefits on writing quality are greater (Graham, McKeown, Kiuhara, & Harris, 2012). However, even though there is plenty of research to point out the benefit of strategy instruction and self-regulation, teachers do not apply these approaches in their classrooms (Graham, 2019; Cutler & Graham, 2008).

Several explanations may be provided for this disconnect and the absence of research-based approaches from classroom settings. One is that teachers do not have a clear understanding of strategy instruction and may confuse it with the application of similar approaches to instruction on planning and revision. Thus, even though they know about planning and its importance, they may not know how to teach planning for a specific genre and how to gradually release the responsibility from themselves to their students. Another explanation is that teachers may not know the pedagogy behind effective strategy instruction. Therefore, they may know that modeling is important and provide modeling in a mini-lesson. However, in strategy instruction, modeling is done by explicitly explaining how to complete the cognitive task and how to manage the process by explicitly explaining how to problem-solve anticipated challenges. Teachers, in this form of modeling, make their thinking visible and model how to overcome challenges by using their strategy. Then through gradual release and transition from modeling to collaborative practice and guided practice, students independently apply the taught strategies. Furthermore, rather than brief modeling in a mini-lesson, teachers model the entire process for students to see how their plan translates into sentences (by considering the needs of the genre) and then into an essay that is reread and evaluated, revised, and edited before being shared. In addition, teachers may not be aware of genres and that instruction should not only address organizational structure but also relevant syntax, vocabulary, and linguistic needs related to a genre (McCutchen, 1986). Another possible explanation is that teachers are using a program that includes writing but incorporates only mini-lessons and responses to reading, but does not support teachers in applying pedagogically sound approaches and systematically teaching the writing process to respond to content learned. Furthermore, teachers may not have received instruction in their college teacher preparation programs on evidence-based practices on writing and may not be aware of what this term means and what practices it entails (Brindle, Graham, Harris, & Hebert, 2016; Cutler & Graham, 2008; Gilbert & Graham, 2010; Kiuhara, Hawken, & Graham, 2009; Ray, Graham, Houston, & Harris, 2016). Finally, teachers may not have received PD on writing instruction that addresses the application of evidence-based practices in general and in strategy instruction in particular (Philippakos & Moore, 2017; Troia & Graham, 2016).

Prior Research on PD for Writing

Recent reviews of research on PD in writing instruction (Kennedy, 2018; McCarthey & Geoghegan, 2016) have concluded that the research is limited but evolving. For instance, a comprehensive review by McCarthey and Geoghehan (2016) found that widely used models of PD on writing lack evidence of effectiveness and did not produce findings that show increases in students' writing quality.

In recent years, studies have evaluated writing PD using the instructional approach of self-regulated strategy development (SRSD; Graham & Harris, 2005) for persuasive or narrative writing (e.g., Festas et al., 2015; Harris, Graham, & Adkins, 2015; Harris et al., 2012; McKeown, Brindle, et al., 2016; McKeown,

FitzPatrick, et al., 2019). SRSD offers strong evidence of the effects on writing quality (Graham et al., 2012). In one study, Harris and colleagues (2012) studied the effects of PD on SRSD on persuasive and narrative writing in primary grades with 20 teachers and 262 second- and third-grade students. Participants were randomly assigned to teach either a planning strategy for writing stories or for opinion essays. Trained in teams of five, teachers received lesson plans, watched videos of each lesson, observed the instructor model lessons, and practiced teaching lessons to peers. Then, teachers proceeded with instruction and taught for 24 sessions while they were observed. When questions were raised, the researchers answered by phone or email. Comparisons between story and opinion groups found large positive effects (effect size [ES] >1.0) for both groups on the inclusion of total genre elements in the genre they learned, but effects on writing quality were determined only for the opinion essay group (ES >1.0).

McKeown and colleagues (2019) conducted a quasi-experimental study with 25 teachers across four urban schools ($n = 11$ treatment). Teachers were taught how to provide instruction on persuasive writing using the principles of SRSD through practice-based PD (Ball & Cohen, 1999) that (1) had a focus on content, (2) engaged teachers on active participation and learning of the methods that teachers learn, (3) provided materials that teachers would be using in the classroom, (4) emphasized the strengths and needs of students in their classrooms, and (5) provided opportunities for teachers to see examples of instructional methods. The results showed that teachers did teach the strategies and that students in the treatment group outperformed students in the control group on writing quality. The authors reported that teachers' fidelity of implementation was lower than expected, and also that the effect sizes on the quality of writing for the treatment group were low (ES = 0.15 on a holistic scale and ES = 0.24 on an analytic scale).

With an emphasis on writing through reform efforts, PD is essential in achieving reform goals (Opfer & Pedder, 2001). However, even though significant efforts have been made on the application of evidence-based practices toward PD for writing, research on PD has not addressed more than one genre, been applied across an academic year, and examined the application of strategy instruction. The study we refer to in this work examined PD of strategy instruction in writing for three genres and for an entire academic year (Traga Philippakos, 2020a).

Current Work

The work described was a collaboration initially with a school and then the entire district. The site was a K–5 Title I school identified as being at risk by its state and in need of improvement in reading, writing, and mathematics. The principal of that school had attended a state conference where a researcher presented on the use of evidence-based practices and extended an invitation to schools to participate in research with writing. After planning, the researcher collaborated with the site on a brief intervention with grade 5 that would took place in the spring. This work ended with a call for a larger collaboration as the school identified writing to be a goal for general schoolwide improvement. The next academic year, the researcher collaborated with the same school on the development of a PD model on writing that would support teachers' Tier 1 instruction and last for a year. In the academic year that followed, the researcher collaborated with the entire district in workshops while coaching was provided to one more school site with 33 teachers. The next section further explains the research methodology used and the results of collaboration with the sites. Additional information on the first cycle of implementation and the research study itself may be found at Traga Philippakos (2020a).

Application of DBR

In this work, DBR was employed as it allowed the researcher to examine the application and affordances of principles of effective PD within a school setting, across grades 3–5, and to evaluate teachers' feedback and comments on feasibility. The benefit of DBR, as shared in Chapter 1 of this volume, is the collaboration between practitioners and researchers and the ability not only to begin with theory but also to inform theory through the constant examination of application, analysis of data, reflection, and revisions across iterative cycles of implementation (Brown, 1992; Design-Based Research Collective, 2003; Gravemeijer & Cobb, 2006; Reinking & Bradley, 2008). In their discussion about PD in reading and teacher education, Dillon, O'Brien, Sato, and Kelly (2011) emphasized the importance of conducting formative experiments that can allow the study of teachers and their practices across time (McKenney & Reeves, 2012). To guide this effort to examine the application of a PD model on writing, a theory of change was designed (see Figure 11.1).

Explanation of the Theory of Change

The purpose of this theory of change was to define the long-term goals and, through a backward design, identify how to reach those specific goals. In this instance, the long-term goals are improvements in the quality of students' writing and teachers' instructional practices. An explanation of the model follows.

Student Distal Outcomes

Distal outcomes refer to achievement on Common Core grade-level reading and writing goals. The standards identify three text types and purposes for writing: inform/explain, persuade, and narrate. In grades 3–5, students are expected to produce clear and well-organized opinion, narrative, and informative texts as well as responses to reading. Student writing should respond to specific tasks, audiences,

Initial state	PD intervention components	Knowledge, strategies, and efficacy (teacher outcomes)	Instructional processes	Student discourse knowledge, strategies, and motivation	Student outcomes (distal)
Third-, fourth-, and fifth-grade public school teachers; PD needed for whole-group application of evidence-based practices and for small groups (based on needs)	Workshops on strategy instruction with self-regulation Coaching Professional learning communities (PLCs)	Teacher pedagogical content knowledge (genres, instructional processes, and self-regulation) Teacher efficacy and beliefs Development of new genre lessons	Introduction of genre via read-alouds Evaluation of good and weak examples Explicit explanation and think-aloud modeling Self-regulation and instruction on mini-lessons Collaborative and guided practice Preparation for peer review; self-evaluation and peer review Connect reading and writing through response to reading and summarizing	Knowledge about genres and good writing Knowledge about strategies for planning evaluation to revise, and editing Application of self-regulation Persistence and motivation to write	**Common Core State Standards** Writing achievement as expected in the Standards Reading achievement

FIGURE 11.1. Theory of change.

and purposes. For instance, the writing standards for the fifth grade require students to develop opinion papers in which they introduce a topic, state an opinion, develop and present reasons and ideas in a logical order, and conclude by referring to the initial opinion statement.

Knowledge about discourse and writing strategies is essential in writing achievement (Graham, 2006; Graham et al., 2012; Harris & Graham, 1999; Olinghouse, Graham, & Gillespie, 2015). There are considerable differences between skilled and novice writers in their knowledge of genres and general discourse, writing purposes and goals, and in their views of what counts as quality writing (Graham, Schwartz, & MacArthur, 1993).

Discourse knowledge includes the characteristics of writing across genres (linguistic, syntactic, and text structure). Students' ability to write well is not only the result of knowledge about topics but also the result of their knowledge of text type, its organization, and language that a specific type of writing entails (McCutchen, 1986). Knowledge about discourse affects writers' abilities to develop good-quality writing (Gillespie, Olinghouse, & Graham, 2013; Olinghouse et al., 2015). Good writers understand connections among content, organization, and language features appropriate to various genres. Novice writers think that good writing is associated with mechanics, spelling, and overall use of conventions or handwriting, whereas skilled writers refer primarily to substance and content (Graham et al., 1993). Differences in knowledge and understanding about writing affect all aspects of the writing process and the resulting written products.

Instructional Processes

The instructional processes that teachers were taught to use were firmly grounded in evidence-based practices. The instructional processes included (1) strategy instruction with self-regulation, (2) instruction in multiple genres, (3) use of genres to integrate planning and revising strategies, (4) instruction in evaluation and critical thinking, and (5) integration of reading and writing.

Students can learn strategies used by proficient writers to set goals and generate and organize content and to evaluate their writing for revision. The instructional components drew from a highly effective model of strategy instruction with self-regulation, the SRSD model (Harris & Graham, 2009). Instructional components also draw from the work of Englert and colleagues (1991) on cognitive strategy instruction in writing (CSIW); these researchers were the first to integrate text structure, or genre elements, into planning and revising strategies. Furthermore, the instructional components draw on work on genre-based literacy pedagogy (Martin & Rose, 2012; Rose, 2016). Genre includes more than text structure (McCutchen, 1986). Critical reading is also promoted to support the development of self-evaluation. An emphasis is placed on evaluation and on the role of critical reading using genre-specific evaluation criteria for revision. Instruction should also support reading and writing connections (Graham et al., 2016; Tierney &

Shanahan, 1991; Philippakos, 2021). Complete, developed lessons were provided to teachers with all the materials needed for instruction (Philippakos, MacArthur, & Coker, 2015).

Teacher Outcomes: Knowledge, Strategies, and Efficacy

The ultimate goal is for teachers to develop a deep understanding of the instructional approach and believe in its efficacy. Strategy instruction is complex, so substantial pedagogical content knowledge must be developed (MacArthur, 2011; MacArthur & Graham, 2016). A reciprocal relationship is anticipated between pedagogical content knowledge (PCK) and self-efficacy and belief in the value of the instructional approach.

Pedagogical Content Knowledge. Teachers' PCK includes knowledge of the content and of the process and methodologies of teaching (Shulman, 1986). In the current case, PCK includes knowledge about genres and mastery of the instructional processes. This knowledge would be evident in the application of cognitive strategies for planning and evaluation for revision, application of reading and writing connections, discussion about genre, and the teaching of self-regulation (Philippakos, 2021).

Self-Efficacy and Beliefs. Teachers' lack of knowledge about writing instruction can affect their self-efficacy, or confidence, about teaching writing. Teachers' self-efficacy for teaching writing is linked to teachers' practices as well as students' writing performance (Graham, Harris, Fink, & MacArthur, 2001).

PD Intervention Components

Drawing from principles of effective PD that has duration, is content specific, supports collaboration, uses models of effective practice, and offers feedback and reflection, this work addressed those components (Darling-Hammond, Hyler, & Gardner, 2017; Darling-Hammond & Lieberman, 2012; Desimone, 2009; Desimone & Garet, 2015). First, PD was planned to continue throughout a full school year as teachers taught three genres. This duration also allowed the developer to understand the context and its needs, differentiate according to those needs, and build a relationship of mutual trust, which is important in effective PD (McCarthey & Geoghehan, 2016). Second, collective participation was achieved through grade-based PD—working with all grade 3–5 teachers in a school. Workshops included collaborative discussions that allowed teachers to practice, discuss, reflect, make connections, and comment on grade-level and cross-grade-level practices. In addition, collective participation and active learning strategies were achieved through coaching practices and observation of teachers' application of taught strategies per genre with feedback on those. Finally, the principal was actively involved as research on PD showcases the value and importance of leadership in reform efforts (Birman, Desimone, Porter, & Garet, 2000; Branch, Hanushek, & Rivkin, 2013).

Data Collection and Measures

Since the PD was focused on a specific instructional approach, data were collected both on student improvement in writing quality across time, and also on teacher feedback on the provided PD support through coaching and workshops. Teachers' feedback on the model and on their understanding about the components of strategy instruction was collected across the year as we transitioned from one genre to the next (each genre was a microcycle of implementation).

Writing Quality

Student writing was collected across all genres that were to be taught across the academic year. Thus, at the beginning of the year and after each assessment cycle, teachers assessed opinion, story, and compare–contrast writing for a total of four assessment times and 12 writing samples for each student (3 genres × 4 times). See Figure 11.2 for a depiction of the assessment process.

Participant Observation

The researcher observed teachers during instruction and participated and delivered lessons as part of coaching and on an as-needed basis (Reinking & Bradley, 2008). Observations were meant to examine how teachers applied the taught practices and what they and their students found challenging with the goal to further inform the PD (Gravemeijer & Cobb, 2006).

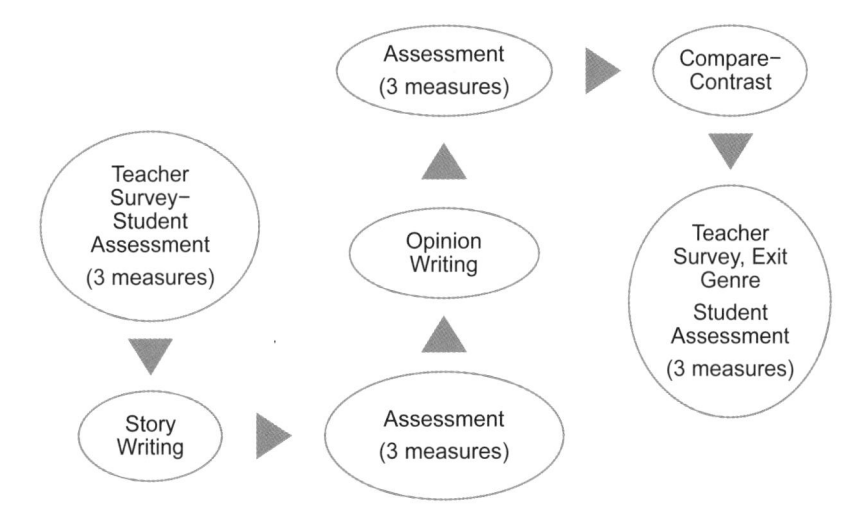

FIGURE 11.2. Assessment plan across the academic year.

Workshops

A cycle of implementation involved instruction on a genre. At the end of each genre, teachers met with the researcher to reflect as a group and record responses to the following questions on a poster (see Figure 11.3):

1. What worked well?
2. What was challenging?
3. What are your goals?
4. What additional PD support do you need?
5. What could support your work better?

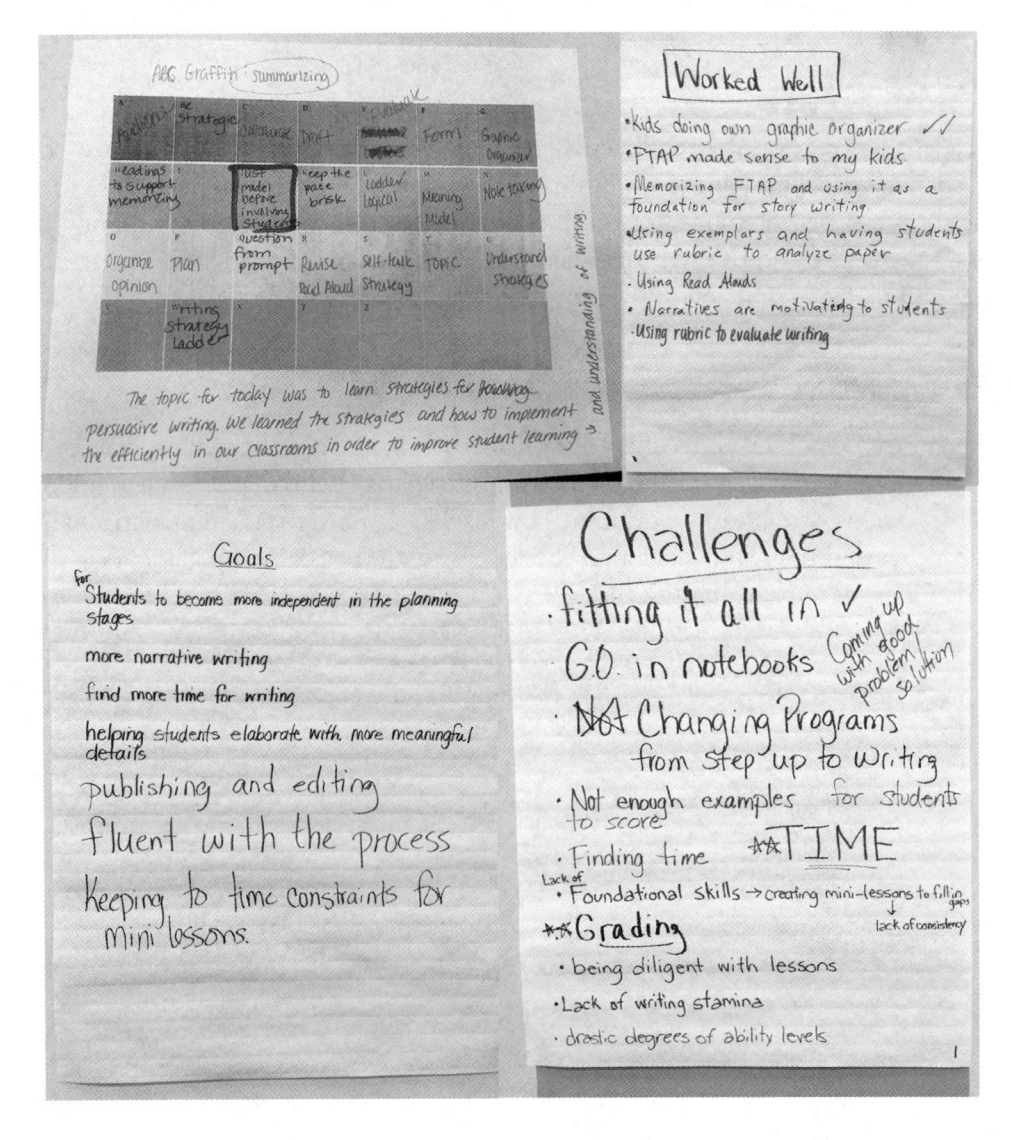

FIGURE 11.3. Reflection and comments at the workshop.

At the end of this reflection, PD was provided on the new genre. The instructional methods were modeled, explained, and demonstrated as applied to the next genre. Prior to the end of the meeting, teachers were asked to complete an ABC table that included all letters of the alphabet in rows. Teachers were asked to record (exchange with a partner and subsequently review) words and phrases that responded to the content of the session and construct a summary that they then shared with the group about their learning. The goal was for them to summarize the session and also to see that even though they all were part of the same workshop, they focused on a different aspect of it based on their interests and learning needs. The process of reflection, discussion, and goal setting was similar to what classroom learners were engaged in at the end of a paper and as they set goals for their next work (Traga Philippakos, 2020b). Information collected during each cycle was used to make revisions in the PD model.

Teacher and Principal Feedback

Teachers provided feedback across iterative cycles and through interviews at the end of the project.

Interviews. At the end of the academic year, teachers were individually interviewed and asked to share their impressions and feedback about the instructional approach, the PD components, and suggestions for improvements. In addition, considering the importance of leadership in reform efforts, the school principal participated in all workshop sessions and was also interviewed at the completion of the first year of the study.

Survey/Questionnaire. Teachers completed a questionnaire before and after the study that provided information about their overall writing practices and about their confidence to teach writing (Graham et al., 2001).

Results

Writing Quality

The results showed that students' writing improved across each genre cycle of implementation (see Traga Philippakos, 2020). Thus, after instruction on story writing, the quality of students' writing improved with regard to story writing ($p < .001$), but no changes were detected on opinion and on compare–contrast writing. After instruction on persuasion, improvements were found on opinion writing ($p < .001$); story-writing quality did not decline, while no statistically significant changes were found on compare–contrast writing. However, a noticeable improvement on compare–contrast writing was seen after instruction on persuasive writing, with

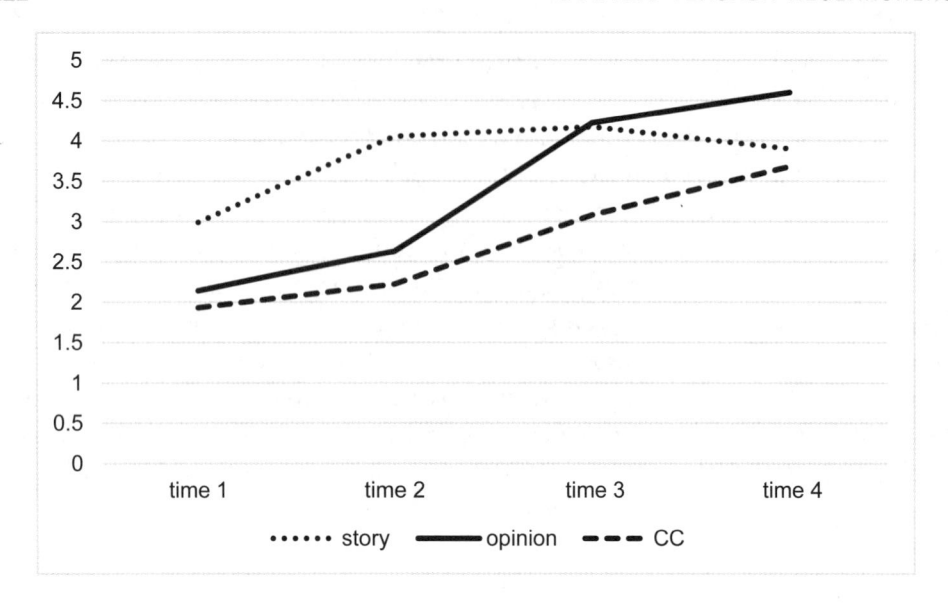

FIGURE 11.4. Quality changes across time.

students providing an organizational structure that included an introduction, main points, and a message to the reader. This observable change in students' work indicated that possibly some knowledge was transferred from one genre to the other. After instruction on compare–contrast writing, improvements were found on compare–contrast writing ($p < .01$) but no change on the other genres (see Figure 11.4).

Teachers' Feedback

Teachers provided positive feedback (across cycles, in a survey at the end of the project, and in interviews at the end of the project) on the instructional approach and on the provided PD. Primarily, teachers appreciated the timely feedback by the researcher and positively commented on the trust that was cultivated between them. Teachers further explained that they appreciated the specificity of the approach and its rigor. Some of them shared that this rigor was challenging initially as they were not able to move away from their previous practices; however, once they transitioned to the new practices, they were convinced to continue applying them after observing changes in students' performance and in their confidence.

Based on the information provided during the iterative cycles, the questions to teachers were changed to address challenges their students faced separately from their own challenges in an effort to work with them to identify instructional goals (reteaching opportunities or mini-lesson development) and professional goals (information they needed to expand their professional understanding about the approach and the writing process). Thus, the questions took the following format:

- What worked for you?
- What worked for your students?
- What was challenging to you?
- What was challenging to your students?
- What are your instructional goals?
- What are your professional goals?
- What additional PD support do you need? What could support your work better?

Principal's Feedback

The principal also positively commented on the approach and on the components of PD. He found that this approach demystified writing and gave all learners the opportunity to be writers, and all teachers the opportunity to develop as teachers of writing. He shared that one particularly powerful aspect for him was to observe his teachers' instruction and to recognize how much their confidence had improved across time. He also commented on the willingness of teachers to gradually include clips of their videos in workshops and how this practice also affected their confidence:

> "Personally, being able to see my teachers in the professional development videos was very powerful. I think it was very empowering to show not only myself, but the other teachers, that they're not only doing the work, but showing it. I think people get scared off from writing at times because they might not have good background or [were] not taught well, but I think through the book as well as constant communication, the confidence level has grown so much in my teachers. When they got the feedback and your stamp of approval, their confidence was so much higher and you could see the quality improve as well."

With regard to teachers' adaptation process, the principal commented on observed differences between veteran and new teachers (in the profession and in the district). He also shared his own learning points: for the hiring process as well as expectations developed for future instructional and professional growth:

> "What I see and what I'm always reflecting on is that we have professionals who have a ton of studies done who have come in and been very successful teachers . . . those are the ones I think are the most difficult to push into change because it hurts their ego and their confidence. They've never had to be pushed in that sense. Looking back, those were the toughest conversations. I think I had to be the buffer to both worlds, but helping them keep in mind that this is best for kids and trying to keep that focus. So yeah, some people's feelings got hurt, but ultimately we'll continue to grow and as professionals, I think we

can see that. For my newer teachers and teachers that came, whether they're brand new or from a different district, they're the ones who jumped right in. So I think as we continue to turn over, I don't see it being as much of an issue. I think we [got] tied up sometimes with contracts and veteran teachers, but some of those really tough teachers are starting to move on to other places. So as we're filling in, we'll ask about their philosophy on writing and professional development and being videotaped, because it won't be an option next year, it'll be an expectation."

Learning Points and Revisions

Through this collaboration with teachers, information was retrieved on not only the effects of applying a PD model for an entire year on a site, but also components that could be further explored and applied in future PD research. The teacher-level data showed that teachers appreciated the PD support and found the instructional approach effective. Overall, the student-level data demonstrated that the instructional approach was effective and stable across the academic year, providing strong evidence of PD's effectiveness.

In the process of working with teachers, and in order to be able to observe them at a higher frequency and to provide them with coaching support, videos were used. Teachers would video-record their instruction, the researcher would share feedback, and if needed a second video would be requested with a new cycle of feedback and application on a third day (if needed). The use of videos was something that supported the PD model as teachers were able to immediately receive feedback. Furthermore, the volume of teachers who were observed daily was higher than what the researcher would have been able to observe if she had only physically visited the site. Within a day, the researcher observed 10 to 13 teachers, whereas in an onsite visit, she could not have observed more than 6 teachers (and this with significant changes made to teachers' schedules to allow the transition of the researcher from classroom to classroom).

Even though in this first implementation, there was an expectation that writing was part of the instructional schedule, writing was not consistently taught by teachers. It was after the first cycle that the principal required all teachers to apply the approach and to teach writing for a minimum of 25 minutes. A schedule was developed that teachers shared with him; it allowed him to observe instruction or monitor the writing instruction that took place in their classrooms. This was an important point that was applied in future work.

The principal's participation in PDs was a necessity for him to be an advocate of the approach and, as he shared at times, to function as a buffer between what was the reform effort and teachers' application of the approach. The enthusiasm, persistence, and increased knowledge this principal showed supported the implementation of the approach and further demonstrated the importance of administrative support in reform efforts. This specific principal was goal oriented, with a positive learning disposition, and tried to apply the approach in the classrooms of his school, encouraging his teachers to offer their feedback. Even though this was initially considered unconventional practice, its pedagogical implications were great. First, he modeled how important learning is for all and that there is always an opportunity to learn. Second, he demonstrably shared the needed knowledge to apply the approach and valued the related strategies. Third, he modeled the idea that everyone should work together as a community to support students' learning and that the overarching goal is always to find ways to support students. This persistent attitude on the part of the principal was innovative and also effective for his own growth as a teacher of writing and evaluator/coach of his teachers.

Future Steps and Current Research

The information on the use of videos supported a follow-up study by the researcher on the examination of teacher fidelity of implementation, and of improvements in students' writing quality by designing an online PD model for second-grade teachers on procedural writing. In this instance, the PD was provided online and videos of instruction were used so teachers might see samples of instruction. Feedback to teachers was provided after the researcher watched their videos and sent them written feedback (Traga Philippakos & Voggt, under review).

Currently, the model of PD is applied in a large district with 10 elementary schools. Since it is a challenge to collect papers from all sites, papers of students' performance are collected from two sites; however, interviews are collected from a sample of teachers per grade and site in order to better understand how they experienced the PD support and from all principals (Traga Philippakos, in press). In this current work, prior to the beginning of the academic year, a curriculum map was developed in consultation with the district's assistant superintendent and curriculum coordinator. The map aligned instruction on reading and writing across grades K–5. Furthermore, assessments were conducted across grades K–5 and cycles of assessments were designed in order for teachers to collect progress monitoring data and determine what they needed to reteach when they revisited the taught genre.

Closing Thoughts

PD on writing requires time and funding in order to be conducted well. Furthermore, the incorporation of technology is needed as students are expected to use technological applications to develop their ideas, collaborate during ideation and composition, and peer-review in order to receive the feedback of readers. In this first cycle of DBR on a PD model, it was possible to closely collaborate with teachers and the administration to examine the affordances and feasibility of PD. The allocation of time for meetings and for teachers to share their comments with the researcher was valuable in establishing trust and a common vision for change. Furthermore, teachers' and administrator's feedback, observations, and writing samples resulted in revisions to the PD model and emphasis on specific instructional aspects for the next cycle of implementation. Moreover, the key principle was the ability to collaborate with teachers who were partners in this work, and this was something they equally appreciated as their voices were heard. This collaboration would not have been possible without the use of the DBR methodology that created the space for a constructive relationship.

REFERENCES

Ball, D. L., & Cohen, D. K. (1999). Developing practice, developing practitioners: Toward a practice-based theory of professional education. In G. Sykes & L. Darling-Hammond (Eds.), *Teaching as the learning profession: Handbook of policy and practice* (pp. 3–32). San Francisco: Jossey Bass.

Birman, B. F., Desimone, L., Porter, A. C., & Garet, M. S. (2000). Designing professional development that works. *Educational Leadership, 5*, 28–33.

Branch, G., Hanushek, E., & Rivkin, S. (2013). School leaders matter: Measuring the impact of effective principals. *Education Next, 13*(1), 1–8.

Brindle, M., Graham, S., Harris, K., & Hebert, M. (2016). Third and fourth grade teacher's classroom practices in writing: A national survey. *Reading and Writing: An Interdisciplinary Journal, 29*, 929–954.

Brown, A. L. (1992). Design experiments: Theoretical and methodological challenges in creating complex interventions in classroom settings. *Journal of the Learning Sciences, 2*(2), 141–178.

Cutler, L., & Graham, S. (2008). Primary grade writing instruction: A national survey. *Journal of Educational Psychology, 100*, 907–919.

Darling-Hammond, L., Hyler, M. E., & Gardner, M. (2017). *Effective teacher professional development*. Palo Alto, CA: Learning Policy Institute.

Darling-Hammond, L., & Lieberman, A. (Eds.). (2012). *Teacher education around the world: Changing policies and practices*. New York: Routledge.

Design-Based Research Collective. (2003). Design-based research: An emerging paradigm for educational inquiry. *Educational Researcher, 32*(1), 5–8.

Desimone, L. M. (2009). Improving impact studies of teachers' professional development: Toward better conceptualizations and measures. *Educational Researcher, 38*(1), 181–199.

Desimone, L. M., & Garet, M. S. (2015). Best practices in teachers' professional development in the United States. *Psychology, Society and Education, 7*(3), 252–263.

Dillon, D. R., O'Brien, D. G., Sato, N., & Kelly, C. M. (2011). Professional development and teacher education for reading instruction. In M. L. Kamil, P. D. Pearson, E. B. Moje, & P. P. Afflebach (Eds.), *Handbook of reading research* (4th ed., pp. 629–660). New York: Routledge.

Drew, S., Olinghouse, N., Luby-Faggella, M., & Welsh, M. (2017). Framework for disciplinary writing in science, grades 6–12: A national survey. *Journal of Educational Psychology, 109*, 935–955.

Englert, C. S., Raphael, T. E., Anderson, L. M., Anthony, H. M., & Stevens, D. D. (1991). Making strategies and self-talk visible: Writing instruction in regular and special education classrooms. *American Educational Research Journal, 28,* 337–372.

Festas, I., Oliveira, A. L., Rebelo, J. A., Damiao, M. H., Harris, K., & Graham, S. (2015). Professional development in self-regulated strategy development: Effects on the writing performance of eighth grade Portuguese students. *Contemporary Educational Psychology, 40*(1), 17–27.

Gilbert, J., & Graham, S. (2010). Teaching writing to elementary students in grades 4–6: A national survey. *Elementary School Journal, 110,* 494–518.

Gillespie, A., Olinghouse, N. G., & Graham, S. (2013). Fifth-grade students' knowledge about writing process and writing genres. *Elementary School Journal, 113*(4), 565–588.

Graham, S. (2006). Strategy instruction and the teaching of writing: A meta-analysis. In C. A. MacArthur, S. Graham, & J. Fitzgerald (Eds.), *Handbook of writing research* (pp. 187–207). New York: Guilford Press.

Graham, S. (2019). Changing how writing is taught. *Review of Research in Education, 43*(1), 277–303.

Graham, S., Bollinger, A., Booth Olson, C., D'Aoust, C., MacArthur, C., McCutchen, D., & Olinghouse, N. (2012). *Teaching elementary school students to be effective writers: A practice guide* (NCEE 2012-4058). Washington, DC: National Center for Education Evaluation and Regional Assistance, Institute of Education Sciences, U.S. Department of Education.

Graham, S., Bolinger, A., Olson, C., D'Aoust, C., MacArthur, C., McCutchen, D., & Olinghouse, N. (2012). Teaching elementary school students to be effective writers. Retrieved from *http://ies.ed.gov/ncee/wwc/PracticeGuide.aspx?sid=17*

Graham, S., Bruch, J., Fitzgerald, J., Friedrich, L., Furgeson, J., Greene, K., . . . Smither Wulsin, C. (2016). *Teaching secondary students to write effectively* (NCEE 2017-4002). Washington, DC: National Center for Education Evaluation and Regional Assistance (NCEE), Institute of Education Sciences, U.S. Department of Education.

Graham, S., & Harris, K. R. (2005). Improving the writing performance of young struggling writers. *The Journal of Special Education, 39,* 19–33.

Graham, S., Harris, K. R., & Chambers, A. B. (2016). Evidence-based practice and writing instruction: A review of reviews. In C. A. MacArthur, S. Graham, & J. Fitzgerald (Eds.), *Handbook of writing research* (2nd ed., pp. 211–226). New York: Guilford Press.

Graham, S., Harris, K. R., Fink, B., & MacArthur, C. (2001). Teacher efficacy in writing: A construct validation with primary grade teachers. *Scientific Study of Reading, 5,* 177–202.

Graham, S., McKeown, D., Kiuhara, S., & Harris, K. R. (2012). A meta-analysis of writing instruction for students in the elementary grades. *Journal of Educational Psychology, 104,* 879–896.

Graham, S., & Rijlaarsdam, G. (2016). Writing education around the glove. *Reading and Writing: An Interdisciplinary Journal, 29*(1), 781–792.

Graham, S., Schwartz, S., & MacArthur, C. (1993). Knowledge of writing and the composing process, attitude towards writing, and self-efficacy for students with and without learning disabilities. *Journal of Learning Disabilities, 26,* 237–249.

Graham, S., Wijekumar, K., Harris, K., Lei, P., Fishman, E., Ray, A., & Houston, J. (2019). Writing skills, knowledge, motivation, and strategic behavior predict students' persuasive writing performance in the context of robust writing instruction. *The Elementary School Journal, 119*(3), 487–510.

Gravemeijer, K., & Cobb, P. (2006). Design research from the learning design perspective. In J. van den Akker, K. Gravemeijer, S. McKenney, & N. Nieveen (Eds.), *Educational design research: The design, development and evaluation of programs, processes and products* (pp. 17–51). London: Routledge,

Grenner, E., Johansson, V., van de Weijer, J., & Sahlén, B. (2020). Effects of intervention on self-efficacy and text quality in elementary school students' narrative writing. *Logopedics, Phoniatrics, Vocology*, 1–10.

Harris, K. R., & Graham, S. (2009). Self-regulated strategy development in writing: Premises, evolution, and the future. *British Journal of Educational Psychology Monograph Series II*, 6, 113–135.

Harris, K. R., Graham, S., & Adkins, M. (2015). Practice-based professional development and self-regulated strategy development for Tier 2, at-risk writers in second grade. *Contemporary Educational Psychology*, 40(5), 5–16.

Harris, K. R., Lane, K. L., Graham, S., Driscoll, S. A., Sandmel, K., Brindle, M., & Schatschneider, C. (2012). Practice-based professional development for self-regulated strategies development in writing: A randomized controlled study. *Journal of Teacher Education*, 63(2), 103–119.

Hertzberg, F., & Roe, A. (2016). Writing in the content areas: A Norwegian case study. *Reading & Writing: An Interdisciplinary Journal*, 29, 555–576.

Hsiang, T., Graham, S., & Yang, Y. (2020). Teachers' practices and beliefs about teaching writing: A comprehensive survey of grades 1 to 3 teachers. *Reading and Writing*, 33(1), 1–38.

Individuals with Disabilities Education Act. (2004). 20 U.S.C. § 1400.

Kennedy, M. M. (2005). *Inside teaching: How classroom life undermines reform*. Cambridge, MA: Harvard University Press.

Kennedy, M. M. (2018). How does professional development improve teaching? *Review of Educational Research*, 86(4), 945–980.

Kiuhara, S. A., Hawken, L. S., & Graham, S. (2009). Teaching writing to high school students: A national survey. *Journal of Educational Psychology*, 101(1), 136–160.

MacArthur, C. A. (2011). Strategies instruction. In K. R. Harris, S. Graham, & T. Urdan (Eds.), *Educational psychology handbook: Vol. 3. Applications of educational psychology to learning and teaching* (pp. 379–401). Washington, DC: American Psychological Association.

MacArthur, C. A., & Graham, S. (2016). Writing research from a cognitive perspective. In C. A. MacArthur, S. Graham, & J. Fitzgerald (Eds.), *Handbook of writing research* (2nd ed., pp. 24–40). New York: Guilford Press.

MacArthur, C. A., Schwartz, S. S., & Graham, S. (1991). Effects of a reciprocal peer revision strategy in special education classrooms. *Learning Disabilities Research and Practice*, 6(1), 201–210.

Martin, J. R., & Rose, D. (2012). *Learning to write, reading to learn: Genre, knowledge and pedagogy in the Sydney School*. Sheffield, UK: Equinox.

McCarthey, S. J., & Geoghegan, C. M. (2016). The role of professional development for enhancing writing instruction. In C. A. MacArthur, S. Graham, & J. Fitzgerald (Eds.), *Handbook of writing research* (2nd ed., pp. 330–348). New York: Guilford Press.

McCutchen, D. (1986). Domain knowledge and linguistic knowledge in the development of writing ability. *Journal of Memory and Language*, 25, 431–444.

McKenney, S. E., & Reeves, T. C. (2012). *Conducting educational design research*. New York: Routledge.

McKeown, D., Brindle, M., Harris, K., Graham, S., Collins, A., & Brown, M. (2016). Illuminating growth and struggles using mixed methods: Practice-based professional development and coaching for differentiating SRSD instruction in writing. *Reading and Writing: An Interdisciplinary Journal, 29*(6), 1105–1140.

McKeown, D., FitzPatrick, E., Brown, M., Brindle, M., Owens, J., & Hendrick, R. (2019). Urban teachers' implementation of SRSD for persuasive writing following practice-based professional development: Positive effects mediated by compromised fidelity. *Reading and Writing, 32*(2), 1483–1506.

National Commission on Writing. (2003). *The neglected "R": The need for a writing revolution.* Washington DC: College Board.

National Governors Association Center for Best Practices & Council of Chief State School Officers. (2010). *Common Core State Standards for English language arts & literacy in history/social studies, science, and technical subjects.* Retrieved from www.corestandards.org/assets/CCSSI_ELA%20Standards.pdf

No Child Left Behind Act of 2001. (2002). Public Law No. 107–110, § 115, Stat. 1425.

Olinghouse, N. G., Graham, S., & Gillespie, A. (2015). The relationship of discourse and topic knowledge to fifth graders' writing performance. *Journal of Educational Psychology, 107*, 391–406.

Opfer, V. D., & Pedder, D. (2011). The lost promise of teacher professional development in England. *European Journal of Teacher Education, 34*(1), 3–24.

Philippakos, Z. A. (2017). Giving feedback: Preparing students for peer review and self-evaluation. *The Reading Teacher, 7*(1), 13–22.

Philippakos, Z. A. (2021). Writing–reading integration. In S. Parsons & M. Vaughn (Eds.), *Principles of effective literacy instruction* (pp. 163–180). New York: Guilford Press.

Philippakos, Z. A., & MacArthur, C. A. (2016a). The effects of giving feedback on the persuasive writing of fourth- and fifth-grade students. *Reading Research Quarterly, 51*(4), 419–433.

Philippakos, Z. A., & MacArthur, C. A. (2016b). The use of genre-specific evaluation criteria for revision. *Language and Literacy Spectrum, 2*(1), 41–52.

Philippakos, Z. A., MacArthur, C. A., & Coker, D. L. (2015). *Developing strategic writers through genre instruction: Resources for grades 3–5.* New York: Guilford Press.

Philippakos, Z. A., & Moore, N. (2017). The literacy coach's role in supporting teachers' implementation of the common core state standards in writing. In S. Lawrence (Ed.), *Literacy program evaluation and development initiatives for P–12 teaching* (pp. 114–137). Hershey, PA: IGI-Global.

Ray, A., Graham, S., Houston, J. D., & Harris, K. (2016). Teachers' use of writing to support students' learning in the middle school: A national survey in the United States. *Reading and Writing: An Interdisciplinary Journal, 29*, 1039–1068.

Reinking, D., & Bradley, B. (2004). Connecting research and practice using formative and design experiments. In N. Duke & M. Mallette (Eds.), *Literacy research methods* (pp. 149–169). New York: Guilford Press.

Reinking, D., & Bradley, B. (2008). *On formative and design experiments.* New York: Teachers College Press.

Rose, D. (2016). New developments in genre-based literacy pedagogy. In C. A. MacArthur, S. Graham, & J. Fitzgerald (Eds.), *Handbook of writing research* (pp. 227–242). New York: Guilford Press.

Shulman, L. (1986). Those who understand: Knowledge growth in teaching. *Educational Researcher, 15*(2), 4–14.

Tierney, R. J., & Shanahan, T. (1991). Research on the reading-writing relationship: Interactions, transactions, and outcomes. In R. Barr, M. L. Kamil, P. Mosenthal, & P. D. Pearson (Eds.), *Handbook of reading research* (Vol. II, pp. 246–280). New York: Longman.

Traga Philippakos, Z. (2019). Effects of strategy instruction with an emphasis on oral language and dramatization on the quality of first graders' procedural writing. *Reading & Writing Quarterly, 35*(5), 409–426.

Traga Philippakos, Z. A. (in press). *Guidelines for effective professional development on genre-based strategy instruction: Principals' voices.*

Traga Philippakos, Z. A. (2020a). A yearlong, professional development model on genre-based strategy instruction on writing. *The Journal of Educational Research, 113*(3), 177–190.

Traga Philippakos, Z. A. (2020b). Developing strategic learners: Supporting self-efficacy through goal setting and reflection. *The Language and Literacy Spectrum, 30*(1), 1–24.

Traga Philippakos, Z. A., & MacArthur, C. A. (2020). Integrating collaborative reasoning and strategy instruction to improve second graders' opinion writing. *Reading & Writing Quarterly, 36*(4), 379–395.

Traga Philippakos, Z. A., & Voggt, A. (in press). The effects of a virtual professional development model on teachers' instruction and the quality of second graders' procedural writing. *Reading and Writing: An Interdisciplinary Journal.*

Troia, G. A., & Graham, S. (2016). Common Core writing and language standards and aligned state assessments: A national survey of teacher beliefs and attitudes. *Reading and Writing: Am Interdisciplinary Journal, 29,* 1719–1743.

Yoon, K. S., Duncan, T., Lee, S. W.-Y., Scarloss, B., & Shapley, K. (2007). Reviewing the evidence on how teacher professional development affects student achievement (Issues & Answers Report, REL 2007–No. 033). Washington, DC: U.S. Department of Education, Institute of Education Sciences, National Center for Education Evaluation and Regional Assistance, Regional Educational Laboratory Southwest. Retrieved from *http://ies.ed.gov/ncee/edlabs*

Zumbrunn, S., & Bruning, R. (2013). Improving the writing and knowledge of emergent writers: The effects of self-regulated strategy development. *Reading and Writing: An Interdisciplinary Journal, 26*(1), 91–110.

CHAPTER 12

Improving Disciplinary Literacy Teaching

A Formative Experiment Exploring Professional Development in Disciplinary Settings

Phillip Wilder, Emily Howell, Lorraine Jacques, Susan Cridland-Hughes, and Mary-Celeste Schreuder

Nationally, educators have focused on adolescent literacy as a remedy for the decline in reading assessment scores in the United States (Moje, 2008). In recent years, this focus spurred increased attention on how literacy practices relate to academic disciplines and specific school subject areas (Moje, 2008; Shanahan & Shanahan, 2008). However, as research and literature has increasingly called for supporting youth disciplinary literacies, teachers in K–12 schools struggle to contend with implications for teaching practice (Alvermann, Friese, Beckmann, & Rezak, 2011). At a state level, when reading assessments found South Carolina students lagged behind compared to national norms (Education Oversight Committee [EOC], 2011), South Carolina literacy policy mandated additional graduate coursework in content-area reading for inservice teachers (South Carolina Department of Education, 2014). An analysis concluded the policy narrowly defined literacy and effective literacy instruction for adolescents within school subject areas (in fact, the law did not even mention *disciplinary literacy*), while also assuming a single, state-supplied, 7-week online course would lead to *highly qualified literacy teachers* "despite a deep empirical research base validating the importance of professional learning which supports ongoing teacher learning in practice" (Cridland-Hughes & Wilder, 2016).

Stimulation for Design-Based Research in the Field of Literacy

Within this context, a group of literacy scholars partnered with one large, urban school district to address the limitations in the policy's underlying theory of change (TOC) and to develop a model of professional learning on disciplinary literacies for secondary teachers. In particular, the district we worked with wanted to develop a model of professional development (PD) to address disciplinary literacy needs in their district.

This study will present findings from a formative experiment conducted during a semester-long PD course at one urban high school in this school district which aimed to improve the disciplinary literacy instruction of the 35 participating teachers representing nine subject areas. Recognizing the challenges with a content-area reading approach (O'Brien, Stewart, & Moje, 1995) and the underdeveloped understanding of disciplinary literacy (Moje, 2008; Shanahan & Shanahan, 2008), we sought to understand the limitations and supports involved with improving disciplinary literacy teaching at one high school (see also Chapter 8 on disciplinary literacy). The formative methodology used in this study allowed the researchers to initially design the PD in this course and make modifications based on the enhancing and inhibiting factors, which then led to implementation of a PD model at a districtwide level (see also Chapter 11, this volume).

Relevant Perspectives

As students progress in secondary schools, the challenge to improve subject-area literacy increases just as texts and ways of knowing within disciplines become more complex and differentiated (Shanahan & Shanahan, 2008). Content knowledge and the language used to learn it are entwined (Schleppegrell, Achugar, & Oteíza, 2004), while texts and discourses both reflect disciplinary epistemic beliefs (Manderino, 2011) and function as tools to mediate thinking during disciplinary inquiry and knowledge production (Billman & Pearson, 2013; Moje, 2008). Secondary school youth, then, need teachers who can apprentice students into the literate thinking of the discipline (McConachie & Petrosky, 2010), while providing youth with opportunities to critique mainstream disciplinary knowledge (Moje, 2008).

Many challenges may be faced when intending to use meaningful professional learning to alter literacy beliefs and practices to improve student literacy. Teachers often resist PD when initiatives appear counter to their own beliefs (Opfer & Pedder, 2011) or expose possible weaknesses (Hobson & McIntyre, 2013). Further teacher resistance can occur when student impact is not observed (Mohamed, 2008; Yan, 2015), professional learning focuses on teacher deficits (Musanti & Pence, 2010), or proposed literacy instructional practices ignore local curricular, pedagogical, or cultural factors (O'Brien et al., 1995).

A perceived lack of support from school leadership can stifle teacher voices (Carpenter, 2015), leaving teachers feeling undervalued (Hardy & Lingard, 2008) and frustrated when PD emphasizes student mastery of discrete skills (Powell & Kusuma-Powell, 2015). Accountability pressures and administrative policies overvaluing high-stakes achievement scores often decrease teacher motivation and efficacy (Mausethagen, 2013), creating a teachers-versus-administrators feeling within the school (Allard & Doecke, 2014). Even when teachers desire to improve practice, the pressure to increase test scores foregrounds attempts at quick fixes (Allard & Doecke, 2014; Skerrett, 2010; Yan, 2015) and exacerbates teacher avoidance behaviors (Hobson & McIntyre, 2013). Additionally, externally imposed standardization, such as scripted curriculum or end of course assessments, diminishes teacher efforts to improve practice (Skerrett, 2010) out of fear of isolation from other teachers or conflict with administrators (Achinstein & Ogawa, 2006; Allard & Doecke, 2014).

Even when teachers have support, changing practice is difficult. Learning a new idea can be difficult for teachers if they feel unconnected to the materials, instructors, or assignments (Raider-Roth, Stieha, & Hensley, 2012). Finding resources and shifting curriculum is time-consuming (Pozuelos, González, & de León, 2010), leaving teachers feeling incapable of modifying practices (Buczynski & Hansen, 2007; Yan, 2015). Not seeing immediate success with a new technique decreases teacher persistence (Mohamed, 2008). Practices to improve learning, such as peer evaluation, may feel judgmental even when the teachers acknowledge their value (Musanti & Pence, 2010).

Thus, design-based research (DBR) in the form of a formative experiment was an ideal methodology for this study as it allowed us to ameliorate many of these challenges in the literature related to teachers not feeling supported in changing their practice. Thus, it allowed the researchers to treat teachers in the disciplines as collaborators, obtain their insight and feedback on the essential elements of the intervention, and make modifications to the intervention prior to scaling it to the district level.

Process of DBR

To identify and understand how particular elements restrain or enhance professional learning and teacher efforts to improve disciplinary literacy instruction, this study is guided by a framework for formative experiments as outlined in Reinking and Bradley (2008; see also Reinking, Colwell, & Ramey, 2013). In this framework, collaborators work toward a pedagogical goal by implementing an intervention with the potential of reaching that goal. The aim of this study was to improve responsive disciplinary literacy instruction for high school teachers participating in the PD studied. Our project was guided by the following inquiry: How can PD, focused on (1) inquiry, (2) assessment, and (3) responsive instructional practices, be instantiated to improve teachers' disciplinary literacy instruction? Because this inquiry question guided the project at the urban high school and would inform the ongoing dilemma facing the school district, a formative experiment made methodological, empirical, and pragmatic sense. Formative experiments are similar to research under a variety of terms, such as DBR and design studies (Cobb, Jackson, & Dunlap, 2016). Cobb et al. (2016) discussed design studies in three different categories: classroom design studies, PD design studies, and organizational design studies. Our formative experiment aligns with Cobb et al.'s definition of a PD design focus as we concentrated on "particular forms of instructional practice" (2016, p. 216) outlined subsequently in our essential elements and sought to understand how these practices could be supported through PD. Cobb et al. (2016) suggested that the limited number of such studies and the need for further research focused on studying interventions centered on particular teacher practices warranted understanding how to support those practices with PD.

Intervention

The intervention included a site-based course, which employed elements of high-quality PD (Darling-Hammond & Richardson, 2009; Garet, Porter, Desimone, Birman, & Yoon, 2001), student-centered coaching (Schen, Rao, & Dobles, 2005), and cycles of collaborative practitioner inquiry (Cochran-Smith & Lytle, 1999). The course was enacted with participating teachers grouped into disciplinary teacher teams to support teacher efforts to conceptualize, enact, and improve disciplinary literacy instruction. The intervention studied was composed of three essential elements: (1) design of a disciplinary inquiry curriculum unit with a focus on disciplinary texts, tasks, and talk (McConachie & Petrosky, 2010); (2) collaborative formative assessment of student literacy practices in disciplinary classes; and (3) use of responsive literacy instructional practices (i.e., modeling and flexible grouping). The intervention was implemented in two different cycles of inquiry: (1) teachers discussed what it meant to be literate in their respective disciplines, and (2) teachers planned how to enact responsive teaching in their discipline. The first cycle of inquiry lasted for 5 weeks, and the second cycle of inquiry lasted for 10 weeks, for a total intervention length of 15 weeks. A formative experiment was chosen both for its affiliation in literacy (Bradley et al., 2012; Howell, Butler, & Reinking, 2017; Howell, Perez, & Abraham, 2020; Ivey & Broaddus, 2007; Jiménez, 1997) and its pragmatic implementation of a school-based intervention (Reinking & Bradley, 2008).

Data Sources and Analysis

Thirty-five participants took part in the PD enacted as a part of this study. These participants came from a variety of disciplines and experience: English/language arts (7), math (3), science (5), social studies (6), special education (6), working with English language learners (2), electives (3), and literacy coaching (3). We focused our data collection on five focal teacher participants (see Colwell, Hunt-Barron, & Reinking, 2013), whom we interviewed and observed enacting their learning during the intervention. Because we embedded ourselves in disciplinary teacher groups listening to conversations, supporting instructional design, and using questioning to support teacher reflection upon practice, our role resembled that of active participant-observers (DeWalt & DeWalt, 2002; Glesne, 2011), which is typical of formative experiments (Reinking & Bradley, 2008).

Data sources included teacher reflections and survey responses, course documents and writings, focus group semi-structured interviews, and classroom observations. Table 12.1 lists the different types of data, gives a description of these data, when data were analyzed, and what method of coding was conducted. These multiple data points support data triangulation, which is called for in formative experiments to develop rigor (Reigeluth & Frick, 1999; Reinking & Bradley, 2008).

Data were analyzed during the intervention to note the enhancing and inhibiting factors of the intervention, unexpected outcomes of the intervention, modifications needed to the intervention, and progress toward the goal of the intervention (Reinking & Bradley, 2008). The research team met on a weekly basis throughout the intervention to discuss emerging codes and necessary modifications to the intervention. Following the completion of data collection, we conducted a holistic, retrospective analysis of the data (Gravemeijer & Cobb, 2006). Portions of the data were coded grounded theory and constant comparison analysis in which the researchers formed initial, focused, and theoretical codes, gathering more data when necessary (Charmaz, 2014; Glaser, 1965). Initial codes such as *designing student inquiry*, *disciplinary text selection*, *formative assessment practices*, and *teacher modeling* were some of the codes used in association with responsive disciplinary literacy teaching and that began to form during the intervention. These codes further developed and informed focused and theoretical codes in the retrospective analysis. In addition, some *a priori* coding was used in the retrospective analysis, on qualitative survey responses and literacy position statements, to determine changes in teacher thinking toward disciplinary literacy.

Results

We organize results first by describing the enhancing and inhibiting factors and modifications made during the intervention as a result of these factors. We also discuss progress emerging due to the intervention and unanticipated outcomes. Then, we report the results of our retrospective analysis addressing remaining inhibiting and enhancing factors and what modifications those factors suggest for future iterations. Table 12.2 (pp. 238–239) demonstrates the initial findings that led to more focused coding and where those focused codes fit within the formative framework. These initial findings appearing in Table 12.2 ultimately informed how we implemented the intervention cycles, each time attempting to improve the "fit" of the intervention with the observed professional learning needs and expertise of participating teachers.

Enhancing and Inhibiting Factors Leading to Modifications

Researchers using formative experiments make instructional adaptations in both micro- and macrocycles (Reinking & Bradley, 2008). The researchers observed how

TABLE 12.1. Data Sources and Analysis

Data source	Description	Point of analysis	Analysis
Eyes on Students observation protocol	Observation protocol in which teachers formatively assessed disciplinary literacy practices of students in their respective classrooms—each participating teacher completed at least 10 observations.	During intervention	Teachers and PD providers used during intervention to inform modifications
Literacy teaching plan	At three points throughout the intervention, teachers collaboratively designed a series of lessons to respond to literacy needs of their students.	During intervention	Teachers and PD providers used during intervention to inform modifications
Literacy teacher position statement ($n = 30$)	At the beginning and end of the intervention, teachers developed a vision for literacy teaching within their disciplines.	Retrospective analysis	A priori coding for changes in their pre- and post-intervention response
Focus group interviews ($n = 2$)	Interview of focus group of participants at both the beginning and end of the intervention	During intervention for first focus group and retrospective analysis of both focus groups	Emergent, grounded theory coding
Fieldnotes and observations ($n = 26$)	Research team notes and observations of research meetings, PD sessions, and classroom observations of individual teachers	During intervention in research team meeting and retrospective analysis	Emergent, grounded theory coding
Survey responses ($n = 24$ that were matched for both pre- and post-intervention responses)	Qualitative responses regarding definition of disciplinary literacy, assessment, and response to student needs	Retrospective analysis	A priori coding for changes in pre- and post-intervention responses to each of the three qualitative questions

the stated intervention was implemented and adapted at the micro level during one iteration of the intervention. In this section, we discuss adaptations made during this iteration based on enhancing and inhibiting factors. In a subsequent section, we make recommendations for future iterations and more macrocycle adaptations. Table 12.3 (p. 240) summarizes all of the micro-level adaptations made during this iteration of the intervention.

Teacher Modeling

The role of teacher modeling took on increasing significance during the unfolding of the intervention in two key areas: responsive teaching and technology. Although responsive teaching and its discussion during the intervention were essential elements of the intervention, their implementation in teachers' classrooms was an inhibiting factor. Responsive teaching was built into the PD as teachers discussed the definition of responsive teaching in the first round of inquiry and thought of how to design and implement this responsive teaching in the second round of inquiry; however, they struggled with distilling which strategies pertained to being responsive in their respective disciplines.

For example, one science teacher exhibited his confusion with a class discussion of SOAPS, a reading and writing strategy where students attend to the speaker, occasion, audience, purpose, and subject of writing and whether this strategy fit within a science domain. This teacher discussed knowing how he found written sources to buttress a written argument, but admitted not being able to apply it to the terms of his discipline, chemistry.

In addition, there was a wide variance in teachers' willingness to adopt their learning from the PD in their classrooms. For instance, we detailed in our fieldnotes that teachers were capable of using formative assessment to identify student learning needs and apply appropriate disciplinary strategies, but we also recognized how teachers described students' needs in the classroom with no clear recourse to address such needs. Thus, we asked teachers to develop models of their own responsive teaching that modified disciplinary literacy pedagogy according to the observable disciplinary literacy needs of students and to present those to their peers during the PD.

For instance, one art teacher had been conducting a week-long collaboration with the literacy coach and agreed to share this collaborative process with the class. Over the course of multiple, sequential lessons, Sarah (all names are pseudonyms) desired for the freshmen and sophomore students in her Art I course to use several paintings to analyze the artistic decisions of several prominent painters in history, with each student group charged with sharing a presentation on an artist with the class. The literacy coach, Linda, visited the class on several consecutive days while students prepared class presentations to gather formative assessment observations of students and use these with Sarah to decide on the appropriate instructional responses in the next day's lesson. These instructional responses took the form

TABLE 12.2. Coding Matrix

Enhancing/inhibiting factors and modifications made (during intervention)		Progress toward goal	
Focused codes	Initial codes	Focused codes	Initial codes
Modification made: teacher modeling	• Differentiation in teacher adoption • Understanding disciplinary literacies in course • Inhibiting factors to implementing disciplinary literacy strategies in teachers' classrooms • Modifications needed for course • Teachers modeling for teachers • Tools as needed discussion	Evidence of progress—from deficit thinking to implementation of strategies	• Student learning • Teacher learning • Process decision as enhancing factor • Teacher focus prior to intervention • Teacher use of strategy as enhancing factor • Teachers attempting disciplinary literacy strategies • Deficit thinking
Modification made: clarification of disciplinary literacy terms	• Ability to define terms • Understanding disciplinary literacies in course • Modifications needed for course		
Modification made: increased significance of research team	• Modifications needed for course • Enhancing factor: formative assessment		
Modification made: less distinction between learning in course and teaching	• Modifications needed for course • Modifications needed for teachers' classes • Structure of course		

Unanticipated outcomes			Enhancing/inhibiting factors and possible future modifications (retrospective analysis)	
Focused codes	Initial codes		Focused codes	Initial codes
Collaboration	<ul><li>Collaboration among teachers</li><li>Students collaborating as enhancing factor</li><li>Unanticipated outcome of course</li><li>Unanticipated outcomes in classrooms of teachers</li></ul>		Systematic impediments to change	<ul><li>Influence of standardized assessment</li><li>School curriculum</li><li>Teacher beliefs</li><li>District policy initiatives</li><li>Potential future modifications</li></ul>
Formative assessment	<ul><li>Enhancing factor: formative assessment</li><li>Using formative assessment</li><li>Unanticipated outcome of course</li><li>Unanticipated outcomes in classrooms of teachers</li></ul>		Future modifications	<ul><li>Desire for expertise</li><li>Disparities in expertise</li><li>Lack of experience</li><li>Reluctance to change</li><li>Potential future modifications</li></ul>
Technology and disciplinary literacies	<ul><li>Technology as enhancing factor</li><li>Tools as needed discussion</li><li>Resistance to new practice</li></ul>			

TABLE 12.3. Modifications Made during Intervention

Inhibiting/enhancing factor	Modification
Inhibiting: Need for teachers to focus on texts and tasks and reflect on how their knowledge of these has changed as a result of course. Workload of class and need to balance teaching and PD/structure of course.	Cancelling collaborative inquiry plan
Inhibiting: Teachers' lack of clarity of terms in disciplinary literacy; systematic impediments to change. Noticed lack of clarity in initial lesson plan and wanted to distinguish between those terms and when they were actually implementing for responsive teaching.	Further clarification of disciplinary literacy terms: inquiry, texts, tasks, and responsive teaching
Inhibiting/enhancing: Tools seen as both needed discussion and enhancing factors when researchers observed teachers' classrooms.	Teachers model for other teachers specifically concerning connections between technology and disciplinary literacies.
Enhancing: Initial codes relating to teachers attempting to use disciplinary literacies in their classes and barriers to such implementation.	Teachers model responsive teaching for other teachers.
Inhibiting: No one to challenge assumptions about disciplinary literacies teachers may have when they are removed from course. In addition, coaches aren't readily available due to standardized testing. *Enhancing:* Ability to collaborate closely due to formative assessment.	Research team works more closely with teachers in classrooms, rather than following coaches' lead with teachers.
Inhibiting: Special education teachers, for example, didn't have specific discipline or were working with students across disciplines. In addition, many teachers lacked foundational understanding of content-area literacy.	Differentiating content of course curriculum by content reading versus disciplinary literacy
Enhancing: Disciplinary literacy couldn't be learned apart from teaching. Teachers really started to learn once they started using disciplinary literacy in own teaching. *Inhibiting:* Time to learn what it means to be literate in their discipline takes far longer than assumed.	Started course thinking that they would identify disciplinary literacies and then teaching in discipline, but modification is that they had to be engaged in both simultaneously.
Inhibiting: Diversity of disciplines and teacher needs in the course and time needed for collaboration in course.	Additions to research team and close collaboration between research team and teachers

of a focus lesson, a redirection of collaborative student work time, and the use of example presentations for students to use as organizers. In the PD, Sarah and Linda shared the process of this collaboration and how their collective attempt to garner feedback from students became actionable and supported the increased disciplinary literacies of students. This sharing with fellow teachers became a response to the recognition many teachers in the PD were struggling to understand: how data-driven instruction could inform disciplinary literacy instruction.

In addition to using strategies for responsive teaching, the teachers also utilized the tools of their discipline, which varied in technological sophistication, from rulers and calculators to websites. Thus, one of the enhancing factors we saw in some teachers' classrooms was their ability to use tools to address student needs. For instance, the art teacher was an expert at addressing students' lack of agency, not feeling artistically capable of attempting the techniques of the discipline. By scaffolding complex tasks using simple tools like a ruler, she built students' confidence in their ability to succeed in such tasks. However, technology was also an inhibiting factor because it was not an essential element immediately addressed in the PD. Thus, we asked teachers to model their use of technology in their discipline and how this technology was used to address needs seen in the formative assessment of students. Teachers of electives modeled for the other teachers how they used tools in their classroom: rulers for perspective in art and Google Forms and Sites to teach students the relevance of their résumés in business education, which led to a discussion that would not otherwise have occurred during the PD about using tools and technology for specific disciplinary tasks.

Clarification of Terms

Another inhibiting factor addressed during the intervention was teachers' lack of clarity regarding disciplinary literacy. Teachers were familiar with the need and emphasis for disciplinary literacy without clarity as to how that term translated into implementation in their practice. For instance, one teacher discussed years of hearing the term without ever enacting disciplinary literacy instruction as she was involved in multiple district initiatives supposedly dedicated to disciplinary literacy that instead focused on standards, the target verbs within those standards, and how to design tasks that implemented those key verbs into action.

This description of teaching as compliance with systematic trends and requirements was reflected in one of our other focused codes, *systematic impediments to change*. Whereas we had organized the first inquiry cycle of the PD to define and discuss the texts, task, and talk of the discipline, we had to modify this discussion, spending more time with terms of disciplinary literacy and focusing on how they related to inquiry and responsive teaching implemented in the respective teachers' classrooms. We also had to add lessons to this part of the course, which clearly defined terms such as *inquiry, texts, tasks,* and *responsive teaching*.

Another focus of discussion during the intervention was not only defining disciplinary literacy but also discussing when it differed from content literacy and how differentiation related to the instruction in various disciplines. For example, one inhibiting factor identified was that disciplinary literacy was not uniform in its relevance to the disciplines as areas such as special education needed to focus more on content literacy than disciplinary literacy to be responsive in their teaching. In addition, many teachers needed further development of content literacy, so we included more focus than originally planned on building a foundation of content literacy before developing knowledge of disciplinary literacy. These discrepancies repeatedly occurred to form the initial code *inhibiting factor: disparities in expertise and disciplines*. One example of this code is a teacher grappling with the need to teach content versus disciplinary literacy based on the ability level of a student as she deals with students whom she believed were not interested in becoming future experts in the discipline.

Increased Significance of Research Team Members

When we initially started the intervention, we had planned to work closely with the three literacy coaches participating in the intervention and observe them as they worked with teachers to enact disciplinary literacy lessons in their respective classrooms. However, we soon realized this would not be possible due in part to data reflected in the initial code, *systematic impediments to change*, which we will discuss in a subsequent section. In sum, the systematic impediment that prevented this plan from working was the literacy coaches were too steeped in administrative responsibilities in the school, especially the administration of standardized testing, to fulfill their genuine desire to work toward their coaching goals. This conflict is represented in one of the coach's literacy position statements where she discusses the reality of her position often conflicting with the goals for that position, especially with unanticipated demands of paperwork and testing. To compensate for the multiple directions the coaches were being pulled, we not only expanded our research team, but also their role in working with teachers to enact disciplinary literacy lessons in their classrooms. The role of the coach was needed to challenge teachers' assumptions about disciplinary literacies, concepts in which they seemed to have metacognitive discrepancy, thinking they understood the term, but this thinking not being evident in their practice. In addition, there was a wide variety of disciplines that needed attention beyond the focus of the major disciplines (math, English, social studies, and science). When we asked teachers what should be modified in an early focus group interview, they asked we respond to this variety of discipline expertise. We added members of the research team who had experience in multiple disciplines, and each member of the research team worked with small groups of teachers in their classrooms. In this way, the methodology of formative experiments was instrumental in not just collecting and observing data, but also allowing for teachers' PD as has been noted by Reinking and Bradley (2008).

Integration of the PD Course and Literacy Teaching

When we designed the PD course, we intended that teachers would identify disciplinary literacies during the initial round of inquiry and then design and implement disciplinary lessons enacted in their classroom. In reality, teachers had to start enacting disciplinary literacy strategies in their classrooms to identify the literate practices of their discipline. In other words, there was not a neat division between learning and enacting; they were interdependent. For example, as Sarah designed literacy pedagogy for her students in her 9th- and 10th-grade art class, she focused on creating authentic disciplinary tasks, formulating an inquiry question meaningful to students, selecting appropriate texts suitable for her students, and using ongoing formative assessment practices to identify when and how students needed additional levels of scaffolding. Yet, her design and enactment of this disciplinary literacy pedagogy occurred in unison with meetings with teaching colleagues and research team members. In fact, as she brought her uncertainties and questions to this collaborative group, the group, in turn, shaped how she designed these elements, how she reflected on formative assessment data, and created suitable scaffolding. Her ongoing inquiry encompassed her enactment and participation in conversations with teaching colleagues and research team members. Still, an inhibiting factor we had not anticipated was the time necessary for teachers to learn both in the PD and in their classrooms the texts, tasks, and talk of their discipline. Thus, we had to focus more time on those terms, both their definition and their relevance to classrooms, so we had to eliminate one major assignment originally on our syllabus: a collaborative inquiry plan, which was intended to include planning for how teachers would continue the PD inquiry after we finished working with them.

Progress toward Goal

There was evidence throughout the intervention of teachers moving from a deficit view of students to a focus on how to implement disciplinary literacy practices. Teachers' deficit view of student learning was seen in the first focus group interview, which emerged in the initial code, *deficit thinking*. Teachers described students in this code with words such as *roadblocks*, *hard*, and *unprepared*. This language seemed to purely place the blame of students being successful or not in their learning on the students. However, this language contrasted sharply with the teachers' final literacy position statements in which they discussed teaching literacy in their discipline. In these statements, the focus of the teachers' discussions was disciplinary strategies and formative assessment. One teacher said strategies such as frontloading had an enormous impact. Another teacher demonstrated the change from her first literacy position statement to her final one. In her initial statement, this teacher wrote from a deficit perspective, focusing on how it was difficult to retain a positive outlook. However, in her final statement, this teacher revised this same comment with a focus on her change in perspective, now seeing students as demonstrating knowledge and expertise during disciplinary reading and her focus on building value and putting relevance in place through scaffolding.

Unanticipated Outcomes

Researchers conducting formative experiments focus on the intervention's essential elements; however, they also pay attention to unanticipated outcomes that may arise out of the implementation of these elements. Three unanticipated outcomes consistently arose during this intervention: (1) the necessity of teacher collaboration, (2) the success of formative assessment, and (3) the connection between technology and disciplinary practices.

Collaboration

In the second focus group interview, a teacher expressed his hope to continue the teacher collaboration developed during the PD, describing how his colleagues provided needed counterbalance to his own limitations as a teacher. Not only did codes emerge for teachers using collaboration to implement disciplinary literacy, such as *collaboration among teachers*, but so did codes suggesting collaboration was important when students enacted disciplinary literacy practices in practicing teachers' classrooms, emerging in the code, *students collaborating as enhancing factor*. Thus, although not an essential element of the intervention, teachers collaborating together during the course in related disciplines worked well. Each week, teachers in the same or similar disciplines came together to form inquiry questions and implement those questions in their teaching practice.

Formative Assessment

Although formative assessment was an essential element of the intervention, and thus not unanticipated in its inclusion in our results, we have listed it as an unanticipated outcome because of the extent of its importance to the teachers. Seventeen out of 30 teachers completing both a pre- and post-intervention literacy position statement discussed formative assessment as an instrumental part of their practice of disciplinary literacy. During the intervention, teachers were required to partner with another teacher and complete an Eyes on Students observation form (Wilder & Herro, 2016) for their partner teacher, in which they observed a student at the request of the instructing teacher. The instructing teachers then used these observations of focal students to make decisions about instruction. In addition to appearing to be a positive access point for teachers practicing disciplinary literacy in their literacy position statements, the code also emerged from our qualitative data as an *enhancing factor: formative assessment*. In these data, teachers discussed this type of assessment giving them a more active, pragmatic role for assessment in the classroom. Some characteristic comments of this observation protocol for assessment included a description of it being productive, a way to focus on students at the individual level, and giving them needed information about their students' literacy ability. Although the feedback on Eyes on Students was mostly positive, teachers also noted that it needed to be paired with assessment that gauged student feedback as this was limited to observations of students.

Technology and Disciplinary Literacy

One element we did not account for specifically in having teachers plan their inquiry was how they would use the tools of their discipline. However, we noticed teachers used tools that were often essential to their scaffolding of disciplinary learning, from rulers in art, websites in business, and graphic calculators in math. Thus, we made a modification to bring this discussion into the PD by having teachers model their use of technology that was specific to their discipline. This modification led to a discussion of how tools may help teachers be more responsive in their teaching and the importance of tools for disciplinary learning. This discussion also emerged in our qualitative coding under the following initial codes: *technology as enhancing factor*, *tools as needed discussion*, and *resistance to new practice*. The need for this discussion, particularly in disciplinary literacies, is reflected in the disparity in the relevant literature. While literature in educational technology frequently addresses the TPACK framework, or knowledge in technology, pedagogy, and content knowledge (Mishra & Koehler, 2006), much of the literature in disciplinary literacy and PD focuses on content and pedagogy without including technology, even though new literacies were a driving force in initial discussions of disciplinary literacy, such as observed by Moje (2008). This gap leads us to the subsequent discussion of future modifications.

Remaining Enhancing and Inhibiting Factors and Future Modifications

Our retrospective analysis of the data revealed remaining enhancing and inhibiting factors not able to be addressed in the micro-level modifications of this intervention (Reinking & Bradley, 2008). Thus, these factors suggest modifications needed for future iterations of this type of PD, focused on teachers' enactment of disciplinary literacy in secondary classrooms.

Throughout the course, there was some resistance to change from the participating teachers and coaches; however, this resistance typically stemmed from barriers that were systematic, rather than teacher beliefs or agency regarding disciplinary literacy. The barriers included initial codes such as *standardized assessment*, *school curriculum*, and *district policy initiatives*. Thus, resistance came in the form of institutional barriers, somewhat out of the teachers' control. This institutional-level resistance is somewhat surprising considering that our PD was initiated by the school district in an effort to integrate a districtwide emphasis on adolescent literacy. However, as teachers tried to meet this new district goal, they were inhibited by interlocking bricks of curriculum and assessment, forming a wall of standardization that was at times insurmountable in the teachers' quest to refine their practice. As we worked with teachers to design new inquiry in their classrooms, we noted in our observations, "There is little freedom in the curriculum since they draw primarily from released test questions" and "The teachers feel the end of year exam doesn't assess literacy and has so much other stuff that literacy doesn't fit in the curriculum." Thus, although teachers embraced disciplinary practices such as formative assessment and Eyes on Students observations, they were also torn between changing practice and conforming to standardized measures, both of which seemed required, although impossible to simultaneously achieve.

As discussed throughout this section, there were modifications that might be considered for future iterations of this intervention. These modifications include accounting for technology more intentionally in disciplinary inquiry, and getting more district-level support to overcome systematic impediments, such as assessment and curriculum that seemed standard though counter to disciplinary literacy initiatives in the district. Other future modifications relate to making sure the design of the PD is sustainable considering the needs of the participating teachers and ensuring that leaders with initiative have an adequate variety of domain knowledge to support the development of teachers enacting disciplinary literacies.

Discussion

Researchers conduct formative experiments to consider grand theoretical concepts but challenge those perspectives in the crucible of a pedagogical context. Thus, the goal of this research is to form local or humble theory that makes pragmatic connections to teaching practice (Gravemeijer & Cobb, 2006). From our emerging focused codes and *a priori* coding of pre- and postsurvey and literacy statements, we have formed these localized theoretical assertions, which have precedence in formative experiments (see Colwell & Reinking, 2016; Howell et al., 2017). These assertions and the data leading to them are described in Table 12.4.

- *Assertion: The Eyes on Students observation protocol provides an entry point for high school teachers to clarify what makes a student literate in their discipline.* Providing teachers with tools, such as the Eyes on Students protocol, and specific strategies for disciplinary literacy creates an entry point for teachers to implement disciplinary literacy practices in their classrooms. These tools allow teachers to focus on responsive teaching strategies, rather than the deficits of their students, and gives them a sense of agency (Buczynski & Hansen, 2007) while respecting the limited time teachers have for implementing change (Pozuelos et al., 2010). Unanticipated outcomes in this intervention including teacher need for both collaboration and assessment of student outcomes suggest a tool such as Eyes on Students that allows teachers to work collaboratively to formatively assess student participation in

TABLE 12.4. Data Leading to Assertions

Focused codes and multiple data points	Assertions
• Focused code: formative assessment • Focused code: collaboration • Literacy position statements • Pre- and postsurvey responses	The Eyes on Students observation protocol provides an entry point for high school teachers to clarify what makes a student literate in his or her discipline.
• Focused code: evidence of progress—from deficit thinking to implementation of strategies • Literacy position statements • Pre- and postsurvey responses	Disciplinary literacy practice aided teacher agency and overcoming deficit thinking.
• Focused code: systematic impediments to change • Focused code: increased significance of research team • Literacy position statements	Systematic impediments limited the ability of teachers and coaches to work together to enact disciplinary literacy.
• Focused code: modification made—teacher modeling • Focused code: modification made—less distinction between learning in course and teaching	PD focused on disciplinary literacy should align to teachers' current curriculum context.
• Focused code: modification made—clarification of disciplinary literacy terms • Focused code: future modifications • Focused code: technology and disciplinary literacies • Literacy position statements	Future modifications of this PD should further emphasize differentiation of literacy practices with disciplinary expertise.

literacy activities of the discipline are not only helpful, but also give teachers a way to access disciplinary literacy as a teaching practice, rather than purely a theoretical concept. Thus, this finding supports the call by Cobb et al. (2016) for more PD design studies providing "means of supporting" (p. 229) teacher learning.

• *Assertion: Disciplinary literacy practice aided teacher agency and overcoming deficit thinking.* Both the qualitative data and analysis of teachers' literacy position statements at the beginning and end of the intervention showed the progress of teachers overcoming a deficit mind-set toward their students. Two practices of disciplinary literacy seemed to catalyze this change: assessment and knowledge of literacy strategies. Once teachers focused on students' progress of specific tasks of the discipline, their focus changed from blaming students for a lack of progress to focusing on how to address where students were to help them succeed in the tasks of the discipline.

• *Assertion: Systematic impediments limited the ability of teachers and coaches to work together to enact disciplinary literacy.* The professional learning of teachers must complement or compensate for testing and administrative practices appearing to counteract what teachers are trying to do. When coaches are reassigned as test monitors and teachers are required to teach discrete topics for the state assessment, teachers may not feel able to enact disciplinary literacy (Achinstein & Ogawa, 2006; Allard & Doecke, 2014; Skerrett, 2010). Multiple data points revealed that teachers faced extrinsic barriers to their implementation of disciplinary literacy. Literacy coaches who were supposed to aid teachers in understanding and implementing literacy practices with discipline experts were relegated to playing the role of test administrators. Thus, we had to add members of our research team to account for the varying discipline expertise of the participating teachers. Although this addition does support the notion that formative experiments are a methodology supportive of teacher development (Reinking & Bradley, 2008), it also suggests future iterations of PD must include a system in which standardized assessments and curriculum are supportive of disciplinary literacy. This finding is especially important considering the limited studies that devote "up-front attention to how teachers' developing practice is situated in school settings" (Cobb et al., 2016, p. 221) as we not only documented the impediments that occurred within this setting, but also how those impediments were modified in this iteration and suggest future modifications to assuage those impediments.

- *Assertion: PD focused on disciplinary literacy should align with teachers' current curricular context.* Several of our modifications included steps to more closely align the coursework and teaching involved in this PD. We had teachers model their teaching during the course time of the PD, and we realized teachers could not necessarily define the texts, tasks, and talk of their disciplines apart from their teaching in classrooms. Thus, our intended cycles of inquiry of defining and then enacting disciplinary literacy were not neatly separated, nor should they be. In addition, this PD also had to be enacted where teachers were in their response to curriculum, standards, and assessment that they were held accountable to in their school district. For example, we tried to help teachers see how they might develop inquiry and develop authentic tasks and negotiate these within the standards they and their students were held accountable to and discussed how these might prepare students for existing assessments.

- *Assertion: Future modifications of this PD should further emphasize differentiation of literacy practices with disciplinary expertise.* Several of our modifications throughout the intervention, including increased time and attention to distinguishing between content and disciplinary literacy and modeling how teachers might use the tools and disciplinary tasks of their disciplines within the PD, show that enacting disciplinary literacy is complicated by the significance of domain knowledge of each discipline. We had to account for this as well by encouraging members of our research team to work more closely with the different disciplines of the participating teachers in this study. In future modifications, those enacting PD on disciplinary literacy may take this differentiation for discipline expertise a step further.

To accommodate disciplinary expertise, we learned teachers may need an *expert peer* to help them bridge the gap between what they learn about disciplinary literacy and how they can implement this learning in their classrooms. This expert peer would be someone who understands the discipline's pedagogy, is knowledgeable about the literacy practices in that discipline, and collaborates with, rather than evaluates, the teacher. This person would help the teacher identify strategies and tools appropriate to the learning goals and literacy needs of the students in ways that connect modifying practice with the teacher's beliefs about learning (Musanti & Pence, 2010; O'Brien et al., 1995; Opfer & Pedder, 2011; Raider-Roth et al., 2012).

Conclusion

Student improvement in disciplinary literacy practice hinges on the ability to design responsive and impactful PD and professional learning for teachers. Connecting teacher learning with disciplinary experts and tools while being responsive to administrative restrictions and cultural norms supports teachers in meeting the literacy needs of their students. This study suggests PD focused on disciplinary literacy can improve teachers' disciplinary instruction. For example, the collaborative formative assessment implemented in this study with the Eyes on Students observation protocol provided teachers with an access point to participate collaboratively with disciplinary literacy. In addition, as teachers learned how to implement the tasks and literacy strategies of their discipline, they were less likely to have deficit thinking toward their students, and more likely to focus on what teaching to provide students to be successful in these tasks. However, this study also identified the challenges that remain to providing successful PD specifically for disciplinary literacy. As Moje (2015) described, disciplinary literacy is more than skills to be mastered as each discipline includes social and cultural dimensions as well as a need to integrate learning across disciplines. We saw these needs as we sought to help teachers grapple with practicing disciplinary literacy inside a school construct that had certain standardized demands regarding goals, assessments, and curriculum that did not allow for flexibility. Until these standardized barriers can be renegotiated to reflect literacy practices unique to each discipline, it is important to help teachers negotiate their current context. This navigation requires collaboration with colleagues who have domain-specific knowledge and expertise. This study begins to fill the gap highlighted by Cobb et al. (2016) that calls for more design studies specifically focused on PD. Through our implementation of such a study, we were able to suggest needed PD support of specific teacher practices, such as the Eyes on Students protocol supporting teachers' practice of disciplinary literacy. This study also suggests further research, such as assessments and standards that are supportive of disciplinary literacy and how expert peers might be used to support teachers' disciplinary expertise. To what extent does formative assessment provide a critical lever for teacher responsiveness during disciplinary literacy pedagogy and how might the PD need to bring greater intentionality to the type and frequency of teacher conversations around student formative assessment data—particularly given the situated realities of literacy within specific educational contexts in specific disciplines with specific teachers and specific students? This proposed research would modify the design features of PD on disciplinary literacies, while attending to the particularities of context and commonalities of disciplines. Ultimately, PD on disciplinary literacies must fit within the local teaching and learning context.

REFERENCES

Achinstein, B., & Ogawa, R. (2006). (In)Fidelity: What the resistance of new teachers reveals about professional principles and prescriptive educational policies. *Harvard Educational Review, 76*(1), 30–63.

Allard, A., & Doecke, B. (2014). Professional knowledge and standards-based reforms: Learning from the experiences of early career teachers. *English Teaching: Practice and Critique, 13*(1), 39–54.

Alvermann, D., Friese, E., Beckmann, S., & Rezak, A. (2011). Content area reading pedagogy and domain knowledge: A Bourdieusian analysis. *Australian Educational Researcher, 38*(2), 203.

Billman, A., & Pearson, P. (2013). Literacy in the disciplines. *Literacy Learning: The Middle Years, 21*(1), 5–33.

Bradley, B., Reinking, D., Colwell, J., Hall, L., Fisher, D., Frey, N., & Baumann, J. (2012). Clarifying formative experiments in literacy research. In P. Dunston, S. King Fullerton, C. Bates, K. Headley, & P. Stecker (Eds.), *61st yearbook of the Literacy Research Association* (pp. 410–418). LaGrange, GA: Literacy Research Association.

Buczynski, S., & Hansen, C. B. (2007). Impact of professional development on teacher practice: Uncovering connections. *Teaching and Teacher Education, 26*, 599–607.

Carpenter, D. (2015). School culture and leadership of professional learning communities. *International Journal of Educational Management, 29*(5), 522–538.

Charmaz, K. (2014). *Constructing grounded theory*. Thousand Oaks, CA: SAGE.

Cobb, P., Jackson, K., & Dunlap, C. (2016). Conducting design studies to investigate and support mathematics students' and teachers' learning. In J. Cai (Ed.), *Compendium for research in mathematics education* (pp. 208–233). Reston, VA: National Council of Teachers of Mathematics.

Cochran-Smith, M., & Lytle, S. L. (1999). Relationships of knowledge and practice: Teacher learning in communities. In A. Iran-Nudged & P. D. Pearson (Eds.), *Review of research in education* (pp. 249–305). Washington, DC: American Educational Research Association.

Colwell, J., Hunt-Barron, S., & Reinking, D. (2013). Obstacles to developing digital literacy on the internet in middle school science instruction. *Journal of Literacy Research, 45*(3), 295–324.

Colwell, J., & Reinking, D. (2016). A formative experiment to align middle-school history instruction with literacy goals. *Teachers College Record, 118*(12), 1–29.

Cridland-Hughes, S., & Wilder, P. (2016). Guiding principles for pre-service teacher literacy education in light of Read to Succeed. *Reading Matters, 16*, 75–80.

Darling-Hammond, L., & Richardson, N. (2009). Teacher learning: What matters? *Educational Leadership, 66*(5), 46–53.

DeWalt, K. M., & DeWalt, B. R. (2002). Learning to be a participant observer: Theoretical issues. In *Participant observation: A guide for fieldworkers* (pp. 16–34). Walnut Creek, CA: AltaMira Press.

Education Oversight Committee of South Carolina. (2011). 2011 Annual report. Retrieved from *www.eoc.sc.gov/InformationforEducators/PastAnnualReports/2011AnnualReport3012011.pdf*

Garet, M. S., Porter, A. C., Desimone, L., Birman, B. F., & Yoon, K. S. (2001). What makes professional development effective? Results from a national sample of teachers. *American Educational Research Journal, 38*, 915–945

Glaser, B. G. (1965). The constant comparative method of qualitative analysis. *Social Problems, 12*(4), 436–445.

Glesne, G. (2011). *Becoming qualitative researchers: An introduction* (4th ed.). Boston: Pearson.

Gravemeijer, K., & Cobb, P. (2006). Design research from a learning design perspective. In J. van den akker, K. Gravemeijer, S. Mckenney, & N. Nieveen (Eds.), *Educational design research* (pp. 17–51). New York: Routledge.

Hardy, I., & Lingard, B. (2008). Teacher professional development as an effect of policy and practice: A Bourdieuian analysis. *Journal of Education Policy, 23*(1), 63–80.

Hobson, A., & McIntyre, J. (2013). Teacher fabrication as an impediment to professional learning and development: The external mentor antidote. *Oxford Review of Education, 39*(3), 345–365.

Howell, E., Butler, T., & Reinking, D. (2017). Integrating multimodal arguments into high school writing instruction. *Journal of Literacy Research, 49*(2), 181–209.

Howell, E., Perez, S., & Abraham, W. T. (2020). Toward a professional development model for writing as a digital, participatory process. *Reading Research Quarterly, 56*(1), 95–117.

Ivey, G., & Broaddus, K. (2007). A formative experiment investigating literacy engagement among adolescent Latina/o students just beginning to read, write, and speak English. *Reading Research Quarterly, 42*, 512–545.

Jiménez, R. T. (1997). The strategic reading abilities and potential of five low-literacy Latina/o readers in middle school. *Reading Research Quarterly, 32*(3), 224–243.

Manderino, M. (2011). Disciplinary literacy in new literacies: Expanding the intersections of literate practice for adolescents. In P. Dunston, S. Fullerton, C. C. Bates, K. Headley, & P. Stecker (Eds.), *Literacy Research Association 61st Annual Yearbook* (pp. 119–133). LaGrange, GA: Literacy Research Association.

Mausethagen, S. (2013). A research review of the impact of accountability policies on teachers' workplace relations. *Educational Research Review, 9*, 16–33.

McConachie, S. M., & Petrosky, T. (Eds.). (2010). *Content matters: A disciplinary literacy approach to improving student learning*. San Francisco: Jossey-Bass.

Mishra, P., & Koehler, M. J. (2006). Technological pedagogical content knowledge: A framework for teacher knowledge. *Teachers College Record, 108*, 1017–1054.

Mohamed, N. (2008). "I have been doing things this way for so many years; why should I change?" Exploring teachers' resistance to professional learning. *New Zealand Studies in Applied Linguistics, 14*(1), 110–124.

Moje, E. B. (2008). Foregrounding the disciplines in secondary literacy teaching and learning: A call for change. *Journal of Adolescent & Adult Literacy, 52*(2), 96–107.

Moje, E. B. (2015). Doing and teaching disciplinary literacy with adolescent learners: A social and cultural enterprise. *Harvard Educational Review, 85*(2), 254.

Musanti, S., & Pence, L. (2010). Collaboration and teacher development: Unpacking resistance, constructing knowledge, and navigating identities. *Teacher Education Quarterly, 37*(1), 73–89.

O'Brien, D. G., Stewart, R. A., & Moje, E. B. (1995). Why content literacy is difficult to infuse into the secondary school: Complexities of curriculum, pedagogy and school culture. *Reading Research Quarterly, 30*, 442–463.

Opfer, V. D., & Pedder, D. (2011). Conceptualizing teacher professional learning. *Review of Educational Research, 81*(3), 376–407.

Powell, W., & Kusuma-Powell, O. (2015). Overcoming resistance to new ideas: Even the best teachers can become resistant to new learning. Deep reflection that reveals visible and invisible commitments to the status quo can yield progress. *Phi Delta Kappan, 96*(8), 66–69.

Pozuelos, F., González, G., & de León, P. (2010). Inquiry-based teaching: Teachers' conceptions, impediments and support. *Teaching Education, 21*(2), 131–142.

Raider-Roth, M., Stieha, V., & Hensley, B. (2012). Rupture and repair: Episodes of resistance and resilience in teachers' learning. *Teaching and Teacher Education, 28*, 493–502.

Reigeluth, C. M., & Frick, T. W. (1999). Formative research: A methodology for creating and improving design theories. In C. M. Reigeluth (Ed.), *Instructional-design theories and models: Vol. II. A new paradigm of instructional theory* (pp. 633–651). Mahwah, NJ: Erlbaum.

Reinking, D., & Bradley, B. A. (2008). *On formative and design experiments: Approaches to language and literacy research*. New York: Teachers College Press.

Reinking, D., Colwell, J., & Ramey, D. (2013). *A framework for conceptualizing, planning, conducting, and reporting a formative experiment*. Study group presented at the 2013 Literacy Research Association Conference, Dallas, TX.

Schen, M., Rao, S., & Dobles, R. (2005). *Coaches in the high school classroom: Studies in implementing high school reform*. New York: Carnegie Corporation of New York.

Schleppegrell, M. J., Achugar, M., & Oteíza, T. (2004). The grammar of history: Enhancing content-based instruction through a functional focus on language. *TESOL Quarterly, 38*(1), 67–93.

Shanahan, T., & Shanahan, C. (2008). Teaching disciplinary literacy to adolescents: Rethinking content-area literacy. *Harvard Educational Review, 78*(1), 40–59.

Skerrett, A. (2010). There's going to be a community, there's going to be knowledge: Designs for learning in a standardized age. *Teaching and Teacher Education, 26*(3), 648–655.

South Carolina Department of Education. (2014). Read to Succeed. Retrieved from *www.scstatehouse.gov/sess120_2013-2014/bills/516.htm*

Wilder, P., & Herro, D. (2016). Lessons learned: Collaborative symbiosis and responsive disciplinary literacy teaching. *Journal of Adolescent & Adult Literacy, 59*(5), 539–549.

Yan, C. (2015). We can't change much unless the exams change: Teachers' dilemmas in the curriculum reform in China. *Improving Schools, 18*(1), 5–19.

CHAPTER 13

Purposeful Clinical Practices in Teacher Preparation through Design-Based Research

Anthony Pellegrino

"You can't do that with this class. Save it for the smart kids."

I bet reading the statement above made many of you cringe. I felt that way too when I heard it from a teacher who was assigned to mentor one of our social studies teacher candidates in a yearlong internship at a local high school. The mentor was referring to the candidate's efforts to include analysis of primary sources in a lesson that challenged students to discern whether the pre-Civil War abolitionist and provocateur John Brown was a hero or a terrorist. It was a well-designed lesson with a rich, compelling question and opportunities for students to engage in practices to strengthen their historical thinking skills while also attending to state history standards. And, the candidate had included various scaffolds such as graphic organizers and clear assessment points and expectations to support the lesson objectives and the diverse learners and needs in the class. The mentor teacher, however, dismissed the lesson as far too advanced for general education students.

It was my first semester as a teacher educator at the University of Tennessee, and I was learning about how clinical experiences worked in this specific program. But in that pre-observation meeting to discuss the lesson and its outcomes, besides thinking about its content, I was also problematizing why this teacher was one of our mentors, and what the mentor training and placement process looked like (or should look like). Based on this experience and other feedback from colleagues, it seemed that the system by which we placed our candidates was dysfunctional. I learned that there was a mentor-training workshop, but it was not mandatory and never well attended. Moreover, the time was spent with mentors from all grade levels and content areas to learn superficial information, such as paperwork-submission protocols rather than any method and models for mentoring practices or attention to the frameworks and evidence-based practices we were emphasizing in coursework. Likewise, the placement process itself was often haphazard with administrators from the university communicating with school-based administration to determine placements. These practices were driven by numbers of candidates, rather than ensuring purposeful placements based on the specific needs of candidates. From these experiences, work to ensure that our clinical practices for candidates were purposeful and robust became paramount.

Based in part on these early experiences, I and my colleagues affiliated with the program began to consider ways to strengthen our partnerships with local school districts, schools, and teachers in an effort to reconsider our clinical model based on what we hoped for and drawing on the expertise of the educators in the schools where our candidates were placed. We knew this could be a long-term effort, and we committed to emphasizing clinical experiences as central to our program. We employed a design-based research (DBR) approach because of its iterative nature and general tenets of collaboration. Together, these elements matched what we believed would be most appropriate to address the complicated challenges related to clinical practice in teacher education. Moreover, the democratic nature of DBR, which includes authentic collaboration around a shared purpose and vision (Reinking & Bradley, 2008), hewed to the focus we have on democratic education in our social studies education program. Specific to that democratic perspective, we began with myriad conversations with stakeholders, including our candidates, university faculty, school-based administration, and teachers, and a new model began to take shape that included some training and professional development, but, more importantly, allowed the voices of all parties to be part of the process. This chapter includes highlights on the process and outcomes of this formative study. The next section includes relevant perspectives on teacher education, the preparation of social studies teachers, and clinical experiences.

Relevant Literature

Scholarship on teacher preparation, clinical practice, and the importance of school partnerships dates back more than a century. Broadly, the field addressed the rise and importance of teacher training and apprenticeship in normal schools and has continued through more complex configurations of school/university partnerships that have emerged in recent decades (Clifford & Guthrie, 1988; Conant, 1963; Fraser, 2007). Looking at these historical antecedents through current literature on clinical experiences for teacher candidates may offer some insight into the ways teacher preparation has sought to ensure teacher candidates have the appropriate experiences to help them in their development to be highly effective.

Teacher Preparation

Over a decade ago, Marilyn Cochran-Smith and Kelly Demers (2008) provided a historical look at teacher preparation and how changes were manifested through research and practice. They noted how, beginning in the 1960s, a paradigm shift from positivism to postmodernism in education research generally fostered a view of "pedagogy as a social exchange among participants rather than simply the transmission of information from teacher to pupils" (p. 1010). Such a change in understanding of teaching and learning affected the premises about the ways in which teachers were prepared (Wilson & Tamir, 2008). From cognitive psychology, scholars recognized a need for prospective teachers to understand practice that is mindful of student prior knowledge and experiences (Driscoll, 2005). Likewise, meeting the needs of diverse learners through culturally relevant pedagogy (Ladson-Billings, 2005) and collaboration with learning specialists (Friend & Cook, 2013) emerged as critical to teacher preparation. As such, educational theory, content knowledge in the context of practice, and clinical experiences were emphasized as the primary means through which quality teachers should be developed (Zeichner & Conklin, 2008). Moreover, this historical look uncovered the importance of fostering the related yet distinct skills from these domains to include purposeful collaboration with colleges of arts and sciences and PreK–12 schools in which teacher educators become the initiating collaborative partners, working with arts and sciences colleagues on content knowledge, and engaging PreK–12 schools to cultivate clinical placement sites where teacher candidates can practice working with learners.

Perhaps the most enduring concept in the campus/field nexus was the professional development school (PDS) model, where collaboration across these stakeholders would be cultivated. First advocated by the Holmes Group (1986) report, it was premised on the teaching hospitals found in medical education. What it represented, however, was the building of a profession where teacher candidates learn to practice in sites intentionally committed to a new relationship between the campus and the field. According to the report, teacher preparation would be fundamentally based on four principles: reciprocity, experimentation, systematic inquiry, and attention to the development of strategies that include all learners, which it observed would require "new structures" (Holmes Group, 1986, pp. 66–67). These new structures necessarily entailed traversing into research and practice collaborations where all participants would be involved in the joint planning of preparation programs using their local knowledge of teaching and learning in their communities. They would also include work with university faculty on research initiatives that sought to unlock more effective practices in both teaching and in teacher education. The report was rather explicit in its conception that there would be inter-institutional working groups that would collaborate on, and even govern, new program designs for teachers who wanted to remain in the classroom, build new curricula, and design new forms of evaluating teachers that would blur the lines between teaching and teacher education for both groups of collaborators. The authors further envisioned teacher educators actively working in PreK–12 classrooms and practicing teachers being fully immersed in preparing beginning teachers.

In its 2001 report, the American Association of State Colleges and Universities (AASCU; 2001) elaborated on this model and called on teacher educators to create high-quality and sustained professional development (PD) responsive to the needs of the profession and local school contexts. The report lamented that universities and PreK–12 schools continue to be interdependent but operate independently of one another. Specifically, the report asserted that "the universities' outputs (teachers) are the inputs to the PreK–12 system, and the PreK–12 outputs (students) are inputs to the university system" (p. 8), yet collaboration between these entities is typically scant and ill coordinated. To remedy these challenges, AASCU (2001) also recommended deep collaborations favored in the Holmes Group report, and the intentionality was palpable; education schools, under this model, would be research-to-practice entities and no longer places where teachers were prepared in isolation from the places where they work. By 2010, most of these shifts of language, concepts, and recommendations were synthesized by the National Council for Accreditation of Teacher Education (NCATE), whose blue-ribbon panel report *Transforming Teacher Education through Clinical Practice* (2010) called on teacher educators to establish mutually rewarding collaborative relationships with PreK–12 schools that help ensure the seamless learning of content and pedagogy with clinical practice.

In order to accomplish this, NCATE called on schools of education to create strategic partnerships with PreK–12 school districts, practitioners, and state and federal policymakers as a means for developing new teacher education programs centered on the practice of teaching for student achievement and accountability, by tying PreK–12 student learning to teacher education. The report recommended that clinical preparation be integrated throughout all aspects of teacher education: "The core experience in teacher preparation is clinical practice. Content and pedagogy are woven around clinical experiences throughout preparation, in coursework, in laboratory-based experiences" (NCATE, 2010, p. 5). The panel directed schools of education to ensure that effective practitioners are coaching and guiding teacher candidates during their preparation and induction in ways fully understood by all participants: a theme that may be traced back to Joyce and Clift (1984) and the Holmes Group (1986). The recommendations of the blue-ribbon panel became a primary motivation for change when they were enshrined as part of the new standards for professional accreditation by the Council for the Accreditation of Educator Preparation (CAEP; 2013). Honoring this work through inquiry and designing research to study various levels of teaching, learning, and the collaboration efforts between stakeholders are essential to help determine the effectiveness and viability of these collaborations. In social studies education, for example, looking at the ways evidence-based practices are supported in clinical experiences and mentor teacher preparation are just two of the innumerable issues to explore through a reimagined program based on these principles of teacher preparation.

Social Studies Teacher Preparation

As scholarship in teacher education evolved to emphasize clinical practice and collaboration between schools and educator preparation programs, scholarship in social studies education moved toward an inquiry-based approach that leverages disciplinary knowledge and skills developed in preparation coursework and practiced in authentic classrooms with highly engaged and effective mentors. In social studies education programs, candidates now learn about practices related to historical thinking as well as frameworks related to civic mindedness, geographic awareness, economic perspectives, and global education. In history, for example, rather than a static chronicle of names, events, and dates that often permeate students' social studies classroom experiences, a more effective approach to learning is one that includes purposeful reading, analysis, and interpretation of a variety of pertinent primary sources that offer evidence about past events, people, and perspectives (Drake & Nelson, 2005; VanSledright, 2011). Primary sources, after all, are firsthand accounts of events and thus serve as fundamental building blocks for thinking historically (Stearns, 2000). Using primary sources allows individuals to more authentically experience the lives of people at a particular time and place, to better understand the decisions and actions they take, and to explore the motives and values that led them to those decisions (Brooks, 2011; Endacott, 2014).

In other disciplines found under the social studies umbrella, including civics, economics, geography, and the behavioral sciences, social studies educators rely on similar frameworks that encourage constructivist and critical orientations to learning. In civics, for example, we seek to engender civic mindedness that is action-oriented and steeped in understanding of how the mechanisms of power work and how people can exercise agency (Parker, 2008; Pellegrino & Zenkov, 2013). Likewise, in economics and geography, we encourage students to challenge a simple knowledge-level understanding of the content and move to critical exploration of the structures that undergird the disciplines. So, rather than memorizing state capitals and the physical shapes of countries on a map, this practice may include using demographic data to examine patterns of racism and discrimination to discern how and why those affect economic opportunities people have with respect to where they work and live.

What these education movements have in common is an approach that calls on students to use evidence in their efforts to respond to relevant questions, engage in disciplinary literacy practices, and produce authentic artifacts that lead to taking informed action. To support these transformations in social studies pedagogy, in 2013, the National Council for the Social Studies (NCSS), the largest professional organization for social studies teaching and learning, published the results of a collaborative effort by state social studies curriculum leaders and other social studies–related organizations to reimagine social studies curriculum and assessment structure. The resulting College, Career, and Civic Life (C3) framework provided information, guidelines, and benchmarks for teachers to reorient their instruction toward this approach and served to support state-level social studies curriculum leaders to develop state standards around its principles. Taken together, this work is both challenging and exciting as it requires students to interpret and corroborate evidence and make decisions about bias and truth in ways offered in few other school experiences (Barton, 2011; Wineburg, 2001).

Undertaking this work in classrooms is, by extension, a complex endeavor, and requires a robust clinical experience model in which opportunities for prospective teachers to apply their knowledge, skills, and other competencies with learners with support from faculty, their educator preparation program, their school-based mentors, and the school community in which they work (Grossman, Hammerness, & McDonald, 2009). With the complexity and relative newness of these initiatives, there remains an incongruity between the teaching approaches advocated by social studies education scholars and those typically practiced in schools—even by their own program graduates. This has been a source of consternation for those involved in the preparation of teachers (Ball & Forzani, 2009; Zenkov & Pytash, 2019).

University/School Partnerships through DBR

Establishing university/school partnerships that leverage the expertise of university faculty and school-based mentors, while also accommodating the voices of the teacher candidates themselves, is a means through which we may actualize the broad recommendations from teacher education scholarship and the research base of social studies education practices. Undertaking this work through DBR affords researchers the opportunity to bring these elements together in ways offered by few other research approaches (Freedman & Kim, 2019). Exploring these partnerships that emerge as part of our efforts to bring teacher candidates into classrooms for rich clinical experiences where they can learn from and work with effective teachers is worthwhile. Drawing on the sentiments of Gutiérrez and Penuel (2014), "studying 'side by side' with research partners jointly engaged in work to transform systems is more likely to produce more sensitive and robust measurement and ecologically valid accounts of cultural production and institutional change" (p. 20). To that end, our project was guided by the tenets of DBR articulated by Anderson and Shattuck (2012), who suggested (1) research is situated in a real education context, (2) there is a focus on the design and testing of a significant intervention, (3) "interventions are assessed on a wide variety of indices using multiple methodologies" (p. 17), (4) multiple iterations are involved in the research, and (5) the research involves a collaborative partnership. Through this DBR model, we sought to explore the effects of designing and implementing a new model of clinical experiences based on the development of a school/university partnership with school-based mentors, university faculty, and teacher candidates. (For a review on DBR, see Chapter 1 of this volume.)

Design-Based Principles

Initial Preparation

This project began with an evaluation of the existing program for prospective middle and high school social studies teachers offered at our university, where we prepared approximately 20 candidates annually. Broadly, the program was a fifth-year licensure program with an optional master's degree. Candidates completed an education major in a content area and a minor in education by taking general courses in education psychology, special education, and general methods. The fifth year consisted of the internship where candidates also took courses in content-area methods and disciplinary literacy. The optional master's degree courses were offered the summer before and after the internship. Based on an audit of the courses and a general evaluation of the program, we had initiated our DBR work to consider changes to the fundamental structures and approach to our work with teacher candidates. Specifically, we drew on the process outlined by Anderson and Shattuck (2012), who called for an initial survey of the context, followed by analysis of the need in the context of the current processes in place. The program evaluation that helped launch the project focused on course requirements, clinical practice opportunities, and state licensure expectations.

The three faculty involved in the evaluation were all members of the program and taught courses as well as supervised candidates in their yearlong internships. Evidence from internal surveys, course grades, program-related standardized assessments, including a project-related research report and edTPA data, and observation assessments related to clinical practice indicated a lack of preparedness on the part of our candidates in the program structure at the time. One notable aspect of the program was that the primary teaching methods course was completed during the first semester of a yearlong internship. While this structure has offered some benefits for clinical practice, we found that it led to a situation in which our candidates were underprepared, including understanding theoretical bases for historical thinking and practical applications thereof. Moreover, from the evaluation, we learned about mismatches between university and school-based expectations and the challenges candidates experienced in addressing both entities.

Intervention and Data Sources

In order to address challenges we discerned from our program evaluation, we looked to utilize our data as an introductory step to initiate collaboration with potential school partners. We began with conversations with central office curriculum coordinators from our collaborating district, who knew the teachers well and would be crucial collaborators to help overhaul our clinical model. Through initial conversations, we shared our evaluation data and prior mentor lists, and learned more about the expectations of the district. Collectively, we determined that the program would require supplemental coursework in methods along with additional clinical experiences that were purposeful and robust. One new course was developed that would be a methods course with an associated project-based clinical experience (Pellegrino, Daoud, & Zurawski, 2018). The project orientation of the clinical component to the class would flow through the school-based partners, and the teacher candidates would work to support mentor teachers in planning and executing the projects.

Coursework

The first iteration of this course, which was not yet a formal program requirement, included 8 candidates, while the second year included 14 candidates. Historical thinking along with resources and practices related to teaching with primary sources framed this course. Specifically, candidates addressed tenets of historical thinking, including multiple perspectives and interpretation of evidence (Barton, 2011), to ground lessons and activities. From this course, we examined course activities and artifacts, where candidates address the importance of primary sources to learning history and lessons and activities using primary sources.

To complement learning about the theoretical perspectives of historical thinking and application strategies of using primary sources, this new methods course also included a clinical component where candidates engage in project-based clinical experiences (see Pellegrino & Zenkov, 2016). This aspect of the course included candidate creation of standards-based, content-informed learning experiences integrating primary sources and emphasizing inquiry-based and student-centered instructional practices using primary sources. Each project was tailored to the curricular needs and intentions of the mentor teacher and focused on using primary sources that the mentor and teacher candidates will implement together during the clinical experience. Projects were reviewed for content alignment to course expectations and meeting the needs of mentor teachers, inclusion of authentic assessment activities, also co-developed by mentors and teacher candidates, as practice opportunities to assess historical thinking. Notably, we decided to require that candidates work in small groups with these mentor teachers. This aspect allowed us to be more selective with the mentors we chose and allowed candidates to work with peers in this clinical environment.

Coursework, Cycle 2

This first iteration of the clinical experience changed considerably based on teacher reflections and feedback. The clinical experience would evolve into even fewer mentor teachers. Rather than six mentor teachers having just a few candidates, we narrowed our pool to three mentor teachers the second year and only two for the third year. This change allowed candidates to be more involved in the projects they were executing and have the experience of working with small groups of students across a significant amount of time. Another change was that we encouraged more leeway for mentors to initiate projects that matched their curriculum needs at the time. For example, in the first year of the project, we determined the topic and scope of projects the candidates would work on well ahead of time. But, unexpected days off from school disrupted the mentors' pacing, and they felt pressure to implement the project because of the work the candidates had already done. The second and third years included more emphasis on the design of the project, rather than the specific topics covered. The candidates also took more of a lead on these designs and utilized online sharing tools to collaborate with the mentors even before they had stepped into their classrooms.

Internship

The initial design of the new program would also involve a robust focus on the year-long internship and PD designed to address mentor teachers, who would work with teacher candidates and their potential mentees. The PD associated with the internship included a summer face-to-face workshop and follow-up activities over the course of a school year that supported the evidence-based principles and practices on which we were focusing in our coursework. The workshop included activities that allow candidates and their mentors to discuss communication and collaboration and reflect on how they approach curriculum (see Swalwell, Pellegrino, & View, 2015, for details on these activities). Partners also began a co-planning inquiry-based activity modeled on the hybrid university-level history course "Teaching Hidden History." The premise of the project was for students to discover a unique primary source and seek to uncover the "hidden" story behind it through other primary sources. Together, the resources, and annotations thereof, became a module designed for secondary history students (Schrum, Sleeter, Pellegrino, & Tyong Vy Sharpe, 2018). One student in the course, for example, began with images of a historic boundary marker near Washington, D.C., and found other primary resources to tell the story of the tensions of the slave trade between the District and neighboring Virginia. Using this model for our project, mentors and mentees worked together to co-develop their digital *hidden history* module to be used with secondary social studies students. Data collected from this workshop included pre- and post-questionnaires regarding mentoring perceptions and experiences, quarterly reflections written by both mentors and candidates, and artifacts related to the co-developed project.

Internship, Cycle 2

The most significant revision of the workshop emerged by design. Having a group of interns and mentors who had completed the PD and internship year project allowed us to draw on their experiences for revisions and to share what they had learned with the second cohort of mentors and teacher candidates. Ultimately, two mentors and two candidates from the first cohort were selected to lead conversations around the internship. In a brief workshop segment where mentors and candidates met in separate groups to discuss issues and practices germane to their respective roles, these "experts" shared what worked for them. They also answered questions that ranged from logistical ones about when candidates should be prepared to lead lessons to strategies to address fundamental differences in approaches to teaching. This iteration also allowed more time for the paired teams of mentor and candidate to think about their yearlong pacing and plan for the inquiry-based Teaching Hidden History project.

Data Analysis

Our data analysis included examining mentor and candidates' questionnaires, projects from the clinical experience, and reflections from before and after internship from both cohort years. Our analysis has included content review of short-answer responses as well as categorizing descriptive data. We conducted content analysis of reflections from the cohorts. To do this, we took a holistic view of the process from program evaluation through cohorts of teacher candidates. Through an inductive approach, we attempted to bring together various sources to explain the complex phenomena of teacher candidates navigating coursework and clinical practice (Yin, 2003).

Learning Points

This multiyear project emerged from an opportunity to reimagine one social studies teacher preparation program with clinical practices as more central to our mission. To that end, we employed DBR principles that guided our process. In addition to working closely with our school-based partners in every step of the process, we have worked to establish a reflective orientation toward the program and a focus on continually exploring the impact of the program on our candidates, our school-based partners, and ourselves (Barab & Squire, 2004). From this work, we significantly revised the program our candidates experience and have become far more driven by clinical practice and a responsiveness to our school and teacher partners. Specifically, we added a clinical-based methods course for candidates in the semester prior to their yearlong internship. We also included mentor/intern PD focused on effective social studies practices, communication skills, and collaboration in the weeks before internship began. This workshop included a focus on skills, practices, and knowledge coming from social studies education research and emphasized practices of effective mentoring and collaboration. The workshop was followed by quarterly reflections and artifacts from co-planned, inquiry-based projects launched during the internship. In this section, we present a general overview of findings from the analysis of the questionnaires, projects, and reflections in two themes: applications of practice and relationship building. These themes help explain what we found through DBR on establishing university and school partnerships that leverage the candidates' clinical practice in ways that support the application of theory and practice to ultimately support young learners in social studies.

Applications of Practice

The theme of applications of practice in social studies speaks to the first objective for our project, which was to ensure that the teacher candidates graduating from our program, as well as their mentor teachers helping to train them, recognize the importance of using evidence-based social studies pedagogies in ways that support student learning. This theme addresses the teacher candidates' and mentors' willingness, comfortability, and knowledge to leverage instructional practices that involve employing primary sources in the classroom. Based on data from pre-internship questionnaires and early reflective opportunities, the contrast between candidates and interns was stark.

From pre-internship questionnaires, it was evident that coursework supported candidates' understanding of pedagogies involving disciplinary practices, including analysis and interpretation of primary sources as the essence of lessons in history. Candidates specifically expressed a number of skills they want their students to attain by using and working with primary source documents, including sourcing, critical analysis, inferencing, and evaluating evidence. They added that they anticipated the skills needed to read and interpret a wide variety of primary sources would help their students *reconstruct* the past, rather than take a textbook or traditional narrative version as the entire story. Likewise, candidates saw primary sources as an opportunity to challenge students to interpret a variety of perspectives to gain a deeper, more contextualized understanding of the past. One candidate likened this approach to *building blocks* that helped students construct a new understanding. In terms of support needed to implement effective social studies instructional practices, candidates indicated that while they believed they needed less support in discerning the utility of primary sources, they were very interested in gaining experiences using these practices in classroom situations. And, they were looking to mentors to provide such opportunities. In addition to these specific needs expressed by candidates, they also focused on broader approaches to teaching. Collaborative research and student choice used in the planning of an inquiry-based project illuminated this perspective. One candidate shared her experience regarding those opportunities:

> "Last semester when I covered the French Revolution I used a mix of direct instruction with supporting activities based on my mentor's previous lessons. Utilizing this inquiry based project allowed for my students to develop key content specific skills, specifically analysis. We were able to cover writing, presenting, analyzing, and examine bias in different historical perspectives. From this, I have noticed my students are developing into greater historical thinkers and questioners on the following unit of imperialism." (Candidate Reflection, February 4, 2019)

In the same questionnaire, mentors shared a more limited view of primary sources. Not only did they limit the types of primary sources to mainly text-based documents, but they also noted that time to utilize instructional practices beyond whole-class direct instruction was limited. Primary sources, therefore, were luxuries used sparingly and done so mostly to supplement traditional narratives. One mentor, for example, said the Emancipation Proclamation was an important primary source to use in teaching U.S. history because "it provided details of how slaves were freed" (Mentor Reflection, September 6, 2018). What we glean from this is that mentors largely see primary sources as ways to inform, rather than ways to build understanding of historical narratives.

The contrasts expressed by the candidates and mentors in this project were valuable to us and our school partners. It was evident that bringing both of us together before an intensive clinical experience like an internship was a useful first step to strengthen our program. It provided us with the opportunity to talk about the different perspectives and approaches to teaching that each brought with them. Not only would interns learn a great deal from their experience, but also mentors could learn from candidates about how primary sources can and should be used to engender historical thinking, and ways to include skills of analysis and interpretation of evidence and perspective taking to foster the habits of mind that enable such thinking. Additionally, the importance of effective collaboration practices to support this relationship became clear to us (Friend & Cook, 2013).

Building Relationships

In the spirit of the collaboration we sought to build through this DBR project, we also learned that talking through the different perspectives teacher candidates and mentor teachers bring to the clinical experience brought out important learning opportunities from both. What has been achieved from the project thus far has been done through relationship building. With a specific focus on problems of practice, we have been able to keep the scope of the project relevant to our candidates, their mentors, and the partner schools (Coburn, Penuel, & Geil, 2013). Likewise, relationships at the university/district level provided the foundation of the placement process and PD and allowed utilization of intentional strategies to support the collaboration necessary to facilitate positive outcomes for all parties (Coburn et al., 2013; Gates-Duffield & Stark, 2001). And at the ground level, the relationships between mentors and interns were nurtured at a variety of levels and through a variety of means, and those were perhaps the most significant relationships we have seen in the project. Mentors, for example, learned from candidates to *not get bogged down in the minutia of teaching*, and to bring back the joy in teaching. Candidates likewise noted that their mentors encouraged the resourcefulness candidates displayed in planning instruction and saw this as *a critical skill for new teachers . . . in a climate of reduced funding and restrictions on time to cover all standards*. Together, these represented the mutually beneficial relationships that were

Purposeful Clinical Practices in Teacher Preparation

captured in reflections. And generally, the reflections have demonstrated the positive relationships these educators have developed. Table 13.1 summarizes general themes expressed by mentors and candidates across the reflections.

Universally, candidates noted that they valued the time to collaborate with their mentor teachers. Early in the internship, one candidate expressed that she "learned so much from watching (her mentor) plan lessons." Many also lamented, however, that time for true collaboration was limited and finding time to work together in person was difficult during the school day. Relatedly, at the same early point in the internship, mentors expressed that they were feeling trust being built with their

TABLE 13.1. Mentor and Candidate Reflections

Early	Midyear	End of year
Mentors		
Building trust	Time to reflect, plan, and provide feedback	Divergent levels of trust: outliers get the most attention.
Establishing routines, norms, and communication plans	Refining mechanisms for communication and feedback	Co-teaching to learn with interns
Learning new role	Discerning expectations versus reality	More purposeful and long-term planning
Balancing new school year and intern's needs simultaneously	Navigating the transfer of authority in the classroom	Reflecting on purpose and relationships
	Introducing interns to ancillary teacher roles	
Interns		
Learning school and classroom culture	Finding ways to apply Educator Preparation Program (EPP) coursework ideas	Co-teaching to learn with mentors
Understanding and managing student perceptions	Straining to problem-solve communication issues with mentor, students, colleagues	Sharing resources and lesson ideas with mentor and colleagues
Liminal space: moving from student to teacher (and back)	Aligning expectations of EPP and mentor	Increased informal mentors and mentoring
Balancing schedules to collaborate with mentor	Feeling unsupported, unmoored	Developing deep commitment to students and school
	Balancing "do my own thing" with relying on mentor support	Preparing for the next school year (applying for jobs, interviewing)

mentee even through brief exchanges they had on planning and few opportunities they had to co-teach portions of lessons. Overall, data surrounding this theme are informative indicators regarding how mentors and teacher candidates were impacted by this idiosyncratic partnership, as well as how they will use the clinical experience to shape their practice of integrating effective social studies practices.

Implications for Future Research Using DBR Methodologies

Our study sought to improve social science educator preparation by establishing a robust university and school partnership that leveraged the clinical experience as a PD learning opportunity grounded in historical thinking and teaching/learning with primary sources. After evaluating the emerging impact of the restructuring of our program, we found that our study had significant implications for both teaching and learning social studies as well as clinical practice as it related to our program. Notably, it was our approach using DBR principles that helped us understand the challenges and find ways to address them. Drawing on the parameters by which DBR is defined (Anderson & Shattuck, 2012), we believe we have begun an iterative cycle that will allow us to continually improve the experiences of our teacher candidates. Below we share what we believe was most impactful.

Situated in a Real Educational Context

From the initial experiences with the clinical model for our program, it was clear that any reforms would have to begin with an understanding of the relationships between the program faculty and clinical experiences. The program evaluation helped us see deficiencies that would inform our communication with potential school partners. We learned, for example, that the placement process was done at administrative levels and that classroom teachers learned about potential mentoring opportunities from their school leaders with little regard for appropriate placements. From this information, we determined that building relationships with teachers and content-area specialists in this target district would be integral to any revised process.

Focusing on the Design and Testing of a Significant Intervention

From our relationship-building process with social studies district leaders and classroom teachers, we co-developed a model of PD that would begin well before candidates begin their internships and extend all the way through the academic year. Likewise, we committed to an iterative cycle of PD that we would reflect on with each new cohort of candidates. The model now included a pre-internship course with a project-based clinical experience (Pellegrino & Zenkov, 2016) where candidates go out in groups to a few mentor teachers and help plan and execute a group project. This model allows candidates to work together in planning and instruction and collaborate with mentor teachers. Through this experience, candidates and mentors share "critical incidents" they found in the experience. We use that information to help us determine internship placements and the objectives of the PD. Making those placements now comes through full collaboration with mentor teachers and content-area social studies leaders at the district level. Those placements are now carefully chosen based on a variety of factors we have learned from our candidates and mentors. Importantly, working with the district social studies specialist has also given us insights into upcoming curricular changes and other policy initiatives that may inform our placements. After placements are made, but well before the internship commences, candidates and mentors come together with us to talk about expectations and experiences, and learn about the ways communication and collaboration can maximize the effectiveness of the internship. They engage in activities to consider their own proclivities in terms of communication and orientation toward the curriculum (Swalwell et al., 2015). The intervention also consists of a co-planning and co-teaching project that they begin in the workshop and continue through execution during the academic year. This inquiry-based project challenges the candidates and mentors to rethink their practice, with a focus on compelling questions, use of disciplinary practices such as engagement with primary sources, through authentic assessments that challenge students to take informed action based on their learning (NCSS, 2013). Periodic reflections are also part of the intervention. These reflections, the prompts of which were co-developed with university faculty and district content leaders, challenge interns and mentors to consider ideas of communication, collaboration, and the challenges thereof across the internship. One midyear prompt, for example, asks that both parties reflect on communication challenges they have faced and ways they have sought to remedy them. Overall, we believe the breadth and depth of the components of the intervention have led us to a deeper understanding of our program and the experiences of our candidates in it.

Using Mixed Methods

Pre- and post-internship questionnaires provide bookends that have helped us recognize the ways both interns and mentors have transformed. Seeing responses to Likert scale questions have led us to realize how impactful the internship is on the ways our candidates see themselves as teachers. In addition to those data, we also collect critical incidents from pre-internship clinical experiences, reflections, classroom observation data, lesson plans, and even student artifacts related to the inquiry-based project. The nature of these data has allowed us to see our program from multiple perspectives and consider how we can continue to improve the preparation of our candidates.

Involving Multiple Iterations

We are currently in the third year of this formative project. Each cycle has, of course, given us more valuable data, but beyond that, it has allowed us to reflect on the data and consider opportunities for improvement. The relationships we have built with mentor teachers and district leaders have helped us learn more about collaboration and communication for us, as well as between mentors and interns. In Year 1, for example, we learned from communication with mentors that the project-based clinical experiences would work better with a more concentrated collection of candidates working with fewer mentor teachers. We have also revised the workshop considerably as we have learned more about the strengths that interns bring to the relationship. We no longer approach the workshop with the traditional model of interns learning from mentors, but now utilize the experiences from both parties in a way that facilitates a mutually beneficial relationship.

Involving a Collaborative Partnership between Researchers and Practitioners

Perhaps the most exciting aspect of this project has been the collaborative partnerships we have developed between mentors and interns, schools and the university faculty, and faculty and mentors. Through this work, we have found that by nurturing a robust partnership between universities and schools that leverages the clinical experience as a PD opportunity is extremely beneficial. We have determined that during the internship, teacher candidates need space to practice and refine their freshly obtained skills with young learners with the support of not only university faculty but also their school-based mentors. Relatedly, we find that mentors can benefit from this unique partnership because they will not only be gaining an asset in their classroom, they will also receive PD to help them grow in their pedagogical practice as well. Through this partnership and framework, we also found that an opportunity exists to transform the clinical experience into a mutually beneficial collaborative experience for the triad of teacher candidates, mentor teachers, and university faculty.

As with any project involving the complexities of teacher preparation and clinical experiences, this project has not been without its challenges. Although we now have full-throated support from our district partners, involving people at that level took considerable effort. Heretofore, clinical placements were made at the school level. Engaging in this partnership would take more effort from people with already full plates. Likewise, more attention from school-based leaders to see our program faculty as partners and our candidates as assets to their students required a rethinking of candidates as not just additional students to be taught but as engaged and energized partners willing to learn and pitch in. Relatedly, the long-term nature of the project we are undertaking was important to explain. We were not interested in a one-time project to learn more about our candidates, but instead sought to reform the clinical model toward a more collaborative and purposeful one that involved sustained partnerships. In terms of the research, this project was also challenging to explain for Institutional Review Board approval. The complexities of working with teachers, candidates, their students, as well as district leaders, for an indeterminate amount of time was difficult to communicate. However, we believed that the research was a necessary component of the work and persistence paid off.

Conclusion

I began this chapter with a quote from a mentor teacher who did not think his students were able to engage in the type of learning we espouse in our social studies education program. While not representative of all the mentor teachers who worked with our candidates at the time, his comments were, nonetheless, reflective of the challenges we faced with a program where clinical experiences were disconnected from coursework. Through DBR, we have been able to drastically change our program to one that is led by school/university partnerships and an approach whereby we all learn from and with each other. And rather than conclude with a focus on the quote that led off the chapter, here is a comment from a current mentor teacher that captures some of the fruits of the project and reveals the benefits of this partnership on all members of this collaboration:

> "[I] just wanted to shoot you a quick email and let you know that Cassidy [candidate pseudonym] had a great first week! We got her out in front of the students a lot, trained her on [the district's software applications], had her make her first parent phone calls, and spent a lot of time getting to know the students and planning for future [lessons]. She also observed multiple teachers last week and will observe several more this week. I want to get her out in front of different teachers as much as possible before her [university] classes start back up. I think this has been valuable for her and she has already gotten a lot of ideas based on what she has observed and what we worked on in the workshop. (Personal Communication, August 9, 2019)

REFERENCES

American Association of State Colleges and Universities. (2001). *To create a profession: Supporting teachers as professionals*. Washington, DC: Author.

Anderson, T., & Shattuck, J. (2012). Design-based research: A decade of progress in educational research? *Educational Researcher, 41*(1), 16–25.

Ball, D. L., & Forzani, F. M. (2009). The work of teaching and the challenge of teacher education. *Journal of Teacher Education, 60*, 497–511.

Barab, S. A., & Squire, B. (2004). Design-based research: Putting a stake in the ground. *Journal of the Learning Sciences, 13*(1), 1–14.

Barton, K. C. (2011). History: From learning narratives to thinking historically. In W. B.

Russell (Ed.), *Contemporary social studies: An essential reader* (pp. 109–139). Charlotte, NC: Information Age.

Brooks, S. (2011). Historical empathy as perspective recognition and care in one secondary social studies classroom. *Theory & Research in Social Education, 39*(2), 166–202.

Clifford, G. J., & Guthrie, J. W. (1988). *A brief for professional education: Ed school.* Chicago: University of Chicago Press.

Coburn, C. E., Penuel, W. R., & Geil, K. E. (2013). *Research–practice partnerships: A strategy for leveraging research for educational improvement in school districts.* New York: William T. Grant Foundation.

Cochran-Smith, M., & Demers, K. E. (2008). How do we know what we know? Research and teacher education. In M. Cochran-Smith, S. Feiman-Nemser, D. J. McIntyre, & K. E. Demers (Eds.), *Handbook of research on teacher education: Enduring questions in changing contexts* (pp. 1009–1016). New York: Routledge/Taylor Francis Group.

Conant, J. B. (1963). *The education of American teachers.* New York: McGraw-Hill.

Council for the Accreditation of Educator Preparation. (2013). Accreditation standards. Retrieved from *http://caepnet.org/standards/caep-commission/standards*

Drake, F. D., & Nelson, L. R. (2005). *Engagement in teaching history: Theory and practices for middle and secondary teachers.* New York: Prentice Hall.

Driscoll, M. (2005). *Psychology of learning for instruction* (3rd ed.). New York: Pearson.

Endacott, J. (2014). Negotiating the process of historical empathy. *Theory & Research in Social Education, 42*(1), 4–34.

Fraser, J. W. (2007). *Preparing America's teachers: A history.* New York: Teachers College Press.

Freedman, E. B., & Kim, J. (2019). Introduction. In B. C. Rubin, E. B. Freedman, & J. Kim (Eds.), *Design research in social studies education: Critical lessons from an emerging field* (pp. 3–27). New York: Routledge.

Friend, M., & Cook, L. (2013). *Interactions: Collaboration skills for school professionals* (7th ed.). New York: Pearson.

Gates-Duffield, P., & Stark, C. (2001). Recipes for professional development schools: A metaphor for collaboration. In R. Ravid & M. G. Handler (Eds.), *The many faces of school–university collaboration: Characteristics of successful partnerships* (pp. 45–55). Englewood, CA: Teachers Ideas Press.

Grossman, P., Hammerness, K., & McDonald, M. (2009). Redefining teaching, re-imagining teacher education. *Teachers and Teaching: Theory and Practice, 15,* 273–289.

Guba, E. G., & Lincoln, Y. S. (2005). Paradigmatic controversies, contradictions, and emerging confluences. In N. K. Denzin & Y. S. Lincoln (Eds.), *The SAGE handbook of qualitative research* (pp. 163–188). Thousand Oaks, CA: SAGE.

Gutiérrez, K., & Penuel, W. (2014). Relevance to practice as a criterion for rigor. *Educational Researcher, 43*(1), 19–23.

Holmes Group. (1986). *A report of the Holmes Group: Tomorrow's teachers.* East Lansing, MI: Author.

Joyce, B., & Clift, R. (1984). The phoenix agenda: Essential reform in teacher education. *Educational Researcher, 13,* 5–18.

Ladson Billings, G. (2005). Toward a theory of culturally relevant pedagogy. *American Education Research Journal, 32,* 465–491.

National Council for Accreditation of Teacher Education. (2010). *Transforming teacher education through clinical practice: A national strategy for preparing effective teachers.* Washington, DC: Author.

National Council for the Social Studies. (2013). *The college career, and civic life (C3) framework for social studies state standards: Guidance for enhancing the rigor of K–12 civics, economics, geography, and history.* Silver Spring, MD: Author.

Parker, W. C. (2008). Knowing and doing in democratic citizenship education. In L. S. Levstik & C. A. Tyson (Eds.), *Handbook of research in social studies education* (pp. 65–79). New York: Routledge.

Pellegrino, A., Daoud, N., & Zurawski, L. (2018). Citizenship & power: Perspectives from a critical, project-based clinical experience. In K. Zenkov & K. E. Pytash (Eds.), *Clinical experiences in teacher education: Critical, project-based interventions in diverse classrooms* (pp. 191–207). New York: Routledge.

Pellegrino, A., & Zenkov, K. (2016, February). The connective power of project-based clinical experiences [Web blog post]. Retrieved from *www.edutopia.org/blog/connective-power-project-based-clinical-experiences-anthony-pellegrino*

Pellegrino, A. M., & Zenkov, K. (2013). Pay attention and take some notes: Middle school youth, multimodal instruction and notions of citizenship. *The Journal of Social Studies Research, 37,* 128–151.

Reinking, D., & Bradley, B. A. (2008). *On formative and design experiments.* New York: Teachers College Press.

Schrum, K., Sleeter, N., Pellegrino, A., & Tyong Vy Sharpe, C. (2018). Teaching hidden history: Student outcomes from a distributed hybrid history course. *The History Teacher, 51,* 573–596.

Stearns, P. N. (2000). Getting specific about training in historical analysis: A case study in world history. In P. N. Stearns, P. Seixas, & S. Wineburg (Eds.), *Knowing, teaching, and learning history: National and international perspectives* (pp. 419–435). New York: New York University Press.

Swalwell, K., Pellegrino, A., & View, J. (2015). Teachers' curricular choices when teaching histories of oppressed people: Capturing the U.S. Civil Rights Movement. *The Journal of Social Studies Research, 39*(2), 79–94.

VanSledright, B. (2011). *The challenge of rethinking history education: On practices, theories, and policy.* New York: Routledge.

Wilson, S. M., & Tamir, E. (2008). The evolving field of teacher education: How understanding challenge(r)s might improve the preparation of teachers. In M. Cochran-Smith, S. Feiman-Nemser, D. J. McIntyre, & K. E. Demers (Eds.), *Handbook of research on teacher education: Enduring questions in changing contexts* (3rd ed., pp. 908–935). New York: Routledge/Taylor Francis Group.

Wineburg, S. (2001). *Historical thinking and other unnatural acts: Charting the future of teaching the past.* Philadelphia: Temple University Press.

Yin, R. K. (2003). *Case study research: Design and methods* (3rd ed.). Thousand Oaks, CA: Sage.

Zeichner, K., & Conklin, H. G. (2008). Teacher education programs as sites for teacher preparation. In M. Cochran-Smith, S. Feiman-Nemser, D. J. McIntyre, & K. E. Demers (Eds.), *Handbook of research on teacher education: Enduring questions in changing contexts* (3rd ed., pp. 269–289). New York: Routledge/Taylor Francis Group.

Zenkov, K., & Pytash, K. (2019). Critical, project-based clinical experiences: Their origins and their elements. In K. Zenkov & K. E. Pytash (Eds.), *Clinical experiences in teacher education: Critical, project-based interventions in diverse classrooms* (pp. 1–17). New York: Routledge.

CHAPTER 14

Graduate Students Writing Design-Based Research Dissertations

Susan McKenney and Thomas Reeves

Whenever we have conducted workshops or given invited presentations focused on design-based research (DBR) over the past 25 years, the majority of faculty members, graduate students, and others in attendance have responded favorably to our call for what we promote as a more socially responsible approach to educational research (McKenney & Reeves, 2019; Reeves, 2000). But inevitably, there is some degree of pushback that comes down to "This sounds like a great idea, but it just doesn't seem feasible for a dissertation." The reasons given include:

- It is too time-consuming to accomplish within the temporal constraints that most graduate students have allocated for their research.
- It is too difficult for graduate students to find practitioners willing and able to join students in tackling a serious problem in a real-world educational context.
- Graduate student supervisors and committees are unfamiliar with DBR and are reluctant to endorse this genre of educational inquiry.
- Funding sources are unfamiliar with DBR and lack the criteria for assessing the worthiness of support for DBR proposals.
- It is not clear how DBR studies can be reported in doctoral dissertations or master's theses.

Particularly the latter concern (lack of clarity on how to write dissertations that report DBR) provides the impetus for this chapter. It is our hope and conviction that supporting graduate students in writing high-quality DBR dissertations will also contribute to demonstrating how the other objections can be addressed. The examples of DBR work by graduate students described in this chapter illustrate how various students successfully completed DBR initiatives despite temporal constraints and the real-world challenges of identifying and maintaining collaboration with practitioners. Hopefully, these powerful DBR dissertation precedents can inspire not only graduate students but also their supervisors, committees, and funding panels.

This chapter begins with brief reflections on the nature of graduate work as well as the nature of DBR, before describing formats commonly used for (DBR) dissertations along with affordances, limitations, and examples for each. Thereafter, tips and tools for writing DBR dissertations are offered. It should be noted that while this chapter draws primarily on our work with doctoral students, the same basic principles can be applied to master's theses.

About Graduate Research

Reeves and Oh (2017) described six important goals for educational researchers: (1) theory development and/or synthesis, (2) exploratory and/or hypothesis testing, (3) descriptive and/or interpretivist, (4) critical and/or postmodern, (5) design and/or development, and (6) action and/or evaluation. This chapter is primarily intended for graduate students (or their mentors) who pursue design and/or development goals, alongside other ones. As such, their scholarship seeks to create and improve effective solutions to serious education problems as well as identify new knowledge related to those problems, often in the form of reusable design principles related to teaching, learning, and performance. Research with design and/or development goals is ideally conducted in close collaboration with practitioners, the people who "own" the problems being addressed.

The goals of one's research initiative wield considerable influence on the pathway to completion of graduate research in general and doctoral research in particular. At the same time, this work is also substantially shaped by the institutional context in which it takes place, and such contexts vary tremendously. Especially for doctoral work, the norms and routines vary by country, university, and even discipline. For example, some doctoral programs require master's diplomas for entry, while others do not; some doctoral students receive stipends, while others pay tuition; and some dissertations are dozens of pages long, while others are hundreds. Our experience has taught us that three contextual factors are particularly influential in shaping dissertation work, and that they hold true for DBR dissertations as well: time, community, and methodological preferences.

Formally, the time spent on a PhD typically varies between 3 and 5 years, but extensions are not at all rare. For example, in most U.S. universities, doctoral students typically complete 2 or more years of coursework before they begin to prepare their research prospectus in earnest and start the process of collecting data for their dissertations. By contrast, in some parts of the world (e.g., Commonwealth countries such as Australia, Canada, and New Zealand as well as many countries in

Europe), it is common for more than 80% of the time to be spent on research, with limited coursework being undertaken to inform the research work. There are many variations on these two extremes, and some programs grant students extra time in exchange for taking on teaching tasks, but in general PhD students may have anywhere from 1 to 5 years to conduct the research on which their dissertation is focused (Barnett, Harris, & Mulvany, 2017).

The communities in which PhD researchers conduct their work contribute significantly to how it is undertaken and the overall doctoral experience. Some PhD studies are embedded in larger projects, such as funded research projects awarded to supervising faculty members. Existing research projects often have the benefits of clear goals, structure, and team momentum as well as facilitated entry into the community involved. Other research projects are primarily initiated by the candidates themselves, but it is beneficial to align PhD work with the existing research agendas of potential supervisors. For example, Richard E. Mayer, Distinguished Professor of Psychology at the University of California, Santa Barbara, has supervised many doctoral studies related to multimedia learning, and Val Shute, the Mack and Effie Campbell Tyner Endowed Professor of Education at Florida State University, has mentored many doctoral studies on immersive game-based learning and assessment. Additionally, in settings where research–practice connections are already in place, practitioners from schools, nonprofits, businesses, and the like may initiate collaboration with a university for conducting research. Sometimes organizations facilitate the doctoral work of their own employees as a form of capacity building, other times external researchers are preferred. Such settings can provide meaningful contexts for doctoral work that has real-world impact.

Last but certainly not least, the methodological preferences held by individual PhD students and those closest to them (notably, supervisors and fellow PhDs) bear mention. Methodological preferences are shaped by many factors, including research paradigms, domain-specific traditions, existing levels of expertise, and degree of interest in exploring new approaches. Research approaches are steered by these factors, as well as fitness for purpose in terms of accuracy (collecting the specific kinds of information needed to answer the research question well) and productivity (making sense within the constraints of the project in terms of finances, time, and obtrusiveness). Obtaining fitness for purpose requires flexibility. This requires a broad and rich methodological repertoire, and often—especially in the case of DBR—includes blending both quantitative and qualitative methods. Understanding and honoring existing methodological convictions are crucial prerequisites to undertaking work that stands to expand them (Markauskaite, Freebody, & Irwin, 2011).

We mention these considerations here because they hold implications for writing (DBR) dissertations. Recognizing the philosophical and epistemological stance from which a study departs enables authors to position theirs in light of existing research. Clarifying the goals of one's research does this as well, while also making it possible to critique the chosen approach. Finally, recognizing the salient differences in PhD pathways (notably, time, community, and methodological preferences) is useful for reflecting on and portraying one's own unique work. While the ideas shared in this chapter are not offered as *one-size-fits-all* solutions, the remainder of this chapter endeavors to demonstrate that DBR dissertations can be undertaken on shorter or longer timelines, within existing or newly created projects, and that describing the work in written form requires a solid understanding of what constitutes accurate and productive methods for achieving the goals of a given (sub)study.

About DBR

Other chapters in this volume describe the nature of DBR as well as its applications in various fields of education. For that reason, we discuss only a few aspects of DBR here, and focus on those that are most salient for understanding our approaches to dissertation writing. To structure the chapter, we begin by briefly presenting a generic model for conducting this kind of research (Figure 14.1). While we use the term *DBR* here to maintain consistency with others in this volume, our own work features the term *educational design research*, which refers to a family of approaches that connect basic and applied educational research in, on, and/or through design, including design experiments, formative research, development research, design-based research, and design-based implementation research.

The model shown in Figure 14.1 depicts a flexible, iterative process that features three core phases (squares), which occur in constant interaction with practice (trapezoid) and yield both practical and scientific outcomes (rectangles). Theoretical understanding may be harvested from individual phases as well as from the overall trajectory. Thus, taking the time to consolidate the insights gained from a given phase in writing before taking subsequent steps is well worth the investment. This holds true for DBR projects in general, as well as both the long-form and article-based dissertations described below.

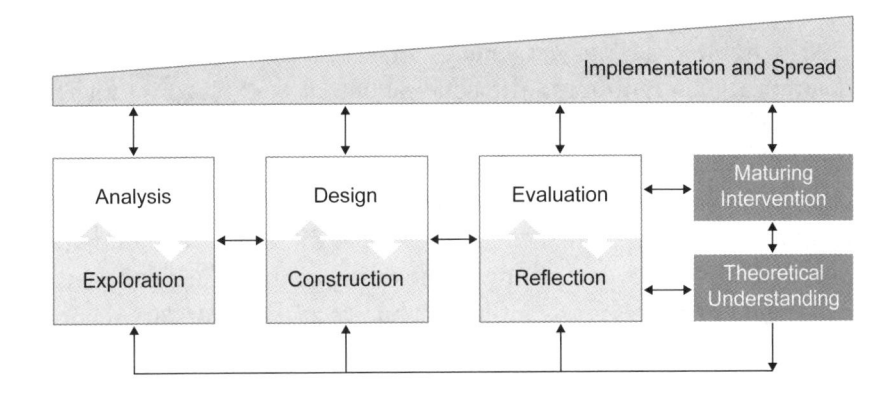

FIGURE 14.1. A generic model for conducting DBR. Reprinted by permission from McKenney and Reeves (2019). Copyright © 2019 Routledge.

During *analysis and exploration,* collaboration is sought with practitioners, literature review is undertaken, and fieldwork is conducted to gain a better understanding of the problem, the context, and stakeholder perspectives. This phase is crucial at the start of a project and is often revisited after design challenges are encountered, or evaluation findings give rise to new questions. While this phase provides inputs for design, it can also generate valuable scientific insights that support the work of others. Here are two examples of articles in PhD dissertations resulting from this phase of DBR (*italicized* author name denotes the PhD candidate):

- Synthesizing existing scientific understanding: *Goldberg,* Sklad, Elfrink, Schreurs, Bohlmeijer, and Clarke (2019) presented a meta-analysis of interventions adopting a whole-school approach to enhancing social and emotional development, and identified key factors that moderate educational and social outcomes.
- Understanding stakeholder views: *Hopster-den Otter,* Wools, Eggen, and Veldkamp (2017) described the findings from questionnaires that were used to analyze the types of actions for which primary school stakeholders (including teachers, principals, and parents) want to use test results and focus groups that were held to determine which information is needed to perform these actions.

During *design and construction,* (prototype) interventions are explored, mapped, and built. As insights mature (through interactions with practice, analysis, or evaluation), this phase is revisited and interventions are revised. This phase does not necessarily involve empirical fieldwork (though it can), but it typically does involve literature review and should include the articulation of the designer theory of action as well as the foundational ideas on which the intervention is based. As such, the results of this phase can constitute theoretical understanding that is valuable to others. Here are two examples of PhD-authored publications that center on the results of this phase of DBR:

- Design framework: *van der Linden* and McKenney (2020) described the theoretical underpinnings, instructional design, and blueprint for research-based video coaching of early career teachers in their article written for educational technology researchers and developers.
- Design decision making: *Krijtenburg-Lewerissa,* Pol, Brinkman, and van Joolingen, (2019) shared their findings from a Delphi study undertaken to inform the selection of teaching and learning content during the creation of curriculum materials for quantum mechanics at the secondary school level.

During *evaluation and reflection,* interventions that have been designed (i.e., imagined but not yet built) or constructed (i.e., embodied in initial, partial, or final form) are empirically tested, and the findings are considered in light of how they inform or refute the core ideas on which they are built. This phase can yield new questions for analysis/exploration as well as inputs for (re)design; it can also produce scientific understanding that serves the work of others. Here are two examples of PhD-authored publications resulting from this phase of DBR:

- Successive formative evaluations: *Vanderhoven* & Schellens (2015); *Vanderhoven*, Schellens, and Valcke (2014, 2016a, 2016b); and *Vanderhoven*, Schellens, Valcke, and De Koning (2014) described five different iterations/evaluations of an intervention in Belgian secondary schools to raise risk awareness and change unsafe behavior on social network sites (once in conference proceedings, once as a book chapter, and thrice as journal articles).
- Summative evaluation: *van Dijk,* Eysink, and de Jong (2020) described the detailed evaluation of one component of an intervention, developed by a PhD candidate, aiming to support cooperative dialogue in heterogeneous groups in elementary education.

Graduate researchers in programs that allocate 1 year or less to fieldwork rarely engage in all phases of the DBR process but can still make valuable contributions. For new projects, this could entail initial analysis/exploration and early iterations of design/construction. Such was the case with a 6-month study that yielded a master's thesis (Anand, 2011) as well as a journal article titled "Professional Development Needs: Early Childhood Teachers in Public Child Care Centers" (Anand & McKenney, 2015). For existing projects (of faculty members, or of projects launched by other graduate students), shorter-term engagement could also entail design/construction and evaluation/reflection. Alternatively, if a design is ripe for testing, it may involve evaluation/reflection, possibly followed by (re)design/construction. This was the case with the thesis of Teunis (2013), which also contributed a journal article titled "School Characteristics Influencing the Implementation of a Data-Based Decision Making Intervention" (van Geel, Visscher, & Teunis, 2017).

Graduate researchers in programs that allocate 2 years or more for their fieldwork might begin with analysis/exploration, but could also enter at the phases of design/construction or evaluation/reflection, if a project is already under way. While these candidates are more likely to engage in all three phases (sometimes more than once), the time spent on each phase (and attention given to each in the resulting dissertations) varies per case. For example, Lucero's (2013) DBR study titled *Considering Teacher Cognitions in Teacher Professional Development: Studies Involving Ecuadorian Primary School Teachers* was truly responsive in nature and demonstrated the importance of investing in thorough understanding of the existing situation. Simply put, her first substudy (Lucero, Valcke, & Schellens, 2013) gave rise to the need for further needs analysis (second substudy) as well as a context analysis (third substudy), all of which were used to shape the design and evaluation of an intervention on questioning behavior (fourth substudy).

The descriptions above demonstrate that not only the DBR process, but also the options for reporting DBR, are quite flexible. Specifically, it is both possible and common to report the results of individual phases or of multiple phases together. Accounts of entire trajectories are possible and can be informative if told well. But for external audiences (e.g., practitioners or researchers not directly associated with the project), article-sized pieces are more likely to be palatable than book-sized ones. One approach to telling the overall story succinctly is to refer to previously published accounts of substudies. Below are two examples of publications based on PhD studies, which communicate the insights gleaned from entire DBR trajectories:

- An article written primarily for technology coordinators shared overarching lessons learned from investigation of teacher talk during the collaborative design of technology-enhanced learning (McKenney, Boschman, Pieters, & Voogt, 2016).
- Two articles were published with overarching lessons learned from an award-winning PhD trajectory through which an interactive learning environment about managing vaccines was developed: one for researchers and developers of interactive learning environments (Kartoğlu, Vesper, & Reeves, 2017), and another for vaccine-handling professionals (Kartoğlu, Vesper, Teräs, & Reeves, 2017).

As mentioned previously, consolidating understanding through writing is important for any DBR endeavor. Building on these ideas, specific recommendations in light of two dominant dissertation formats are given next.

Dissertations Reporting DBR

DBR is, by nature, a collaborative endeavor. While graduate students conducting DBR collaborate with practitioners as well as their supervisors and possibly broader teams, they sometimes also work with each other. To ensure the level of independent work that is required for master's or doctoral research, this is commonly achieved by working closely together on different facets of the same project. In some cases, this may be achieved by distinguishing focal areas in the data collection (e.g., one person focuses primarily on teacher data, while another focuses primarily on learner data). It may also be achieved by taking on different roles (e.g., one person serves as consultant, developer, or project assistant, while another serves as researcher and collects data for a thesis or dissertation).

For example, 10 different master's students contributed to McKenney's (2001) PhD study on computer-based support for curriculum developers (elaborated later in this chapter). While four collaborated with stakeholders, McKenney, and an additional supervisor, six of them also worked in pairs. Two pairs conducted the research together and wrote single master's theses (Nijhof & Wagenaar, 1999; van

Daele & van Keulen, 1998). Of the third pair, one graduate student positioned the work as an internship, while it served as the thesis topic for the other (Wuisman, 2001).

At the PhD level, Keuning and van Geel (2016) collaborated with a broader team over the course of 4 years to design, implement, and evaluate a schoolwide data-based decision-making intervention. By being meticulous in clarifying the individual contributions, they wrote one dissertation, which featured four substudies led by each researcher, resulting in a total of eight journal articles. They defended their dissertations in back-to-back sessions with the same committee of examiners.

Whether writing individually or together, most reports of master's or doctoral research in the field of education will include common elements: introduction, context, theoretical framework, intervention, methods, results, conclusions, and discussion. The amount of detail devoted to each element is likely to vary based on the case at hand, the habits of the academic group providing the supervision, and the format of the dissertation being used. While hybrid dissertations and other forms can also be feasible, two of the most common forms are described next. As with data collection and analysis, the form of the dissertation should be chosen with regard to fitness for purpose. In the case of doctoral work, the purposes are writing to learn, and writing to make an original and relevant contribution to the existing body of knowledge (Duke & Beck, 1999).

Long-Form Dissertations

We use the term *long-form dissertation* to refer to the reports of master's- or PhD-level work that tend to describe the elements mentioned above (introduction, context, theoretical framework, intervention, methods, results, conclusions, and discussion) one chapter at a time. These reports typically position the work as a single study, possibly with multiple phases. For example, the theoretical framework in the long-form dissertation is typically the focus of one entire chapter. The first three chapters are sometimes (heavily) based on the prospectus or proposal for the study.

While it is possible for journal articles to be distilled from graduate work written in long form, this is more common after the fact than along the way. This format is primarily useful for graduate students in programs that devote less than a year to the research component (as opposed to coursework). Still, recognizing that the long-form dissertation is often a requirement and not an option for many doing more than 1 year of research work, an example of a multiyear, multi-iteration PhD study reported this way is given next.

Long-Form Example: Computer-Based Support for Curriculum Developers

This example of DBR was conducted by Susan McKenney. For her PhD, she investigated computer-based support for developers of science and mathematics curriculum materials in southern Africa. In the 1990s, many countries in the southern African region made educational policy decisions that necessitated the production of new or more appropriate lesson materials, such as the creation of locally relevant textbooks, or increasing the number of qualified science and mathematics teachers. Often, projects were initiated to engage existing teachers in the materials development process, since this has been considered to be a viable, effective, and practical form of professional development that simultaneously fulfills needs for new materials. However, expertise for shaping such projects was not readily available on the ground, which is why McKenney's university had been affiliated with multiple development cooperation initiatives, for example, in Lesotho, Namibia, Zimbabwe, Tanzania, and Botswana. Typically, the funding for these projects covered initial development work, with limited resources for the institutionalization or maintenance. As such, the goal of this study was to explore the potential of the computer to provide additional technical assistance in a sustainable way.

Three main research questions guided the study. Respectively, they concerned the validity, practicality, and effectiveness of the (to be) designed support, which eventually contained three components: software, website, and user manual. Over 500 respondents from eight different countries contributed to the study, which took place throughout a 4-year period and involved data collection through interviews, questionnaires, focus groups, observations, logbooks, and document analysis. The research was subdivided into phases, cycles, and circuits of data collection and analysis. The needs and context analysis phase lasted for about 9 months and consisted of two iterations: literature review and concept validation (conducted in four circuits) and site visits (three circuits). The phase of design, development, and formative evaluation of prototypes took about 30 months and involved four prototypes (and four, three, ten, and six circuits, respectively). The 9-month semi-summative evaluation included live field testing of the support package (three circuits) as well as a remote surveylike query about the final version.

As was customary in her department at the time, McKenney's (2001) dissertation was written in long form. The introductory chapter described the origins, context, and aim of the study, alongside the research approach and overall structure of the dissertation. The second chapter described the theoretical framework (weaving together literature on curriculum development, teacher professional development, exemplary materials, and computer-based performance support) as well as implications for the study. The third chapter described the research design. After introducing the overall DBR approach, attention was given to sampling, data collection phases and strategies, and data analysis. The fourth chapter described the evolution of the resulting software package in terms of foundational tenants, development guidelines, and product specifications; and although limited attention was given to prototype descriptions, the final version was portrayed in detail. Chapter 5 contained the results, reported through separate sections for analysis, design, and evaluation, respectively. It also provided an overview of key findings from each phase and how they shaped program development. The sixth and final chapter gave a recap of the main findings, reflections in light of literature, and recommendations. In addition to many appendices, the dissertation also included a CD-ROM with the support package that had been developed.

Following defense of the dissertation, three journal articles were distilled about this study. The first one (McKenney & van den Akker, 2005) told the overarching story as a case of DBR (at that time, referred to as *developmental research*). The second article (McKenney, 2005) reported on the evaluation of the final version of the program, with emphasis on its effectiveness. The third article (McKenney, 2008) gave comparatively less attention to the research methods and findings, as the main focus was describing the software and the design principles that emerged from the study.

Article-Based Dissertations

We use the term *article-based dissertation* to refer to the reports of master- or PhD-level work that tend to encompass the elements mentioned above (introduction, context, theoretical framework, intervention, methods, results, conclusions, and discussion) in multiple papers. These reports typically position the work as a collection of substudies. For example, in article-based dissertations, multiple theoretical frameworks are often described, notably one for the overarching project and (slightly) different ones for each substudy.

In addition to the efficiency of producing articles along the way, this format inherently encourages interim writing and, as such, consolidation of emerging insights. For that reason, we highly recommend this format for graduate students in programs that devote a year or more to research (as opposed to coursework). With this format, each substudy stands on its own but the collection as a whole presents a story. Often, but not always, the story element and overarching contributions are articulated in introductory and concluding chapters, checklists for which are given at the end of this chapter.

Article-Based Example: Collaborative and Constructivist Learning in Preservice Teacher Education

This example of DBR conducted by a doctoral student examined how collaborative learning methods and constructivist learning theory could be applied to an undergraduate course for preservice teachers in Oman. Porcaro's DBR initiative focused on the problem of overreliance on traditional instructivist pedagogical methods in Middle Eastern countries and that these teacher-centered approaches contributed to a gulf between common educational outcomes (rote knowledge) and the critical capabilities needed in the 21st-century labor force (problem solving, groupwork, and creativity skills). More specifically, university graduates in the Middle East were unable to find work due to lack of relevant and practical skills and their limited capacity to engage in collaborative teamwork.

Porcaro's dissertation took a linguistic cognitive anthropology design research approach (Bell, 2004), focusing on the role of culture in adopting pedagogical methods designed in one context (the West) and adapted to another (the Middle East). His two semesters of research on the ground in the College of Education at Sultan Qaboos University in Oman were funded by a Fulbright Fellowship (*https:// us.fulbrightonline.org/about/types-of-awards/study-research*). Mixed methods were used, including student questionnaires, observations, individual and focus group interviews with students and teaching staff, document analysis, and online data analysis. Data collection took place over three consecutive semesters at Sultan Qaboos University, the first two by Porcaro himself and the third time by his primary Omani collaborator. The study yielded several design principles for preparing collaborative learning environments for use in a setting like Oman, where collaborative learning was very uncommon.

Porcaro utilized a multiple-article dissertation format (2011a), consisting of four journal-ready manuscripts. The first paper described the conceptual framework for introducing constructivist methods into an instructivist-based learning culture such as Oman (Porcaro, 2011b). The second paper reviewed the literature, focusing on the limited application of computer-supported collaborative learning (CSCL) and face-to-face collaborative learning in the Arab Middle East (Porcaro, 2011c). The relative lack of CSCL studies suggested that a DBR study could help fill a gap in the field, as well as provide a sustainable CSCL designed for Omani higher education. The third manuscript described the three iterations of the efforts to test and refine the CSCL intervention, focusing on student reactions to a technology integration course for preservice teachers that incorporated constructivist pedagogy and the CSCL learning environment. This paper also delineated the Omani cultural elements that supported or hindered collaborative knowledge building in the course (Porcaro & Reeves, 2013). The fourth manuscript was written with a practitioner audience in mind. Coauthored with the primary collaborating Omani professor, this publication provided an overview of lessons learned from the study (Porcaro & Al-Musawi, 2011). In addition, this paper described design principles that can be applied in similar learning contexts that could help facilitate CSCL adoption in other Arab nations. These principles include design considerations, teacher considerations, and technical considerations. All four manuscripts sought to further understanding of educational change in Oman as well as to document the efforts to link higher education coursework with much needed workforce skills.

Tips and Tools to Guide Doctoral Studies in DBR

This chapter has been written to support graduate students in writing high-quality DBR dissertations. The previous section described feasible approaches to dissertation writing, and demonstrated that graduate-level DBR work can be conducted and reported on shorter or longer timelines, for existing or new projects, and across varied methodological orientations. The following recommendations build on these ideas, while also attending to the importance of recognizing the philosophical or epistemological stance from which a study departs, and in light of that, clearly articulating its scientific contribution.

In so doing, we stress the importance of writing for understanding (of self, project team, or others), and observe the crucial role played by interim reporting throughout the trajectory. This can be done in the form of project reports or journal articles. We therefore conclude this chapter with 10 tips related to content, flow, and readability, as well as three tools for dissertation writing: an introductory chapter checklist, a generic article outline, and a concluding chapter checklist. These are different from but complementary to other tools that we have published previously (McKenney & Reeves, 2019), which are openly accessible at *https://tinyurl.com/yblxj69h*.

Ten Tips: Supporting Content, Flow, and Readability

DBR dissertations must adhere to the same publication standards as other dissertations. At the same time, DBR studies tend to be so rich that it can be quite challenging to determine what to report, how much to report, and which structures will serve best. This section offers tips for addressing such challenges.

1. *Separate the front office from back office stories.* Front offices are typically public, whereas back offices are not. Inevitably, much of the learning during DBR reflects the researcher's own professional growth. While a few "back office" insights may be useful to others, this is rarely the case for the majority of them. Thus, it is crucial to review research insights in light of identifying those that can serve the work of others, that is, those best fit for the "front office." It is this information, and not necessarily a painstaking process account of all the activities undertaken in a project, that should be foregrounded in reporting.

2. *Choose the scope.* There are often multiple ways to cluster subtasks of DBR trajectories (such as a literature review about the problem and context, literature review about the kind of intervention, data collection and analysis relating to the context, the stakeholders, the intervention or its use). It is important to recognize this and to carefully select those combinations that render the most relevant and useful contribution(s). Across and within single publications, it can be useful to distinguish phases or substudies. In publications foregrounding individual substudies, describing the overall DBR endeavor can be more distracting than helpful to the audience, and can also detract from helping readers understand the significant contribution made by the substudy at hand.

3. *Situate the case.* Because DBR takes place in specific contexts, the value of its findings to others outside the research setting may seem limited unless the work is clearly situated. Clarify why this particular study holds significance for a broader

audience. Readers need to know "What is the phenomenon being investigated here and how prevalent is it?" Audiences also crave sufficient information to help them ascertain if and to what extent a given study is relevant to their own purposes, a process referred to as *case-to-case generalization*.

4. *Know the audience.* All good writing for others requires empathy to attune key messages to the concerns of the readership. While most readers of academic journals can be expected to have a basic understanding of research approaches and methods, different communities value different elements in varying ways. DBR studies often produce results that are relevant to multiple audiences (e.g., practitioners, researchers, policymakers). Reading the target journal(s) and attending the related conferences are among the best ways to become familiar with different audiences. This should be done before writing, not afterward. We highly recommend identifying target publication outlets at the start of the writing process so that the papers can be tailored to their requirements and styles.

5. *Know the genre.* Choose the reporting approach that best fits the kind of study being reported. DBR studies can use quantitative, qualitative, or mixed methods (see Chapter 1, this volume). They may include case studies or experiments, combinations, or other designs. Study design often holds implications for reporting. For example, ethnographic studies often feature rich and detailed descriptions of individual participants, whereas randomized controlled field trials tend to emphasize sampling procedures and characteristics of populations more than those of individuals. It is important to aptly characterize the approach used and to clarify how the study at hand attends to valued procedures or concepts inherent in that approach.

6. *Seek inspiring examples.* Study and deconstruct sample dissertations, articles, and other reports. Examples are more beneficial when it is clear how they can be used. In our work, we regularly seek multiple examples at the beginning of writing projects for the following purposes: to understand reporting conventions within a particular journal; to get ideas about how to report specific methods; or to learn from how others have positioned similar topics. For examples of how to report (phases of) DBR, we note that many have been given throughout this chapter (and are denoted as such in the reference list), as well as elsewhere (McKenney & Reeves, 2019; McKenney, 2016; McKenney & Reeves, 2013).

7. *Leverage prior knowledge.* A powerful way to leverage reader prior knowledge is to use standard reporting elements and sequences. While the flow of argumentation for conceptual and theoretical papers (often resulting from the design and construction phase) tends to vary, there is more consensus about the main elements of empirical papers (typically resulting from the analysis and exploration or evaluation and reflection phases). Using these structures helps readers position the research in light of their existing paradigms and helps them make sense of the work.

8. *Outline, elaborate, and revise.* Develop and elaborate an outline before starting to write the prose. The outline itself helps stimulate the consideration

of hierarchy; makes redundancies and consistencies visible; and clusters or tracks information. The outlining process helps to refine argumentation, as it requires the definition of paragraphs, each making a main point. Furthermore, this process supports within-paragraph structuring, as it prompts consideration of main versus supporting details. Finally, it helps with cross-paragraph structuring, as ideas can easily be moved around until the outline is organized into an easy-to-follow sequence. Outlining is also efficient, because it enables rapid, small revision cycles that are particularly useful in early stages, thus mitigating the need to rewrite when sequencing is changed. Outlines make it easier to see the overall flow and alignment, and to decide which elements of the rich and complex DBR best support reader comprehension, and which pose potentially distracting tangents. For example, if reporting on one phase of research, describing the overall DBR endeavor might actually confuse the reader.

9. *Take the reader through an hourglass.* Publications typically need to take the reader through a journey that might be characterized as zooming in, exploring, and zooming out. This can be visualized in the shape of an hourglass. The reader is gradually brought into the focus of the research through the presentation of background knowledge, known facts, and areas of uncertainty. In DBR, this is often done by articulating the practical problem (in a way that demonstrates it is not idiosyncratic in nature, but rather, experienced more widely), and enumerating both what the existing knowledge base offers and lacks for addressing it. In the body of the report, the aims, methods, and results of a given study are typically more narrowly focused. Thereafter, reports tend to widen back out again, putting the study into perspective through comparison with literature and discussion of limitations and implications for policy, practice, or research.

10. *Develop visual support.* Visual support is as valuable to the author as it can be to the readers. For the author, it demands careful consideration and selection of key ideas, and helps refine the messages to be communicated. For the readers, visual support can be useful for many purposes, including advanced organization. Here, we give three examples of helpful visuals that address frequent struggles encountered by PhD students reporting on DBR. Illustrating one way to leverage prior knowledge and clarify structure, Figure 14.2 shows the graphical preview provided at the beginning of a theoretical article that resulted from the design and construction phase. Figures 14.3 and 14.4 offer two approaches to helping readers of introductory dissertation chapters understand the structure of the dissertation (also mentioned in the introductory chapter checklist). This is particularly important when DBR is unfamiliar to committee members, as it helps them identify aspects that they expect or value in dissertations. Moreover, we have found that creating and iteratively refining these visual overviews constitute a crucial reflection and learning process for the PhD candidate. Figure 14.3 separates a methodological overview from a conceptual overview, whereas Figure 14.4 (pp. 288–289) combines these into one figure.

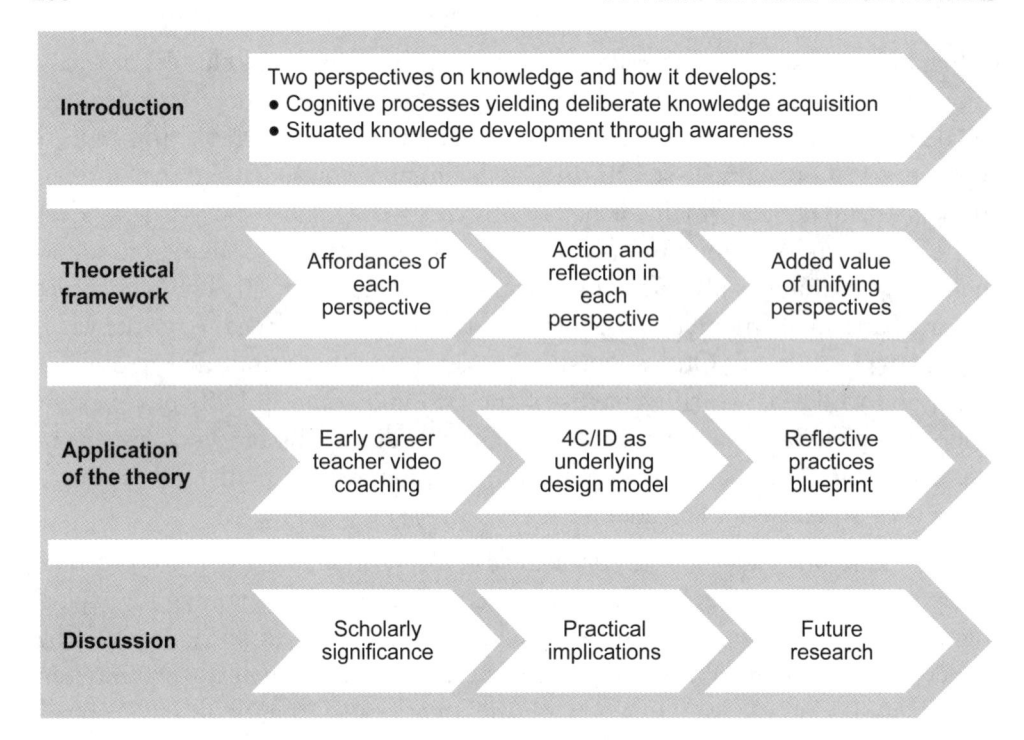

FIGURE 14.2. Graphical preview of theoretical journal article. From van der Linden and McKenney (2020). Reprinted by permission of the authors.

Three Tools for Article-Based and Long-Form Dissertation Chapters

Tool 1: Introductory Chapter Checklist

- Holistic impressions of the chapter
  - *Flow:* The chapter starts with broad societal issues (i.e., positions the study) and ends with narrow scientific concerns (i.e., focuses the study).
  - *Writing:* The tone is scholarly, and the language is easy to follow.
  - *Reasoning:* The argumentation is clear, crisp, and relevant to understanding the overall DBR study.
- Positioning
  - *Connection to the world:* This section describes current issues and trends in society, education, or the broad field to which this dissertation is relevant.
  - *Key issues:* It unpacks several key issues that should be returned to in final chapter.
  - *Intervention:* If there is an intervention or the goal of designing one, it might be briefly characterized at the end of this section.

	RO	Methodology	Data collection	Analysis
1	General introduction			
2	RO1	Literature review	Exploring literature on parent–teacher communication	Literature review
	RO2	Qualitative	Video-based instrument ($n = 269$)	Content analysis
3	RO1 + RO2	Quantitative	Student teacher survey ($n = 581$)	Factor analyses (EFA CFA); Reliability analysis
4	RO3: *RQ3a*	Literature review	Exploring literature on clinical simulations	Literature review
	RO3: *RQ3b*	Quantitative	Student teacher survey ($n = 323$)	Independent-samples t-tests
		Qualitative	Student teacher survey ($n = 323$)	Content analysis
5	RO3: *RQ3c*	Quantitative	Student teacher survey ($n = 33$)	Paired-samples t-tests
		Qualitative	Video-based instrument ($n = 33$)	Content analysis; paired-samples t-tests
			Video recordings ($n = 33$)	Content analysis; repeated measures ANOVA
6	RO3: *RQ3c*		Pretest/Posttest intervention study with online ($n = 181$) and face-to-face ($n = 95$) intervention group	
		Quantitative	Student teacher survey	Independent-samples and paired-samples t-tests
		Qualitative	Video-based instrument	Content analyses, independent-samples and paired-samples t-tests
7	General discussion and conclusion			

Chapter 1
General introduction

RO1 & RO2

Chapter 2
A measurement of student teachers' PTCC: the design of a video-based instrument

Chapter 3
Measuring student teachers' self-efficacy beliefs about parent–teacher communication: scale construction and validation

RO3

Chapter 4
RO3a–RO3b
Bridging the theory–practice gap in teacher education: the design and construction of simulation-based learning environments

Chapter 5
RO3c
Developing student teachers' PTCC via face-to-face clinical simulations: an intervention study

Chapter 6
RO3c
Exploring the effectiveness of online and face-to-face clinical simulations to develop student teachers' PTCC

Chapter 7
General discussion and conclusion

FIGURE 14.3. Separate methodological and conceptual overviews. From de Coninck (2019).

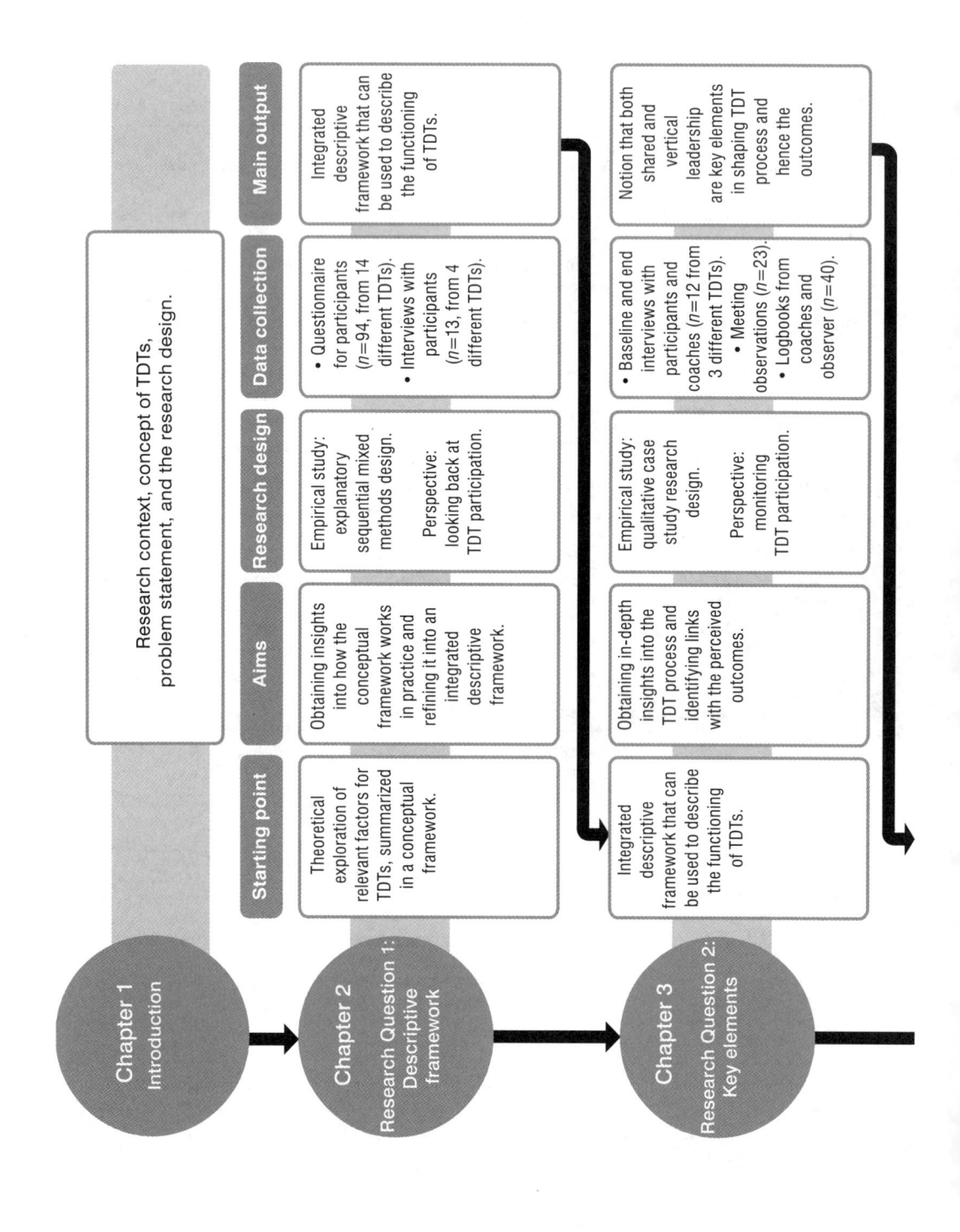

	Starting point	Aims	Research design	Data collection	Main output
Chapter 1 Introduction	Research context, concept of TDTs, problem statement, and the research design.				
Chapter 2 Research Question 1: Descriptive framework	Theoretical exploration of relevant factors for TDTs, summarized in a conceptual framework.	Obtaining insights into how the conceptual framework works in practice and refining it into an integrated descriptive framework.	Empirical study: explanatory sequential mixed methods design. Perspective: looking back at TDT participation.	• Questionnaire for participants ($n=94$, from 14 different TDTs). • Interviews with participants ($n=13$, from 4 different TDTs).	Integrated descriptive framework that can be used to describe the functioning of TDTs.
Chapter 3 Research Question 2: Key elements	Integrated descriptive framework that can be used to describe the functioning of TDTs.	Obtaining in-depth insights into the TDT process and identifying links with the perceived outcomes.	Empirical study: qualitative case study research design. Perspective: monitoring TDT participation.	• Baseline and end interviews with participants and coaches ($n=12$ from 3 different TDTs). • Meeting observations ($n=23$). • Logbooks from coaches and observer ($n=40$).	Notion that both shared and vertical leadership are key elements in shaping TDT process and hence the outcomes.

Chapter 4
Research Question 3: Intervention

- Notion that both shared and vertical leadership are key elements in shaping TDT process and hence the outcomes.
- Developing shared and vertical leadership guidelines and an intervention that integrates these leadership behaviors.
- Theoretical study: theoretical exploration.

  Perspective: examining existing literature.
- Literature about teacher teams and literature about management and organization.
- Ten leadership guidelines and a 9-step method that integrates shared and vertical leadership in TDT processes.

Chapter 5
Research Question 4: Enactment

- Ten leadership guidelines and a 9-step method that integrates shared and vertical leadership in TDT processes.
- Understanding how shared and vertical leadership were exhibited while applying this method and how this supported the process.
- Empirical study: qualitative case study research design.

  Perspective: monitoring TDT participation when using the 9-step method.
- Baseline and end interviews with participants and coaches ($n=10$ from 2 different TDTs).
  - Meeting observations ($n=17$).
  - Logbooks from coaches and observer ($n=34$).
- Overview of how shared and vertical leadership are exhibited in TDTs and how they support the process.

  Insights into the remaining TDT leadership challenges.

Chapter 6
Conclusion and discussion

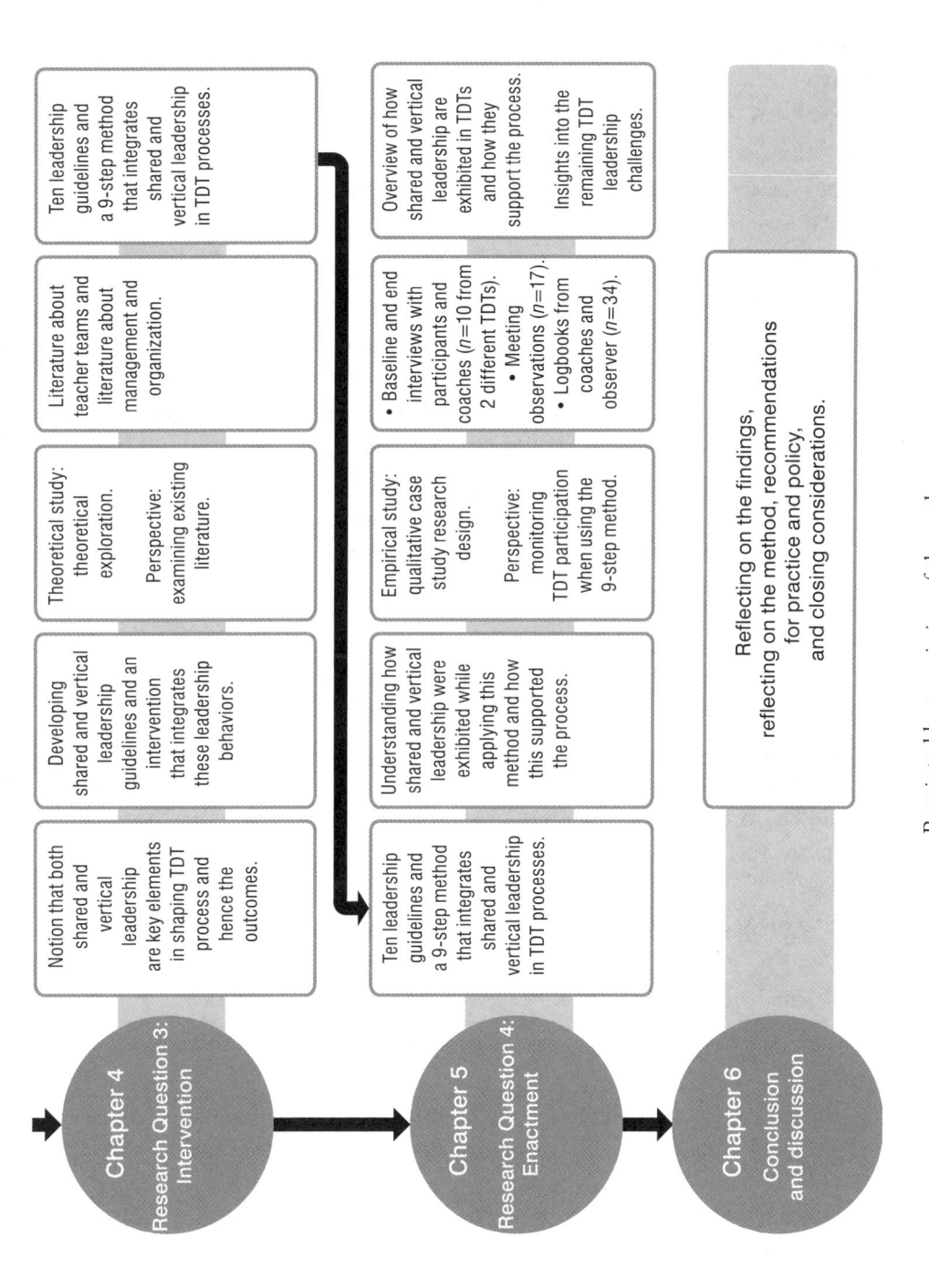

Reflecting on the findings, reflecting on the method, recommendations for practice and policy, and closing considerations.

Reprinted by permission of the author.

- Theoretical framework (NB: An overarching theoretical framework is usually a separate chapter in long-form dissertations.)
  - *Main ideas:* Core constructs from each substudy are presented.
  - *Coherence:* The core ideas are knit together to form a unified set of ideas.
  - *(Visual) synthesis:* A (visual) synthesis is given to help readers see how the studies are connected conceptually.
  - *Broadly applicable:* This is presented in a way that readers can apply to their own similar situation (i.e., it is relevant to similar work, not only this case).
- Problem statement
  - *Clarifies what is known and not known:* This section contains one to three paragraphs that address: (1) what we know about the main issues (X, Y, Z); and (2) what we don't know about them (A, B, C).
  - *Clarifies why we need to fill the gap:* This section explains why we need that knowledge (of A, B, C) for theory building and (if applicable) practical reasons. It describes research that does not adequately address the gap.
  - *Broadly applicable:* To clarify the scientific contribution, the theoretical statement is given in general terms (not tied specifically to one setting).
- Research approach
  - *Goal:* The main goal of the study is clear.
  - *Context:* The setting of the study has been described, and it is clear why this is fitting.
  - *Research questions:* This section introduces the questions guiding the overall study, typically one to four. (There could be one for each substudy, but at least one should be overarching.) The questions clearly tie to the theoretical framework presented previously (and align with the A, B, C elements of the problem statement).
  - *Approach:* This section characterizes the approach(es) used for the study as a whole.
- Structure of the dissertation
  - *Chapter overview:* Each upcoming chapter is briefly summarized in about one paragraph each.
  - *Visual overview:* At or near the end of this section is a visual that summarizes the type of study, goal(s), population, instrumentation and focus of data analysis, and possibly also mentions the key outcomes, while also linking to each chapter. (NB: For long-form dissertations, such a visual might make more sense in the methods chapter.)

Tool 2: Generic Outline Template for Empirical Article

1. Abstract (250 words)
2. Introduction (750 words)
   2.1. What background info is needed to understand this?
   2.2. What is the main problem addressed by this DBR?
3. Theoretical framework (1,500 words)
   3.1. What are the core ideas in this study?
   3.2. How do they relate to one another?
   3.3. How do they relate to what is ongoing in the field?
   3.4. What are the overall research questions?
4. Context/design (750 words)
   4.1. What does the reader need to know about the setting and/or the design to be able to follow this DBR?
5. Methods (1,000 words)
   5.1. What are the detailed research questions?
   5.2. What approach was used?
   5.3. What instruments were used?
   5.4. Which people were involved?
   5.5. What is the link between the research questions and the instruments?
   5.6. What techniques were used for data analysis?
6. Results (2,000 words)
   6.1. What are the findings in relation to the research subquestions?
7. Conclusion (1,000 words)
   7.1. What were the main findings and answers to the research questions?
   7.2. What noteworthy aspects of the findings bear mention? What does the literature say about this?
   7.3. What noteworthy aspects of the fieldwork bear mention? What were the strengths and limitations of this approach? Are there alternative interpretations for the findings?
   7.4. What recommendations can be given for future research, for policy, or for practice?
   7.5. What is the scientific relevance of this DBR? What is the social relevance?
8. References (1,000 words)

Tool 3: Concluding Chapter Checklist

- Holistic impressions of the chapter
  - *Flow:* The chapter focus starts close to the findings and ends with the broad scientific and societal significance.
  - *Writing:* The tone is scholarly, and the language is easy to follow.
  - *Reasoning:* The argumentation is clear, crisp, and relevant to understanding the work that was undertaken and its significance.
- Revisiting the overall project
  - *Goals and approach:* This section recaps the goal and basic approach of the overall DBR.
  - *Key findings:* This section recaps the key findings from each substudy.
- Conclusions
  - *Answer each question:* This section returns to the research questions posed in the first chapter and answers each.
- Discussion
  - *Reflection on the methods:* This section critically discusses strengths and limitations of the approach(es) used, and what those could imply for interpreting the findings.
  - *Reflection on the findings:* This section typically looks at themes that cut across multiple studies or emerged from the overall project. The reflection is given in light of relevant literature.
- Recommendations
  - *Practice:* Implications and recommendations for practice are given. They are clearly rooted in the findings.
  - *Policy:* Implications and recommendations for policy are given. They are clearly rooted in the DBR process.
  - *Further research:* Implications and recommendations for further research are given. They are clearly rooted in the findings and/or the research process.
- Closing considerations
  - *Contribution:* The main contributions of this study are stated clearly and succinctly.
  - *Connection to the world:* The closing remarks do so in light of the broad societal issues (where this dissertation started) and any new developments since this study was undertaken.

Closing Thoughts

Graduate research in the field of education is typically undertaken for qualification purposes and/or for personal fulfilment. DBR offers outstanding opportunities for each of these goals. All scientific research is a human social activity that is expected to meet certain standards and norms, and graduate projects using DBR are no exception. This chapter has offered considerations for reporting DBR in ways that reveal how such socially responsible research adheres to basic principles, while at the same time addressing real-world challenges. Graduates who succeed in writing high-quality DBR-based dissertations will lead the way for others, thereby contributing to science as well as the quality of life for individuals and groups in society.

REFERENCES

Anand, G. (2011). *Needs and context analysis for a public preschool para-teacher professional development program in India*. Unpublished master's thesis, University of Twente, Enschede, the Netherlands.

Anand, G., & McKenney, S. (2015). Professional development needs: Early childhood teachers in public child care centers. *Staff and Educational Development International*, 19(2–3), 85–104.

Barnett, J. V., Harris, R. A., & Mulvany, M. J. (2017). A comparison of best practices for doctoral training in Europe and North America. *FEBS Open Bio*, 7(10), 1444–1452.

Bell, P. (2004). On the theoretical breadth of design-based research in education. *Educational Psychologist*, 39(4), 243–253.

Binkhorst, F. (2017). *Connecting the dots: Supporting the implementation of teacher design teams*. Unpublished doctoral dissertation, University of Twente, Enschede, the Netherlands.

de Coninck, K. (2019). *Conceptualizing, measuring and developing parent-teacher communication competence is: Clinical simulations in teacher education*. Unpublished doctoral dissertation, University of Ghent, Ghent, Belgium.

Duke, N. K., & Beck, S. W. (1999). Research news and comment: Education should consider alternative formats for the dissertation. *Educational Researcher*, 28(3), 31–36.

Goldberg, J. M., Sklad, M., Elfrink, T. R., Schreurs, K. M., Bohlmeijer, E. T., & Clarke, A. M. (2019). Effectiveness of interventions adopting a whole school approach to enhancing social and emotional development: A meta-analysis. *European Journal of Psychology of Education*, 34, 755–782.

Hopster-den Otter, D., Wools, S., Eggen, T. J. H. M., & Veldkamp, B. P. (2017). Formative use of test results: A user's perspective. *Studies in Educational Evaluation*, 52, 12–23.

Kartoğlu, U., Vesper, J. L., & Reeves, T. C. (2017). On the bus and online: Instantiating an interactive learning environment through design-based research. *Interactive Learning Environments*, 25, 624–633.

Kartoğlu, U., Vesper, J. L., Teräs, H., & Reeves, T. C. (2017). Experiential and authentic learning approaches in vaccine management. *Vaccine*, 35, 2243–2251.

Keuning, T., & van Geel, M. (2016). *Implementation and effects of a school-wide data-based decision making intervention: A large scale study.* Unpublished doctoral diss., University of Twente, Enschede, the Netherlands.

Krijtenburg-Lewerissa, K., Pol, H. J., Brinkman, A., & van Joolingen, W. R. (2019). Key topics for quantum mechanics at secondary schools: A Delphi study into expert opinions. *International Journal of Science Education, 41,* 349–366.

Lucero, M. (2013). *Considering teacher cognitions in teacher professional development: Studies involving Ecuadorian primary school teachers.* Unpublished doctoral dissertation, University of Ghent, Ghent, Belgium.

Lucero, M., Valcke, M., & Schellens, T. (2013). Teachers' beliefs and self-reported use of inquiry in science education in public primary schools. *International Journal of Science Education, 35,* 1407–1423.

Markauskaite, L., Freebody, P., & Irwin, J. (Eds.). (2011). *Methodological choice and design: Scholarship, policy and practice in social and educational research.* New York: Springer.

McKenney, S. (2001). *Computer based support for science education materials developers in Africa: Exploring potentials.* Unpublished doctoral dissertation, University of Twente, Enschede, the Netherlands.

McKenney, S. (2005). Technology for curriculum and teacher development: Software to help educators learn while designing teacher guides. *Journal of Research on Technology in Education, 38*(2), 167–190.

McKenney, S. (2008). Shaping computer-based support for curriculum developers. *Computers and Education, 50*(1), 248–261.

McKenney, S. (2016). Researcher–practitioner collaboration in educational design research: Processes, roles, values & expectations. In M. A. Evans, M. J. Packer, & K. Sawyer (Eds.), *Reflections on the learning sciences* (pp. 155–188). Cambridge, UK: Cambridge University Press.

McKenney, S., Boschman, F., Pieters, J., & Voogt, J. (2016). Collaborative design of technology-enhanced learning: What can we learn from teacher talk? *TechTrends, 60*(4), 385–391.

McKenney, S., & Reeves, T. C. (2013). Educational design research. In M. Spector, M. Merrill, J. Elen, & M. Bishop (Eds.), *Handbook of research on educational communications & technology* (pp. 131–140). London: Springer.

McKenney, S., & van den Akker, J. (2005). Computer-based support for curriculum designers: A case of developmental research. *Educational Technology Research and Development, 53*(2), 41–66.

McKenney, S. E., & Reeves, T. C. (2019). *Conducting educational design research* (2nd ed.). New York: Routledge.

Nijhof, N., & Wagenaar, A. (1999). *The usefulness of CASCADE-SEA at Ponhofi Osekundoskola in Namibia.* Master's thesis, University of Twente, Enschede, the Netherlands.

Porcaro, D. S. (2011a). *Omani undergraduate student reactions to collaborative knowledge building.* Unpublished doctoral diss., University of Georgia, Athens, GA.

Porcaro, D. S. (2011b). Applying constructivism in instructivist learning cultures: A conceptual framework. *Multicultural Education and Technology Journal, 5*(1), 39–54.

Porcaro, D. S. (2011c). Reviewing the literature of computer-supported collaborative learning (CSCL) to determine its usefulness in Omani education development. *International Journal of Education and Development using ICT, 7*(3), 102–120. Retrieved from *www.learntechlib.org/p/187993*

Porcaro, D. S., & Al-Musawi, A. S. (2011). Lessons learned from adopting computer-supported collaborative learning in Oman. *Educause Quarterly, 34*(4). Retrieved from https://er.educause.edu/articles/2011/12/lessons-learned-from-adopting-computersupported-collaborative-learning-in-oman

Porcaro, D. S., & Reeves, T. C. (2013). Educational design research for collaborative learning: Challenges and opportunities in Oman. In T. Plomp & N. Nieveen (Eds.), *Educational design research—Part B: Illustrative cases*. Enschede, the Netherlands: Netherlands Institute for Curriculum Development (SLO).

Reeves, T. C. (2000). Socially responsible educational technology research. *Educational Technology, 40*(6), 19–28.

Reeves, T. C., & Oh, E. (2017). The goals and methods of educational technology research over a quarter century (1989–2014). *Educational Technology Research and Development, 65*(2), 325–339.

Teunis, B. (2013). *Bevorderende en belemmerende facyoren bij de implementatie van opbrengstgericht werken* [Supporting and hindering factors during the implementation of outcomes-based education]. Unpublished master's thesis, University of Twente, Enschede, the Netherlands.

van Daele, E., & van Keulen, A. (1998). *Inservice education in Tanzania: Supply and demand*. Master's thesis, University of Twente, Enschede, the Netherlands.

van der Linden, S., & McKenney, S. (2020). Uniting epistemological perspectives to support contextualized knowledge development. *Educational Technology Research & Development, 68*, 703–727.

van Dijk, A. M., Eysink, T. H. S., & de Jong, T. (2020). Supporting cooperative dialogue in heterogeneous groups in elementary education. *Small Group Research, 51*(4), 464–491.

van Geel, M., Visscher, A. J., & Teunis, B. (2017). School characteristics influencing the implementation of a data-based decision making intervention. *School Effectiveness and School Improvement, 28*, 443–462.

Vanderhoven, E., & Schellens, T. (2015). How authentic should a learning context be? Using real and simulated profiles in a classroom intervention to improve safety on social network sites. *International Journal of Cyber Society and Education, 8*(1), 1–18.

Vanderhoven, E., Schellens, T., & Valcke, M. (2014). Educating teens about the risks on social network sites: Useful or pointless? An intervention study in secondary education. *Comunicar, 22*(43), 123–132.

Vanderhoven, E., Schellens, T., & Valcke, M. (2016a). Changing unsafe behaviour on social network sites. Collaborative learning vs. individual reflection. In M. Walrave, K. Ponnet, E. Vanderhoven, J. Haers, & B. Segaert (Eds.), *Youth 2.0: Social Media and Adolescence* (pp. 211–226). Cham, Switzerland: Springer.

Vanderhoven, E., Schellens, T., & Valcke, M. (2016b). Decreasing risky behavior on social network sites: The impact of parental involvement in secondary education interventions. *Journal of Primary Prevention, 37*(3), 247–261.

Vanderhoven, E., Schellens, T., Valcke, M., & De Koning, E. (2014). Involving parents in school programs about safety on social network sites. *Procedia—Social and Behavioral Sciences, 112*, 428–436.

Wuisman, N. (2001). *Moving towards computer assisted curriculum and teacher development for better teaching practices: CASCADE-SEA research project at the Shoma center in Soweto, South Africa*. Master's thesis, University of Leiden, Leiden, the Netherlands.

CHAPTER 15

Fostering Techno-Mathematical Literacies in Higher Technical Education
Reflections on Challenges and Successes of Design-Based Implementation Research

Nathalie J. van der Wal, Arthur Bakker,
Albert Moes, and Paul Drijvers

In this chapter, we describe the challenges and successes in the implementation phase of a design study using a design-based implementation research (DBIR) approach. Implementations of research-based innovations in education have proven to be difficult and often unsuccessful (Fishman & Penuel, 2018). This gap between research and practice is under-represented in educational literature, where scalability and sustainability of innovations are scarcely addressed and typically left to practitioners (e.g., Akkerman, Bronkhorst, & Zitter, 2013; Farley-Ripple, May, Karpyn, Tilley, & McDonough, 2018; Snow, 2016). Furthermore, innovation is a process rather than a single act, and many stakeholders, such as teachers, teacher educators, school management, and policymakers, are involved. Because teaching contexts differ between schools, regions, and countries, it is crucial to understand how innovations can be adapted to local situations (Maass, Cobb, Krainer, & Potari, 2019).

A bridge between *"what works"* in design research and *"what works where, when and for whom"* (Means & Penuel, 2005, p. 181, emphasis in the original) is provided by DBIR. Where design research focuses on design, DBIR can be seen as an expansion supporting usability and effectiveness of the sustainable implementation of educational innovations (Penuel & Fishman, 2012). To this end, DBIR aims to break down barriers between disciplines of educational research and reconfigures the roles of researchers and practitioners to bring about systemic change (Fishman, Penuel, Allen, Cheng, & Sabelli, 2013). Four key principles of DBIR (p. 332) are:

1. A focus on persistent problems of practice from multiple stakeholders' perspectives
2. A commitment to iterative, collaborative design

3. A concern with developing theory and knowledge related to both classroom learning and implementation through systematic inquiry
4. A concern with developing capacity for sustaining change in systems

Faced with this aspiration of DBIR, Cobb, Jackson, Smith, Sorum, and Henrick (2013) noted, "Given DBIR's current status as an emerging methodology and the limited guidance for instructional improvement at scale provided by current research, it is reasonable to expect that the systematic inquiry to which Penuel et al. (2011) refer will be a bootstrapping process" (p. 342). As the word *bootstrapping* refers to achieving something without necessary external input, Cobb et al. emphasize here that DBIR requires large effort with limited guidance from the literature. Furthermore, DBIR needs multiple theoretical frameworks to work from (DiSessa & Cobb, 2004), and these theories need to be networked, that is, coordinated and integrated (e.g., Alberto, Bakker, Walker-van Aalst, Boon, & Drijvers, 2019; Bikner-Ahsbahs, Bakker, Haspekian, & Maracci, 2018).

It is challenging for the teaching community to benefit from research insights. Literature, for example, can be less accessible because of jargon, high level of abstraction, paywalls, or lack of actionable knowledge (see other publication challenges in Chapter 2, this volume). Therefore, the gap between educational research and practice can be seen as a barrier for education reform. Also, vice versa, teachers' practical expertise is critical for curriculum reform, but teachers' voices are not often part of research design or implementation (see Chapter 3, this volume).

To create alignment between academic research communities and professional teaching practices, teacher-researchers, as so-called *brokers*, can cross boundaries between those two worlds (Wenger, 1998). Such brokers face many challenges, occupying an ambiguous position operating in the very different cultures of school and academia—each culture bearing different expectations (Bakx, Bakker, Koopman, & Beijaard, 2016).

In this chapter, we describe our DBIR project as a case study, in which a teacher-researcher (van der Wal), in the role of broker, gained insights into how theory and practice can be brought together by both designing and implementing an educational innovation while being assisted by a team of lecturers. Many challenges and successes were experienced, and this chapter presents a variety of factors and mechanisms that play a role in such an adventure.

Professional Development and Agency

Because all organizations need to innovate to keep up with social and technological developments, change is a requirement in teachers' professional lives. However, transformations in practices and teachers' identities are difficult to achieve (Vähäsantanen, 2015). Success in educational innovations highly depends on the teachers who shape them (Lieberman & Pointer Mace, 2008). Visnovska, Cobb, and Dean (2012) and Goodchild (2014) stated it might be too ambitious to expect teachers to engage in the design process from the start, but Hargreaves (2003) argued that innovations that are only based on volunteers are less sustainable. Teachers benefit from involvement in innovation in terms of professional learning, but they also make sure that aspects such as practicality and authenticity are not neglected (Wake, Swan, & Foster, 2016).

Professional development (PD) is widely seen as the center of innovation (Heck, Plumley, Stylianou, Smith, & Moffett, 2019), and evidence is growing that quality PD improves student learning (Desimone, 2009; see Chapters 3, 11, and 12, this volume). Not all PD formats, however, are equally efficient (Kennedy, 2016), and they are not always based on how teachers learn. Learning outcomes that teachers report in terms of changes in knowledge and beliefs are attained mostly by experimenting and reflection on their own teaching practices and less by literature or input from colleagues. However, there are substantial differences between teachers, and some experience friction, struggling not to revert to old ways and avoiding learning (Bakkenes, Vermunt, & Wubbels, 2010). Little (2007) advised that teachers exchange experiences with one another for personal growth.

Teacher beliefs and values influence teaching practices (e.g., Philip, 2007) but also drive professional agency (Meirink, Imants, Meijer, & Verloop, 2010). Agency is defined as the opportunity to influence one's work, have the power to act, think for oneself, make decisions and choices, and take stances (Ketelaar, Beijaard, Boshuizen, & den Brok, 2012; Priestley, Edwards, & Priestley, 2012). In agency, people express their personal power, and it can be developed (Eteläpelto, Vähäsantanen, Hökkä, & Paloniemi, 2013; Holland, Lachicotte, Skinner, & Cain, 2001).

There is an emerging tendency to acknowledge the importance of teachers' agency (Biesta, Priestley, & Robinson, 2015). Agentic teachers perceive themselves as active learners, as pedagogical experts, and are able to implement and develop their own expertise (Toom, Pyhältö, & Rust, 2015). When opportunities for participation and influence are absent, teachers' agency is strongly reduced (Vähäsantanen, 2015). Therefore, agency can manifest itself in line with an innovation but also in criticism and resistance, and it is constructed in the middle of dilemmas and pedagogical uncertainties (Pyhältö, Pietarinen, & Soini, 2012).

In this chapter, we address the following research question: Which challenges may arise in the relation between teachers' agency and the aim of PD, and the goal of a sustainable implementation of an innovation?

Project Context: Implementation of a New Mathematics Course for Future Engineers

The implementation of a new course in applied mathematics was part of a larger design study to improve mathematics education in the technical domain of higher technical professional education in the Netherlands. Mathematics curricula are a topic of ongoing discussion because of variation in topics and level, and employer expectations (van Asselt & Boudri, 2013). This is the situation also at Avans University of Applied Sciences, where the study took place. At the School of Life Sciences and Environmental Technology and other technical schools, low success rates and motivation of students were encountered, and a wide variety in students' mathematical background levels provided additional problems. Mathematics curricula focused on abstract mathematics, and most teaching was transmission-based. So, our project started from the multiple issues (low student motivation and performance, diverse entrance levels of students) we faced in mathematics education and therefore aligns with the first principle of DBIR.

Because one of our goals was to improve the connection between mathematics education and workplace practices, we decided to introduce the development of *techno-mathematical literacies* (TmL) as central learning goals in the course. The term TmL was introduced by Kent, Bakker, Hoyles, and Noss (2005). Bakker, Hoyles, Kent, and Noss (2006) defined TmL as "functional mathematical knowledge mediated by tools and grounded in the context of specific work situations" (p. 343). They include mathematical, workplace, and software knowledge; multistep calculation and estimation; and the ability to interpret abstract data and communicative skills (Hoyles, Noss, Kent, & Bakker, 2010, 2013).

To identify which TmL engineers use in their daily work practices, we conducted an interview study in a range of technical domains (van der Wal, Bakker, & Drijvers, 2017). With these TmL categories as central learning goals, a new course in applied mathematics for technical schools was developed by the researcher-lecturer in collaboration with an interdisciplinary design team of three lecturers from the School for Life Sciences and Environmental technology, the School of Built Environment and Infrastructure (both part of Avans University of Applied Sciences), and the Institute for Engineering and Design (HU University of Applied Sciences Utrecht). These lecturers helped create support for innovations, contributed expertise from different technical domains, and provided the technical contexts.

By designing and implementing a new course in applied mathematics in higher technical education, we aimed to gain insights into how to better align mathematics education with workplace practices. This involved creating learning materials, adjusting domain-specific pedagogy, and designing PD of lecturers, as well as formulating prerequisite conditions for the course. Designing the course materials was labor-intensive but without insuperable difficulties. To promote the development of TmL, we had reasonably clear learning goals in mind, based on interviews with engineers (van der Wal et al., 2017). However, involving lecturers who had not taken part in the design process proved the most substantial challenge. We, therefore, broadened our initial focus on the design of the course to include the support of all lecturers who would teach the course. We added evaluation interviews after the first (2016–2017) and second cycles (2017–2018) of the implementation, in which we investigated the lecturers' experiences, opinions, dilemmas, feelings, and beliefs regarding teaching the new course.

Our experiences underpin the importance of Engeström's (2011) critique of most interventionist research, namely, that it adopts a linear model with assumptions about control and prediction that do not hold in a setting where people have agency and sometimes are resistant to change. In this work, we focus on the lecturers and the support we provided, while student learning outcomes are a topic for a future report.

Course Specifics

In the designed course, we focused on the application of mathematics by using context-based cases, to improve recognition of mathematics in technical practices and enhance motivation in students. Because basic, abstract knowledge of mathematics is essential for successfully working on these cases, we added a learning track using ALEKS[TM,1] software. Furthermore, we changed our pedagogical approach; transmission teaching was limited, and inquiry-based learning (IBL) was introduced during so-called *feedback hours*. The choice for IBL was based on the premise that TmL are inquiry-based by nature. An extended description of the course can be found in van der Wal, Bakker, and Drijvers (2019).

The new mathematics course was implemented for all students of the School of Life Sciences and Environmental Technology at Avans University of Applied Sciences in the Netherlands. After a pilot in the spring of 2016 with 59 chemistry students, two iterative cycles (the second principle of DBIR) were administered, monitored, evaluated, and adjusted in the years that followed. We started with eight lecturers and 400+ students in the fall of 2016 and proceeded with nine lecturers and 500+ students in the 2017 cohort.

Lecturers

Our design team's setup resembles a teacher design team (TDT), a type of emerging PD in which a group of teachers focuses on the design of educational materials (also see Chapter 3). Because participation in such a team stimulates ownership, TDT can be the basis of a successful implementation. Enthusiasm is key; teachers in TDTs are often motivated and ambitious (Binkhorst, Handelzalts, Poortman, & van Joolingen, 2015). To support sustainability of the innovation, it is advised to involve all teachers (Hargreaves, 2003).

In our case, however, for multiple reasons, most lecturers involved in teaching the course could not be a member of the design team. We did not precisely know

---

[1] Assessment and LEarning in Knowledge Spaces is a Web-based, artificially intelligent assessment and learning system. ALEKS uses adaptive questioning to quickly and accurately determine exactly what a student knows and doesn't know in a course. ALEKS then instructs the student on the topics he or she is most ready to learn. As a student works through a course, ALEKS periodically reassesses the student to ensure that topics learned are also retained.

which and how many lecturers would be teaching. Over the last few years, the student population has grown; therefore, more lecturers have been required each year. Also, some lecturers left because of other tasks and priorities, and others joined later; thus, we did not have a steady teaching team during the project. Also, we introduced many innovations in the design. This would not have been possible had too many people been involved.

Teachers are the most important agents in educational change and many innovations have failed due to lack of teacher learning (Borko, 2004; Guskey, 2002). "Top-down" approaches from policymakers or researchers to teachers do not work (Altrichter, Feldman, Posch, & Somekh, 2008; Tirosh & Graeber, 2003). Therefore, in our suboptimal circumstances, not being able to involve all lecturers in the design process was a significant challenge. Although the lecturers in the design team were very motivated and ambitious, not all teaching lecturers were enthusiastic about starting the new course with different content and pedagogy. They were asked by management to participate, but most of them were used to teaching "old-school" mathematics for years. The design team was conscious of this situation and tried to provide as much support as possible to assist with the necessary changes.

Support Kit for Teaching Lecturers

To support the teaching lecturers, the design team developed a support toolkit for them. The choice of tools was based on the experiences of the two lecturers, the researcher-lecturer and the design lecturer of the School of Life Sciences and Environmental Technology, in the pilot of the new course. We provided materials such as manuals and written information about IBL and TmL and sent weekly emails with instructions, suggestions, and tips to the teaching lecturers. Support via phone, email, or live with the researcher-lecturer was available. We also provided the lecturers with a reflection form to monitor their own experiences. Most importantly, we organized lecturer meetings 3 times each in the first and second year, with a seventh, final meeting in the third year, moderated by a coach-lecturer from the School of Life Sciences and Environmental Technology. These meetings, designed to prepare and support the lecturers, addressed a range of topics, all presented in Table 15.1.

By conducting iterative design cycles, we developed knowledge about factors that influence an implementation's success (the third principle of DBIR). In applying changes to the innovation's design to support sustainable implementation in the curriculum, our project aligns with the fourth principle of DBIR.

Interviews

The first cycle (2016–2017) of implementing the new course led us to discover that the teaching lecturers were the most critical factor in successful implementation.

TABLE 15.1. Lecturers' Meetings in 3 Years of Implementation

Time of meeting	Content of meeting
Beginning of Year 1, Meeting 1	Working on case and reflect. Presentation of theory on IBL and TmL, rationale behind the course, results engineer-field study. Explanation of course details and video examples of feedback hours from pilot study.
Half-way Year 1, Meeting 2	Working on another case and reflect. Discussion of factors that influence the feedback hours. More video examples for motivation and support.
End of Year 1, Meeting 3	Evaluation. Discussion of first round of interviews. Inventory of ideas and wishes for adjustments.
Beginning of Year 2, Meeting 1	Discussion of changes in the course, based on the first round of interviews and the evaluation Meeting 3 of previous year.
Half-way Year 2, Meeting 2	Experiencing TmL and IBL by working on assignment in pairs.
End of Year 2, Meeting 3	Evaluation. Sharing students' success rates and other facts. Inventory of ideas and wishes for adjustments.
End of Year 3, Meeting 1	Evaluation.

We also realized that our support toolkit did not suffice. We needed to deeply understand the lecturers' experiences, opinions, dilemmas, feelings, and beliefs to apply necessary changes in the design. Therefore, as mentioned above, in the spring of the first cycle, interviews with the six teaching lecturers were conducted by the member of the design team from HU University of Applied Sciences Utrecht (Moes). This choice was based on the teaching lecturers and the design lecturer not being acquainted, which provided a certain distance whereby lecturers would be able to speak more freely. The interview questions originated from DBIR principles 2, 3, and 4, by gaining insights for the design (both materials and support) and in lecturers. The interview questions are listed in Table 15.2. The approximately 1-hour-long semi-structured interviews were audio-recorded, transcribed, and coded according to the method of Boeije (2005) by the design lecturer. The assigned codes were guided by the interview questions, but also emerged from the material and were grouped by theme. A total of 321 fragments in 2017 and 93 in 2018 was coded. Frequent discussions took place with the researcher-lecturer regarding interpretation of findings.

Although we originally planned to conduct these interviews once, we decided to add a second round, to determine the lecturers' experiences with the design changes (see Table 15.5 on p. 310) after the first implementation cycle. This illustrates a need for flexibility in conducting this kind of research that goes beyond the four key principles of DBIR. These informal, short interviews with the six teaching lecturers from the previous year and two new lecturers were conducted by the

TABLE 15.2. Interview Questions for the Teaching Lecturers

Theme	Questions
Classes	You have taught the course Applied Mathematics. I'm curious as to how classes went. Can you tell me a bit about that? • What were the students mainly doing? • What were you mainly doing? • What went well? • What went less well? Were you able to teach the classes in a way that suits you? • Can you explain that? • If not, what would suit you better? Were you able to teach the classes as intended by the design team? • Can you explain that?
The design of the course	How would you explain to colleagues what this course is about? What is new or different about this course?
Support for the lecturers	How did you prepare for the lessons? • Did you work out any problems in ALEKS™? • Have you worked out the cases yourself? • Did you do any other things to prepare yourself? Support has been offered in several ways. I have them printed on these cards. For you, some of those ways will have been more effective than others. Would you please lay out the cards, in order of effectiveness? • Can you explain this order? [cards: lecturer meetings, feedback form, asking questions via email, asking questions via telephone, weekly email] For your colleagues and yourself, what would be effective ways to be supported in teaching these classes in the future?
Lecturers' input in the redesign	(Only for lecturers that have taught the course before) You have taught the course for the second time. What have you done differently? Next year, the course Applied Mathematics will be taught again. In the next months, the design of the course will be reviewed and adjusted. • What suggestions do you have for improvement of the course? • Would you change anything about the content of the course? • Would you change anything about the teaching methods? • Would you change anything about the cases? • Would you change anything about testing and assessment? What else could help to make this course a success?

researcher-lecturer in the spring of the second cycle (2017–2018). The researcher-lecturer asked for experiences, opinions, and feelings about teaching the course that year. These interviews were not audio-recorded but were summarized on-the-spot on a laptop. The notes were coded and interpreted by the design lecturer using the same approach as in the first round.

The former director of the School of Life Science was involved at the beginning of this research project and was supportive and facilitating during its process. Thus, we decided to organize a semi-structured interview with him to identify his role in stimulating a successful implementation. This interview was also conducted by the design researcher, audio-recorded, and transcribed, but because of the different goals of this interview, we decided not to code it, but interpret and draw conclusions directly from the transcription. The interview questions for the director can be found in Table 15.3. After the second cycle of implementation, the director retired, and we were pleased that the new director continued support for our project.

Insights into Challenges and Successes Gained from the Interviews

The Former Director

The former director of the School of Life Sciences and Environmental Technology turned out to be quite valuable in the implementation of the new course and was an important stakeholder (the first principle of DBIR). He had a clear vision and ideas on needed improvements to the mathematics curriculum. He addressed the problems with the differences in the level of mathematical skills between students and the fact that abstract mathematics does not stimulate students' and lecturers' motivation. At the beginning of the project, he suggested that we should investigate what the mathematical needs of the workplace are to improve student motivation,

TABLE 15.3. Interview Questions for the Director

Theme	Questions
Goals of the course	What purpose did you have in mind with this course? • Why is that important? • When would you call it a success?
Role in the implementation of the course	What role did you have in the implementation process? • How would you describe that yourself? • By what means can you influence this process?
Supporting lecturers	What does it require of a lecturer to be able to teach this course? • How can you manage this? • What kind of support can you offer? • What kind of support can you facilitate? • Which conditions are necessary?

design the course accordingly, add technology to support differences in students, and use appropriate pedagogical tools.

Indicators of success were, according to him, satisfaction in lecturers and students, and a strong connection between the course, the rest of the curriculum, and the workplace. He hoped lecturers would be happy with a new approach, and motivation would improve. He also suggested that, after this intervention, other courses could be adjusted accordingly.

Although he did not share his vision extensively with all lecturers, he recruited lecturers to participate and to conform to the prerequisites of the course, allocated task hours, and provided support to the researcher-lecturer. He also facilitated the PD of the teaching lecturers to support the learning of the required pedagogy.

The most striking aspect of the interview was his conjecture that the lecturers, especially the younger ones, were reflective professionals who wanted to develop professionally, would be motivated by the domain-specific context in mathematics, and thus would be able to motivate students. He also hypothesized that younger lecturers, more recently educated in teaching, would be more enthusiastic about new courses with new content and pedagogy.

The First Round of Lecturer Interviews

The purpose of the lecturer interviews was to identify their experiences, opinions, dilemmas, feelings, and beliefs and therefore gain insight into factors that play a role in the success of the implementation. We shall discuss the most distinctive, surprising, and influential themes and illustrate these with excerpts from the interviews. The themes emerged from the data, as we combined open codes to selective codes (Boeije, 2005). Some themes are only discussed in one round, but most are addressed in both. Table 15.4 shows the percentage breakdown. In the first round, most codes and most comments by the lecturers concerned learning outcomes, the feedback hour, the support toolkit, and the students.

The theme feedback hour menu is only discussed in the second round of interviews and is addressed in the section: the second round of lecturer interviews.

Inquiry-Based Learning

Lecturers experienced many difficulties with using IBL during the feedback hours. In general, most lecturers in higher professional education have worked in industry before switching to teaching and receive only a course of 6 European Credit Transfer and Accumulation System on pedagogy. They tend to teach in the way they were taught in their own school days, with a focus on sending information and explaining procedures. Conducting feedback hours with IBL questions, addressing TmL, managing classroom discussions, and creating a safe atmosphere in the class are complex tasks. They require taking on multiple teacher roles, something most lecturers are not used to, and that some do not prefer, as they explained in

TABLE 15.4. Percentages of Fragmented Codes in the First and Second Round of Interviews

	First round (spring 2017)	Second round (spring 2018)
Learning outcomes	15%	8%
Cases	8%	4%
ALEKS	6%	9%
First hour: instruction	5%	3%
Second and third hours: collaborative work	10%	7%
Fourth hour: feedback hour	13%	9%
Assessment	3%	14%
Lecturer preparation	6%	
Support toolkit	12%	
Teacher roles	7%	13%
Students	11%	5%
Feedback hour menu		22%
Miscellaneous	4%	8%
Total	100%	100%

Note. Fragmented codes include experiences, opinions, dilemmas, feelings, and beliefs of the lecturers. Percentages above 10 are highlighted.

the lecturer meetings. Although all lecturers received the same support toolkit, we noticed their interpretations of, for example, the approach of IBL were very different. All lecturers tried to administer the classes as they thought they were meant to, but some lecturers assumed instruction and explaining were not allowed anymore, while others used all teacher roles freely. In the following example, we hear from one lecturer (L1) struggling with the desire of students to know whether an answer is correct and her effort to focus on the approach, rather than the answer.

L1

"And then they asked: 'Is it correct?' I got asked that question a lot. And then I said: 'Does everyone agree that it has to be solved like this?' Then everyone said: 'Yes, that must be correct.' Then I said: 'If everyone agrees, then it must be correct.' They did not like that."

Content and Pedagogy

In the School of Life Sciences and Environmental Technology, mathematics courses are not taught by mathematicians or mathematics teachers, but by biologists, chemists, and chemical engineers who have an affinity with mathematics or statistics.

We expected their background would turn out to be an advantage for the new applied mathematics course, as contexts provide meaning for these professionals. As mentioned above, the school's director shared this expectation.

However, we did not see this conjecture confirmed. It is very challenging for many mathematics teachers to transform from an instructor teaching procedures for solving specific tasks to a more facilitating role, supporting both conceptual understanding and procedural fluency (Swan, 2007). Some lecturers preferred to teach abstract mathematics, and we suspect that context-based cases are actually mathematically more difficult. According to Heck et al. (2019), mathematics is often seen as a static body of knowledge of rules and procedures, while an inquiry-oriented approach stimulates a more dynamic view and actively engages students to construct knowledge. This aligns with the view of Freudenthal (1973), who perceives teaching mathematics as a human activity in his principle of realistic mathematics education. Pozzi, Noss, and Hoyles (1998) state that the key idea is mathematization, which they define as a complex set of relations (including mathematical relations) between resources, activities, and settings as they are operationalized to achieve a particular goal at work.

In the next example, we present a lecturer (L2) who experiences a lack of mathematical content and misses teaching his specialty in basic mathematics (*students study basic mathematics in ALEKS outside class*). His drive to help students is challenged by the shifted content and pedagogy of the course:

L2

"For myself, I miss the content component very much and I wonder: Do you need me, or should you use someone who is better in process coaching and perhaps less mathematically educated? That would work for this class, too. I cannot teach my specialty, [which is] basic mathematics. It [the new approach] is something I struggle with, and I would like to teach that. To share my knowledge, this is how you can approach this, and you can use these methods to solve this problem. I want to be able to use and teach my mathematical expertise. Those mathematical skills [in students] are not yet developed. I can contribute to that development, [and offer] a significant contribution. I would like to have a possibility for that. To provide mathematical support to students, which is not asked of me. Students don't ask for it, but it would be beneficial to them."

Because the teaching load of lecturers is generally high, most had limited preparation time for teaching the new course. From informal conversations with the lectures, it appeared that almost all lecturers in both cycles did not work out the cases by themselves and did not study or even open the trajectory of abstract mathematics in ALEKS. We suspect this lack of preparation played a significant role in lecturers feeling less confident with the content of the course. We also noticed that some lecturers tended to turn to abstract mathematics and calculation rules. In this example, the lecturer is more comfortable with basic differentiation rules than the applied mathematics content:

L1

"It's getting accustomed for me. You [usually] just say 'x square is 2x' and go for it. Not this kind of teaching. This takes getting used to, this content."

Feedback Hour

All lecturers struggled to engage students during the feedback hour. A lecturer describes below her challenges with the different levels of understanding and some lack of motivation among her students:

L3

"During the feedback hour, it is challenging to keep everyone engaged. That is hard work. Some students want to listen carefully to what is going on, because they don't understand it very well. However, there are also some who are noisy, and then you have to ask for quiet continuously. They are obligated to be there and then motivation is not always very high. They are noisy because they already get it. When we talk more about a specific topic because some students struggle with it and some don't, then the engagement is gone. I try to keep them engaged, but it costs a lot of energy."

Cases and TmL

We considered the lecturer meetings to be an essential tool in the support kit, hoping to educate the lecturers in TmL and IBL. We saw, however, that lecturers were not focused on these meetings, but appreciated the more practical tools of the kit. Short-term support in the form of informal phone calls and weekly emails was experienced as most helpful. Although lecturers reported positive experiences with students learning to work with Excel and estimations, which are TmL, the concept of TmL appeared to be challenging for the lecturers; we thus observed limited engagement with it. Here, we have an example of a lecturer who focuses on mathematical content rather than TmL, but then realizes TmL was, in fact, part of it:

L4

"The lecturers' version of the cases gave theory: Learning goals and the skills students work on. I did not read that well. There were all kinds of abbreviations and difficult concepts I could not understand directly. Nathalie [first author] did explain that in the lecturer meetings, however. Something with numbers and getting a sense of numbers, but it was all in English. Something with a letter . . . [Interviewer says TmL.] Uh, yes, TmL. Those were present in the lecturers' version of the cases, but in class we didn't do anything with that. That would be too vague for the students, too. That is how I dealt with it; I focused on the content, the math, the Excel, the lesson itself. The thoughts behind, I did not occupy myself with that. . . . Perhaps then I am not right if I say that the name of the course [applied mathematics] is misleading because that TmL is part of it. But when I say mathematics, then it is about topics, and how much they come up."

There were also some doubts about desired learning outcomes in using these cases, but most lecturers believed they were useful and suitable tasks for students to work on: mathematical applications in the technical domain. One lecturer explains how students have to really think instead of applying procedural rules:

L1

"This is interesting because you let them really think about something instead of giving them some rules to learn by heart. Because they forget those, you see that with me, too. But anyway, do you become a good biologist by this? I think you can be one without, but on the other hand, I do think it is important that they learn to think a certain way, and I think you can accomplish that with such cases."

Revision of the Design

Not many changes were made to the original design of the course in the iterative cycles of the implementation. There were small adjustments in the cases on the level of text or added pictures, the construct of two learning trajectories comprising the use of ALEKS, and the cases were maintained, because the purposes and learning goals of the course appeared to match. The only substantial change we implemented was the form of assessment. In the initial design of the first cycle, cases were submitted by the students and reviewed by the lecturers. Because we experienced some cases of cheating by students and reviewing the cases appeared to be too time-consuming for the lecturers, we decided to introduce a digital assessment after the first year, consisting of TmL questions regarding the cases. Lecturers viewed this as a considerable improvement. In general, lecturers at the School of Life Sciences and Environmental Technology are accustomed to written assessments and value this form as the most reliable to test students' knowledge.

We learned from the interviews and the evaluation meeting at the end of the first cycle that the whole-class feedback hours with students presenting their work were the most substantial challenge. The amount of work students had finished during the collaborative second and third hours varied enormously, which raised the difficulty of administering this hour. We, therefore, introduced a menu with different options for the feedback hour (see Table 15.5). This local adjustment in the design was in line with formative interventions (Engeström, 2011) but also corresponded to the second principle of DBIR. For more advanced students, alternative and extra assignments were developed. We also suggested to the lecturers that they vary the length of the collaborative second and third hours as they saw fit.

The Second Round of Lecturer Interviews

During the second cycle, in the spring of 2018, informal interviews with the researcher-lecturer were conducted. Table 15.4. shows a shift toward codes regarding assessment form, teacher roles, and the menu of feedback. Lecturers were positive toward the feedback-hour menu. Adding more options in teaching allowed for more autonomy and professional agency. We chose not to audio-record these interviews but to take notes, because we did not want to possibly disturb the collegial relationship between the researcher-lecturer and the teaching lecturers. This interview round provided less data, as the interviews were shorter; because no audio-recording took place, we cannot present excerpts.

In the support toolkit for the teaching lecturers, a reflection form was provided to be completed after every class. The aim was to provide support and to gain insight into the experiences, thoughts, and feelings of lecturers. Only one lecturer used this form and reported that it helped to improve her teaching in successive classes. This lecturer also held the most positive opinions about the new course and reported extensive content preparation.

We considered whether changing both mathematical content and pedagogy by introducing a new course was too ambitious in a college where lecturers are used to more traditional ways of teaching. Most lecturers appeared to be ill equipped for the pedagogical choices in the design. However, content and pedagogy are often intertwined. Because TmL are inquiry-based by nature, IBL seemed to be the preeminent choice for learning these skills. Therefore, although administering IBL in the classroom is complex, we did not want to abolish this approach in the course. It became apparent that additional PD for the lecturers was inevitable to achieve a sustainable and successful implementation.

TABLE 15.5. Menu for Organizing a Feedback Hour

- Option 1. Two or three groups of presenting students and whole-class discussion using IBL
- Option 2. Visit all groups and discuss using IBL
- Option 3. Alternate options 1 and 2 per week
- Option 4. Peer review per two groups and proceed with whole-class reflection
- Option 5. Option 2 in Weeks 1–6 and with short presentations of products in Week 7

In the third cycle (2018–2019), two lecturers left the team, and two others joined. There was no official PD available anymore, but new lecturers were supported and trained individually by the researcher-lecturer. We tried to recruit new lecturers who fit the profile of a reflective practitioner. We also continued with conducting an evaluation meeting at the end of each year. We saw that, after two cycles, the lecturers were getting more used to the course, and although some lecturers deviated from the design, we also observed more confidence in lecturers and fresh ideas and successes in newcomers. It became more and more apparent that sustainable implementation required a long-term effort.

Conclusion and Discussion

While design studies are developed in a specific local context, researchers should try to create general knowledge that can be of value to other researchers and contribute to theory (Anderson & Shattuck, 2012; McKenney & Reeves, 2013). In this chapter, we shared the lessons learned in a DBIR project and illustrate why this kind of research is complicated and challenging as there is not just one theoretical frame to work from. However, we also shared successes and have implemented a new course in the curriculum that may endure for many years. While our first efforts focused on the design of the course, over time, we encountered the influence of many practical constraints; the importance of continuous PD for lecturers thus became apparent.

We conjectured that lecturers would appreciate applied mathematics in their domain in contrast to abstract mathematics. Students are focused on answers and ask confirmation explicitly. It seems that both lecturers and students share a belief in mathematics containing problems that have one correct solution. TmL provides a perspective of mathematics as an activity with multiple solutions and with less certainty. We wanted to keep our focus on these skills because of their importance in the workplace. However, we do think this contrast might be part of why many obstacles in the implementation occurred.

Design components were considered successful if they worked as conjectured and intended, or could be made to work effectively after small adjustments, and were positively received by the lecturers. The most substantial success we can point at in the implementation is the menu for the feedback hour. The factors we could not predict and struggled with, or could not find an immediate solution for during the process, we consider as challenges. We saw that the act of interviewing added to the positive experience of being seen and heard. Reflection on theory, which we did not accomplish during the lecturer meetings, was stimulated by the interviews. Therefore, listening and trying to adjust the design, but avoiding lethal mutations (Brown & Campione, 1996), were both our most significant successes and challenges with regard to the lecturers. Therefore, a design should have a certain amount of robustness so that it can survive small changes (Roschelle, Tatar, Shechtman, & Knudsen, 2008).

Although we knew from the literature that it is advisable to involve all lecturers in the design process, this was not practically possible. Even with this knowledge, we were surprised by the enormous impact of lecturers' beliefs regarding mathematics content, learning outcomes, and pedagogy on the success of the implementation. Our support toolkit did not provide enough basis for successful implementation, and we did not expect the limited effect of the lecturers' meetings, which were appreciated less than the more practical tools in the support kit. Can we accommodate lecturers by operating more closely in agreement with their beliefs and preferences? Cole and Engeström (2007) state, in line with Vygotsky and followers, that practice is essential for testing and improving theory, and that activity should be the unit of analysis. Although DBIR includes practice by using iterative cycles of implementation, we do think that we should move toward formative interventions, in which Vygotsky's principle of a second stimulation fosters learner's agency (Engeström, 2011). Alternatively, perhaps, designs should be more *half-baked*, as Kynigos (2007) defines his microworlds, which are pieces of software, to be built on and changed by all their users. This allows a design to be both robust and flexible.

In this chapter, we did not report on students' experiences and learning outcomes. In student evaluations, we saw a direct correlation between confident and content lecturers and content students. As for learning outcomes, we administered a pre- and posttest, and those results will be the topic of a future report.

Based on the experiences in this project, the lecturers and researcher-lecturer recently formulated a plan for the coming years. Long-time management support for implementation is imperative, and fortunately, the green light was given for more official, external PD and peer feedback going forward, with a plan to recruit more lecturers with an innovative mind-set. We hope these actions will contribute to more success and a sustainable future for the course and will have a positive influence on other courses as well.

Within our design study, it appeared that the implementation phase was the most challenging, and we needed to focus on PD of the lecturers. On one side, we have a course and ideas for pedagogy, but on the other, we have some teaching lecturers who are not comfortable and need agency and autonomy. Although Luckner, Purgathofer, and Fitpatrick (2018) provide design research advice, every project has different challenges, and the authors emphasize the unpredictability of "research in the wild" (p. 818). Research is always directed backward, but life is forward, and one has to consider how much leeway there is. Our project aligns with the four principles of the theory of DBIR (Fishman et al., 2013). Yet, Engeström and Sannino (2010) warn that researchers should not expect "nicely linear results from their efforts." And even with the DBIR principles in mind, implementation of innovation requires, most of all, flexibility of the researchers; one cannot blindly follow abstract guidelines. In the nonideal circumstances of real practice, we should expect the unexpected.

ACKNOWLEDGMENTS

This work is part of the research program Doctoral Grant for Teachers, with Project No. 023.009.061, which is financed by the Netherlands Organisation for Scientific Research (NWO). We would like to thank Edwin Melis, Paul van Hal, and the mathematics lecturers of the School of Life Sciences and Environmental Technology at Avans University of Applied Sciences.

REFERENCES

Akkerman, S. F., Bronkhorst, L. H., & Zitter, I. (2013). The complexity of educational design research. *Quality & Quantity, 47,* 421–439.

Alberto, R. A., Bakker, A., Walker-van Aalst, O., Boon, P. B. J., & Drijvers, P. H. M. (2019). Networking theories in design research—An embodied instrumentation case study in trigonometry. In U. T. Jankvist, M. van den Heuvel-Panhuizen, & M. Veldhuis (Eds.), *Proceedings of the Eleventh Congress of the European Society for Research in Mathematics Education* (pp. 3088–3095). Utrecht, the Netherlands: Freudenthal Group & Freudenthal Institute, Utrecht University, and ERME.

Altrichter, H., Feldman, A., Posch, P., & Somekh, B. (2008). *Teachers investigate their work: An introduction to action research across the professions* (2nd ed.). London: Routledge.

Anderson, T., & Shattuck, J. (2012). Design-based research: A decade of progress in education research? *Educational Researcher, 41*(1), 16–25.

Bakkenes, I., Vermunt, J. D., & Wubbels, T. (2010). Teacher learning in the context of educational innovation: Learning activities and learning outcomes of experienced teachers. *Learning and Instruction, 20,* 533–548.

Bakker, A., Hoyles, C., Kent, P., & Noss, R. (2006). Improving work processes by making the invisible visible. *Journal of Education and Work, 19,* 343–361.

Bakx, A., Bakker, A., Koopman, M., & Beijaard, D. (2016). Boundary crossing by science teacher researchers in a PhD program. *Teaching and Teacher Education, 60,* 76–87.

Biesta, G., Priestley, M., & Robinson, S. (2015). The role of beliefs in teacher agency. *Teachers and Teaching, 21,* 624–640.

Bikner-Ahsbahs, A., Bakker, A., Haspekian, M., & Maracci, M. (2018). *Introduction to the papers of TWG17: Theoretical perspectives and approaches in mathematics education research.* In *Proceedings of CERME 10,* Dublin, Ireland, February 2017 (hal-01948870).

Binkhorst, F., Handelzalts, A., Poortman, C. L., & van Joolingen, W. R. (2015). Understanding teacher design teams—A mixed methods approach to developing a descriptive framework. *Teaching and Teacher Education, 51,* 213–224.

Boeije, H. R. (2005). *Analyseren in kwalitatief onderzoek: Denken en doen* [Analysis in qualitative research]. Amsterdam, the Netherlands: Boom onderwijs.

Borko, H. (2004). Professional development and teacher learning: Mapping the terrain. *Educational Researcher, 33*(8), 3–15.

Brown, A. L., & Campione, J. C. (1996). Psychological theory and the design of innovative learning environments: On procedures, principles, and systems. In L. Schauble & R. Glaser (Eds.), *Innovations in learning: New environments for education* (pp. 289–325). Mahwah, NJ: Lawrence Erlbaum Associates.

Cobb, P., Jackson, K., Smith, T., Sorum, M., & Henrick, E. (2013). Design research with educational systems: Investigating and supporting improvements in the quality of mathematics teaching and learning at scale. *National Society for the Study of Education Yearbook, 112,* 320–349.

Cole, M., & Engeström, Y. (2007). Cultural-historical approaches to designing for development. In J. Valsiner & A. Rosa (Eds.), *The Cambridge handbook of sociocultural psychology* (pp. 484–507). Cambridge, UK: Cambridge University Press.

Desimone, L. M. (2009). Improving impact studies of teachers' professional development: Toward better conceptualizations and measures. *Educational Researcher, 38*(3), 181–199.

DiSessa, A. A., & Cobb, P. (2004). Ontological innovation and the role of theory in design experiments. *Journal of the Learning Sciences, 13*(1), 77–103.

Engeström, Y. (2011). From design experiments to formative interventions. *Theory & Psychology, 21,* 598–628.

Engeström, Y., & Sannino, A. (2010). Studies of expansive learning: Foundations, findings and future challenges. *Educational Research Review, 5*(1), 1–24.

Eteläpelto, A., Vähäsantanen, K., Hökkä, P., & Paloniemi, S. (2013). What is agency? Conceptualizing professional agency at work. *Educational Research Review, 10,* 45–65.

Farley-Ripple, E., May, H., Karpyn, A., Tilley, K., & McDonough, K. (2018). Rethinking connections between research and practice in education: A conceptual framework. *Educational Researcher, 47,* 235–245.

Fishman, B., & Penuel, W. (2018). Design-based implementation research. In F. Fischer, C. E. Hmelo-Silver, S. R. Goldman, & P. Reimann (Eds.), *International handbook of the learning sciences* (pp. 393–400). New York: Routledge.

Fishman, B. J., Penuel, W. R., Allen, A. R., Cheng, B. H., & Sabelli, N. (2013). Design-based implementation research: An emerging model for transforming the relationship of research and practice. *National Society for the Study of Education, 112*(2), 136–156.

Freudenthal, H. (1973). *Mathematics as an educational task.* Dordrecht, the Netherlands: Reidel.

Goodchild, S. (2014). Mathematics teaching development: Learning from developmental research in Norway. *ZDM: International Journal on Mathematics Education, 46,* 305–316.

Guskey, T. R. (2002). Professional development and teacher change. *Teachers and Teaching, 8,* 381–391.

Hargreaves, A. (2003). *Teaching in the knowledge society: Education in the age of insecurity.* New York: Teachers College Press.

Heck, D. J., Plumley, C. L., Stylianou, D. A., Smith, A. A., & Moffett, G. (2019). Scaling up innovative learning in mathematics: Exploring the effect of different professional development approaches on teacher knowledge, beliefs, and instructional practice. *Educational Studies in Mathematics, 102*(3), 319–342.

Holland, D. C., Lachicotte Jr., W., Skinner, D., & Cain, C. (2001). *Identity and agency in cultural worlds.* Cambridge, MA: Harvard University Press.

Hoyles, C., Noss, R., Kent, P., & Bakker, A. (2010). *Improving mathematics at work: The need for techno-mathematical literacies.* London: Routledge.

Hoyles, C., Noss, R., Kent, P., & Bakker, A. (2013). Mathematics in the workplace: Issues and challenges. In A. Damlamian, J. F. Rodrigues, & R. Sträßer (Eds.), *Educational interfaces between mathematics and industry* (pp. 43–50). London: Springer.

Kennedy, M. M. (2016). How does professional development improve teaching? *Review of Educational Research, 86,* 945–980.

Kent, P., Bakker, A., Hoyles, C., & Noss, R. (2005). Techno-mathematical literacies in the workplace. *Mathematics Statistics and Operational Research, 5*(1), 5–9.

Ketelaar, E., Beijaard, D., Boshuizen, H. P. A., & den Brok, J. (2012). Teachers' positioning towards an educational innovation in the light of ownership, sense-making and agency. *Teaching and Teacher Education, 28,* 273–282.

Kynigos, C. (2007). Half-baked logo microworlds as boundary objects in integrated design. *Informatics in Education—An International Journal, 6,* 335–359.

Lieberman, A., & Pointer Mace, D. H. (2008). Teacher learning: The key to educational reform. *Journal of Teacher Education, 59,* 226–234.

Little, J. W. (2007). Teachers' accounts of classroom experience as a resource for professional learning and instructional decision making. In P. A. Moss (Ed.), *Evidence and decision making* (2007 NSSE Yearbook, Vol. 106, Issue 1, pp. 217–240). Boston: Blackwell Synergy.

Luckner, N., Purgathofer, P., & Fitzpatrick, G. (2018, June). Reflecting on challenges of conducting design-based research in large university courses. In *EdMedia+ Innovate Learning* (pp. 807–821). Waynesville, NC: Association for the Advancement of Computing in Education.

Maass, K., Cobb, P., Krainer, K., & Potari, D. (2019). Different ways to implement innovative teaching approaches at scale. *Educational Studies in Mathematics, 102,* 303–318.

McKenney, S., & Reeves, T. C. (2013). Systematic review of design-based research progress: Is a little knowledge a dangerous thing? *Educational Researcher, 42*(2), 97–100.

Means, B., & Penuel, W. R. (2005). Research to support scaling up technology-based innovations. In C. Dede, J. P. Honan, & L. C. Peters (Eds.), *Scaling up success: Lessons from technology-based educational improvement* (pp. 176–197). New York: Jossey-Bass.

Meirink, J. A., Imants, J., Meijer, P. C., & Verloop, N. (2010). Teacher learning and collaboration in innovative teams. *Cambridge Journal of Education, 40*(2), 161–181.

Penuel, W. R., & Fishman, B. J. (2012). Large-scale science education intervention research we can use. *Journal of Research in Science Teaching, 49,* 281–304.

Penuel, W. R., Fishman, B. J., Cheng, B. H., & Sabelli, N. (2011). Organizing research and development at the intersection of learning, implementation, and design. *Educational Researcher, 40,* 331–337.

Philipp, R. (2007). Mathematics teachers' beliefs and affect. In F. Lester (Ed.), *Second handbook of research on mathematics teaching and learning* (pp. 257–318). Reston, VA: National Council of Teachers of Mathematics.

Pozzi, S., Noss, R., & Hoyles, C. (1998). Tools in practice, mathematics in use. *Educational Studies in Mathematics, 36*(2), 105–122.

Priestley, M., Edwards, R., & Priestley, A. (2012). Teacher agency in curriculum making: Agents of change and spaces for manoeuvre. *Curriculum Inquiry, 42*(2), 191–214.

Pyhältö, K., Pietarinen, J., & Soini, T. (2012). Do comprehensive school teachers perceive themselves as active professional agents in school reforms? *Journal of Educational Change, 13,* 95–116.

Roschelle, J., Tatar, D., Shechtman, N., & Knudsen, J. (2008). The role of scaling up research in designing for and evaluating robustness. *Educational Studies in Mathematics, 68*(2), 149–170.

Snow, C. E. (2016). The role of relevance in education research, as viewed by former presidents. *Educational Researcher, 45*(2), 64–68.

Swan, M. (2007). The impact of task-based professional development on teachers' practices and beliefs: A design research study. *Journal of Mathematics Teacher Education, 10*(4–6), 217–237.

Tirosh, D., & Graeber, A. O. (2003). Challenging and changing mathematics teaching practices. In A. Bishop, M. A. Clements, C. Keitel, J. Kilpatrick, & F. Leung (Eds.), *Second international handbook of mathematics education* (pp. 643–688). Dordrecht, the Netherlands: Kluwer.

Toom, A., Pyhältö, K., & Rust, F. O. C. (2015). Teachers' professional agency in contradictory times. *Teachers and Teaching, 21*, 615–623.

Vähäsantanen, K. (2015). Professional agency in the stream of change: Understanding educational change and teachers' professional identities. *Teaching and Teacher Education, 47*, 1–12.

van Asselt, R., & Boudri, J. C. (2013). *Versterking van de doorstroom en de kwaliteit an het technisch HBO; adviezen vanuit het onderwijswerkveld* [Reinforcing flow and quality of higher technical professional education; advice from educational practices]. Nieuwekerk aan de IJssel, the Netherlands: Landelijke Werkgroep HBO Wiskunde.

van der Wal, N. J., Bakker, A., & Drijvers, P. (2017). Which techno-mathematical literacies are essential for future engineers? *International Journal of Science and Mathematics Education, 15*(Supplement 1), 87–104.

van der Wal, N. J., Bakker, A., & Drijvers, P. (2019). Teaching strategies to foster techno-mathematical literacies in an innovative mathematics course for future engineers. *ZDM Mathematics Education, 51*, 885–897.

Visnovska, J., Cobb, P., & Dean, C. (2012). Mathematics teachers as instructional designers: What does it take? In G. Gueudet, B. Pepin, & L. Trouche (Eds.), *From text to "lived" resources: Mathematics curriculum materials and teacher development* (pp. 323–341). Berlin: Springer.

Wake, G., Swan, M., & Foster, C. (2016). Professional learning through the collaborative design of problem-solving lessons. *Journal of Mathematics Teacher Education, 19*(2–3), 243–260.

Wenger, E. (1998). *Communities of practice, learning, meaning and identity*. Cambridge, UK: Cambridge University Press.

Index

Note. *f* or *t* following a page number indicates a figure or a table.

Academic language, 170
Accountability pressures, 232–233
Accreditation, 256. *See also* Teacher preparation
Action, 66–67. *See also* Pragmatic approach
Actual learning trajectory, 86. *See also* Learning
Administrators, 232–233
Agency of participants
    assertions from the DBR process with disciplinary literacy teaching and, 247
    considerations for design researchers regarding, 15–16
    design-based implementation research (DBIR) and, 297–298
ALEKS software, 300
Analysis/revision, 86, 87, 95–98, 96*f*. *See also* Data analysis; Revision of a design
Answerability, 15–16
AP coursework, 171–173, 182–183. *See also* Ascend Program
Applied mathematics course for future engineers
    design-based implementation research (DBIR) and, 298–312, 302*t*, 303*t*, 304*t*, 306*t*, 310*t*
    interviews, 301–311, 303*t*, 304*t*, 306*t*, 310*t*
    overview, 300–301, 302*t*, 311–312
Argumentation writing. *See also* Reading and writing instruction; Writing
    Ascend Program and, 176–182, 177*t*
    Camp Questions and, 150–151
    dialogic principles and, 118
    genre-based strategy instruction and, 116–121
    multilingual students and, 169–170
    overview, 104–105
    writing instruction in middle school and, 108–112, 111*f*, 112*f*, 113*f*
Argumentative grammar, 14–15
Article-based dissertations, 281–282, 286, 290–292. *See also* DBR graduate dissertations

Artifact design, 70–78, 71*f*, 74*f*
Ascend Program. *See also* Multilingual students
    collecting information to understand the context, 173, 174*t*, 175
    consolidating data and refining theory, 174*t*, 176–182, 177*t*
    gathering baseline data, 174*t*, 175
    implementing and refining, 174*t*, 175–176
    overview, 171–173, 182–183
    post-assessment, 174*t*, 175–176
    research partnership, 173, 174*t*
    using DBR with, 173–183, 174*t*, 177*t*
Assessment. *See also* Assessment of comprehension; Assessment of writing
    Ascend Program and, 175, 178, 180
    disciplinary literacy instruction and, 244–245, 246
    Finnish educational context and, 67–68
    genre-based strategy instruction and, 120
    Literacy Is Transformative Lab (LIT Lab) and, 131, 135–137, 136*f*
    science curriculum development and, 115–116
Assessment of comprehension. *See also* Assessment; Comprehension; Reading and writing instruction
    challenges of, 187–188
    overview, 187–188, 203–204
    using DBR with, 191–202, 191*t*, 195*t*, 199*t*
Assessment of writing. *See also* Assessment; Reading and writing instruction; Writing
    evidence-based practices and, 211
    genre-based strategy instruction and, 120
    PD model on writing and, 218–224, 219*f*, 220*f*, 222*f*
    reading and writing instruction and, 104
    science curriculum development and, 115–116
Asset-based approaches, 169
Audience, 284
Automated essay scoring (AES), 120

317

Background knowledge. *See also* Knowledge
  comprehension and, 187–188
  comprehension assessment and, 192, 200
  genre-based strategy instruction and, 117
  tips for writing graduate dissertations, 284
Baseline data collection, 175. *See also* Data collection
Bias
  genre-based strategy instruction and, 119
  multilingual students and, 175
Book publishing. *See* Publication
Bootstrapping, 297

Camp Questions. *See also* Digital literacies; Intervention
  influence of DBR on learning and, 163–164
  overview, 147–148
  results of the DBR, 155–163, 161f
  using DBR to design, 149–154, 150t, 152t
Carceral thinking, 16
Case-to-case generalization, 284
Choice
  genre-based strategy instruction and, 117
  teacher preparation and, 263–264
Citation of sources, 118–119
Classroom practices. *See also* Classroom-DBR (C-DBR); Implementation; Instructional processes; Teachers
  curriculum design and, 50
  design-based implementation research (DBIR) and, 297
  Finnish educational context and, 79–80
  overview, 83–85
  pragmatic framework for DBR and, 66–67
Classroom-DBR (C-DBR). *See also* Classroom practices; Design-based research (DBR) in general; Teachers
  cycle of, 85–86
  examples that illustrates, 87–98, 91f, 94f, 96f
  overview, 84–86, 99–100
  process of DBR with disciplinary literacy instruction and, 233–234
  ratio and proportion design phase, 89–95, 91f, 94f
  stable instruction learning theory and, 98–99
  timeline of, 87–98, 87t, 88t, 91f, 94f, 96f
Coaching
  comprehension assessment and, 198–200, 199t
  disciplinary literacy instruction and, 237, 241
  process of DBR with disciplinary literacy instruction and, 234
  teacher preparation and, 256
Cognitive-strategy instruction in writing (CSIW), 106, 217–218. *See also* Reading and writing instruction; Strategy instruction; Writing
Cohesion, 56–57
Co-learning, 193
Collaboration. *See also* Researchers; Teacher design teams (TDTs); Teachers
  advice to authors regarding writing about DBR and, 35–37, 36f
  applied mathematics course for future engineers and, 300–301, 302t
  comprehension assessment and, 191
  curriculum design and, 50–54
  DBR graduate dissertations and, 278–279
  design-based implementation research (DBIR) and, 297
  disciplinary literacy instruction and, 244
  genre-based strategy instruction and, 116–117
  methodological affordances of DBR and, 25
  overview, 276
  PD model on writing and, 225–226
  pragmatic framework for DBR and, 66–67
  support for teachers and, 232–233
  teacher preparation and, 263–266, 265f, 268–269
  writing instruction in middle school and, 110
Collaborative design, 147–149. *See also* Camp Questions
Collaborative learning
  DBR graduate dissertations and, 281–282
  teacher design teams (TDTs) and, 55–56
Collaborative school culture
  curriculum design and, 60
  teacher design teams (TDTs) and, 56–57
Collection of data. *See* Data collection
College, Career, and Civic Life (C3) framework, 257–258
Common Core State Standards (CCSS)
  digital literacies and, 148–149
  literacy achievement and, 103
  overview, 210
  PD model on writing and, 216f
  reading and writing instruction and, 104–105
Comprehension, 118, 187, 192. *See also* Assessment of comprehension
Computer-based support for curriculum developers, 279–281. *See also* Technology
Computer-supported collaborative learning (CSCL), 282
Conceptual framework, 33–34
Conference proceedings, 38–39. *See also* Publication
Conjecture. *See also* Design principle
  considerations for design researchers regarding, 14–15
  critiques of DBR and recommendations for publications and, 33–34
  reviewing DBR research and, 29–30
Constructively responsive reading theory, 192, 196
Constructivist learning theory, 281–282
Content knowledge building. *See also* Knowledge
  applied mathematics course for future engineers and, 307–308
  Literacy Is Transformative Lab (LIT Lab) and, 143–144
Context
  Ascend Program and, 173, 175
  critiques of DBR and recommendations for publications and, 33–34
  science curriculum development and, 70–78, 71f, 74f
  tips for writing graduate dissertations, 283–284
Continuous practice, 110, 112
Co-teaching, 162
Council for the Accreditation of Educator Preparation (CAEP), 256
Critical perspectives, 4–5, 14–17, 30–35
Crosscutting features of DBR, 5–14. *See also* Iterations and iterative processes; Theory and knowledge development
Culturally responsive teaching (CRT) practices, 169
Curricular design research (CDR). *See also* Curriculum design
  knowledge production and, 57–58
  overview, 45–46
  scaling results from, 58–60
Curricular spider's web, 46–47, 47f
Curriculum coherence-making, 56
Curriculum design. *See also* Curricular design research (CDR); Science curriculum development; Teachers
  overview, 45–49, 47f, 64–65
  scalability and, 58–60
  school context and, 54–57
  teachers and, 49–54

Index

Curriculum material
   assertions from the DBR process with disciplinary literacy teaching and, 248
   overview, 45
   when DBR would be a good approach, 5

Data analysis
   advice to authors regarding writing about DBR and, 35–37, 36f
   Ascend Program and, 176–182, 177t
   assertions from the DBR process with disciplinary literacy teaching and, 246–249, 247t
   Camp Questions and, 153–154, 163–164
   comprehension assessment and, 191–194, 197
   critiques of DBR and recommendations for publications and, 34–35
   cycle of C-DBR and, 86, 87, 95–98, 96f
   genre-based strategy instruction and, 115–116
   Literacy Is Transformative Lab (LIT Lab) and, 130, 133, 137–139, 139f
   methodological affordances of DBR and, 25–26
   overview, 276
   PD model on writing and, 218–221, 219f, 220f
   process of DBR with disciplinary literacy instruction and, 234–235, 236t, 238t–239t
   teacher design teams (TDTs) and, 52–53
   teacher preparation and, 262

Data collection
   advice to authors regarding writing about DBR and, 35–37, 36f
   Ascend Program and, 173, 175
   Camp Questions and, 153–154
   comprehension assessment and, 191–194, 197
   critiques of DBR and recommendations for publications and, 32, 34–35
   Literacy Is Transformative Lab (LIT Lab) and, 130, 135–137, 136f
   methodological affordances of DBR and, 25–26
   PD model on writing and, 219–221, 219f, 220f
   process of DBR with disciplinary literacy instruction and, 234–235, 236t
   teacher design teams (TDTs) and, 54
   teacher preparation and, 259–262

Data-based decision making (DBDM), 133–134

DBR graduate dissertations. *See also* Graduate research; Publication
   article-based dissertations, 281–282
   long-form dissertations, 279–281
   overview, 272–273, 278–282, 293
   tips and tools for, 282–292, 286f, 287f–289f
   tools for writing long-form and article-based dissertations, 286, 290–292

Decentralization, 67–70

Design principle, 6, 29–30, 33–34

Design teams. *See* Research teams

Design-based implementation research (DBIR). *See also* Implementation
   applied mathematics course for future engineers and, 298–312, 302t, 303t, 304t, 306t, 310t
   overview, 25, 296–297, 311–312
   professional development (PD) and agency and, 297–298

Design-based research (DBR) in general. *See also* Classroom-DBR (C-DBR); DBR graduate dissertations
   considerations for design researchers regarding, 14–16
   features of, 5–9
   methodological affordances of, 24–26
   overview, 3–4, 16–17, 23–24, 39–40, 64–65, 83–84, 275–278, 275f
   science curriculum development and, 70–78, 71f, 74f
   when DBR would be a good approach, 4–5

Devaluing, 128. *See also* Motivation

Dialogic instruction
   argument writing and, 118
   Ascend Program and, 177, 177t, 179, 181–182
   multilingual students and, 170

Differentiation, 120

Digital literacies, 147–149. *See also* Camp Questions; Technology

Digital Youth Divas (DYD) project, 7

Disciplinary expertise, 248–249

Disciplinary literacy teaching. *See also* Literacy teaching; Reading and writing instruction; Strategy instruction
   assertions from the DBR process with, 246–249, 247t
   overview, 231, 249–250
   using DBR with, 231–235, 236t, 237, 238t–240t, 241–246

Discourse, 217

Dissertation writing. *See* DBR graduate dissertations; Graduate research

Distal outcomes, 215, 217

Doctoral research. *See* DBR graduate dissertations; Graduate research

Documentation, 52–53

Domain knowledge, 248–249. *See also* Knowledge

Ecological perspective, 25, 170–171

Educational programs for teachers. *See* Teacher preparation; Training

Emergent perspective, 86

Empirical testing, 52–53

Engineers, applied mathematics course for. *See* Applied mathematics course for future engineers

English language learners (ELLs), 131–132, 168–169. *See also* Multilingual students

Epistemic authority, 12

Equality, 67–68

Ethnography, 3–4

Evaluation of sources, 119

Evidence, 119

Evidence-based practices
   professional development (PD) and, 214
   writing instruction and, 210–213

Evolutionary curriculum design approach, 55. *See also* Curriculum design

Experiential representations, 48

Experimental learning, 55

Experimental research, 4–5

Experimentation, 255

Expert appraisal, 53. *See also* Focus group

Expertise, 248–249

Explanation, 110

Explicit instruction, 179–180, 181–182. *See also* Strategy instruction

Extracurricular interventions, 171–173. *See also* Ascend Program; Intervention

Eyes on Students observation protocol, 246–247

Features, crosscutting, 5–14

Feedback
   Ascend Program and, 179–180
   PD model on writing and, 221, 222–224
   writing instruction and, 211

Feedback hour, 300, 308, 310, 310t, 311–312

Finnish educational context, 64–65, 67–70, 79–80
Flexibility
    comprehension assessment and, 204
    curriculum design and, 46–47, 47f
    disciplinary literacy instruction and, 240t
Focus group, 53, 54
Formative assessment and evaluation. *See also* Assessment of comprehension
    DBR graduate dissertations and, 277
    design of a tool for, 192
    disciplinary literacy instruction and, 244–245, 249–250
    teacher design teams (TDTs) and, 52, 54
    using DBR with, 190
4-day organizers used with Camp Questions, 157–160. *See also* Camp Questions
Framework for K–12 Science Education (NRC, 2012), 9–11
FTAAP (form, topic, audience, author, purpose) acronym for writing
    reading instruction in middle school and, 112, 114
    writing instruction in middle school and, 109, 111f
Funds of knowledge, 171
Future-orientation of DBR, 6, 10, 12

Generalizability
    critiques of DBR and recommendations for publications and, 32–33
    curriculum design and, 58
    tips for writing graduate dissertations, 284
Genre. *See also* Genre-based strategy instruction
    overview, 217–218
    reading instruction in middle school and, 114
    tips for writing graduate dissertations, 284
    writing instruction in middle school and, 109
Genre-based strategy instruction. *See also* Reading and writing instruction; Strategy instruction
    data analysis and findings and, 115–116
    evaluation measures, 115
    methods, 108–115, 111f, 112f, 113f
    overview, 103, 106–108, 116–121
    PD model on writing and, 214–226, 216f, 219f, 220f, 222f
    reading instruction and, 112, 114
    teachers and, 114–115
    writing instruction and, 108–112, 111f, 112f, 113f
Goals, 4–5, 215–217, 216f
Gradual release of responsibility
    Camp Questions and, 152
    writing instruction and, 212–213
Graduate research, 272–275, 282–292, 286f, 287f–289f, 293. *See also* DBR graduate dissertations
Graphic organizers
    argumentation writing and, 111f
    4-day organizers used with Camp Questions, 157–160
Graphs, 119
Guided practice, 110

Help teams, 56
High fidelity, 59
High schools. *See also* Literacy Is Transformative Lab (LIT Lab); Secondary schools
    literacy achievement and, 103–104
    reading and writing instruction and, 104–108
    science curriculum development and, 69–70
High-stakes testing, 232–233
Human–computer interaction, 3–4, 8. *See also* Technology
Humble theory, 171, 181–182
Hypothetical learning trajectory (HLT), 85–86, 87, 87t, 89–95, 91f, 94f. *See also* Learning

Implementation. *See also* Design-based implementation research (DBIR)
    Camp Questions and, 151–152
    comprehension assessment and, 194–202, 195t, 199t
    critiques of DBR and recommendations for publications and, 35
    cycle of C-DBR and, 85–86, 87, 89–95, 91f, 94f
    disciplinary literacy instruction and, 243
    overview, 296–297
    PD model on writing and, 224–226
    scalability and, 58–60
    teacher preparation and, 263–264
Individuals with Disabilities Education Act (IDEA), 210
Innovation
    comprehension assessment and, 190
    professional development (PD) and, 298
Inquiry-based approach, 75–78, 257–258. *See also* Systematic inquiry
Inquiry-based learning (IBL), 300, 305–306, 308–309, 310–311
Inquiry-based science teaching (IBST), 78
InquiryHub research–practice partnership, 9–11
Institute of Education Sciences (IES), 210–212
Instruction theory, 84–85, 98–99
Instructional processes, 216f, 217–218
Instructional technology, 141. *See also* Technology
Integrating writing and reading, 104, 211–212. *See also* Reading and writing instruction
Interactive approaches, 53
Internships, 259–269, 265f
Intervention. *See also* Ascend Program; Camp Questions; Literacy Is Transformative Lab (LIT Lab)
    challenges in designing, 129–130
    critiques of DBR and recommendations for publications and, 34–35
    DBR graduate dissertations and, 276
    disciplinary literacy instruction and, 245–246
    overview, 128–129
    PD model on writing and, 218–219
    process of DBR with disciplinary literacy instruction and, 234
    reading intervention team in the LIT Lab, 140
    teacher preparation and, 259–262
    when DBR would be a good approach, 4–5
Iterations and iterative processes
    applied mathematics course for future engineers and, 312
    Ascend Program and, 175–176, 177–178
    comprehension assessment and, 203, 204
    critiques of DBR and recommendations for publications and, 35
    examples that illustrate, 11, 13–14
    Literacy Is Transformative Lab (LIT Lab) and, 133
    overview, 8–9, 275, 275f
    PD model on writing and, 222–223
    reviewing DBR research and, 29
    science curriculum development and, 70–78, 71f, 74f
    teacher design teams (TDTs) and, 53, 55
    teacher preparation and, 260–262, 268

Journal publication, 38–39. *See also* Publication

Knowledge. *See also* Background knowledge; Content knowledge building; Pragmatic approach; Theory and knowledge development
    assertions from the DBR process with disciplinary literacy teaching and, 248–249
    multilingual students and, 170–171
    pragmatic framework for DBR and, 66–67

Index

Landscape model of reading, 192, 204
Learning. *See also* Hypothetical learning trajectory (HLT); Learning environments
   applied mathematics course for future engineers and, 312
   Camp Questions and, 163–164
   curriculum design and, 47–49
   cycle of C-DBR and, 92–95, 94f
   pragmatic framework for DBR and, 66–67
   professional development (PD) and, 298
   revision of a design and, 95–98, 96f
Learning and development research
   Literacy Is Transformative Lab (LIT Lab) and, 139–143
   when DBR would be a good approach, 5
Learning environments. *See also* Learning
   DBR graduate dissertations and, 278
   future-orientation of DBR and, 6
   reviewing DBR research and, 30
   teacher design teams (TDTs) and, 55
Lecturers
   applied mathematics course for future engineers and, 300–301, 302t, 311–312
   interviews, 301–311, 303t, 304t, 306t, 310t
Levels of education, 47–48
Limited English proficient (LEP), 168–169. *See also* Multilingual students
Literacies, digital. *See* Digital literacies
Literacy achievement. *See also* Digital literacies; Reading and writing instruction; Struggling students
   genre-based strategy instruction and, 115–116
   overview, 127–128, 231
   secondary schools and, 103–104
Literacy Is Transformative Lab (LIT Lab). *See also* Intervention
   learning points from, 139–143
   overview, 130, 143–144
   phases of, 132–134
   progress monitoring and, 135–137, 136f
   results from, 137–139, 139f
   using DBR to design, 130–137, 136f
Literacy teaching, 231–233. *See also* Disciplinary literacy teaching; Instructional processes; Reading and writing instruction; Strategy instruction
Literature reviews, 54, 89–90
Long-form dissertations, 279–281, 286, 290–292. *See also* DBR graduate dissertations
Long-term English language learners (LTELs), 168–169. *See also* Multilingual students

Macro level of education, 47
Mastery experiences, 170
Materials Science Project, 72–75, 74f
Mathematics education, 87–98, 88t, 91f, 94f, 96f. *See also* Applied mathematics course for future engineers; Classroom-DBR (C-DBR); Realistic Mathematics Education (RME)
Meaning-making activities, 55–56
Measures of Academic Progress (MAP), 115
Memory, 192
Mentors. *See also* Professional development (PD); Training
   future research using DBR and, 266–269
   overview, 253–254
   teacher preparation and, 259–266, 265f
Meso level of education, 47
Metacognitive strategies. *See also* Strategy instruction
   comprehension assessment and, 204
   genre-based strategy instruction and, 119–120

Methodology
   critiques of DBR and recommendations for publications and, 31–32, 33–34
   genre-based strategy instruction and, 108–115, 111f, 112f, 113f
   graduate research and, 274
   methodological affordances of DBR and, 24–26
   overview, 23–24, 39–40
   rigor and, 14–15
   teacher design teams (TDTs) and, 52–54
Micro level of education, 47
Microevaluation, 53
Middle schools. *See also* Secondary schools
   literacy achievement and, 103–104
   reading and writing instruction and, 104–108
   science curriculum development and, 69–70
Mini-lessons, 118
Mixed methods, 267
Modeling. *See also* Think-alouds
   disciplinary literacy instruction and, 237, 241
   genre-based strategy instruction and, 116–117, 119–120
   strategy instruction and, 105
   writing instruction in middle school and, 109–110
Model–practice–reflect instructional cycle, 104, 211
Models of inquiry, 162
Motivation
   Literacy Is Transformative Lab (LIT Lab) and, 144
   literacy levels and, 128
   science curriculum development and, 75–78
   of teachers, 232–233
   writing instruction and, 211
Motivational inquiry-based curriculum, 75–78
Multilingual students. *See also* Ascend Program; English language learners (ELLs)
   argument writing and, 169–170
   asset-based views of, 169
   challenges faced by, 168–169
   overview, 167–168
   using DBR with, 170–171, 173–183, 174t, 177t
Multiracial democracy, 17
Mutual action, 65
Mutual adaptation, 59

Nano level of education, 47
Nanomaterials, 72–75, 74f
National Council for the Social Studies (NCSS), 257–258
National-level curriculum. *See also* Finnish educational context
   pragmatic framework for DBR and, 66–67
   science curriculum development and, 67–70, 72–75, 74f, 78–79
Networked improvement communities, 60
Next Generation Science Standards (NGSS), 148–149. *See also* Science curriculum development
No Child Left Behind Act of 2001, 210
Note taking, 114
NRC framework. *See* Framework for K–12 Science Education (NRC, 2012)

Opportunity gaps, 171–172. *See also* Ascend Program; Multilingual students
Organizational design studies, 233–234
Outcomes
   assertions from the DBR process with disciplinary literacy teaching and, 246–249, 247t
   Finnish educational context and, 67–68, 69–70
   literacy levels and, 128

Outcomes *(cont.)*
  science curriculum development and, 70–78, 71*f*, 74*f*
  teacher design teams (TDTs) and, 53
Outlining process
  tips for writing graduate dissertations, 284–285
  tools for writing long-form and article-based dissertations, 291

Parents, 65
Participants, agency of. *See* Agency of participants
Participatory design, 3, 25
PD design studies, 233–234. *See also* Professional development (PD)
Pedagogical content knowledge (PCK), 218
Peer devaluing, 128. *See also* Motivation
Peer review
  genre-based strategy instruction and, 107
  writing instruction in middle school and, 110
Perceived difficulty, 128. *See also* Motivation
Perceived representations, 48
PhD research and dissertations. *See* DBR graduate dissertations; Graduate research
Point of view, 119
Power
  considerations for design researchers regarding, 16
  critical pragmatism and, 16–17
Pragmatic approach
  genre-based strategy instruction and, 107
  overview, 16–17, 65–67
  when DBR would be a good approach, 5
Pre-interviews, 90–91, 91*f*
Preliminary investigation, 52
Preservice education, 83–84
Primary schools, 60
Primary sources
  genre-based strategy instruction and, 119
  social studies education and, 257–258
  teacher preparation and, 263–264
PRIMES project (Parents Rediscovering and Interacting with Math and Engaging Schools project), 11–14
Prior knowledge. *See* Background knowledge
Privilege, 175
Problem solving
  comprehension assessment and, 194
  writing instruction in middle school and, 110
Product assessments. *See* Assessment
Professional development (PD). *See also* Teacher preparation; Teachers; Training
  applied mathematics course for future engineers and, 310–311
  assertions from the DBR process with disciplinary literacy teaching and, 246–249, 247*t*
  curriculum design and, 50, 51, 59
  design-based implementation research (DBIR) and, 297–298
  disciplinary literacy instruction and, 233–235, 236*t*, 237, 238*t*–240*t*, 241–246, 249–250
  Finnish educational context and, 68
  genre-based strategy instruction and, 107–108, 114–115
  literacy teaching and, 231–233
  overview, 45, 83–84, 209, 224–226
  PD model on writing and, 214–226, 216*f*, 219*f*, 220*f*, 222*f*
  previous research on in writing instruction, 213–214
  support for teachers and, 232–233
  teacher preparation and, 256
  when DBR would be a good approach, 5
Professional development school (PDS) model, 255–256

Professional learning, 140–141, 143. *See also* Professional development (PD)
Professional learning communities (PLCs). *See also* Professional development (PD)
  curriculum design and, 52
  Literacy Is Transformative Lab (LIT Lab) and, 142–143
Programme for International Student Assessment (PISA), 68
Progress monitoring
  genre-based strategy instruction and, 120
  Literacy Is Transformative Lab (LIT Lab) and, 135–137, 136*f*
Promotion and tenure guidelines, 37–38. *See also* Graduate research
Prototypes, 54
Publication. *See also* DBR graduate dissertations
  advice to authors regarding, 35–37, 36*f*
  article-based dissertations, 281–282
  book publishing, 39
  critiques of DBR and recommendations for, 30–35
  current state of, 26–27, 28*t*
  journal and conference proceedings and, 38–39
  long-form dissertations, 279–281
  methodological affordances of DBR and, 24–26
  overview, 39–40
  promotion and tenure guidelines and, 37–38
  reviewing DBR research and, 29–30
  tips for writing graduate dissertations, 282–292, 286*f*, 287*f*–289*f*
Purposes for writing, 109, 114. *See also* Writing

Qualitative data, 131
Quality, curriculum, 48–49. *See also* Curriculum design
Quantitative data, 131

Racial justice, 16
Read-alouds
  genre-based strategy instruction and, 117
  writing instruction in middle school and, 109
Reading and writing instruction. *See also* Assessment of comprehension; Assessment of writing; Genre-based strategy instruction; Literacy achievement; Literacy teaching; Writing
  evidence-based practices and, 210–213
  overview, 211–212
  PD model on writing and, 225–226
  previous research on professional development in writing instruction, 213–214
  reading instruction in middle school and, 112, 114
  in the secondary classroom, 104–108
  writing instruction in middle school and, 108–112, 111*f*, 112*f*, 113*f*
Reading comprehension. *See* Assessment of comprehension; Comprehension
Reading intervention. *See* Intervention
Reading motivation, 129–130. *See also* Motivation
Reading selection, 117
Reading specialists, 189, 191–193, 194, 197–198, 202–203. *See also* Teachers
Realistic Mathematics Education (RME), 6, 91–92
Real-world settings, 25
Reciprocity, 255
Redesign, 86
Reflection
  comprehension assessment and, 202–203
  PD model on writing and, 220–221, 220*f*
  science curriculum development and, 70–78, 71*f*, 74*f*
  teacher design teams (TDTs) and, 53

Index

Reform policies, 209–210
Reporting on a DBR study. *See also* Publication
   advice to authors regarding, 35–37, 36f
   journal and conference proceedings and, 38–39
   overview, 39–40
   tips for writing graduate dissertations, 282–292, 286f, 287f–289f
Research teams, 84, 85–86. *See also* Classroom-DBR (C-DBR); Researchers; Teachers
Researchers. *See also* Collaboration; Research teams
   advice to authors regarding writing about DBR and, 35–37, 36f
   Camp Questions and, 153, 163–164
   Finnish educational context and, 79
   journal and conference proceedings and, 38–39
   pragmatic framework for DBR and, 66–67
   promotion and tenure guidelines and, 37–38
   science curriculum development and, 65
Responsive teaching, 237, 241
Retrospective analysis, 180–182. *See also* Data analysis
Revision of a design
   applied mathematics course for future engineers and, 309–310
   cycle of C-DBR and, 86, 95–98, 96f
   overview, 8–9
Rigor, 14–15

Scaffolds
   disciplinary literacy instruction and, 243–244
   genre-based strategy instruction and, 120
   multilingual students and, 169–170
   strategy instruction and, 105
Scalability, 49, 58–60
School context
   curriculum design and, 59–60
   Literacy Is Transformative Lab (LIT Lab) and, 142
   teacher design teams (TDTs) and, 54–57
School culture
   curriculum design and, 60
   teacher design teams (TDTs) and, 56
School of Life Sciences and Environmental Technology at Avans University of Applied Sciences in the Netherlands, 300. *See also* Applied mathematics course for future engineers
School/university partnerships, 258, 262–263, 269. *See also* Teacher preparation
Schoolwide data-based decision-making intervention, 279
Science curriculum development. *See also* Curriculum design; Next Generation Science Standards (NGSS)
   digital literacies and, 148–149
   examples that illustrate, 70–78, 71f, 74f
   Finnish educational context and, 68–70
   overview, 78–80
   pragmatic framework for DBR and, 65–67
Screening, 53, 54
Secondary schools. *See also* High schools; Middle schools; School context
   curriculum design and, 60
   literacy achievement and, 103–104
   reading and writing instruction and, 104–108
   science curriculum development and, 69–70
Second-language students. *See* English language learners (ELLs); Multilingual students
Self-efficacy beliefs
   Ascend Program and, 177t, 180
   multilingual students and, 170, 176
   PD model on writing and, 218
   of teachers, 232–233
   writing instruction and, 211
Self-evaluation
   Finnish educational context and, 67–68
   genre-based strategy instruction and, 107
   writing instruction in middle school and, 110
Self-regulated strategy development (SRSD) model, 106, 213–214, 217–218
Self-regulation
   genre-based strategy instruction and, 119–120
   strategy instruction and, 105
   writing instruction and, 110, 212–213
Sense-making, 50–51
Shared reading, 117
Signature methodology, 3
Situated learning, 51–52
SOAPS (speaker, occasion, audience, purpose, and subject) strategy, 237
Social justice
   Ascend Program and, 182–183
   multilingual students and, 175
Social persuasions, 170
Social practice, 48–49
Social studies education
   future research using DBR and, 266–269
   teacher preparation and, 256, 257–258, 259–266, 265f
Socioecological justice, 16
Solution-orientation, 190
Special education, 132. *See also* Struggling students
Stable learning trajectory, 87, 88t, 98–99
Stakeholders, 276, 278–279
Standards, 210. *See also* Common Core State Standards (CCSS); Next Generation Science Standards (NGSS)
Statewide context, 83–84
STEM (science, technology, engineering, and mathematics)
   Digital Youth Divas (DYD) project and, 7
   inquiryHub research–practice partnership and, 9–11
   when DBR would be a good approach, 5
Strategy development, 255
Strategy for Teaching Strategies (STS), 109–112, 111f, 112f, 113f
Strategy instruction. *See also* Disciplinary literacy teaching; Explicit instruction; Genre-based strategy instruction; Reading and writing instruction
   Ascend Program and, 179–180, 181–182
   overview, 105–106
   PD model on writing and, 214–226, 216f, 219f, 220f, 222f
   professional development (PD) and, 214
   writing instruction and, 108–112, 111f, 112f, 113f, 212–213
Strong and weak model examples, 109–110
Structured Academic Controversy (SAC) discussions, 177, 177t, 179
Struggling students, 127–129, 243–244. *See also* Intervention; Literacy Is Transformative Lab (LIT Lab)
Student confidence, 138–139, 144
Student-centered coaching, 234
Students, 152–153, 193
Students, graduate. *See* DBR graduate dissertations; Graduate research
Subject matter learning, 4
Summarization
   genre-based strategy instruction and, 107
   reading instruction in middle school and, 114
Summative evaluation, 277
Summer enrichment interventions. *See* Camp Questions; Intervention
Support, 55, 232–233

Supra level of education, 47
Sustainability, 49
Synthesizing scientific understanding, 276
Systematic inquiry, 52, 255. *See also* Inquiry-based approach

Teacher design teams (TDTs). *See also* Collaboration; Curriculum design; Teachers
  applied mathematics course for future engineers and, 300–301
  curricular design research (CDR) results and, 58–60
  embedding in the school context, 54–57
  overview, 50–54
Teacher preparation. *See also* Professional development (PD); Training
  future research using DBR and, 266–269
  overview, 253–254, 255–256, 269
  university/school partnerships through DBR, 258
  using DBR with, 259–266, 265f
Teachers. *See also* Classroom-DBR (C-DBR); Collaboration; Curriculum design; Professional development (PD); Reading specialists; Research teams; Teacher design teams (TDTs); Teacher preparation
  curriculum design and, 49–54
  design-based implementation research (DBIR) and, 297–298
  Finnish educational context and, 65, 67–70, 79–80
  genre-based strategy instruction and, 114–115, 116
  Literacy Is Transformative Lab (LIT Lab) and, 132, 133–134, 140–141, 142–144
  overview, 45
  PD model on writing and, 218–224, 219f, 220f, 222f
  pragmatic framework for DBR and, 66–67
  school and district leadership and, 232–233
  science curriculum development and, 65, 70–78, 71f, 74f, 79
  social studies education and, 257–258
Teaching experiment, 3
Teaching literacy. *See* Literacy teaching
Team composition
  reading intervention team in the LIT Lab, 140
  teacher design teams (TDTs) and, 56
Technology. *See also* Digital literacies
  applied mathematics course for future engineers and, 298–312, 302t, 303t, 304t, 306t, 310t
  computer-based support for curriculum developers, 279–281
  computer-supported collaborative learning (CSCL), 282
  disciplinary literacy instruction and, 237, 241, 245
  Literacy Is Transformative Lab (LIT Lab) and, 141
  technology-enhanced learning, 278
Techno-mathematical literacies (TmL), 299–300, 308–309. *See also* Applied mathematics course for future engineers
Tenure, 37–38. *See also* Graduate research
Testing, 232–233
Theoretical framework, 33–34, 52
Theory and knowledge development
  about learning and design, 7
  Ascend Program and, 176–182, 177t
  comprehension assessment and, 189–190

critiques of DBR and recommendations for publications and, 32–34
curriculum design and, 57–58
examples that illustrate, 10–11, 12–13
multilingual students and, 171
teacher design teams (TDTs) and, 52–53
usability of DBR and, 7–8
when DBR would be a good approach, 4–5
Theory of change
  literacy teaching and, 231–233
  PD model on writing and, 215–217, 216f
Think-alouds. *See also* Modeling
  comprehension assessment and, 189, 196
  genre-based strategy instruction and, 116–117, 119–120
  writing instruction in middle school and, 110
TPACK framework (technology, pedagogy, and content knowledge), 245
Training. *See also* Professional development (PD); Teacher preparation
  genre-based strategy instruction and, 114–115
  Literacy Is Transformative Lab (LIT Lab) and, 142–143
  overview, 253–254
  reading intervention team in the LIT Lab, 140–141
  university/school partnerships through DBR, 258
Transformation of systems, 4–5
Translanguaging practices, 178, 182–183
Tryout, 53

University/school partnerships, 258, 262–263, 269. *See also* Teacher preparation
Upper secondary schools, 60. *See also* School context
Usability of DBR
  considerations for design researchers regarding, 15
  examples that illustrate, 11, 13
  overview, 7–8
Use-inspired research, 17

Variation, 56–57
Verbal protocols in comprehension assessment, 189–190, 193, 194, 196, 197–198, 200–202. *See also* Assessment of comprehension
Vicarious experiences, 170
Visual support, 48, 285
Vulnerability of curriculum, 46–47, 47f

Walkthroughs, 53
Writing. *See also* Argumentation writing; Assessment of writing; Reading and writing instruction
  evidence-based practices and, 210–213
  PD model on writing and, 214–226, 216f, 219f, 220f, 222f
  previous research on professional development in writing instruction, 213–214
  reform policies and, 209–210
Writing dissertations. *See* DBR graduate dissertations
Writing performance. *See* Argumentation writing; Literacy achievement; Reading and writing instruction
Writing Self-Efficacy Scale (WSES), 180
Written representations, 48

Zone of proximal development (ZPD), 4, 48, 60